Understanding Morphological Rules

Studies in Morphology

VOLUME 1

Managing Editors:

Adam Albright; *MIT, USA*
Geert Booij; *University of Leiden, The Netherlands*
Ingo Plag; *University of Siegen, Germany*

For further volumes:http://www.springer.com/series/8804

Stela Manova

Understanding Morphological Rules

With Special Emphasis on Conversion and Subtraction in Bulgarian, Russian and Serbo-Croatian

Stela Manova
University of Vienna
Department of Slavic Studies
Universitätscampus AAKH
Spitalgasse 2-4, Hof 3
1090 Vienna
Austria
stela.manova@univie.ac.at

ISBN 978-90-481-9546-6   e-ISBN 978-90-481-9547-3
DOI 10.1007/978-90-481-9547-3
Springer Dordrecht New York Heidelberg London

Library of Congress Control Number: 2010938974

© Springer Science+Business Media B.V. 2011
No part of this work may be reproduced, stored in a retrieval system, or transmitted in any form or by any means, electronic, mechanical, photocopying, microfilming, recording or otherwise, without written permission from the Publisher, with the exception of any material supplied specifically for the purpose of being entered and executed on a computer system, for exclusive use by the purchaser of the work.

Printed on acid-free paper

Springer is part of Springer Science+Business Media (www.springer.com)

Foreword

Conversion and subtraction are morphological operations which have not aroused as much concern in morphological theories and descriptions as concatenative operations, but have proven to be of great theoretical interest. One main goal of Stela Manova's monograph is to achieve a theoretically deeper analysis of both operations (techniques) and to describe them in more detail and more exhaustively at least in three languages. One example of her results is the well-argued distinction between conversion proper, formal conversion and syntactic conversion in its application to several languages, also beyond Bulgarian, Russian and Serbo-Croatian.

Manova's approach is functionalist and integrates basic tenets of Cognitive Linguistics with semiotically-based Natural Morphology. The main contribution of Natural Morphology to her approach consists in differentiating, and elaborating on, relevant dimensions of its three subtheories:

(a) In regard to universal morphological preferences she deals especially with the parameters of iconicity and transparency and develops a new scale of constructional iconicity, which helps her to refine and subclassify the concepts of conversion and subtraction.
(b) In regard to typological adequacy, she elaborates on various morphological aspects of the inflecting-fusional type which is rather closely approached by Russian, Serbo-Croatian (both especially in nominal inflection) and Bulgarian (especially in verb inflection).
(c) In regard to language-specific system adequacy, she deals with language-specific generalisations, for example in the domain of similar Russian and Bulgarian, as opposed to Serbo-Croatian, agent formation or of Bulgarian diminutive formation. In this respect she can explain also why diachronic rule inversions have emerged, resulting in subtractive morphology. Thus universal and typological preferences can be overridden, if the solution fits to clear generalisations of language-specific system adequacy. It should also be noted that Manova, in contrast to many other morphologists, systematically pays attention to prosodic patterns, including Serbo-Croatian intonation.

The main contribution of Cognitive Linguistics to her approach lies in Manova's appeal to standard prototype theory, whereby all members of a category clustered around the most salient prototype must share at least one single property. Here she equates the prototype of a category of morphological technique with the most salient representative of it. First she establishes a scale of prototypical morphological techniques, according to constructional iconicity, ranging from pure affixation (the most natural one on the parameters of iconicity and transparency) over partial substitution, modification, conversion or zero affixation to subtraction (with emphasis on the latter techniques), thus excluding suppletion as a non-morphological technique. Then she describes graded clines between these prototypes, e.g. affixations accompanied by more or less substitution or modification.

Manova applies the concept of the prototype again in contrasting prototypical word-based morphology to non-prototypical stem-based and root-based morphology and in using the concept of a cline from prototypical inflection (similar to G. Booij's later contextual inflection) over non-prototypical inflection (cf. Booij's inherent inflection) to non-prototypical derivation (e.g. in diminutive formation) to prototypical derivation. This allows her, furthermore, to apply prototype theory to her concept of the morphological template of Slavic words and word forms which has the format: (prefix)-base-(derivational suffix)-(thematic marker)-(inflectional suffix). As expected, prototypical derivational suffixes fill only the derivational-suffix slot, prototypical inflectional suffixes only the inflectional-suffix slot, whereas non-prototypical ones may violate such strict one-to-one mappings. In such ways Manova can ascribe to clines subtle gradualness, which consists in discrete steps, not a rather unmanageable real continuity. Such elaborate interplay among her concepts adds consistency to her accounts and preempts potential objections of circularity. Moreover, interesting new generalisations are possible, e.g. that subtraction appears to be excluded from both prototypical inflection and root-based morphology.

This monograph felicitously mixes properties of item-and-arrangement grammars and of item-and-process grammars. For the former I want to cite again the concept of a morphological template of Slavic words and word forms, which is useful for the inflecting-fusional morphological type at large. The latter dimension holds, beyond the thorough theoretical and descriptive analysis of morphological operations, also for the subtle and innovatory discussion of criteria for establishing the direction of change in conversion and subtraction (vs. addition). Another example is Manova's detailed account of rule competition/rivalry. Her account predicts that more natural and especially prototypical operations have precedence over less natural ones in terms of productivity, semantic scope or stylistic restrictions.

The descriptive focus is on three Slavic languages which are typologically similar but differ in their proximity to the inflecting-fusional morphological type (Bulgarian less so than Russian and Serbo-Croatian) and pose so far underrated challenges to morphological analysis. Both conversion and subtraction, plus various shortening devices, exhibit different patterns than those well-known from discussions of English and other Western European languages.

Manova's analysis is not strictly bound to any linguistic school, but easily accessible to readers of any linguistic persuasion. Thus she is able to bridge the gap between contemporary West European and North American approaches and East European Slavicist traditions.

Vienna, Austria   Wolfgang U. Dressler

Acknowledgements

The present book is a revised and expanded version of my 2003 Ph.D. thesis in General Linguistics, *Conversion and Subtraction in Bulgarian, Russian and Serbo-Croatian*, from the University of Vienna. Therefore, first and foremost, I would like to thank Wolfgang U. Dressler, the principal adviser of my Ph.D. research and this book. Many thanks for all our turbulent but insightful discussions; for always reading my texts quickly and carefully; for the financial support in terms of numerous lunches (and not only); for the periods of not speaking to me because of always taking linguistics and related matters seriously, and in particular for speaking to me afterwards. The enormous intellect Dressler possesses, supplemented with the obligatory for a powerful mind original character, spreads much outside linguistics and influenced my development in many respects.

Many thanks are due also to the second adviser of my Ph.D. thesis, Heinz Miklas, for all his academic help during my Ph.D. programme, as well as for hosting my postdoctoral project on Bulgarian morphology, Grant 10366 from the Austrian National Bank (OeNB). The financial support of OeNB is hereby gratefully acknowledged.

I thank two anonymous reviewers and the series editors for the profound and thought-provoking reviews of my text. I am particularly indebted to Ingo Plag from whom in the last two years I also learned how to edit a peer-reviewed journal. It was always a pleasure to work with him.

I would also like to thank the following colleagues who contributed to the completion of this book in one way or another: Mark Aronoff, Matthew Baerman, Hans Basbøll, Laurie Bauer, Pier Marco Bertinetto, Dunstan Brown, Bernard Comrie, Greville G. Corbett, Bogdan Dabić, Marina Dzhonova, Heiner Eichner, Gordana Ilić-Marković, Zrinka Jelaska, Jagoda Kappel, Aleksandr Kibrik, Ferenc Kiefer, Roman Krivko, Martin Neef, Gerhard Neweklowsky, Johanna Laakso, Klaus Laalo, Gary Libben, Greg Stump, Ruselina Nitsolova, Vladimir Plungian, Franz Rainer, Johannes Reinhart and Maria Voeikova. Over the past ten years I had the pleasure to meet some of these colleagues at conferences, discussed with others during their stay as Visiting Professors in Vienna, and engaged still others in written correspondence (e-mail and even real letters). My 2003 colleagues from the Linguistic department of the University of Vienna, Adriana Galwan, Antigone Katičić and Markus Pöchtrager, helped me with the data in the present book. Ares George Manos and Kimberley Winternitz proofread the manuscript. I thank them all.

I am also grateful to the Austrian Science Fund (FWF) for the generous support I have received since 2007, grant V64-G03 (Elise Richter Fellowship).

Finally, I would like to thank Jolanda Voogd and Helen van der Stelt from the Springer editorial office and Leah Paul, who managed the typesetting, for all their help and patience with me.

This book is dedicated to my family and to the memory of the Bulgarian poet Михаил Берберов[1] (1934–1989). (I can still hear your voice: "Птици пеят. Нека пеят. Птиците са оптимисти.")[2]

---

[1] Mihail Berberov and Mikhail Berberov in Latin script on the Internet.

[2] 'Birds are singing. Let them sing. Birds are optimists.'

Contents

1	**Preliminaries**		1
	1.1 Introduction		2
		1.1.1 Conversion and Subtraction in Slavic: History of Research	5
		1.1.2 Organization of the Book	8
	1.2 Bulgarian, Russian, and Serbo-Croatian		10
		1.2.1 Phonological and Morphonological Features	11
		1.2.2 Morphological Features	13
	1.3 Word as a Basic Linguistic Unit		25
	1.4 Word-, Stem- and Root-Based Morphology		29
	1.5 Thematic Markers, Aspectual Suffixes and Root Extensions		31
2	**Theoretical Background**		35
	2.1 Natural Morphology		35
		2.1.1 Universal Naturalness	36
		2.1.2 Typological Adequacy	39
		2.1.3 System-Dependent Naturalness	40
	2.2 Cognitive Linguistics (CL)		41
	2.3 Prototype Theory (PT): Prototypes and Clines		42
	2.4 Morphological Techniques		44
	2.5 Derivation-Inflection Continuum		50
3	**Conversion**		55
	3.1 Terminology		55
	3.2 Definition		59
	3.3 Delimiting Conversion		62
		3.3.1 Homophony, Polysemy, Metaphor, Metonymy	62
		3.3.2 Conversion and Related Techniques	64
	3.4 Direction of Conversion		67
		3.4.1 Marchand's Criteria	68
		3.4.2 Criteria by Other Authors	70
		3.4.3 Conversion with a Clear Direction	72

		3.4.4	Reversible Conversion vs. Cross-Linguistic Semantic Pattern	72
	3.5	Classification of Conversion		74
		3.5.1	Conversion in Derivation	74
		3.5.2	Conversion in Inflection	103
		3.5.3	Syntactic Conversion	111
	3.6	Conclusion		121
4	**Subtraction**			**125**
	4.1	Terminology and Definition		125
	4.2	Delimiting Subtraction		130
		4.2.1	Phonological Shortening	131
		4.2.2	Backformation	133
		4.2.3	Haplology	134
		4.2.4	Hypocoristics	136
		4.2.5	Clipping	139
		4.2.6	Blends	142
		4.2.7	Acronyms	143
		4.2.8	Subtraction of Meaning	144
		4.2.9	Zero Sign	145
		4.2.10	Truncation	146
	4.3	Subtraction and Rule Inversion: Ethnicity Terms		147
	4.4	Classification of Subtraction		156
		4.4.1	Subtraction in Derivation	156
		4.4.2	Subtraction in Inflection	166
	4.5	Conclusion		170
5	**Typological and Language-Specific Adequacy of Conversion and Subtraction**			**173**
	5.1	Typological Adequacy of Conversion and Subtraction		173
	5.2	Language-Specific Adequacy of Conversion and Subtraction		177
		5.2.1	Conversion as a Language-Specific Morphological Technique	178
		5.2.2	Subtraction as a Language-Specific Morphological Technique	184
	5.3	Conclusion		190
6	**Conclusions**			**191**

Appendix A: Bulgarian Noun Inflection 201

Appendix B: Bulgarian Adjective Inflection 203

Appendix C: Bulgarian Verb Inflection (Synthetic Forms) 205

Appendix D: Russian Noun Inflection 207

Appendix E: Russian Adjective Inflection 209

Appendix F: Russian Verb Inflection (Synthetic Forms) 211

Appendix G: Serbo-Croatian Noun Inflection 213

Appendix H: Serbo-Croatian Adjective Inflection 215

Appendix I: Serbo-Croatian Verb Inflection (Synthetic Forms) 217

References 219

Author Index 233

Subject Index 237

List of Tables

Table 1.1	Serbo-Croatian accentuation	11
Table 1.2	Nominal categories in Bg., R. & SC.	18
Table 1.3	Verbal categories in Bg., R. & SC.	18
Table 1.4	Non-finite verbal forms in Bg., R. & SC	23
Table 3.1	Types of prototypical conversion in regard to intervention of inflection	102
Table 3.2	Types of conversion and their distribution in Bg., R. & SC.	122
Table 4.1	Bulgarian noun inflection (based on Manova and Dressler 2001).	154
Table 4.2	Types of subtraction according to their scope	170
Table 4.3	Types of subtraction according to their bases	171
Table 5.1	Feminine and masculine nouns with the suffix -*k-(a)* denoting animals.	185
Table 5.2	Diminutives from nouns in -*k-(a)* denoting animals.	186
Table 5.3	Adjectives from nouns in -*k-(a)* denoting animals	187
Table 6.1	Word-, stem- and root-based conversion in Bg., R. & SC.	194
Table 6.2	Root-, stem- and word-based subtraction in Bg., R. & SC.	196
Table 6.3	Types of subtraction and their productivity.	197

Abbreviations

ACC	accusative
ACT	active
ADJ	adjective
ADV	adverb
AOR	aorist
ASUFF	aspectual suffix
attr.	attributive
AUG	augmentative
Bg.	Bulgarian
colloq.	colloquial
COMP	comparative
DAT	dative
DEF ART	definite article
DIM	diminutive
DSUFF	derivational suffix
E.	English
FEM	feminine
F.	Finish
Fr.	French
G.	German
GEN	genitive
GSUFF	gender suffix
H.	Hungarian
HYP	hypocoristic
IMP	imperative
IMPF	imperfect
IMPFV	imperfective
IMPFV1	primary imperfective
IMPFV2	secondary imperfective
INSTR	instrumental
ISUFF	inflectional suffix
It.	Italian
Lat.	Latin

LOC	locative
MASC	masculine
metaph.	metaphoric
N	noun
NEUT	neuter
NM	Natural Morphology
NOM	nominative
OCS	Old Church Slavic
OBg.	Old Bulgarian
PART	participle
PASS	passive
PEJ	pejorative
PF	perfect
PFV	perfective
PL	plural
PRES	present
PRO	pronoun
PT	Prototype Theory
R.	Russian
REFL	reflexive
S.	Serbian
SC.	Serbo-Croatian
SG	singular
Sp.	Spanish
SUFF	suffix
SUP	superlative
T.	Turkish
TM	thematic marker
V	verb
VOC	vocative
WF	word-formation
Ø	zero

Transliteration from Cyrillic

Language	Letter	Transliteration
	a	*a*
	б	*b*
	в	*v*
	г	*g*
	д	*d*
S.	*ђ*	*đ*
	е	*e*
R.	*ё*	*ë*
	ж	*ž*
	з	*z*
	и	*i*
S.	*j*	*j*
Bg., R.	*й*	*j*
	к	*k*
	л	*l*
S.	*љ*	*lj*
	м	*m*
	н	*n*
S.	*њ*	*nj*
	о	*o*
	п	*p*
	р	*r*
	с	*s*
	т	*t*

S.	ћ	ć
	у	u
	ф	f
Bg., R.	х	x
S.	х	h
	ц	c
	ч	č
S.	џ	dž
	ш	š
Bg.	щ	št
R.	щ	šč
Bg.	ъ	ă
R.	ъ	ъ
R.	ы	y
Bg., R.	ь	ʼ
R.	э	è
Bg., R.	ю	ju
Bg., R.	я	ja

Additional Old Church Slavic / Old Bulgarian characters used in the text:

ѣ	ě
ъ	ъ
ь	ь
ѫ	ǫ
ѧ	ę

Notes

1. In this book, all examples from languages that use Cyrillic script (i.e. Bulgarian (Bg.), Russian (R.) and Serbian (S.)) are transliterated, according to the table above.
2. A blank language column indicates that the respective Cyrillic character is found in the alphabets of all three languages, Bulgarian, Russian and Serbian.
3. In the current book, Serbo-Croatian is meant as representing Bosnian, Croatian and Serbian. Of these, only Serbian uses Cyrillic script, Bosnian and Croatian use Latin script, i.e. the transliteration of Serbian is the Bosnian/Croatian spelling (see, however, Section 1.2.1).

Chapter 1
Preliminaries

In June 2005 I had the pleasure to discuss with the well-known psycholinguist Gary Libben on bases of morphological rules. I argued that words are of particular importance to the human brain and that a native speaker discovers morphology via word comparison. Libben, however, argued that the fundamental status of words is not so obvious. He supported his claim with a psycholinguistic experiment he had conducted: having taken both G. *Lauf* 'race, run' and G. *arm* 'poor' as primes to *verlaufen* 'to pass off' and *verarmen* 'to get poor' respectively, he could confirm that priming by the noun *Lauf* (for the verb *verlaufen*) is not as effective as that by the adjective *arm* (for the verb *verarmen*), though both *verlaufen* and *verarmen* have the same structure, which presumes equal paths of parsing and processing. From Libben's explanation, it seemed that not only wordhood of the input but the part of speech it belongs to might impact morphological processing. Although this hypothesis seemed plausible, I found somewhat disappointing the fact that words might not always be what they are expected to be and decided, therefore, to reanalyze the two examples in terms of the categorization effort they require (an approach I applied to conversion and subtraction in my 2003 Ph.D. thesis).

While one can form *verlaufen* in two different ways: either according to the pattern *Lauf – laufen* 'to run' – *verlaufen* or to the chain *Lauf – Verlauf* '(in the) course (of)' – *verlaufen*, there is only a single possibility for *arm* → *verarmen*, since in German, there exists neither an adjective **verarm* nor a verb **armen*. In other words, the relation *Lauf – verlaufen* appears to be cognitively more complex than that of *arm – verarmen*. Moreover, whether one assumes the chain *Lauf - laufen - verlaufen* or the pattern *Lauf – Verlauf – verlaufen*, the relation between the noun and the verb (i.e. between *Lauf – laufen* and *Verlauf – verlaufen*) is reversed in comparison to the natural semantic direction which is from verb to noun, since the definitions of *laufen* and *verlaufen* do not depend on *Lauf* and *Verlauf*, whereas those of *Lauf* and *Verlauf* are based on *laufen* and *verlaufen*. In other words, the result nouns *Lauf* and *Verlauf* are derived from their respective verbs by conversion, and the direction of the above derivations is determined by the semantic dependence of their mates, i.e. *laufen* → *der Lauf* and *verlaufen* → *der Verlauf*. On the contrary, *arm* is directly associated with *verarmen* by the most iconic and cognitively easiest rule of affixation (i.e *arm* →

verarmen), where addition of meaning is mirrored by addition of form. Thus the more complex cognitive nature of conversion, in comparison to addition (cf. Chapter 2), further contributes to the low efficiency of *Lauf* as a prime to *verlaufen*. Surprisingly to me, Libben, who knows well how foolish the morphological parser can be (e.g. it even looks for relations between phonologically similar but semantically unrelated words, cf. Libben and de Almeida 2002) could not find any contra arguments to my cognitively oriented (i.e. excluding any stupidity) analysis.

I decided to mention the discussion with Libben because it seems to me a nice illustration of the possibilities for, and the importance of, alternative methods and analyses in linguistics. Moreover, the arguments I put forward during the discussion are particularly telling in regard to the 'alternative' way that linguistic phenomena are tackled in this book.

1.1 Introduction

The present book merges principles and mechanisms from Cognitive Linguistics and Natural Morphology. The line of research followed connects linguistic structure with principles of human categorization, pragmatic principles, and semiotic and functional principles, such as iconicity, indexicality, biuniqueness, etc. The notion of prototype has a central role in the analysis, and realizations of linguistic phenomena are seen as clustered around best examples or prototypical instances. It will be demonstrated that there is hardly a rule that is entirely uniform in all its realizations, since both the input and the output of the rule in question might vary in comparison to the prototype, i.e. the realizations of the rule constitute a cline.

The assumption of non-discrete morphological rules tolerating deviations does not mean that morphological operations cannot be categorized, i.e. like in the categorization of colours that constitute a continuum, one always has an idea what colour is involved, though the identification of a particular colour may depend on the cultural settings in which one grows up or the language(s) to which one is exposed (i.e. whether or not such language has means to express a large set of different colours and colour shades).

The cognitive aspect of the present theory further differs from Cognitive grammar (and to some extent from Natural Morphology as well) in paying particular attention to the formal side of morphological changes. In the present study, all rules are given in terms of morphotactic structures or templates representing prototypical instances, e.g. X → X + Y represent affixation by addition as in E. *to teach* → *teach-er* and X + Y → X + Z is the prototype of the derivation E. *to nomin-ate* → *nomin-ee*, with affixation by substitution. Categorization of the data is based on a template structure we call a generalized form of a Slavic word: (PREF)-ROOT-(DSUFF)-(TM)-(ISUFF). These are all slots that a Slavic word uses if all possible morphemes that might participate in a word form have a single realization (for a precise definition of the template cf. Section 1.4). This generalized form resembles to some extent schematic structures of Cognitive Grammar, but in contrast to such schemas, it is not semantically defined, but rather, motivated universally (by the principle of constructional iconicity, cf. Dressler 1987b; 2000a) and typologically (i.e. since Slavic languages belong to the inflecting type, they make a clear distinction between derivational and inflectional affixes, cf. Skalička 1979). Indeed, the template has different slots for derivational and inflectional suffixes, which should imply a clear-cut boundary between derivation and inflection, but it does not exclude the possibility that exponents of non-prototypical inflection (in the sense of Dressler 1989) might occupy the derivational slot of the word, and conversely, that the exponents of non-prototypical derivation can be in the inflectional slot of the word, as we will see later. The fact that non-prototypical derivation (such as nominal diminutives) and non-prototypical inflection (such as verbal aspect and nominal gender) use either the derivational or the inflectional slot of the word is evidence of their non-prototypical status. As for the classification of non-prototypical categories, we assume along with Manova (2005a) that there are always facts (typological and/or language-specific) that speak for either derivational or inflectional status. For example, in the inflecting-fusional type, the output of non-prototypical derivation is dispersed within the language's inflectional system, while the output of non-prototypical inflection, since connected with a particular inflectional class or complementary classes, is identifiable inflectionally.

The theory suggested here is also comparable and compatible with what Stump (2001) defines as realizational-inferential approach to inflectional morphology, such as Word-and-Paradigm theories of inflection (e.g. Matthews 1972; Zwicky 1985; Anderson 1992). Roughly, it is not the mere addition of an affix (as is claimed by lexical-incremental theories of word-formation, e.g. Lieber 1992) that produces new words or word-forms, but that 'an inflected word's association with a particular set of morphosyntactic properties licenses the application of rules determining the word's inflectional form; *likes*, for example, arises by means of a rule appending -*s* to any verb stem associated with the properties "3sg subject agreement", "present tense", "and indicative mood" (Stump 2001: 3).

Likewise in word-formation rules the present book acknowledges, that we have, on the one hand, morphological units listed in the lexicon and specified semantically and according to their word class, and, on the other hand, intensional semantics that we would like to derive (Dressler and Manova 2002 and Manova and Dressler 2005 speak of a regular (describable by a rule) semantic change).

The association of a lexical entry with the semantics we wish to derive determines the cognitive mechanism (morphological technique), such as addition, substitution, modification, conversion and subtraction, that operates on the input. For example, if we take the base *to play* from the lexicon and want to produce a noun meaning 'somebody that plays', the mechanism of association will select the morphological technique of addition and the suffix -*er* from the lexicon. A realization rule will then produce *player*. If the semantics we want to express is 'something that is played', the base *to play* will be associated with the morphological technique of conversion, and a realization rule will produce the output *a play*, etc. Thus, if the morphological technique assigned requires a suffix, the suffix will be taken from the lexicon. If not, either conversion (as in the derivation of the noun *a play*) or subtraction, as in the following examples from Bulgarian, apply: Bg. *biologija* 'biology' → *biolog* 'biologist' and Bg. *geografija* 'geography' → *geograf* 'geographer'. Both derivations use bases with similar phonological make-up and express the same semantic change 'science → scientist' and therefore select the same morphological technique. However, Bg. *antologija* 'anthology' → Ø, since *antologija*, though also terminating in -*ija*, does not mean 'a science'. The association between the input and the regular semantic change we pursue is, in this book, sometimes specified only in general, i.e. in terms of word-class relations, such as N → ADJ, and in all cases where the data allow – precisely, as in the above-mentioned Bulgarian pattern 'science → scientist'.

In some instances, two cognitive operations can apply to a single base, as in Bg. *učenik* 'pupil' → *učenič-esk-i* 'pupil's', with affixation and a concomitant *k : č* morphonological palatalization (cf. Dressler 1987b; and morphological meta-generalizations, i.e. combinations of morphophonological and morphological rules, in Stump 2001).

The main advantage of such an approach to morphology is that it successfully accounts for non-concatenative morphology, such as conversion and subtraction as well as adequately categorizing morphological operations in languages with rich inflection, such as Slavic ones, from which most of the data are obtained. Thus, although derivations such as the following from Bulgarian (i) N *krava* 'cow' → ADJ *kravi* 'cow-' and (ii) N *krava* 'cow' → ADJ *kraveški* 'cow-' have the same input and express the same morphological change, they differ when analysed according to the generalized form of the Slavic word: (i) *krav-ø-a* → *krav-ø-i* and (ii) *krav-ø-a* → *krav-ešk-i*. It is clear that (i) represents conversion (the derivational slot of the word is empty and the word-class-change is expressed by inflection change only), whereas (ii) is derived by affixation (an affix is added in the derivational slot of the word, thereby the word-class-change is adequately (prototypically) expressed). As we will see in the discussion (Chapters 3 and 4), in cases where a single output is related to the same intensional semantics by two different rules, the cognitively easier, more iconic, operation (affixation) usually prevails over the cognitively more complex, less iconic, operation (conversion). In Bulgarian, *kravi*-MASC is preferred in idiomatic expressions, such as *krave*-NEUT *sirene*-NEUT 'white cheese made from cow milk' (the typical Bulgarian cheese), whereas *kraveški* expresses the meaning 'cow-' in general.

The theoretical claims made herein will be tested against data of conversion and subtraction from Slavic, with special emphasis on Bulgarian, Russian and Serbo-Croatian. In this book, Serbo-Croatian stands for Bosnian/Croatian/

1.1 Introduction

Serbian, though most of the examples come from Croatian sources. If a particular example is typical of the three languages, Bosnian, Croatian, Serbian, it is classified as Serbo-Croatian. If an example exists only in one or two of these languages, the language(s) that possess(es) the example is/are explicitly specified.

Being of importance to English word formation, the conversion/zero derivation concept developed in the 1960s (Marchand 1960, 1963, 1964a; Kastovsky 1968; Dokulil 1968a–c) and in the 1990s (Cetnarowska 1993; Don 1993; Vogel 1996; Štekauer 1996) whereas the topic of subtraction is primarily connected with the 1980s and 1990s (Dressler 1984, 1987a, b, 1994; Martin 1988, 1994; Mel'čuk 1991). Conversion and subtraction have never belonged to the central topics of the morphological debate, but due to their non-concatenative character, they have become a must to any serious theory of word-formation, cf. for conversion Aronoff (1976), Lieber (1981a, b), Kiparsky (1982), Williams (1981) and Di Sciullo and Williams (1987), Beard (1987, 1995), among others,[1] and for subtraction Dressler et al. (1987), Dressler (2000a, b) and Anderson (1992).

Bulgarian, Russian and especially Serbo-Croatian, approach rather closely the inflecting-fusional type that, as in the examples above, is characterized by addition and deletion of inflectional material in derivation, which makes Slavic conversion and subtraction particularly difficult to analysis. Moreover, the terms conversion and (especially) subtraction are nearly unknown in Slavic linguistics. This fact finds its explanation in the specific development of East-European linguistics, wherin terminology and data description often significantly differ from those in West European and American linguistic traditions, which renders difficult, on the one hand, use of Slavic data by foreign linguists and application of modern linguistic theory to Slavic data, on the other.

Therefore, this book has the following goals:

- to offer a framework for unified analysis of all possible morphological processes that might take place in a language's morphology, demonstrating that all morphological relations are gradual, this with focus on non-iconic and anti-iconic morphology such as conversion and subtraction; and
- to present a considerable amount of Slavic data relevant to conversion and subtraction, i.e. Slavic morphology poses many challenges, the analysis of which may contribute to the definition of conversion and subtraction, to the better understanding of inflecting-fusional-type morphology, and to the ongoing discussion of the nature of word-formation and inflection in general.

1.1.1 Conversion and Subtraction in Slavic: History of Research

Slavic grammars distinguish between zero derivation and conversion and prefer the former to the latter. However, different sources advocate different

---

[1]See the discussion in Don (1993).

understandings of zero and conversion, thereby parallel instances have been classified differently in the three languages.

As for subtraction, since Bulgarian, Russian and Serbo-Croatian grammars do not use the term at all, examples of subtraction can be found under different labels even in one and the same linguistic work, and thus there exists no reliable source of data.

Each of the three languages, however, has an official representative grammar published by the respective academy of sciences. In order to gain some consistency, those Academy Grammars will serve as main sources of data for us: for Bulgarian, Andrejčin et al. (1983); for Russian, Švedova et al. (1980); for Serbo-Croatian, Babić (1991) for word-formation and Babić et al. (1991) for inflection. For the sake of completeness, for each language, a few other grammars also have been consulted: Stojanov (1993 [1964])[2]; Bojadžiev et al. (1999) and Maslov (1981[2]) are the additional sources for Bulgarian; the Russian data is further checked mainly with Vinogradov (1972); for Serbo-Croatian, Stevanović (1978) and Barić et al. (1997) have been used. Of course, grammars of the three languages by other authors, courses in historical, comparative and general linguistics, studies on specific problems, articles as well as textbooks for second language acquisition also have been considered.

The notion of conversion entered the Slavic linguistic area in the 1950s when Aleksandr Smirnickij published two articles on conversion in English (cf. Smirnickij 1953, 1954), wherein he emphasizes the paradigmatic change occurring in conversion (and in word-formation in general). The term 'zero derivation' appears after Marchand (1960,[3] 1969) and becomes a well-established label, especially in Russian and Serbo-Croatian linguistic traditions. Like Marchand, Slavic grammars distinguish between zero suffixation and conversion, i.e. while zero suffixation is a word-formation process, conversion concerns syntax (cf. Section 3.1). Syntactic conversion (in particular substantivization) is the best investigated conversion-related process, especially so in Russian linguistics. Substantivization, whether under the label conversion or as 'usage of adjectives for substantives'/'substantives with adjectival declension', can be found in every Russian grammar. In Russian, the term zero suffixation is first used by Lopatin (1966: 77f), afterwards by the Russian Academy Grammar (1970)[4] and also by Zemskaja (1973a: 38).[5] Babić (1986) discusses zero suffixation in Croatian, dedicating an entire chapter, entitled 'Nulti sufiksi' ['Zero suffixes'] (1986: 283–302), to specific theoretical problems concerning the zero suffixation concept and illustrating the discussion with copious examples, from

---

[2]Stojanov is the author of the part on WF in Andrejčin et al. (1983), therefore Stojanov (1993) is often cited instead of the Bulgarian Academy Grammar.

[3]See Marchand (1969 [1960]) in the references.

[4]In the Russian Academy Grammar (1970), the chapter on word-formation is written by Lopatin and Uluhanov.

[5]For a more detailed history of research on zero derivation in Russian see Vogel (1996: 31ff).

Croatian, that he assigns to different semantic groups. As for Bulgarian, the Bulgarian Academy Grammar does not operate with zero suffixes, therefore Bojadžiev (1999) will be cited instead.

It should be underlined that in the three languages different understandings of zero have been advocated. Whereas the Russian Academy Grammar (Švedova et al. 1980: 219ff, 303f, see also the 1970 edition) allows for addition of inflectional material in cases of zero suffixation, e.g. *xval-i-t'* 'to praise' → *xval-a* 'praise', *sel-i-t'sja* 'to settle' → *sel-o* 'village', *suprug* 'husband' → *suprug-a* 'wife' (Švedova et al. 1980: 222, 224), Barić (1991) and Bojadžiev (1999) postulate zero suffixation only if after a deletion of morphotactic material nothing else is added, i.e. SC. *pogled-a-ti* 'to look (at)' → *pȍglēdØ* 'look, glance' (Babić 1991: 310); Bg. *zal-iv-a-m* '(I) overflow', *zal-iv-a* → *zalivØ* 'bay, gulf' (Bojadžiev 1999: 266). According to Babić (1991: 41) the inflectional suffixes *-a, -o, -e, Ø* combine inflectional and word-formational meaning, therefore he classifies examples such as *suprug* 'husband' → *suprug-a* 'wife', *dobav-i-ti* 'to acquire, obtain' → *dobav-a* 'obtainment', etc. as derivations with overt suffixes (cf. Babić 1991: 65ff). According to Bojadžiev (1999: 266f), in cases where a derivational suffix is expected, but only inflection is added, the zero suffixation turns to morphological conversion (the same claim in Maslov 1981). For Bojadžiev, examples such as *zabrav-j-a* 'I forget', 3 SG *zabrav-i* → *zabrav-a* 'forgetfulness, oblivion', *săprug* 'husband' → *săprug-a* 'wife' are morphological conversions.

As can be seen from the examples in the previous paragraph, parallel output forms have been labelled in three different ways in the three languages: zero suffix, suffixation with an overt suffix and morphological conversion in Russian, Serbo-Croatian and Bulgarian respectively. Moreover Babić (1991: 41) further distinguishes among zeroes, such as different zero suffix for masculine nouns (e.g. $gukØ_1$) and feminine nouns (e.g. $skrbØ_2$ 'sorrow').

The Russian Academy Grammar assumes zero suffixation in cases of addition of nominal (cf. the above-cited examples from Russian) and adjectival inflection (cf. Švedova et al. 1980: 303f; cf. also Valgina et al. 1964: 135), but surprisingly, if only verbal inflection (thematic markers and infinitival suffixes) is attached, the process is classified as normal concatinative derivation (Švedova et al. 1980: 333ff). Following the assumption that nominal and adjectival inflection suffixes that might change word class are derivational, Babić (1991: 463ff) considers all verbs built only by addition of inflection also word formation with overt suffixes.

As for subtraction, the term is entirely unknown to Slavic grammars.[6] (A curious fact: summarizing the history of Russian word-formation research, Uluhanov (2000: 287ff) argues for 77 word-formation types (Wortbildungsarten)

---

[6]Babić (1991: 40) mentions substraction (SC. *supstrakcija*) as a term preceding 'zero suffix' in the terminology of Serbo-Croatian grammars. However, I could not find a source operating with the term.

in modern literary Russian. Despite the great number of types, there is no subtraction among them. A peculiar change called 'desuffixation'[7] could be seen as a kind of subtraction, if it were not strangely restricted to colloquial style only).

Although Bulgarian *săkraštenie* 'shortening' (cf. Bojadžiev 1999: 254f), Russian *usečenie* 'shortening (literally cutting)' (cf. Švedova et al. 1980: 421ff), Serbo-Croatian *skraćivanje osnova* 'stem shortening' (Babić 1991: 220) can be understood as to some extent connected to subtraction, there exists no uniform Slavic term for subtractive rules. Moreover, the three terms appear to be hyperonyms of truncation/substitution, conversion and subtraction (cf. Chapter 2).

1.1.2 Organization of the Book

The book consists of six chapters.

Chapter 1 includes introduction, history of research, organization of the book, and a section on morphological systems of Bulgarian, Russian and Serbo-Croatian where relevant phonological and morphonological features are also tackled. The chapter finishes with the definitions of root, stem and word with the help of which word-, stem- and root-based morphological rules are discussed.

Chapter 2 defines the book's theoretical background, beginning with short surveys of Natural Morphology research and Cognitive Linguistics (including the definition of prototype). Afterwards, a system of cognitively defined morphological techniques is presented. Morphological techniques correspond to all possible cognitive operations that can be performed on a morphological form. If classified according to the mental effort required (or the degree of iconicity they exhibit), the morphological techniques constitute a cline that includes the following operations: (1) Addition X → X + Y, (2) Substitution X + Y → X + Z, (3) Modification X → X', (4) Conversion X → X, and (5) Subtraction XY → X, which is X → X – Y. The formal templates of the techniques represent prototypical instances of morphological rules. In this way, we consider the fact that rules of a language's morphology can be word-based (most prototypical), stem-based (less prototypical) and root-based (least prototypical), as well as that affixation, substitution and subtraction may be accompanied by phonological and morphonological modifications. At the end of the chapter, examples of modified (non-prototypical) realizations of

---

[7]Uluhanov illustrates desuffixation with examples such as: *čaška – čaša* 'cup – big cup', *ložka – loga* 'spoon – big spoon' and *njanja* → *njan'* 'babysitter-FEM – babysitter-MASC', the latter is pointed out as a case of zero desuffixation. For Uluhanov, desuffixation, deprefixation, depostfixation, desubstantivization and decomposition constitute the group of "okkasionelle inverse, reine Wortbildungsarten" ('occasional inverse, pure word-formation strategies') (Uluhanov 2000: 291f).

the techniques are classified according to their prototypicality. In other words, establishment of the prototypicality degree of a rule requires evaluation against various criteria. It becomes clear thereby that the different realizations of a rule are clustered around the prototype of that rule and constitute a cline.

Chapters 3 and 4 tackle conversion and subtraction respectively and have, to a great extent, the same organization: (1) terminology and definition; (2) demarcation of the respective technique where various false examples of the techniques are discussed. Conversion is distinguished from homophony, polysemy, metaphor, metonymy and its neighbour techniques modification and subtraction. The morphological technique of subtraction is set apart from phonological shortening, backformation, haplology, hypocoristics, clippings, blends, acronyms, subtraction of semantics, zero sign, truncation and rule inversion; (3) direction of conversion and subtraction (the subject is dealt with only in the chapter on conversion), i.e. since the output of conversion and subtraction is the same or shorter than their input, a problem with determining the direction of a conversion/subtraction rule arises; criteria by different authors and their reliability are discussed; some new suggestions are also made; (4) classification of the respective technique (each technique is illustrated in derivation as well as in inflection with a rich amount of word-, stem- and root-based realizations, all examples sanctioning formal templates. Further classification criteria take into consideration the word-class of the input and output of conversion/subtraction rules; as well as the presence/absence of modifications in cases of subtraction; and (5) conclusions.

The specific features of Slavic morphology require the discussion of non-prototypical inflectional categories (verbal aspect and nominal gender) that are an exact formal parallel to non-prototypical derivations (without word-class change), which, if expressed without derivational suffixes, represent conversion. For non-prototypical inflection the term formal conversion is used. Formal conversion is addressed in Section 3.5.2.

Syntactic conversion (Section 3.5.3) is discussed in accordance with Slavic linguistic tradition (in particular that of Russian linguistics) for substantivization.

Chapter 5 focuses on the typological and language-specific characteristics of conversion and subtraction. The typological perspective in regard to conversion is primarily in relation to its bases in the two polar morphological types – the isolating and the inflecting-fusional, though examples from agglutinating languages are also considered. In this chapter, cases of conversion and subtraction are explained with language-specific features such as system-adequate stress-patterns, language-specific inflectional productivity, etc. Bulgarian, Russian and Serbo-Croatian belong to the Slavic family and possess nearly the same sets of morphemes, presupposing the same or at least similar morphological solutions. At times, however, the same semantic meaning may be expressed by different morphological techniques in the three languages. Such instances are also in the scope of the chapter.

In Chapter 6 the main ideas of the analysis are summarized and conclusions are drawn.

In order to make the book easier to understand, it ends with nine appendices where the major inflection patterns of Bulgarian, Russian and Serbo-Croatian nouns, adjectives and verbs are exemplified.

1.2 Bulgarian, Russian, and Serbo-Croatian

The three languages belong to the Slavic family and are genealogically related as descendents of a parent language conventionally called Proto-Slavic. The first Slavic texts are, however, written in Old Church Slavic (Old Bulgarian in some authors). The most widely accepted classification of Slavic languages divides them into South, East and West (De Bray 1951, 1980; Schenker and Stankiewicz 1980; Kondrašov 1986; Comrie and Corbett 1993, among others). According to that classification Bulgarian and Serbo-Croatian are South Slavic languages, whereas Russian belongs to the East Slavic group. This implies that Bulgarian and Serbo-Croatian would have more features in common than Bulgarian and Russian, on the one hand, or Russian and Serbo-Croatian, on the other. However, not all of these implications hold, which is due to the fact that the above-mentioned classification has two important disadvantages. First, the classification neglects the strong (historically-conditioned) diachronic relations between Bulgarian and Russian via Old Church Slavic, and second, overlooks the peculiar status of Bulgarian within the Slavic family, since Bulgarian is one of the central languages of the Balkans. Thus taking into consideration the misleading implications of the threefold classification, Mareš (1980: 36) suggests a new fourfold grouping:

(1) South-East Slavic languages with Bulgarian and Macedonian;
(2) South-West Slavic languages with Serbo-Croatian and Slovene;
(3) North-West Slavic languages with Czech, Slovak, Upper and Low Sorbian, and Polish;
(4) North-East Slavic languages with Ukrainian, Belorussian, and Russian.

This less popular classification underlines the central position of Bulgarian in the Balkan Sprachbund, the latter including Bulgarian, Macedonian, Romanian, Albanian and Modern Greek (Serbian being a peripheral Balkan language, cf. Assenova 2002). The most salient balkanism of Bulgarian morphology that distinguishes it from Russian and Serbo-Croatian is the clear tendency towards analytism. In nominal morphology analytism is manifested in uttermost restriction of case as well as in the use of analytic forms for comparatives and superlatives of adjectives and adverbs. In verbal morphology the tendency towards analytism affects the verb infinitive; Bulgarian has lost the infinitive replacing it by a construction with the complementizer *da* and a finite verb. The loss of the infinitive reflects further on the expression of the future tense that in

1.2 Bulgarian, Russian, and Serbo-Croatian

Old Bulgarian consisted of the conjugated form of *iměti* 'to have', *xotěti* 'to want' and *načęti* 'to begin' plus an infinitive. Thus in Modern Bulgarian, in contrast to Russian and Serbo-Croatian, the future tense (affirmative form) is expressed by the particle *šte* (continuant of the Old Bulgarian volitional auxiliary *xotěti* 'to want') and the respective present tense form of the verb, e.g. Bg. *šte piša* (cf. R. *budu pisat'*-INF and SC. *xočem pisati*-INF), whereas the negated paradigm of the future uses the unchangeable *njama* 'don't have' (i.e. from *iměti* 'to have') and a *da*-construction of the conjugated verb in the present, e.g. Bg. *njama da piša*-1SG.PRES 'I will not write', *njama da pišeš*-2SG.PRES 'you will not write', etc.

In Bulgarian, after the loss of the infinitive, 1 SG PRES IND becomes the citation form of the verb. Therefore in the analysis, all Bulgarian verbs are given in the 1 SG PRES IND, while the respective Russian and Serbo-Croatian examples will be cited in the infinitive. In fact, the different citation forms are of no importance for the productive core of the Slavic verb morphology, as most of the Slavic verbs have identical present stem (visible in the present tense) and aorist stem (visible in the infinitive and the aorist), e.g. Bg. *xval-j-a* 'I praise'/3 SG *xval-i*, R. *xval-i-t'* 'to praise', SC. *xval-i-ti* 'to praise'. However, if a verb exhibits two different stems, the situation could seem strange, since it will require different analysis for Bulgarian, e.g. Bg. *piša* '(I) write' (1 SG AOR *pisax*) versus R. *pisat'* (1 SG PRES *pišu*), SC. *pisati* (1 SG PRES *pišem*). A solution to this problem is suggested in Section 1.3 below.

1.2.1 Phonological and Morphonological Features

The stress in Bulgarian and Russian is free, dynamic and mobile. Serbo-Croatian also is characterized by a free and mobile stress, but an automatic rule allows no word-final stress for polysyllabic words (cf. SC. *národ*, *sèstra* vs. Bg. and R. *naród*, *sestrá*). The most interesting characteristic of the Serbo-Croatian vowel system is the accentuation (SC. *naglasak* 'accent'). Vowels (and the syllabic *r*) vary according to length and pitch and can be long and short. Pitch is differentiated only in initial stressed position, where there is an opposition between rising and falling tone. The following four symbols (Table 1.1) indicate the position of stress, tone and length in Serbo-Croatian:

Falling accents are found only on the first syllables of words and can occur on monosyllables. Rising accents occur on any syllable but the last, i.e.

Table 1.1 Serbo-Croatian accentuation

Syllable	Vowel Tone	long	short
stressed	falling	ˆ	˵
	rising	´	ˋ
unstressed		—	

monosyllables cannot have rising tone. Long and short vowels are distinguished under accent or in later syllables in the word (i.e. post-accentual length). Post-accentual length is notated, e.g.: *gòdīnā* 'years -GEN.PL' (the first vowel is stressed, has falling tone and is short; the last two vowels are unstressed and long). Many post-accentual lengths are associated with specific suffixes or grammatical forms, for example, the suffix *-ār* (*matemàtičār* 'mathematician') or genitive plural of nouns (see the previous example).

It should be noted that the symbols in Table 1.1 are used in dictionaries and grammars but are not printed in ordinary texts. Most recent grammars and dictionaries do not notate accents either, and native speakers have difficulties with the assignment of the exact accentuation. Therefore in this book, the accents will be notated only if they entail some change relevant for the discussion, but even in such cases, it will be the placement of the accent and not its exact contour that will be considered.

In Russian, a phonological change called *ákan'e* neutralizes the *o/a* opposition in unstressed syllables, e.g. *vodá* 'water' as [vadá], but the orthography fails to record *ákan'e*.

In comparison to Russian and Bulgarian, Serbo-Croatian has the smallest inventory of palatalized consonants, and some authors even notice an 'absence of a consonantal correlation of palatalization' (Horálek 1992: 439). In other words, palatalized consonants constitute a problem for a comparative morphological analysis of Bulgarian, Russian and Serbo-Croatian, since in Russian, consonants that are followed by *e* and *i* are always palatalized (soft),[8] in Bulgarian *e* and *i* do not palatalize every consonant, and then in Serbo-Croatian there is an extremely restricted set of palatilized consonants. In order to have a unified analysis, we will not notate palatalization (softening), because of *e* and *i* in Russian. We will assume further that the different types of bases such as roots or stems, by rule, terminate in non-palatalized consonants and it is the addition of *e* and *i* initial desinences that palatalizes, e.g. *stekl-o* 'glass' → *stekl-* + *-i-t'* 'to supply with glass', i.e. *stekl-it'* and not *stekl'-it'*, which makes the Russian pair *stekl-o* → *stekl-it'* compatible with Bg. *stăkl-o* → *stăkl-ja* (not *stăkl'-a*) and SC. *sestr-a* 'sister' → *sestr-iti* 'to make a sister'. If the base of the rule terminates in a palatal consonant and the rule adds a palatalizing suffix (e.g. the derivation R. *učitel'* 'teacher' → *učitel'* + *-it'* 'to work as a teacher (colloq.)', where the same palatalizing inflection *-it'* as in *stekl-it'* is added), the palatal character of the base-final consonant is not notated in the derivative, since the attachment of a palatalizing suffix indicates palatalization (i.e. *učitel-it'* and not *učitel'-it'*, by analogy to *stekl-it'*).

Besides the different prosodic alternations, vocalic alternations such as ablaut are typical for conjugation and for nominalizations from verbs, e.g.: Bg. IMPFV *nos-j-a* 'I carry' → PFV *pod-nes-a* 'I present, submit, offer, serve' → IMPFV2 *pod-nas-ja-m*, and from the last two verbs N *pod-nos* 'tray' and N

---

[8]In Russian, *ž, c* and *š* are invariably hard while *č* and *šč* are invariably soft.

pod-nas-ja-ne 'presentation, offer' are derived; SC. IMPFV *ìzvir-a-ti* 'to well' → *ìzvor* 'well', etc.

Palatalizations (in terms of *g, k, x* changes) are perhaps the most characteristic morphonological feature of Slavic languages. *k, g, x* palatalize in nominal and in verbal morphology, and in derivation as well as in inflection, e.g. Bg. N *učenik* 'pupil', PL *učenic-i*, FEM SG *učenič-ka* and ADJ *učenič-eski* 'pupil-'; V PRES *pek-a* 'I bake, roast, scorch', 2 SG *peč-eš* → verbal N *peč-ene* 'baking, roasting, sunbathing' and the noun *pek* 'scorching heat'.

In Serbo-Croatian, if *l* is word-final, it is changed to *o*. This alternation occurs without exception in masculine singular *l*-participles, e.g. *pisa-o* 'written' (← *pis-a-ti* 'to write'), but the feminine singular form is *pisa-l-a*. The change is also wide-spread, though lexicalized, in adjectives and nouns, e.g. ADJ MASC SG *mȋo* 'nice', FEM SG *mȉl-a*; NOM SG *mîsao* 'thought', NOM PL *mîsl-i*, but NOM SG *misāl* 'missal', NOM PL *misáli*.

Serbo-Croatian (Štokavian),[9] depending on the reflex of the Common Slavic *ě* (*jat'*), is divided into three dialect groups: Ikavian (replacing *ě* with *i*), Ekavian (replacing *ě* with *e*) and Ijekavian (replacing *ě* with *ije* in long syllables and with *je* in short syllables), giving *dite, dete* and *dijete* 'child' respectively. Ikavian dialect is no longer used as a literary language. The Serbian literary language is both Ekavian and Ijekavian, while Croatian and Bosnian are Ijekavian. In this book, since Babić (1991), who represents the Croatian (i.e. Ijekavian) standard, is the main source of data, the examples are usually given in Ijekavian, unless an example from a source written in Ekavian is cited.

1.2.2 Morphological Features

As already discussed, in the generalized form of the Slavic word the following slots are distinguished: (PREF) – ROOT – (DSUFF) – (TM) – (ISUFF), of all slots only the root slot is obligatorily occupied. This template form is based on the universal principle of constructional iconicity (see on NM in Chapter 2) and the characteristic features of the inflectional/fusional type morphology (Chapter 2, the section on NM). The form is also in accordance with Greenberg's Universal 28: 'If both the derivation and inflection follow the root, or they both precede the root, the derivation is always between the root and the inflection' (Greenberg 1963: 93).

---

[9]Štokavian is the main dialect of the Bosnian, Serbian and Croatian languages. It is spoken in Serbia, Montenegro, Bosnia and Herzigovina, in part of Croatia and in the southern part of Burgenland (Austria). The name of the dialect comes from the form for the interrogative pronoun 'what', which is *što* or *šta* in this dialect. There are also Kajkavian ('what' is pronounced as *kaj*) and Čakavian ('what' is pronounced as *ča*) dialects, both spoken in different parts of Croatia.

Note, however, that all slots of the Slavic word, except the TM slot, can be realized more than once. For example, a verb can have: more than one prefix (Bg. ***pre-pod**-pisvam*, I resign', ***pre-pod**-pisva*); more than one root (Bg. ***rud**-o-**dob**-iv* 'ore output'; if two roots co-occur, they are usually connected with a linking vowel, in this case -*o*-); more than one derivational suffix (Bg. *uči-**tel-sk**-i* 'teacher's, where both -*tel*- and -*sk*- are derivational suffixes), as well as more than one inflectional suffix (Bg. *žen-**a-ta*** 'woman-SG-DEF', cf. *žen-**i-te*** 'woman-PL-DEF'). In order to account for such multiple realizations of slots, one has to add (a) slot(s) of the respective type to the generalized form of the Slavic word.

Generally speaking, affixation in terms of either addition or substitution of affixes, is the dominant morphological rule in Slavic. There is an interesting, nearly complementary, distribution of prefixation and suffixation changes. Prefixation plays a marginal role in nominal morphology, but prefixes are the main perfectivizing device for Slavic verbs. In contrast, most derivational suffixes are nominalizing, and derivational suffixation is rare in verbal morphology. The set of adjectivizing suffixes is also smaller than that of substantivizing suffixes. Thematic markers (TM) are stem-forming material that appears between the root and an inflectional suffix (R. *čit-a-t'* 'to read' with the root *cit*-, TM -*a*-, and the infinitival inflection -*t'*), and rarely between a derivational suffix and an inflectional suffix, as in derived verbs such as SC. *model-ir-a-ti* 'to model'.

TMs are typical for Slavic conjugation, which can be illustrated by the following present paradigm of the Serbo-Croatian verb *sedeti* 'to sit':

(1) PRESNT
    SG   PL
    1 *sed-i-m*   1 *sed-i-mo*
    2 *sed-i-š*   2 *sed-i-te*
    3 *sed-i*   3 *sed-e*

Since all the forms but 3 PL share the stem *sed-i-* with the TM -*i*, the verb *sedeti* is traditionally classified as an -*im*-verb, which serves to say that according to its present stem, *sedeti* belongs to the *i*-conjugation.

Aorist and imperfect paradigms of a Serbo-Croatian verb display TM in all person/number forms. Consider the aorist paradigm of the perfective verb *viknu-ti* 'to cry, call' and the imperfective paradigm of the imperfective verb *pisa-ti*:

(2) AORIST
    SG   PL
    1. *vik-nu-h*   1. *vik-nu-smo*
    2. *vik-nu*   2. *vik-nu-ste*
    3. *vik-nu*   3. *vik-nu-še*

1.2 Bulgarian, Russian, and Serbo-Croatian

(3) IMPERFECT
SG   PL
1. *pis-a-h*   1. *pis-a-smo*
2. *pis-a-še*   2. *pis-a-ste*
3. *pis-a-še*   3. *pis-a-hu*

Let us compare now the above verb paradigms with the inflectional paradigm of the noun *izvor* 'well':

(4) SG   PL
NOM *izvor*   NOM *izvor-i*
GEN *izvor-a*   GEN *izvor-a*
DAT *izvor-u*   DAT *izvor-ima*
ACC *izvor*   ACC *izvor-e*
VOC *izvor-e*   VOC *izvor-i*
LOC *izvor-u*   LOC *izvor-ima*
INSTR *izvor-om*   INSTR *izvor-ima*

Serbo-Croatian grammars classify this declension type as *a*-stems (Babić 1991: 489; Barić et al. 1997: 103), due to the genitive singular inflection *-a*. However, a comparison with the above conjugation paradigms undoubtedly speaks for word-based inflection. If we assume stems, the genitive would be the only case exhibiting the TM. Likewise for *e*-stems:

(5) *pravda* 'truth'
NOM *pravd-a*   NOM/ACC/VOC *pravd-e*
GEN *pravd-e*   GEN *pravd-a*
DAT/LOC *pravd-i*   DAT/LOC/INSTR *pravd-ama*
ACC *pravd-u*
VOC *pravd-o*
INSTR *pravd-om*

This paradigm is not word-based, but the expected TM (*-e-*) is overt only in the genitive singular and in the syncretic NOM/ACC/VOC plural form.

It seems that *i*-stems are the only declension type organized on thematic markers, i.e. like paradigms in conjugation. Consider the declension of the noun *smrt* 'death':

(6) NOM/ACC *smrt*   NOM/ACC/VOC *smrt-i*
GEN/DAT/VOC/LOC *smrt-i*   GEN *smrt-ī*
INSTR *smrć-u, smrt-i*   DAT/LOC/INSTR *smrt-ima*

The unclear status of thematic markers in declension can be evidenced by the different suggestions for stem differentiation. For example, Browne (1993: 319ff), in analogy to Proto-Slavic declension, assumes that Serbo-Croatian has three main declension types: (1) *o*-stems corresponding to the above-cited *a*-stems (Babić 1991; Barić et al. 1997) and further subdivided into masculine *o*-stems and neuter *o*-stems; (2) *a*-stems corresponding to the aforementioned *e*-stems, and distributed into feminine and masculine *a*-stems; and (3) *i*-stems comprising the same nouns in both classifications.

Russian declension and conjugation represent the same state of affairs. While all studies on Russian verbal morphology agree that there are two patterns of present conjugation, with *e-* and *i-* thematic markers respectively, the descriptions of declension differ considerably. For example, Comrie (1990: 72) postulates *a*-stems, *o*-stems (with subdeclensions for masculines and neuters) and *i*-stems (in fact, Comrie's description of Russian declension classes resembles that of Serbo-Croatian proposed by Browne 1993). Timberlake (1993) accepts hard and soft declension types without thematic markers, whereas Corbett and Fraser (1993: 115) and Fraser and Corbett (1995: 135) postulate four major declensional classes: *zakon, komnata, kost', vino*; Aronoff (1994), based on Jakobson (1984), allows three singular classes and an extra plural class (for a similar but gender-oriented classification see the Russian Academy Grammar):

	Russian inflection classes (Aronoff 1994: 72)			
	Class 1	Class 2	Class 3	Plural
Nominative	Ø/o	a	Ø	i/a
Accusative	a/o	u	Ø	i/a/Ø/ov/ej
Genitive	a	i	i	Ø/ov/ej
Dative	u	e	i	am
Instrumental	om	oj	ju	am'i
Locative	e	e	i	ax
	zakon 'law' *vino* 'wine'	*komnata* 'room'	*kost'* 'bone'	

In this table, there is a clear correspondence to Comrie's stem-oriented declension: Class 1 is parallel to *o*-stems, Class 2 to *a*-stems and Class 3 to *i*-stems. However, the table undoubtedly shows that only Class 3 can be seen as organized on thematic markers in the traditional sense, as, for example, in Latin declension.

Besides the Slavic *i*-stems, clear cases of thematic markers in declension are the continuations of the Old Church Slavic consonantal stems: -*en*-, -*es*-, -*et*-, -*v*- (OCS -*ū*-). They all are consistently marked by a stem marker in Serbo-Croatian and Russian, e.g. SC. SG NOM *uže* 'rope', GEN *užeta*, DAT *užetu*, etc. → PL NOM *užeta*, GEN *užetā*, etc.; SG NOM *rame* 'shoulder', GEN *ramena*, DAT *ramenu*, etc. → PL NOM *ramena*, GEN *ramenā*, etc.; SG NOM *čudo* 'miracle,

1.2 Bulgarian, Russian, and Serbo-Croatian

wonder', GEN *čuda*, DAT/LOC *čudu*, etc. → PL NOM *čudesa*, GEN *čudesā*, etc. (the stem marker appears only in the plural); SG NOM/ACC/VOC *podne* 'noon', GEN *podneva*, etc. → PL NOM *podneva*, GEN *podnēvā*, etc.; R. SG NOM *vremja* 'time', GEN *vremeni*, DAT *vremeni*, etc. → PL NOM *vremena*, GEN *vremën*, etc. It should be mentioned, however, that like *i*-stems, the consonantal stems are unproductive and therefore do not play a significant role in Russian and Serbo-Croatian declension systems (consonantal stems are not even mentioned by most of the above-cited linguists).

In Bulgarian, with the loss of case, a noun exhibits only a few inflected forms. Thus postulation of thematic markers in Bulgarian declension is even more inappropriate than in Russian and Serbo-Croatian.

Note, however, that even in a language such as Latin, which is nearer to the ideal inflecting-fusional type than Bulgarian, Russian and Serbo-Croatian, and in which declension is thus much more stem-oriented than in Slavic, stem vowels are not presented with the same consistency in all declension classes, as Skalička (1979) points out:

> Die 'thematischste' ist die 5. Deklination. Hier findet man das Thema *-ē-* oder *-e-* in allen Kasus. Weniger thematisch ist die 4. Deklination, wo in Dativ und Ablativ Plur. *-u-* wegfällt: *curr-i-bus*.[10] In der 1. Deklination steht das Thema *-a-, -ā-*, man findet hier aber auch mehrere Formen ohne Thema: das Dativ und Ablativ Plur. *femin-īs*, der Genitiv and Dativ Sing., der Nom. Plur. *femin-ae* (heute *féminé* ausgesprochen). In der 2. Deklination sind die thematischen Formen in der Minderheit: *serv-ō, serv-ō-rum, serv-ō-s*. In der 3. Deklination findet man das Thema bei Wörtern mit ursprünglichen *i*-Stamm häufiger (*mar-is, mar-ī, mar-i-a, mar-i-um, mar-i-bus*), bei Wörtern mit ursprünglich konsonantischem Stamm seltener (*trab-i-s, trab-ī, trab-i-bus*). (Skalička 1979: 48).[11]

In summary, Bulgarian, Russian and Serbo-Croatian declension systems do not exhibit thematic markers and are not organized on stems, i.e. inflection classes in declension are defined in terms of sets of inflectional suffixes. In contrast, conjugation shows thematic markers in the classical sense, and conjugation classes are defined in terms of TMs and sets of inflectional suffixes. According to thematic markers, verbs distinguish between the infinitive and present stem.

Whether stem-based or not, Slavic inflectional morphology is undoubtedly very rich. In addition to the inflectional characteristics typical for the whole

---

[10] However, *curr-i-bus* has as a secondary form *curr-u-bus*, the latter with the TM *-u-* (my footnote).

[11] The most thematic of all declensions is declension 5 where the theme *-ē-* or *-e-* is visible in all cases. Less thematic is declension 4 where the theme *-u-* is omitted in Dative and Ablative Plural: *curr-i-bus*. In the first declension, the theme is *-a-, -ā-*, many forms are, however, without the theme vowel: the Dative and Ablative Plural *femin-īs*, the Genitive and Dative Singular, the Nominative Plural *femin-ae* (pronounced as *féminé* today). In the second declension, thematic forms are the minority: *serv-ō, serv-ō-rum, serv-ō-s*. In the third declension, the theme is more frequent in words that belonged to the old *i*-stems (*mar-is, mar-ī, mar-i-a, mar-i-um, mar-i-bus*) and less frequent in words whose origin is in the consonant stems (*trab-i-s, trab-ī, trab-i-bus*). (Skalička 1979: 48). (Translation SM)

family, the different languages possess a range of specific features which are due to the individual diachronic development of each language. In Serbo-Croatian, both declension and conjugation are relatively complex. Bulgarian has lost its case system and moved to a very simple declension, but the verbal conjugation with nine tenses has been left unchanged and is now the most complex one within Slavic. Russian, in contrast, has preserved a complex declension with six cases, but its conjugation has been strongly simplified. Thus, Bulgarian and Russian might be seen as illustrating 'systematic hypertrophy' (Horálek 1992: 162) consisting of a complementary relationship in the evolution of declension and conjugation (see Table 1.2 and Table 1.3 below).

Table 1.2 Nominal categories in Bg., R. & SC.

Noun categories languages	Number & gender		Case	Definiteness
	SG	PL		
Bulgarian	m., f., n.	no	Ø	yes
Russian	m., f., n.	no	6	no
Serbo-Croatian	m., f., n.	m., f., n.	7	no

Table 1.3 Verbal categories in Bg., R. & SC.

Category Language	Tense	Mood	Voice	Aspect	Number	Person
Bulgarian	9	4	ACT & PASS	IMPFV & PFV	SG & PL	3
Russian	3	3	ACT & PASS	IMPFV & PFV	SG & PL	3
Serbo-Cr	7	3	ACT & PASS	IMPFV & PFV	SG & PL	3

Notes:
Bulgarian
Tenses: 1. Present (synthetic), 2. Aorist (synthetic), 3. Imperfect (synthetic), 4. Future (analytic), 5. Present Perfect (analytic), 6. Past Perfect (analytic), 7. Future Perfect (analytic), 8. Past Future (analytic), 9. Past Future Perfect (analytic)
Moods: 1. Indicative, 2. Imperative (synthetic and analytic), 3. Conditional (analytic by default), 4. Renarrated (analytic by default)[12]
Russian
Tenses: 1. Present (synthetic), 2. Past (synthetic), 3. Future (synthetic (from perfective verbs) and analytic (from imperfective verbs)),
Moods: 1. Indicative, 2. Imperative (synthetic and analytic), 3. Conditional (analytic)
Serbo-Croatian
Tenses: 1. Present (synthetic), 2. Aorist (synthetic), 3. Imperfect (synthetic)[13], 4. Future (synthetic[14] and analytic), 5. Perfect (analytic), 6. Pluperfect (analytic), 7. Anterior Future (analytic)
Moods: 1. Indicative, 2. Imperative (synthetic and analytic), 3. Conditional (analytic).

---

[12] Not all linguists recognize Renarrated as a mood, see, for example, Kucarov (1999: 413) who speaks of Mode of Expression ('Vid na izkazvaneto'), instead of Mood.
[13] Imperfect is almost entirely replaced by Perfect; the same is true of Aorist, but to a lesser extent.
[14] Only in Serbian.

1.2.2.1 Noun Morphology

As can be seen in Table 1.2, the grammatical categories shown by declension in Bulgarian, Russian and Serbo-Croatian are number and gender. Russian and Serbo-Croatian also have a category of case, whereas Bulgarian possesses definiteness as a nominal morphological category.

Serbo-Croatian distinguishes seven cases (NOM, GEN, DAT, ACC, VOC, INSTR, LOC) with three genders (MASC, FEM, NEUT) in the singular as well as the plural. Note that Bulgarian and Russian make no gender distinction in the plural (for Russian, see also the appendices at the end of the book). The Vocative case is fully preserved in Serbo-Croatian; Bulgarian has retained only some vestiges of vocative forms; in Russian, the Vocative has been lost completely, though some authors (Yadroff 1996; Daniel and Spencer 2009) assume the existence of the so-called new Vocative. The latter, however, unlike the Serbo-Croatian and Bulgarian[15] vocatives, cannot be derived from any noun (the Russian new Vocative is discussed in detail in Section 4.2.4).

None of the three languages exhibit dual forms, but based on the Old Church Slavic dual, Bulgarian has developed the category of count plural. The count plural is relevant only to masculine impersonal nouns terminating in consonants, e.g.: *stol* 'chair' → PL *stol-ove*, count PL *stol-a*, *kon* 'horse' → PL *kon-e*, count PL *kon-ja*, though in colloquial style all masculines can be inflected for count plural. The count plural is used after cardinal numerals and is still productive in modern Bulgarian. Consider: *mač* 'match' → PL *mač-ove*, count PL *mač-a*, *kompjutăr* 'computer' → PL *kompjutr-i*, count PL *kompjutăr-a*. Residues of dual forms serve to express nouns used after numerals from 'two' to 'four' in Russian and Serbo-Croatian (on the category of number in Slavic see the discussion in Stankiewicz 1986: 113ff, 153ff, cf. also Jakobson 1971: 116).

The category of definiteness has an overt morphological marker only in Bulgarian. The Bulgarian definite article is postposed and has the status of an inflectional suffix, which appears to be a typical feature of the Balkan morphology (cf. Assenova 2002).

The category of animacy seems to be of importance only to the Russian and Serbo-Croatian declension systems. Masculine singular animate nouns have accusative forms identical to the genitive, whereas for inanimate nouns, the nominative and the accusative are identical. In the plural, animacy is expressed only in Russian. Since Russian makes no gender distinction in the plural, for plural animate nouns, regardless of gender, accusative is syncretic with genitive. Serbo-Croatian nominal inflection exhibits syncretism for all genders in the

---

[15]In Modern Bulgarian, like in Serbo-Croatian, one can still derive a vocative from any noun, animate and inanimate alike. Vocatives from inanimates are, however, not really in use whereas vocatives derived from proper names can be used but are felt impolite, especially vocatives from women's names, e.g. the vocative *Elen-o* (Elena-VOC) sounds rude and it is therefore advisable to use *Elena* instead.

plural where the nominative and the vocative are identical, as well as in the dative, locative and instrumental.

The opposition animate vs. inanimate is realized in Bulgarian in terms of the human vs. non-human distinction. It plays a marginal role in declension and, as mentioned above, holds only in connection to the count plural.

An interesting difference between the three languages is the morphological integration of loanwords (cf. Corbett 1990: 134; Doleschal 2000). In Bulgarian and Serbo-Croatian, even loanwords ending in a vowel decline, unless feminine in Serbo-Croatian. (For Bulgarian see the discussion in Manova and Dressler 2001: 78; on loanwords in Serbo-Croatian Filipović 1986). Only in Bulgarian do loanwords seem to be completely integrated in the nominal inflection system. Consider: Bg. *sako* 'coat' → PL *sak-a* (cf. *selo* 'village' → PL *sel-a*), *ragu* 'ragout' → *ragu-ta* (cf. *momče* 'boy' → PL *momče-ta*) vs. Serbo-Croatian *sako* 'coat' → GEN SG *sako-a*, NOM PL *sako-i*, *ragu* 'ragout' → GEN SG *ragu-a*, NOM PL *ragu-i*. However, SC. *auto* 'car' → GEN SG *auta*, NOM PL *auti*, i.e. all three loanwords *sako, ragu* and *auto* have the same declension, but only the final *-o* in *auto* is considered to be inflection, as in indigenous words terminating in *-o*. In Russian, nouns such as *ragu* 'ragout', *pal'to* 'coat', etc., a significant number, usually do not decline (cf. Comrie et al. 1996: 117–120).

1.2.2.2 Adjectival Morphology

While Bulgarian has lost the distinction between Common Slavic long and short form adjectives, in Russian and especially in Serbo-Croatian, the distinction is preserved.

In contrast to Bulgarian, where the category of definiteness has morphotactic markers of its own, Serbo-Croatian expresses definiteness through differentiation between long and short form adjectives. In Serbo-Croatian, both long and short adjectives can be used in attributive position where they differ in terms of definiteness, e.g. *dobri čovek* 'the good man' vs. *dobar čovek* 'a good man'. The long forms terminate in *-i* in NOM SG MASC and are called definite, whereas the short forms are indefinite. Note however that only some adjectives have both forms, the majority of adjectives having either definite or indefinite forms. Since the indefinite form of the adjective is its citation form, if an adjective has no such form, the definite form is used instead. The accent is the main distinctive feature between indefinite and definite feminine and neuter adjectives in the singular as well as of all adjectives in the plural. Definite adjectives follow the pronominal declension. Declension of indefinite adjectives is the same as that of nouns, except in INSTR SG of masculine and neuter nouns and DAT/LOC SG of feminine nouns (cf. Appendix G and Appendix H).

In Russian, short-form adjectives have a restricted syntactic distribution and can be used only predicatively. Long forms can be used in attributive and in predicative positions. Short-form adjectives distinguish only gender and number and that following the nominal inflection of the nominative case, e.g. MASC *krasen* 'red', FEM *krasn-a*, NEUT *krasn-o*, PL *krasn-y*. Long-form adjectives decline like demonstratives and have a full set of case forms. In colloquial speech, usage of long forms takes precedence over that of short forms (cf. Zemskaja 1973: 196–216). Since short adjectives are subject to restrictions, long adjectives serve as citation forms of Russian adjectives and thus are assumed to be bases of all derivations from adjectives.

As mentioned above, Bulgarian has developed analytic forms for the comparative and superlative of adjectives. Both forms are built with the preposed stressed particles: *pó* 'more' and *náj* 'most', e.g.: *krátăk* 'short' → *pó-krátăk* 'shorter', *náj-krátăk* 'the shortest'.

Russian comparatives can be synthetic and analytic. Analytic comparatives can be used attributively and predicatively. They are formed by modifying the adjectives by the adverb *bolee*, e.g.: *bolee krasiv-yj dom* 'more beautiful-MASC house-MASC'. *Bolee* is invariable while the adjective agrees with the noun it qualifies. The synthetic forms end in *-ee (-ej)*, e.g.: *sláb-yj* 'thin' → *slab-ée, krasív-yj* 'beautiful' → *krasív-ee*.[16] There are also a number of adjectives which get only the suffix *-e*: *dorog-oj* 'dear, expensive' → *dorož-e, korotk-ij* 'short' → *koroč-e*. A few adjectives have comparative forms in *-še*, e.g. *dol'g-ij* 'long' → *dol'-še* 'longer', *tonk-ij* 'thin' → *ton'-še* 'thinner' (cf. Section 4.4.2.2.2). The synthetic comparatives cannot be used attributively. The superlative degree of the adjective can be formed in more than one way: *samyj* 'most' can be combined with the positive adjective, e.g.: *sam-yj krasiv-yj dom* 'the most-MASC beautiful-MASC house-MASC', *sam-aja krasiv-aja ženščin-a* 'the most-FEM beautiful-FEM woman-FEM', etc. where *samyj* agrees with the adjective and the noun in gender, number and case, or *-ejšij/-ajšij* 'most extraordinarily' can be used, e.g.: *sil'n-yj* 'strong' → *sil'n-ejš-ij* 'strongest -MASC', *sil'n-ejš-aja* 'strongest -FEM', *blizk-ij* 'near' → *bliž-ajš-ij* 'nearest', etc. Another form of the superlative can be formed with the short form comparative and *vsego* and *vsex*, for singular and plural respectively, e.g. *on bystree vsex* 'he is faster than all, i.e. the fastest'. It is also possible to express the superlative with *nai-* as in *naivysšij* 'the highest' or with *naibolee*, as in *naibolee želatel'nyj rezul'tat* 'the most desirable result'.

In Serbo-Croatian, the comparative is formed by addition of suffixes (MASC *-ji/-iji*, FEM *-ja/-ija*, NEUT *-je/-ije* in the singular and MASC *-ji/-iji*, FEM *-je/-ije*, NEUT *-ja/-ija* in the plural). Three adjectives have *-ši* comparatives: *lak* 'light' → *lakši, mek* 'soft' → *mekši* and *lijep* 'beautiful' → *lijepši*. The superlative requires the addition of the prefix *naj-* to comparatives, e.g.: *kratak* 'short' → *krače* → *najkrače*. Comparative and superlative forms decline like definite forms of adjectives.

---

[16]Some linguists (cf. Vinogradov 1972 [1947]: 204; Isačenko 1982: 158) assume that the short form of an adjective is a base of its synthetic comparative, since the synthetic comparative and the feminine short form of the adjective have the same stress pattern: *sláb-yj* 'thin', short forms: MASC *slab*, FEM *slab-á* → COMP *slab-ée, krasív-yj* 'beautiful', short forms: MASC *krasív*, FEM *krasív-a* → COMP *krasív-ee*.

Note that some of the above-cited Russian and Serbo-Croatian comparatives (and very few Russian superlatives) are formed by subtraction (Section 4.4.2.2).

1.2.2.3 Verbal Morphology

The three languages have finite synthetic and analytic forms expressing tense, voice and mood (see Table 1.3), and non-finite verbal forms such as infinitive (except Bulgarian), verbal adjectives (participles) and verbal adverbs (gerunds), see Table 1.4 below.

The category of aspect is the most salient feature of the Slavic verbal morphology and plays an important role in the conjugations of the three languages. Aspect concerns the internal temporal consistency of a situation: 'the perfective views a situation as a single whole, effectively as a point, while the imperfective views the situation as having internal consistency' (Comrie 1990: 75). In comparison to Russian and Serbo-Croatian, Bulgarian possesses the fullest range of aspect forms (cf. Andrejčin 1962, Maslov 1981). Only very few verbs cannot be paired for aspect in Bulgarian. In this book, verbs will be analysed as organized in triples, consisting of primary imperfective verbs (IMPFV1), from which perfective verbs (PFV) are formed (by prefixation or by suffixation with the semelfactive suffix *-n-*) and which in turn are the bases for secondary imperfective verbs (IMPFV2), i.e. IMPFV1 → PFV → IMPFV2 (cf. Manova 2002). Note that whereas in Bulgarian, nearly all aspectual forms of verbs can be built following the above-cited triple, in Russian and Serbo-Croatian, if the semantic change in perfectivization is not significant, the primary imperfective verbs are often used instead of secondary imperfective ones: Bg. IMPFV1 *piša* 'I write', 3 SG PRES *piše* → PFV *napiša* 'I write (down)', 3 SG *napiše* → IMPFV2 *napisvam*, 3 SG *napisva* vs. R. IMPFV1 *pisat'* 'to write' → PFV *napisat'* 'to write (down)' → IMPFV2 **napisyvat'*, SC. IMPFV *pisati* 'to write' → PFV *napisati* 'to write (down)' → IMPFV2 **napisivati*.

Verbs from foreign bases (recent loanwords) are biaspectual in the three languages. While in Bulgarian they are derived mainly by the suffix *-ira-*, e.g., *organiz-ira-m*, *demonstr-ira-m*, in Russian and Serbo-Croatian other suffixes also occur. In Russian there are *-ova-* and *-irova-* loanwords, e.g. *organiz-ova-t'*, but *demonstr-irova-t'*. In Serbo-Croatian, verbs from foreign bases are derived by *-isa-*, *-ova-* and *-ira-*. Some regional variants allow for competing formations with *-ira-*, on the one hand, against *-isa-* and *-ova-*, on the other hand, e.g. SC. *apel-ova-ti/apel-ira-ti*, *manifest-ova-ti/manifest-ira-ti*, *model-ova-ti/model-ira-ti*, *oksid-isa-ti/oksid-ira-ti*, *telegraf-isa-ti/telegraf-ira-ti* (Mrazović and Vukadinović 1990: 78).

For the sake of completeness, it should be noted that in Bulgarian, verbs from foreign bases may be imperfectivized in colloquial style, e.g.: IMPFV & PFV *organiziram* → IMPFV2 *organizirvam*, IMPFV & PFV *demonstriram* →

1.2 Bulgarian, Russian, and Serbo-Croatian

IMPFV2 *demonstrirvam*, etc. In this way, the aspectual system, according to the aspectual triple, tries to compensate for the missing form.

Bulgarian possesses the richest tense system, in which aorist and imperfect can be formed from perfectives as well as from imperfectives. The aorist and the imperfect tense are both common in modern Bulgarian.

In Serbo-Croatian, the imperfect is found with imperfective verbs and the aorist usually, but not exclusively, with perfectives, and there is a compound past tense usually referred to as a 'perfect', formed from verbs of either aspect. In some dialects, particularly in Croatia, the perfect replaces both the imperfect and aorist, the latter being the better preserved.

Russian has completely lost the old Slavic aorist and imperfect and now has only one past tense. There is no copula in the present tense, giving *ja pisal* 'I wrote'. The form *pisal* is etymologically a participle (i.e. verbal adjective) and therefore agrees in gender and number, rather than in person and number, with its subject. In Russian, only imperfective verbs have present tense meaning (forms from perfective verbs express future), whereas in Bulgarian and Serbo-Croatian, there is also a present from perfectives, which is distinct from the future.

A feature specific to Bulgarian verbal morphology is the so-called 'renarration' (evidential forms, cf. Turkish and Albanian), an innovation using the past imperfect participle to express present and imperfect tenses.

Table 1.4 below presents a survey of all non-finite verbal forms (adjectives and adverbs) in the three languages. Modern Bulgarian has lost the Common Slavic infinitive, and 1 SG PRES IND is used as a citation form of the verb

Table 1.4 Non-finite verbal forms in Bg., R. & SC

Language	Bulgarian	Russian	Serbo-Croatian
non-finite form			
INF		*čita-t'* 'to read'	*čita-ti* 'to read'
		pisa-t' 'to write'	*pisa-ti* 'to write'
PRES ACT PART	*čet-jašt*	*čita-jušč-ij*	
	piš-ešt	*piš-ušč-ij*	
PRES PASS PART		*čita-em-yj*	
		pisu-em-yj	
PAST ACT PART (AOR	*čel*	*čita-vš-ij*	*čita-o*
ACT PART in Bg.)	*pisa-l*	*pisa-vš-ij*	*pisa-o*
IMPF ACT PART	*četja-l*		
	piše-l		
PAST PASS PART	*čete-n*	*čita-nn-yj*	*čita-n*
	pisa-n	*pisa-nn-yj*	*pisa-n*
PRES GER	*čete-jki*	*čita-ja*	*čitaju-ći*
	piše-jki	Ø	*pišu-ći*
PAST GER		*pro-čita-v*	*(pro)čita-v(ši)*
		na-pisa-v	*(na)pisa-v(ši)*
VERBAL N	*čete-ne*	*čte-nie/čita-nie*	*čita-nje*
	pisa-ne/pisa-nie	*pisa-nie*	*pisa-nje*

instead of the infinitive. Russian has no -*l* participle. As mentioned in the previous paragraph, the -*l* participle is used for expressing the Past Tense. The Imperfect Past Active Participle is a Bulgarian innovation. Note also that for convenience the Aorist Past Active Participle is named after the base of the form, which is the aorist/infinitive stem in Bulgarian. In Russian and Serbo-Croatian, this participle is usually called Past (Active) Participle only.

As can be seen in Table 1.4 and from the examples in (7), verbs usually have two stems, present and past (infinitive):

(7)   Bg. PRES *čet-a* 'I read', 3 SG *čet-e*, AOR *čet-o-x* 'I read', 3 SG *čet-e*
R *čit-a-t'* 'to read', PRES *čita-ju* 'I read', 3 SG *čita-e-t*
SC *čit-a-ti* 'to read', PRES *čit-a-m* 'I read', 3 SG *čit-a*

Bg. PRES *piš-a* 'I write', 3 SG *piš-e*, AOR *pis-a-x* 'I wrote', 3 SG *pis-a*
R. *pis-a-t'* 'to write', PRES *piš-u* 'I write', 3 SG *piš-e-t*
SC *pis-a-ti* 'to write', PRES *piš-e-m* 'I write', 3 SG *piš-e*.

Although it is possible to posit a single basic stem from which allostems can be derived (Jakobson 1971), for convenience, two stems, present and infinitive, are usually assigned to the Slavic verbs. In general, the present allostem is used for the present tense, imperative, present active participles, imperfect tense and participles, and the infinitive allostem is a base for infinitive, past tense or aorist, past active participles and passive participles (see Table 1.4).

In Slavic languages, where a verbal stem usually consists of a root plus a thematic marker, the root appears to be more important than the stem, and it is often the case that roots are used instead of stems for the description of verb morphology. Roots are particularly preferred for language-learning purposes, where simplifications are deliberately sought (see Mrazović and Vukadinović 1990: 90), i.e. pedagogically it seems easier to derive a verb from the root than to refer to two listed stems. See also Manova (2008) for a root-based analysis of the Bulgarian verb inflection.

As for verb-to-noun derivations in Slavic, it is also more the root than the stem that is of importance, especially in cases of modifications and conversions to nouns terminating in consonants. For example:

(9)   Bg. *pod-piš-a* 'I sign', 3 SG *pod-piš-e* → *pod-pis* 'signature'
R. *pod-pis-a-t'* → *pod-pis*'
SC. *pot-pis-a-ti* → *pot-pis*

In fact, the great majority of Slavic verbs have the same root in their present and infinitive stems. Different roots constitute a problem only for an unproductive group of verbs. Verbs with two different roots in the paradigm usually have high token frequency (the high frequency of verbs with different roots in the present and in the aorist speaks for listing and is thus supportive of Lieber's 1981a claim that a lexeme can have two stems just in case these stems are irregular and hence listed in the lexicon), e.g. Bg. *kaža* 'I say, tell', *kaže* and *kazax*; R. *skazat'* 'to say, tell' and *skažu, skažeš*; and SC. *kazati* 'to say, tell' and *kažem*. Some of the verbs with two roots also have peculiar infinitive forms, terminating in *-č'* instead of *-t'* in Russian, and in *-ći* instead of *-ti* in Serbo-Croatian, e.g.: R. *moč'* 'to be able', *mogu, možeš'*; SC. *moći* 'to be able', *možem, mogu*, etc. (cf. Bg. *moga* 'I am able to', 3 SG *može* and AOR 1SG *možax*, 3 SG *moža*).

As already discussed, in Slavic conjugation a given paradigm is organized on a particular stem (cf. Carstairs-McCarthy 2000), although within a derivational paradigm, it is difficult to establish a rule of preference for a particular stem. Consider derivations such as Bg. N *peče-ne* 'baking', N *peč-ka* 'stove', N *peč-iv-o* 'baked dish', N *pek-ar* 'baker', and N *pek* 'scorching heat', all formed from the verb Bg. *pek-a* 'I bake, roast', *peč-e* (PRES stem *peč-e-* and AOR stem *pek-o-*). As can be seen from these examples, derivational morphology uses neither verb roots only nor verb stems only. This observation holds even for verbs for which the present and aorist stems coincide. For example, Bg. *uča* 'I learn, study', 3 SG *uči* exhibits the same stem (*uci-*) in the present and in the aorist, but derivations from *uča* can be stem-based (*uč-i-tel* 'teacher', based on the stem *uč-i*) as well as root-based (*uč-eben* 'educational' the base of which is the root *uč-*).

In sum, the three languages under investigation in this book represent different degrees of morphological complexity with respect to inflection: Bulgarian has extremely complex verb inflection but simple noun and adjective inflection; Russian represents the opposite case – complex noun and adjective inflection but simple verb inflection; and in Serbo-Croatian all three types of inflection, nominal, adjectival and verbal, are very rich. Thus the typology this book suggests is based on morphological (inflectional) richness and not on the traditional geographic branching of Slavic languages into East, West and South. No West Slavic language is investigated, but West Slavic languages are very similar in morphological organization (inflectional richness) to Russian.

1.3 Word as a Basic Linguistic Unit

In this section, I am going to question the status of lexemes in morphology. I will show that the word is the basic linguistic unit.

In the literature, a lexeme is defined as an abstract unit of vocabulary realized by words/word forms (Bauer 1988; Aronoff 1994; Carstairs-McCarthy 2000; Booij 2002), 'having both form and meaning, but being neither, and existing outside of any particular syntactic context' (Aronoff 1994: 11). In other words, a lexeme is an abstract unit represented by a set of forms. There is nothing wrong with defining a morphological concept as based on a set of forms. One, however, expects a concept that is represented by a set of forms to be always associated with the same set of forms, which is not the case with the concept of lexeme. Lexeme appears: (1) language specific, (2) word-class specific, and (3) inflection-class specific. For example, the sets of forms of English nouns, adjectives and verbs differ from those of Bulgarian, Russian or Serbo-Croatian nouns, adjectives and verbs. Lexemes with different word-class specifications in the same language have different sets of word forms, i.e. the set of forms of a noun is not the same as the set of forms of a verb. Additionally, in the same language the lexemes of the same word-class may have different sets of forms, due to belonging to different inflection classes. These facts render lexeme a problematic concept, especially in word-formation. While in inflectional morphology a lexeme is usually represented by its inflectional paradigm and one thus has the lexeme's set of forms, in derivational morphology it is not a common practice to give all inflectional forms of the input and output of a rule. The English pairs *to be* → *being* and *to play* → *playing*, though non-derivational, provide a good illustration of the problem. When analyzing *being* and *playing* one assumes that they are formed from the respective infinitives in the same way. In other words, one ignores the fact that the set of forms of the lexeme BE is not the same as that of the lexeme PLAY. The set of BE forms includes 'be, am, are, is, was, were, and been' whereas the set of forms PLAY corresponds to includes only 'play, plays, and played'. Of course, the unification of BE and PLAY in terms of a lexeme does not constitute a problem for the analysis of English morphology where most of the verb lexemes are of the PLAY type and there is no other verb with as many forms as BE. This is, however, not the case in Bulgarian. Recall that a Bulgarian verb has over 50 forms in indicative active. Additionally, Bulgarian verbs are distributed into (at least) eight inflection classes (in different sources). How can we make Bulgarian morphology comparable with English morphology if the basic morphological unit, the lexeme, is not the same in the two languages? Note that a comparison between English and Bulgarian derivational processes is desirable, especially for conversion, since conversion is typical of English word-formation and there is much research on conversion in English. Luckily, although a Bulgarian lexeme differs from an English lexeme, Bulgarian and English words are comparable. They are real units that associate a particular existing form with a particular meaning. Moreover, it should be mentioned that as a rule, word-formation analyses of inflecting-language data do not consider the inflectional pattern of the input and output of a morphological rule. In other words, Bulgarian, Russian and Serbo-Croatian grammars see all morphological changes as relating (basic forms of) words. Thus, we also assume that word-formation rules relate words and not lexemes. A similar claim in Booij (2002: 3):

> Native speakers will discover the existence of a morphological process in their native language on the basis of the comparison of a number of words with systematic form-meaning differences.

If for a language such as English, it is clear which word forms are used as input of morphological rules, for Slavic, one should further decide whether,

1.3 Word as a Basic Linguistic Unit   27

for example, in instances of derivations from verbs, it is the infinitive of the verb or a finite (tense) form that serves as input of a rule. A similar question arises for nouns: Is it the nominative or some other case form that serves as input of a morphological change. For verbs, it seems that the infinitive, since syntactically unmarked, is more likely to be preferred by native speakers to other verb forms. This pattern is assumed for Russian and Serbo-Croatian. For Bulgarian, however, where the infinitive has been lost, that assumption appears somewhat inappropriate. As already mentioned, in Bulgarian there is still an infinitive (aorist) stem, the latter, however, appears too marked morphosyntactically to be the base of all morphological rules that operate on verbs in that language. On the contrary, it is much more likely that a less marked (i.e. less cognitively complex) present tense form is the base of derivations from verbs. Two forms seem the most probable candidates – 1 SG PRES and 3 SG PRES, the latter being the less marked of the two (cf. Mayerthaler 1980). Intriguingly, the Bulgarian grammar tradition uses the 1 SG PRES IND as a citation form of the verb. Moreover, Manova (2008) demonstrates that on the basis of 1 SG PRES IND one can successfully predict the inflection class of a Bulgarian verb, which is not the case if one starts with 3 SG PRES.[17] Therefore, for Bulgarian we assume that 1 SG PRES IND serves as a base of all derivations from verbs. Note, however, that 1 SG PRES IND often lacks a thematic marker, therefore for convenience, 3 SG PRES IND, which coincides with the present stem of the verb (i.e. terminates in the present-tense thematic marker), will be always cited as well.

In cases where the root of the verb displays some morphonological alternation in the present, 1 SG PRES is distinct from 3 SG PRES:

(10) Bg. *peka* 'I bake, roast'
      PRESENT   AORIST
      SG
      1 *pek-á*   *pék-o-x*
      2 *peč-é-š*   *péč-e*
      3 *peč-é*   *péč-e*
      PL
      1 *peč-é-m*   *pék-o-xme*
      2 *peč-é-te*   *pék-o-xte*
      3 *pek-át*   *pék-o-xa*

For such verbs it is assumed, by analogy with verbs without morphonological changes in the root, that 3 SG PRES displays (i.e. coincides with) the present stem of the verb, which implies that the present root is *peč*-. However, a

---

[17] The preliminary results of a comparative psycholinguistic investigation of the organization of Bulgarian and Italian verb paradigms by Manova, Bertinetto, Finocchiaro and Janyan also speak in favour of the citation form of the verb – the infinite in Italian and 1 SG PRES in Bulgarian.

closer look at the present paradigm in (10), shows that the present root is *pek-* and not *peč-*, since the *k* → *č* palatalization occurs only in forms where the inflection added starts with *-e*. The case is relevant to conversion, since from the verb *pek-a* 'I bake, roast' one can derive the result noun *pek* 'scorching heat', which, depending on the present root, is formed either by conversion (of the root *pek-*) or by modification (of the root *peč-*). In instances such as these, we assume that it is the addition of inflection that causes palatalization (cf. morphological metageneralizations in Stump 2001) and therefore speak of conversion.

In sum, from now on in this book all Russian and Serbo-Croatian verbs will be given in their infinitive forms, whereas the Bulgarian verbs will be cited with two forms: 1 SG PRES IND and 3 SG PRES IND, in cases where 1 SG differs from 3 SG, the 1 SG displays the present root.

Such a language-specific presentation of the data is in accordance with the third subtheory of NM, that of language-specific (system-dependent) naturalness (see Chapter 2).

Nouns from languages with a case system (i.e. Russian and Serbo-Croatian) are given in nominative singular, while all Bulgarian nouns are cited in their singular indefinite form, since Bulgarian does not have a category of case for nouns. This presentation of the data is consonant with the results of the psycholinguistic research on the organization of the Serbo-Croatian noun paradigm by Lukatela et al. (1987). Lukatela et al. compare dative/locative singular with instrumental singular and nominative singular and establish that regardless of gender and regularity of a noun, mean lexical decision times are the shortest for the nominative singular. Further evidence for the more special status of the nominative singular provides the Russian nominal inflection. The inflection classes of the Russian noun are often referred to as nominative singular forms, e.g. *zakon* 'law', *komnata* 'room', *vino* 'wine' and *kost'* 'bone' (cf. Corbett 1991). In other words, these nominative singular nouns serve to identify the inflection class of a noun in Russian (which is similar to what Manova 2008 claims for 1 SG PRES IND and the inflection classes of Bulgarian verbs).

According to the descriptive-grammar traditions of the three languages under investigation, adjectives are cited in their nominative singular long forms in Russian, in their nominative singular short forms in Serbo-Croatian (if the adjective does not have a short form, its long form is given), and in their singular indefinite forms in Bulgarian.

Finally, it should be mentioned that our word-based understanding of morphology is consonant with realizational approaches, such as Stump (2001),[18] and word-based analyses, such as those in Blevins (2005, 2006).

In sum, the input and output of a morphological rule relate words (word forms). In Bulgarian, Russian and Serbo-Croatian (as well as in many other

---

[18]Stump (2001: 1ff) provides a detailed overview of realizational approaches to morphology and their advantages over incremental (i.e. entirely compositional) analyses.

languages) the input and output of a word-formation rule[19] coincide with the citation forms of verbs, nouns and adjectives. Using citation forms as bases of morphological rules has a practical side effect, namely a reader can easily find the input and output of any morphological rule in a dictionary.

1.4 Word-, Stem- and Root-Based Morphology

In the previous section, we demonstrated that morphological rules relate well-formed words. Hypothetically, when two words are compared, they might share the same root, the same stem, or might fully coincide. Such an approach is compatible with Blevins' (2006) observation that all realizational morphology is word-based with respect to semantics, i.e. morphosyntax (abstract morphology in his terms), which is not the case if morphological form (i.e. morphotactics) is concerned. Note that while Stump (2001) provides an analysis that is word-based morphosyntactically but root-based and stem-based morphotactically, Blevins (2005, 2006) argues for morphology that is word-based morphosyntactically and morphotactically.

In this book, the (formal) base of a morphological rule (morphological technique) is defined as a morphological unit (root, stem, word) which is presented in the input as well as the output of a morphological change. For example, X is the base of the following rules: (1) X → XY; (2) XY → XZ; and (3) XY → X, and theoretically, X could be a word, a stem, or a root. Although in the literature, both stems and roots are often referred to as stems, the exact differentiation of roots and stems is necessary for the proper understanding of conversion (Chapter 3) and subtraction (Chapter 4). Only stems and words are subject to subtractive rules (root-based subtraction is extremely rare), whereas conversion operates on roots, stems and words.

As already discussed, a word is a basic linguistic unit and as such makes possible the discovering of morphological processes by native speakers. All morphological rules relate words, with respect to semantics, but only word-based morphology operates on words, with respect to form. An example of word-based morphology is R. NOM SG *zakon* 'law' → GEN SG *zakon-a*.

A stem is that part of a word form which remains when a suffix is removed and which, by definition, has at least one suffix more than a root, e.g. the base of the derivation R. *uč-i-t'* 'to teach, learn' → *uč-i-tel'* 'teacher' is the stem *uč-i-*. Thus, this derivation is an example of stem-based morphology. A prototypical stem consists of a root and a TM (i.e. *ič-i-* is a prototypical stem), less prototypical stems lack the TM.

A root is that part of a word form which remains when all suffixes have been removed. Root-based changes (e.g. R. *uč-i-t'* 'to teach, learn' → *uč-enie* 'learning,

---

[19]Inflectional morphology may exhibit peculiarities with respect to the base of a rule, see examples (9) and (10) in Section 4.2.1.

doctrine') are the least natural ones. Since Slavic languages are characterized by right-hand headedness,[20] in this book, only suffixes are taken into consideration for the classification of bases (cf. the discussion on headedness in Stump 2001: 96ff). In other words, the root is the basic part of a multimorphemic word which cannot be further decomposed on the right edge. This means that both Bg. *xód-j-a* 'I go, walk', 3 SG *xód-i* → *xod* 'walk, pace, tread' and Bg. *raz-grom-j-á* 'I rout', 3 SG *raz-grom-í* → *raz-gróm* 'rout' are root-based (*raz-* is a prefix).

According to the above definitions, if the input of a morphological rule collapses a root and a word into a single form, as in R. ADJ *zlo* 'evil' → N *zlo* 'the evil' or Bg. *măž* 'man' → PL *măž-e*, we will speak of a word-based rule instead of a root-based one. This categorization is motivated by the fact that words are primary linguistic signs. Likewise, if a stem and a word coincide, as in the derivation Bg. ADJ *rod-stv-en* 'of family' → N *rod-stv-en-ik* 'relative', where, the input is an existing word, we acknowledge a word-based suffixation rule. In contrast, R. *rabot-a-t'* 'to work' → N *rabot-a* 'work, job, occupation' represents stem-based morphology because here only the stem *rabot-a-* (and not the whole input form *rabot-a-t'*) serves as a base. Similarly, Bg. *xod-j-a* 'I go walk', 3 SG *xod-i* → N *xod* 'gate, walk, move' is root-based.

The fact that morphological rules can be root-based, stem-based and word-based, requires a revision of the generalized form of the Slavic word. The form assumed so far

(11)   (PREF)-ROOT-(DSUFF)-(TM)-(ISUFF)

can serve as a schema only for instances where different slots have single realizations. The template fails to account for more than one realization of slots, as well as for more complex cases of stem-based and word-based morphology, as in the following derivational relations from Bulgarian:

(12)   *uč-a* 'I study', 3SG *uč-i* → *uči-tel* 'teacher' (based on the stem *uc-i-*)
           → *učitel-stv-o* 'all the teachers; working as a teacher' (based on the word *učitel*)
           → *učitelstv-a-m* 'I work as a teacher', *učitelstv-a* (based on the stem *učitelstv-*)

The exact morpheme analysis of *uč-i-tel-stv-a-m*, the output of the last derivation, is: ROOT-TM-DSUFF-DSUFF-TM-ISUFF. The template in (11) allows for more than one slot of the same type (cf. the discussion at the beginning of Section 1.2.2) but cannot explain the existence of two (non-neighboring) TMs in the same word form. Recall that we have observed that a Slavic verb possesses only one TM. Therefore the following slightly changed version of (11):

---

[20] A principle proposed by Williams (1981) that says that the right-hand member of a morphologically complex word is the head of that word, i.e. the rightmost constituent determines all the properties of the word.

1.5 Thematic Markers, Aspectual Suffixes and Root Extensions   31

(13)   (PREF)-BASE-(DSUFF)-(TM)-(ISUFF)

This modified version better accounts for morphological changes than that in (11). The advantage of the template in (13) is that it recognizes the fact that BASE can be a recursive category and treats all types of bases (roots, stems, and words) equally, placing them in the BASE slot. The analysis of the verb *učitelstvam* is now quite easy, to the base *uč-i-tel-stv-*, that is a stem, a TM and an ISUFF are added, both inflectional material. The latter fact defines the derivation of *učitelstvam* as stem-based conversion (Chapter 3).

1.5 Thematic Markers, Aspectual Suffixes and Root Extensions

In this section, we define three types of form that are closely related to morphological stems, namely thematic markers, aspectual suffixes and root extensions. We will demonstrate that the three forms are inflectional material.

The template of the Slavic word in (13) locates a TM between derivational and inflectional suffixes. An aspectual suffix, if overt, is in the derivational slot of the word, i.e. immediately before the TM, e.g. Bg. *podpis-v-a-me* 'we[21] sign', where *-a-* is the TM and *-v-* the aspectual suffix. A root extension can be seen as occupying the same position as an aspectual suffix, e.g. Bg. *igr-a-e-m* 'we play', *-e-* is the TM, *-a-* is a root extension. However, root extensions are, in contrast to aspectual suffixes, empty morphs, i.e. they have form (are vowels by default) but no meaning. Aspectual suffixes derive verbs from other verbs and signal a change in aspect. Thus, the above-mentioned *podpis-v-a-m* '(I) sign'/*podpis-v-a-me* 'we sign' is an IMPFV2 verb derived from the PFV *podpiš-ø-a* '(I) sign'/*podpiš-e-m* 'we sign' by the addition of the aspectual suffix *-v-*, whereas the verb *igr-a-o-ja* '(I) play'/*igr-a-e-m* 'we play' cannot be related to another verb in a similar way. Additionally, a root extension can turn into a TM in some of the verb forms, as is the case with the amplification *-a-* in the aorist tense form *igr-a-xme* 'we played-AOR' of the verb *igr-a-o-ja* '(I) play'. Thus, the classification of an element as either a TM or a root extension depends on the position of that element in the word form as well as on the structure of the paradigm where the element occurs. Consider the following two paradigms of the Bulgarian verb *igraja* '(I) play':

(14)   PRES, Root extension *-a-* , TM *-e-*   AOR, TM *-a-*
       1SG *igra-ø-ja*   *igr-a-x*
       2SG *igra-e-š*   *igr-a*
       3SG *igra-e*   *igr-a*
       1PL *igra-e-m*   *igr-a-xme*
       2PL *igra-e-te*   *igr-a-xte*
       3PL *igra-ø-jat*   *igr-a-xa*

---

[21] 1 PL is cited instead of 1SG in order to have overt TMs and inflectional suffixes in the forms used for illustration.

Compare now these paradigms with the corresponding paradigms of two verbs without root extensions, the above-mentioned Bg. *podpiša* '(I) sign-PFV' and *podpisvam* '(I) sign-IMPFV2':

(15a)   PRES, TM -*e*-   AOR, TM -*a*-
         1SG *podpiš-ø-a*   *podpis-a-x*
         2SG *podpiš-e-š*   *podpis-a*
         3SG *podpiš-e*   *podpis-a*
         1PL *podpiš-e-m*   *podpis-a-xme*
         2PL *podpiš-e-te*   *podpis-a-xte*
         3PL *podpiš-ø-at*   *podpis-a-xa*

(15b)   PRES, TM -*a*-   AOR, TM -*a*-
         1SG *podpisv-a-m*   *podpisv-a-x*
         2SG *podpisv-a-š*   *podpisv-a*
         3SG *podpisv-a*   *podpisv-a*
         1PL *podpisv-a-me*   *podpisv-a-xme*
         2PL *podpisv-a-te*   *podpisv-a-xte*
         3PL *podpisv-a-t*   *podpisv-a-xa*

Thus, based on the template in (13) and the paradigm structure, and in order to provide a unified account of all the above paradigms, we assume that the AOR -*a*- in (14) is a TM. Since TMs are inflectional material, the fact that root extensions can serve as TMs in the verb form assigns inflectional status to root extensions.

In contrast to TMs and root exeinsions, aspectual suffixes are always overt in the verb's paradigm. Aspectual suffixes in IMPFV2 verbs in the three languages, Bulgarian, Russian and Serbo-Croatian, are of the type -*(V)v*- and always combine with the TM -*a*-, which allows for treating the combination of the IMPFV2 aspectual suffix and the following TM as a complex TM of the type -*(V)va*- (Manova 2005a, 2010). In other words, aspectual suffixes, like TMs, serve for identifying the inflectional class of a verb. Therefore, aspectual suffixes are, like TMs, considered inflectional material.

The inflectional character of aspectual suffixes can be further illustrated with the Russian perfectivizer -*nu*-. Note that the Russian *nu*-verbs and their Bulgarian (*n*-verbs) and Serbo-Croatian (*nu*-verbs) equivalents form inflection classes of their own in the three languages (Manova 2005a). While -*nu*- is an aspectual suffix in verbs such as R. *prygat'* 'to jump-IMPFV' → *prygnut'* 'to jump once-PFV SEMELFACTIVE', it is a TM in deadjectival verbs such as IMPFV *soxnut'* 'to become dry', derived from *suxij* 'dry'. The verbs *soxnut'* and *prygnut'* have different aspects, perfective and imperfective respectively, but receive the same inflection, which is due to the marker -*nu*-. In order to have an analysis that accommodates the fact that all -*nu*- verbs

1.5 Thematic Markers, Aspectual Suffixes and Root Extensions   33

in Russian, regardless of their aspect, belong to the same inflection class, we refer to *-nu-* as a TM of the respective class of verbs. Consider:

(16a) *prygnut'* 'to jump once'
 1SG *pryg-n-u*
 2SG *pryg-ne-š'*
 3SG *pryg-ne-t*
 1PL *pryg-ne-m*
 2PL *pryg-ne-te*
 3PL *pryg-n-ut*

(16b) *soxnut'* 'to become dry'
 1SG *sox-n-u*
 2SG *sox-ne-š'*
 3SG *sox-ne-t*
 1PL *sox-ne-m*
 2PL *sox-ne-te*
 3PL *sox-n-ut*

In (16ab), *-nu-* is reduced to *-n-*, which is not typical of aspectual suffixes. Compare with the paradigm of the IMPFV2 verb *podpisyvat'* 'to sign', with the aspectual suffix *-yv-*; the infinitive TM *-a-* is reanalysed as an extension.

(17) *podpisyvat'* 'to sign'
 podpisyva-ø-ju
 podpisyva-e-š'
 podpisyva-e-t
 podpisyva-e-m
 podpisyva-e-te
 podpisyva-ø-jut

In Russian, somewhat similar to the *-nu-* case are verbs with the TM *-ova-/-eva-*. *-ova-/-eva-* was an aspectual suffix diachronically (cf. Isačenko 1982: 227–229). However, in Modern Russian *-ova-/-eva-* derives verbs from nouns and adjectives (Švedova et al. 1980: 337ff), i.e. *-ova-/-eva-* has lost its aspectual function. Since *-ova-/-eva-*verbs constitute an inflection class of their own, the suffix *-ova-/-eva-* behaves like a TM, which is illustrated with the following paradigm where *-ova-/-eva-* changes into *-u-*:

(18) *sovetovat'* 'I advise'
 1SG *sovet-u-ju*
 2SG *sovet-ue-š'*
 3SG *sovet-ue-t*
 1PL *sovet-ue-m*
 2PL *sovet-ue-te*
 3PL *sovet-u-jut*

Note that -*nu*- and -*ova*-/-*eva*- suffixes cannot be seen as derivational material, since the formal reduction they undergo in inflection is not typical for derivational suffixes.

Serbo-Croatian examples parallel to the above cited Bulgarian and Russian ones can be found in Appendix I.

In sum, based on the template of the Slavic word and the paradigm structure of the Slavic verbs, we distinguish among TMs, aspectual suffixes and root extensions. These three types of morphological form are, however, closely related and may replace one another in some instances. We therefore consider all three forms inflectional. This conclusion has consequences for the analyses of conversion and subtraction: the addition and deletion of TMs, aspectual suffixes and root extensions is irrelevant to derivational morphology. As regards inflectional changes, if the paradigm structure presupposes a suffix but the latter is not overt, we will classify such instances as zero-sign (on zero sign see Section 4.2.9). To illustrate, in Russian an imperfective *nu*-verb may undergo a deletion of -*nu*- in the past tense (19a) whereas a perfective semelfective *nu*-verb preserves the suffix -*nu*- in all its past-tense forms (19b):

(19a)   IMPFV
        sóxnut' 'to become dry' → MASC *sox*, FEM *sóxla*, NEUT *sóxlo*,
        PL *sóxli*
        BUT also *sóxnul*/-*a*/-*o*/-*i*

(19b)   PFV SEMELFACTIVE
        prygnut' 'to jump' → *prygnul*/-*a*/-*o*/-*i*.

The deletion of -*nu*- in (19a) resembles subtraction very much, but the change is not subtractive. The forms without -*nu*- are athematic in the past tense and the MASC past inflection of *sox*, the suffix -*l*-, is zero-signed. Thus, none of the short past tense forms in (19a) is derived by subtraction.

Chapter 2
Theoretical Background

The theoretical background to this book merges principles and assumptions that have come to be known as 'Natural Morphology' (NM) (Section 2.1) and 'Cognitive Linguistics' (CL) (Section 2.2). Section 2.3 is devoted to the notion of prototype, which is seen as central to the understanding of the nature of morphological phenomena. Section 2.4 puts forward a set of morphological techniques corresponding to all possible cognitive operations that can be performed on a morphological form. If classified according to the mental effort required (or the degree of iconicity they exhibit), the morphological techniques constitute a cline that includes the following operations: (1) Addition $X \rightarrow X + Y$, (2) Substitution $X + Y \rightarrow X + Z$, (3) Modification $X \rightarrow X'$, (4) Conversion $X \rightarrow X$, and (5) Subtraction $XY \rightarrow X$ (or $X \rightarrow X - Y$). In Section 2.5, the prototype model is discussed in regard to the classification of derivation and inflection.

2.1 Natural Morphology

NM emerged in the late 1970s when 'naturalness' was a fashionable movement in phonology. The theoretical model of NM elaborates on the Prague School concept of markedness (cf. Trubetzkoy 1931; Jakobson 1971), Peircean semiotics (Peirce 1965) and Natural Phonology (cf. Stampe 1973a, b). A complete and coherent platform of the model was first published as 'Leitmotifs of Natural Morphology' in 1987 (Dressler et al. 1987). Since the theory is influential in morphology, it is presented in nearly all sources on general morphology, the most recent being Booij et al. (2000) and Štekauer and Lieber (2005). In both sources, Wolfgang U. Dressler (2005) surveys the model. Linguists outside NM also pay attention to this framework, and Bauer (1988: 187–200) and Carstairs-McCarthy (1992: 215–240) devoted chapters on NM.

In contrast to the 'formalist' Generative Morphology, which postulates autonomy of grammar and concentrates on the development of formalism for the description of the morphology of a particular language, NM focuses on universal preferences and the way in which they are related to basic cognitive and semiotic principles (which makes NM compatible with Cognitive Linguistics, cf. Dressler 1990b). As 'natural' means cognitively simple and easily accessible, evidence external to the language system, but directly connected with the language ontology (such as functional analysis, motivation from first and second language acquisition, language disorders and diachronic change, as well as semiotic motivation), is of particular importance to NM.

Since naturalness derives from markedness, it is a gradual concept and can be described in terms of more or less natural (Dressler 2000a: 288).[1] Gradualness based on markedness can be illustrated with the following examples from Bulgarian noun inflection: *učítel* 'teacher' → PL *učítel-i* is more natural than *stol* 'chair' → PL *stol-óve* where a modificatory prosodic alternation in terms of phonological stress change co-occurs. On the other hand, *učenik* 'pupil' → PL *učenic-i* with a morphonological palatalization is less natural than *stol* 'chair' → PL *stol-óve*, but more natural than *kamăk* 'stone' → PL *kamăni*, with an unpredictably modified plural form (an isolated paradigm in Bulgarian). The least natural is, however, *bălgarin* 'Bulgarian man' → PL *bălgari*, because in this pair the plural form that is morphosemantically more marked is morphotactically shorter. In Bulgarian there exist no plurals such as the English PL *sheep*[2] (← SG *sheep*), but if there were, such morphotactically unchanged forms should be situated between *kamăni* and *bălgari*. (For a detailed account of the Bulgarian declension within the theoretical framework of NM see Manova and Dressler 2001).

The theory of NM consists of the three subtheories of universal naturalness, typological naturalness and language-specific naturalness. These subtheories interact in a hierarchical fashion in the sense that typological naturalness is a filter of universal naturalness, and language-specific naturalness is a filter of typological naturalness, i.e. in case of naturalness conflicts, language-specific preferences have precedence. If language-specific parameters are intact, the typological adequacy has precedence over universal naturalness.

2.1.1 Universal Naturalness

The theory of universal markedness (system-independent naturalness) is a preference theory that operates with a set of naturalness parameters: iconicity, indexicality, transparency (morphotactic and morphosemantic), biuniqueness, preferences for bases of morphological rules, binarity, and optimal shape of a morphological word. (Note that the set of preference parameters considered in this book is that elaborated by Dressler (cf. Dressler 1988, 1989, 1999, 2000a),

---

[1] Note that as Wurzel (1993) underlines, there is a difference between 'marked' (G. markiert) and 'markered' (G. merkmalhaft), 'markful' in Mayerthaler's terminology.

[2] The Old Bulgarian pluralia tantum *usta* 'mouth' and *vrata* 'door' denoting two-part objects may, like the E. *sheep*, take singular and plural agreement, but in both cases morphosemantically they are singular.

2.1 Natural Morphology

rather than that by Mayerthaler 1981.)[3] In accordance with those parameters, degrees of universal preferences are deductively established, i.e. what is more natural is universally preferred and therefore more frequent.

The most important of all universal preference parameters is *iconicity*, also called constructional diagrammaticity. Here diagrams are meant as subtypes of icons in the sense of Peirce (1965) who distinguishes between three fundamental varieties of semiosis based on different relationships between signans and signatum: icons, indices and symbols. An icon is a linguistic sign that resembles its signatum in some respect (e.g. onomatopoeic words). An index refers to its signatum only by contiguity. A symbol is characterized by a learned convention between signans and signatum. In addition, there are three subtypes of icons: images, diagrams and metaphors, of all diagrams being the most important to grammar (cf. Jakobson 1971, II: 349ff, II: 707). An image represents the simple qualities of the signatum (e.g. onomatopoeic words). A diagram reflects the similarities between a signans and signatum in respect to the relations of their parts. A metaphor exhibits only some partial similarities between signans and signatum.

Let us now turn back to the above-cited Bulgarian plurals and grade them in respect to their iconicity. Clearly, there is no instance of an image, but the plural form *učitel-i* 'teachers' (← *učitel*), where addition of meaning (plural) is expressed by addition of form (the affix *-i*), is diagrammatic. The next plural form, that of *učenic-i* 'pupil' (← *učenik*), is diagrammatic (addition of form) and metaphoric (due to the opacifying palatalization), which defines *učenic-i* as less iconic in comparison to *učiteli*. The plural *kamăni* (← *kamăk*) is metaphoric and thus less iconic than *učenic-i*. As for the subtractive plural *bălgari* 'Bulgarians', from *bălgarin* '(a) Bulgarian', it is anti-iconic, since the concept of pluralization is contradicted by the subtraction of form, i.e. *bălgari* is the least iconic of all forms. For the sake of completeness, English plurals of the type *sheep* (← *a sheep*) exemplify non-iconicity, which is more natural that anti-iconicity. Thus, according to the parameter of constructional iconicity, the four Bulgarian plurals above display a decreasing degree of naturalness.

Morphological formations are usually indexical in the way affixes refer to morphological bases to which they are bound. On the parameter of *indexicality*, adjacency is preferred to distance, i.e. the attachment of a marker to an immediately adjacent base is better than a situation in which affix and base are nonadjacent, the latter case being more natural than if no marker occurs.

Biuniqueness holds if one and the same form always corresponds to the same meaning and vice versa. Uniqueness is less natural; it is when one form has two different meanings, e.g. E. *to cut* → *a cut*. Least natural is ambiguity where there are many to many relations between form and meaning, e.g. E. ADJ *better – to better – a better* (Bauer 1988: 30).

---

[3] Mayerthaler's parameters of universal markedness appear problematic in some respects, discussion in Carstairs-McCarthy (1992: 217–223) and Dressler (2000a: 291f).

Full *morphosemantic transparency* means fully compositional meaning. The least natural option according to the parameter of morphosemantic transparency is that of morphosemantic opacity, as in the following example from Bulgarian:

(1)   *bix*   *čel*
       bix-COND.1 SG   read-PAST AOR PART.MASC SG
       'I will/would read'

This conditional form corresponds to English conditionals with real (referring to the future) as well as unreal (referring to the moment of speaking) conditions and does not indicate past. The expression in (1), however, exhibits two constituents both marked for past: the first constituent has the preterit marker *-x* and the second constituents – the past participle marker *-l*.

With respect to *morphotactic transparency*, the most natural forms are those which show no opacifying obstruction for ease of perception. The most transparent case is when no phonological or morphonological alternations occur, i.e. of both morphological relations Bg. *učitel* 'teacher' → *učitel-i* 'teachers' and *učenik* 'pupil' → *učenic-i* 'pupils', the latter is less transparent than the former.

An example of extreme unnaturalness, due to both morphosemantic and morphotactic opacity, are Bulgarian synthetic conditionals (cf. Stojanov 1993: 391f.; Kucarov 1999: 409). In Bulgarian, secondary imperfective verbs that correlate for aspect with semelfactive verbs can be used as conditionals. Consider first the following aspectual oppositions:

(2)   IMPFV *pij-a* 'I drink', 3 SG *pi-e*→ PFV SEMELFACTIVE *pij-n-a*,
       3 SG *pij-n-e* → IMPFV2 *pij-v-a-m*;
       IMPFV *pišt-j-a* 'I shriek', 3 SG *pišt-i* → PFV SEMELFACTIVE
       pis-n-a, 3 SG *pis-n-e* → IMPFV2 *pis-v-a-m*, 3 SG *pis-v-a*.

(Note that verbs without semelfactive mates, such as IMPFV *četa* 'I read' (→ PFV SEMELFACTIVE *četna), do not have syntactic conditional. For the aspectual correlation of semelfactives, which is a language-specific feature of Bulgarian verbs, see Andrejčin 1962, 1978; Stojanov 1993: 340). The verb form *pijvam* exhibits the morphosyntactic properties present, singular and indicative, and has no conditional marker; nevertheless *pijvam* is augmented with some conditional meaning. The first reading *pijvam* receives, if used outside any context (Bulgarian is a pro-drop language), is that of 'I will/would drink (if)...'. The same holds for the second verb above *pisvam* 'I will/would shriek (if)...' in which, in addition, a morphonological change occurs. Thus *pisvam*, having no conditional marker at all and exhibiting a *št : s* alternation, is morphosemantically and morphotactically opaque.

Morphotactic transparency is related to the criterion for *bases of morphological rules*. A base of a morphological rule is a morphological unit which is presented in both the input and output of the rule. According to this criterion, words, being primary signs in semiotic terms, are the most natural type of bases, while of stems and roots, stems are the more natural.

The parameter of *binarity* is motivated by the binary nature of the transmittance of neurological information and assigns the status of 'the most natural' to grammatical relations that are binary.

As for the *optimal shape of a morphological word*, according to Dressler (2000a), the most natural word shape is bi-syllabic, which corresponds to one prosodic foot. Here prosodic phonology motivates morphological naturalness.

2.1.2 Typological Adequacy

Inspired by the ideas in Skalička (1979), Wolfgang U. Dressler elaborates the subtheory of typological naturalness. Dressler understands language type as an ideal construct (cf. also Comrie 1981: 34f; 2001: 33f) whose properties are guiding principles that are never fully realized by actual language.[4] Ideal language types are '(alternative) sets of consistent responses to naturalness conflicts' (Dressler 2000a: 293). Since the greatest naturalness on all parameters is impossible within a single language, a language sacrifices naturalness of certain parameters in favour of others (cf. Dressler 1985a, 1987b). For example, the agglutinating type morphology is constructionally iconic, biunique and transparent, but at the same time the words are very long, i.e. unnatural according to the parameter of optimal word length. Moreover, the great number of affixes presupposes that they cannot be immediately adjacent to the root. Hence, the agglutinating type is also quite unnatural on the parameter of indexicality, insofar as its indexicality is very complex. Thus, rather unnatural options can be typologically adequate because they fit the respective language type.

Slavic morphology represents the inflecting(-fusional) type (see Skalička 1979: 337–339; Dressler 1987b: 120). A prototypical word of the inflecting type consists of a base (root or stem) and an inflectional affix, which means closeness of signans and signatum, i.e. a high degree of indexicality in derivation as well as in inflection. There is a clear differentiation between derivational and inflectional suffix slots, and the words can thus be distinguished according to their semantic and syntactic characteristics. Inflectional categories are expressed in a polyvalent way, with little morphotactic transparency, a high degree of syncretism, and ambiguity instead of biuniqueness. The inflecting type is characterised by inflectional classes, the latter differing either by sets of specific inflectional affixes (e.g. Slavic nominal morphology) or by specific affixes and properties of stem classes (e.g. Slavic verbal morphology). Stem

---

[4]Dressler's understanding of language type can be seen as similar to some extent to the canonical typology of inflectional morphology, cf. recent research by the Surrey Morphology Group (http://www.surrey.ac.uk/LIS/SMG/).

classes are marked by thematic markers (typically vowels) in stem-final position. Although diagrammaticity is not highly valued by this language type, the metaphoric principle of length (what is morphosemantically marked tends to be morphotactically longer (Dressler 1985a)) holds for inflecting languages, in general at least. Affixation (in terms of addition and substitution of affixes) is the dominant morphological technique, though often accompanied by modifications such as stress changes, ablaut, soft/hard consonant alternations or palatalizations. Gender is a type-specific category. In verbal morphology, the category of aspect is family-specific for Slavic languages and the perfective/imperfective opposition characterizes nearly all verb forms.

2.1.3 System-Dependent Naturalness

This third component of morphological naturalness explains the ways an individual language filters data from language typology, in particular when naturalness conflicts arise. The origination and the development of this subtheory is connected with the name of Wolfgang U. Wurzel. Wurzel (1993) defines system-adequacy as based on two main principles: (1) the principle of *system congruity* which reveals the system-defining properties of a language, and (2) the principle of *preferred membership of inflectional classes* (inflectional class stability in Wurzel 1984: 116f).

System-defining structural properties stabilize the language's morphological system and are best visible in cases of competing properties (rules) where the dominating property (rule) is the most system-adequate (system-defining). System congruity prefers systems which are uniformly constructed in respect to particular structural characteristics such as base-form inflection vs. stem inflection, separate vs. cumulative symbolization of categories, etc. (Wurzel 1993: 2597).

The assignment of a form to an inflectional class is governed by paradigm structure conditions (similar to inflection class assignment rules in other models of inflectional morphology). According to Wurzel (1993) the preferential membership of inflectional classes 'prevents the inflectional system from splitting up into too many classes, and over longer periods can actually lead to the complete loss of inflectional classes, as has virtually happened in English' (Wurzel 1993: 2596).

The subtheory of system-dependent naturalness, since devoted to the grammatical organization of a given language, displays much more formalism than the previous two subparts of NM and is compatible with current models of inflectional morphology such as Aronoff (1994) and Stump (2001).

Finally, it should be noted that the original ambition of the subtheory of language-specific naturalness, as formulated by Wurzel, is to account for inflectional morphology only. In this book, however, we will demonstrate repeatedly (Chapters 3, 4 and 5), that language-specific parameters can have an impact on derivational morphology as well (cf. Dressler and Ladányi 2000).

To sum up, 'natural' is a central notion in the theory of NM and means 'universally preferred'. The main assumptions of NM are formulated in three subtheories, the latter representing levels of adequacy related in a hierarchical manner, i.e. typological adequacy is a filter of universal naturalness, and language-specific system adequacy is a filter of typological adequacy. Each of the three subtheories has relevance to both derivation and inflection.

2.2 Cognitive Linguistics (CL)

Cognitive Linguistics emerged as a coherent theoretical approach in the mid 1980s (overviews of the basic ideas of the model in Ungerer and Schmid 1996; Taylor 2003; Tuggy 2005, among others). CL, like NM, is a reaction against the expansion of Chomskian 'formalist' linguistics. The latter regards knowledge of language as an autonomous component of the mind, independent from other cognitive abilities. CL, on the contrary, assumes a close, dialectic relationship between the structure and the function of language, on the one hand, and non-linguistic skills and knowledge on the other (recall that the cognitive perspective of NM is somewhat focused on language ontology; NM, like Chomskian linguistics, also argues for external modularity of the language system (cf. Dressler 1997).[5] CL posits that language reflects, in its structure, more general cognitive abilities, one of the most important being the ability to

---

[5]Dressler (1997), based on Schaner-Wollas (1992) and Schaner-Wollas and Haider (1987) acknowledges evidence for the dissociation of grammatical and cognitive development (i.e. external modularity of the grammar). On the other hand, Dressler confirms that the assumption of external modularity challenges the cognitive orientation of the first subtheory of NM, that of universal naturalness. In order to solve the discrepancy, Dressler distinguishes between extragrammatical morphological operations, such as 'echo-word formation, back formation, various abbreviatory and subtractive devices, surface analogies and blends' (p. 1400) and morphological organization based on universal principles. Since extragrammatical operations are typical for the first phase of language acquisition (called pre-morphological by him) but violate different principles of morphological organization, they cannot be handled by the morphological module of grammar. This leads him to the following conclusions (only those relevant to the discussion are listed here): (1) linguistic modules are not genetically inherited but originate and grow during language acquisition; (2) in the first phase of language acquisition a separate, distinct grammatical module does not yet exist and extragrammatical operations are handled by more general cognitive principles; (3) the system of morphological grammar is developing in the second (proto-morphological) stage of language acquisition; and (4) that modules originate from earlier global systems through dissociation when the task and the structure of a global system become too complex (p. 1401). However, it remains unclear why children, governed by general cognitive principles, start speaking by using cognitively complex operations in terms of reductive formations. It seems to me that subtractive morphology during the first stage of language acquisition indicates either rote-learning (note that extragramamtical morphology is not describable in terms of rules) or what CL recognizes as primary use of language – categorization of the non-linguistic world around us by naming. Extragrammatical morphology during that first stage is cognitively governed only in the sense that a child explores the non-linguistic world and has nothing to do

categorize, i.e. to see sameness in diversity. Categorizing allows access to previously stored knowledge and its application to a new situation. In this way the cognitive ability of categorizing helps us to reduce the complexity of the world.

According to CL, the primary use of language is for categorizing (naming) things, which is categorization of the non-linguistic world. In addition, CL acknowledges the language itself as an object of categorization. It is this type of categorization we will deal with in this book. With CL, we will assume that the structure of the language itself resembles, in many respects, the categories human beings perceive in the non-linguistic world around them, and that grammatical categories, like non-linguistic ones, have an internal structure based on prototypical instances (best examples). This leads us to the next section.

2.3 Prototype Theory (PT): Prototypes and Clines

Cognitive science distinguishes between two basic views of categories: the classical view, also called Aristotelian approach which accepts discrete categories, with clear-cut boundaries, and an alternative view which understands categories as having graded membership and thus structured around prototypical instances. The idea of non-discrete categories is rooted in anthropological linguistics, in particular in the study of colour terms (Berlin and Kay 1969; Kay and McDaniels 1978). The further development of the approach is connected with cognitive psychology and the research on concrete objects carried out mainly by Rosch (1973, 1975, 1977, 1978), who introduces the term 'prototype'. In linguistics, PT first became popular in lexical semantics (cf. Lakoff 1973; Coleman and Kay 1981) from where the model is later expanded to the area of grammar, known as 'Cognitive Grammar' (Langacker 1987, 1991, 1999, 2002 [1991]).

PT knows two versions: standard and extended (cf. Kleiber 1998: 29ff). The extended version of the model (cf. Givón 1986: 78; Kleiber 1998: 109ff) is based on Wittgenstein's idea of family resemblances (Wittgenstein 1953: 66f). A family resemblance relationship may hold between the different members of a category or between the different categories within a supra-ordinate meta-category. Family resemblance links category members in the following way: member *a* may resemble (i.e. share properties with) *b*; *b* may resemble *c*, *c* may resemble *d* etc., so that members *a* and *d* may share no properties at all. Note, however, that

---

with the cognitive organization (i.e. the categorization) of language as a system, which is the second kind of categorization in CL. Categorization by naming also explains the rather unnatural (conversion-like) use of one and the same word as N and V by a child, e.g. Bg. *bu(u)* for 'a car' and 'to drive a car'. Further evidence for naming is the fact that extragrammatical morphology children use seems to be non-derived. For me, *Betty*, for example, cannot be derived via some reduction from *Elisabeth* (as Dressler assumes, p. 1401), since it is not very probable that during the pre-morphological phase the child produces first *Elisabeth* and only afterwards *Betty*.

2.3 Prototype Theory (PT): Prototypes and Clines

in this book, as everywhere in Langackerian Cognitive Grammar, the standard version of PT is meant, i.e. we assume that all the members of a category have at least a single feature in common.

A more recent development of PT explores the notion of 'gestalt', cf. Ungerer and Schmid (1996).

For a definition of a prototype we will assume with Langacker (1987) that:

> A prototype is a typical instance of a category, and other elements are assimilated to the category on the basis of their perceived resemblance to the prototype; there are degrees of membership based on degrees of similarity (Langacker 1987: 371).

Since non-prototypical instances match the category according to the extent to which they approach the prototype, prototypical instances are central whereas non-prototypical ones form a gradation depending on how far they deviate from the prototype. Put differently, cognitive categories are made up of prototypes and periphery (remember the Prague school idea of centre and periphery[6]). A prototype is established on the basis of salient characteristics or typical aspects (called attributes) of the category it represents. Attributes of a given category can be listed. The prototype model does not require that every member of a category possesses all its attributes. In this way, the model allows for a non-discrete continuum space within as well as between categories (Givón 1986: 79) and avoids many characterization problems.

In linguistics, the notion of prototype has usually been applied to phenomena concerning semantics (lexical and categorical), categorization in phonology and to syntactic constructions and language acquisition (cf. Taylor 2003). Morphological forms have being neglected somewhat. Yet, Bybee and Moder (1983) apply the PT to the purely formal elements of morphological description. Studying the morphological behaviour of English strong verbs, Bybee and Moder (1983) claim that 'speakers of natural language form categorization of linguistic objects in the same way that they form categorizations of natural and cultural objects' (p. 263), i.e. psychological principals governing linguistic behaviour are of the same type as those governing other types of human behaviour. Bybee and Moder (1983) evidence their conclusions by English strong verbs, such as *sing* which display the vowel alternation /i/-/æ/-/ʌ/ in the present tense, past tense, and past participle. Other verbs, such as *cling*, have the pattern /i/-/ʌ/-/ʌ/. Both classes have been moderately productive over centuries and have accumulated verbs originally in other classes, such as *ring*, *fling*, *stick* and *dig*. Moreover, verbs with a present tense vowel other than /i/ have been added, e.g. *hang*, *strike*, and for some speakers even *sneak*, *shake* and *drag*. These latter, due to their non-conforming present tense forms, are marginal members of the paradigms. The fact that most of the verbs have as stem final consonant a velar nasal (*cling*, *sing*, etc.) also accounts for a prototype structure of the paradigms, i.e. termination in a velar nasal is a prototypical characteristic, and other verbs that exhibit only partial similarity to the central

---

[6]Cf. *Travaux linguistiques de Prague 2* (1966), in particular the paper by František Daneš.

members of the two paradigms terminate either in a non-velar nasal (e.g. *swim, win*) or in a non-nasal velar (e.g. *stick, dig*).

Although the relation between the gradual concepts of NM, defined according to the different naturalness parameters, and the notion of prototype is obvious (the most natural options represent a prototype and the deviations gradually characterized as less natural, much less natural, unnatural, more unnatural, much more unnatural to most unnatural are non-prototypical instances), NM and CL have not been connected explicitly yet, though Dressler (1989; 1990a, b) could be seen as attempts towards some integration of NM and CL concepts. Thus, one of the challenges for the present book is to relate explicitly the basic principles of NM with those of PT. In line with Bybee and Moder (1983), we will focus on the prototype analysis of morphological forms. However, the perspective of this study differs from that of previous research on the relation between linguistic form and the concept of prototype. Based on the universal preference parameters of NM, the present book shifts the starting point of prototype analysis from concrete paradigms (as in Bybee and Moder 1983, and everywhere in CL) to generalized morphological forms which are cognitively predicted prototypes, as we will see in the next section.

2.4 Morphological Techniques

All operations that can be undertaken with an object (input of a particular process) in the real world, in order to produce a new, different object (output of the process), conceptually based on the primary one, might be predicted. Moreover, thanks to our previous experience (i.e. cognitive knowledge), the expected operations could be graded according to the effort they require:

(1) The easiest way to produce something different is by adding (e.g. by gluing, sewing, etc.) new material to the primary object;
(2) If the nature of the primary object allows, some part of the latter could be substituted with another object, or with a part of another object;
(3) Depending on the primary object, it is also possible to modify it in one way or another (e.g. to change its shape by pressing or twisting), without adding or replacing parts;
(4) Although we need a new, different object, we can try to use the basic object we have without any changes (the process involves re-categorization and thus supposes some additional mental activities);
(5) The original form of the object we have could be reduced. In most cases such a decision appears not very reasonable, since our behaviour might result in an unusable (due to impairment) object;
(6) In case the input object seems inappropriate (or has become unusable) for the task we have to complete, we can replace it with another, entirely different object; and
(7) We can refuse to perform the task and leave it uncompleted.

2.4 Morphological Techniques   45

Recall that we have assumed, with CL, that principles governing linguistic behaviour do not differ from cognitive principles governing human behaviour in real life. Under this assumption, we expect morphology where one creates new words or new forms of words to use the strategies listed in 1–7 above. Therefore, we argue that what happens in morphology, be it derivational or inflectional, is describable in terms of basic morphological techniques (Manova 2003b, cf. also Dressler 1987b), which are analogous to the above non-linguistic solutions. Morphological techniques operate in derivation and inflection and remain for morphological relations describable in terms of morphological rules. In morphology, we will speak of:

(1) Addition, i.e. X → X + Y, e.g. Bg. N *učitel* 'teacher' → ADJ *učitel-ski* 'teacher's'; *učitel* 'teacher' → PL *učitel-i*
(2) Substitution, i.e. X + Y → X + Z, e.g. Bg. N *marks-izăm* 'marksism' → N *marks-ist* 'marksist'; SG *žen-a* 'woman' → PL *žen-i*
(3) Modification (phonological and morphonological alternations), i.e. X → X', e.g. R. *byt* 'to be' → *byt* 'way of life' and Bg. V *podnes-a* 'I present, offer, serve', 3 SG *podnes-e* → N *podnos* 'tray'; PFV *podnes-a*, 3 SG *podnes-e* → IMPFV2 *podnas-ja-m*, 3 SG *podnas-ja*
(4) Conversion, i.e. X → X, e.g. Bg. *sladko* 'sweet' → *sladko* 'marmalade, dessert'
(5) Subtraction, i.e. XY → X (or X → X –Y, since X is the base of the rule), e.g. Bg. *biolog-i-ja* 'biology' → *biolog* 'biologist'; *bălgarin* '(a) Bulgarian' → PL *bălgari*

The last two non-linguistic solutions, those in 6 and 7 above, are known in linguistics as suppletion and defectiveness respectively. The most typical feature of suppletion consists of the fact that it is not rule-governed, which means that suppletion cannot be described by a morphological rule. Therefore, we do not acknowledge suppletion as a basic morphological technique. Defectiveness means that there is no form available, i.e. the grammar refuses to provide a form we would otherwise expect. Defectiveness is usually recognized in inflectional morphology (see, for example, the Surrey Morphology Group research on defectiveness in morphology, http://www.defectiveness.surrey.ac.uk/) since the organization of the inflectional paradigm favours analogical levelling. Defectiveness is, however, hard to define in derivational morphology where idiosyncrasies are much more frequent than in inflection. It is quite normal for a derivational paradigm to be incomplete, i.e. it is seldom the case that all available bases of a particular type lend themselves to a particular type of derivation. Thus, due to the highly unpredictable character of defectiveness, we do not define it as a morphological technique.

Let us return to suppletion now. Dressler (1987b: 103f) defines suppletion as the last (least natural) stage at a scale of modifications and assumes the existence of only affixation, conversion and subtraction rules in WF. Dressler (p.c.) understands substitution as truncation in the sense of Aronoff (1976), where the rule of truncation is defined in the following way:

A truncation rule deletes a morpheme which is internal to an affix, in the following general manner:

[[root + A]$_X$ + B]$_Y$
    1   2   3 → 1 ø 3

where X and Y are major lexical categories (Aronoff 1976: 88).

According to Aronoff, the derivation E. V *nomin-ate* → N *nomin-ee* is an instance of truncation.

Dressler (p.c.) explained to me that the lack of substation in the NM account of WF rules implies that this type of change is considered as a sub-case of addition (affixation in Dressler's terminology). However, we cannot agree with Aronoff (and Dressler) that the truncation rule properly accounts for morphological changes. Consider the following examples from Bulgarian in which addition of the same material, the inflectional suffix *-i*, to the same base truncates two different segments.

(3)   N *miš-k-a* 'mouse' → PL *miš-k-i*
      N *miš-k-a* 'mouse' → ADJ *miš-i* 'mouse (attr.)'

According to Aronoff (1976), both cases involve the same change, namely truncation, due to the addition of *-i*. However, the above examples represent two different rules. The fist rule pluralizes, whereas the second is adjectivizing, and what takes place cannot be explained with homonymy, since the addition of the inflection *-i* deletes different forms in each of the two examples. In contrast, the system of morphological technique suggested herein adequately accounts for both examples.[7] The first example is a case of substitution in inflection (*-i* substitutes *-a* in the inflectional slot of the word), whereas the second rule is subtractive, as the material added (*-i*) is in the inflectional slot, whereas the material deleted (*-k*) is in the derivational slot. Since a derivational change (adjectivization) is expressed by deletion of derivational material, we speak of subtraction in derivation. The morphological technique of subtraction is the topic of Chapter 4 where more such examples can be found.

Truncation also fails to distinguish between derivations such as the following ones from Serbo-Croatian:

(4)   N *žèn-a* 'woman' → V *žèn-iti se* 'to marry'
      N *žèn-a* 'woman' → ADJ *žèn-sk-ī* 'woman's'

---

[7]An alternative solution would assume two *-i* suffixes, *-i$_1$* that pluralizes and *-i$_2$* that adjectivizes. Such a treatment of the examples in (3) is, however, less appropriate than the solution suggested above, since it is difficult to distinguish between *i$_1$* and *i$_2$*. Both suffixes are at the same word slot and select the same base.

2.4 Morphological Techniques

Although both rules are word-class changing, they cannot be classified together, i.e. as truncation, since in the first example inflectional material is replaced by inflectional material, whereas in the second case the derivational suffix *-sk-* is added. Therefore, we assume conversion for the first example and addition, rather than subtraction, for the second.

Note that truncation analysis seems to be avoided in the morphological theory as well. For example, Spencer (1998) speaks of replacive morphology (see the next paragraph) and uses truncation only for changes involving evaluative morphology, such as formation of hypochoristics (see also Lappe 2007), e.g. *Michael – Mike* (consider that in such formations the input and the output do not differ semantically, which would not be the case if a WF rule operates). Becker (1993) labels truncation-like rules either as 'affix-replacing' or as 'substitution', cf. also Sassen (1981).

Spencer (1998: 140f) illustrates replacive morphology (substitution for us) with the derivation *Marxism – Marxist*. He correctly noted that we cannot take the forms *Marxism* and *Marxist* to be derived by adding of either *-ism* or *-ist* to *Marx*, since a Marxist is not just someone with some arbitrary relationship to Marx, but rather one who practices Marxism, i.e. semantically, *Marxist* is motivated by *Marxism*, not by *Marx*. Thus, he concludes that *Marxist* is derived from *Marxism* by replacing *-ism* with *-ist*.

My last argument for substitution instead of truncation comes from inflectional morphology. A prototypical characteristic of inflectional morphology (see the next section), due to its paradigmatic organization, is the substitutability of inflectional affixes within the same word slot, which implies formation by substitution. Of course, here it is fair to say that Aronoff (1976), when suggesting the rule of truncation, did not tackle inflection. On truncation see also Chapter 4.

We will understand the five morphological techniques as prototype answers to the needs of morphology. Put differently, morphological techniques are prototypical instances of morphological rules with the help of which one can model all possible morphological operations, be they concatinative morphology or processes. Moreover, if evaluated for naturalness, according to their iconicity the above techniques constitute a scale beginning with the most iconic (natural) addition (called usually affixation), where addition of meaning (morphosemantic complexity) is expressed by addition of form (morphotactic complexity). Substitution and modification come into play after affixation. The latter two are less iconic than addition (substitution being the more iconic technique of both), but since involving some addition of morphotactic features, they are more iconic than conversion where one and the same form is used for the expression of different meanings. Thus, conversion represents non-iconicity. The last technique, that of subtraction, is even anti-iconic because when applied, addition of meaning is expressed by subtraction of form. This claim in respect to iconicity predicts that more iconic techniques would be preferred to less iconic ones.

The scale of morphological techniques represents more gradual than discrete relations of prototypical rules, which implies that non-prototypical instances of neighbour techniques will show characteristics of both techniques and thus will be difficult to classify (see the discussion below). Such instances are tackled in detail in Chapter 3, where we distinguish conversion from modification and subtraction.

Since the above morphological techniques model morphological changes in general, we expect that they will operate in derivation as well as in inflection, and will have words, stems and roots as bases, word-based realizations being prototypical, whereas stem-based and root-based morphology will be seen as deviating from the prototype, stem-based morphology being less non-prototypical than root-based morphology. (Recall, that in accordance with the NM parameter for bases of morphological rules, words are the most natural type of bases). The prototype status of word-based rules seems best visible in conversion. Consider:

(5) E. V *to cut* → N *cut* (word-based);
R. N *rabot-a-t'* 'to work' → V *rabota* 'labour, task, work, job' (stem-based)
Bg. V *xod-j-a* 'I go, walk', 3 SG *xod-i* → N *xod* 'gate, pace, tread, move, walk' (root-based)
R. V *sel-i-t'sja* 'to settle' → V *sel-o* 'village' (root-based)

Due to the prototype status of the English example, no linguist would hesitate to classify it as conversion, whereas for the Russian and Bulgarian examples of conversion, some explanation is needed, specifically that derivations involving word-class change delete and add inflectional material.

As in conversion and in accordance with the template of addition, word-based suffixation is a prototypical addition (note that this rule holds only for right-hand-headedness), but addition can also mean prefixation, circumfixation, reduplication, interfixation[8] and infixation, all these being non-prototypical addition.

The prototype of modification is also word-based, and since modification comprises phonological and morphonological changes, we can have the following different types of modification (based on Dressler 1987b: 104):

(1) Phonological modifications

    (a) prosodic modifications
    (b) segmental modifications

---

[8]Aronoff and Fuhrhop (2002) analyze German linking elements as stem-forming suffixes, which seems to support the understanding of interfixation as addition, i.e. a derivative has the following structure [[[X + Linking element]$_{stem}$] + Y] and is thus interpretable as derived by (stem-based) addition.

2.4 Morphological Techniques

(2) Morphonological modifications
   (a) leaving the morpheme boundary relatively intact
   (b) completely blurring morpheme boundaries

Note, however, that the prototype of modification exhibits the most radical modification possible (that of 2b) and, as already stated, is word-based, as in R. N *drug* 'friend' → V *druž-i-t'* 'to be friends' (here *-i-t'* is inflection). The prototype status of such modifications is supported by the fact that they have not been confused (or have rarely been confused) with conversion, the neighbour technique of modification, whereas less prototypical modifications such as E. V *to impórt* → N *ímport* are often classified as conversions. Thus, the following examples from Slavic all represent non-prototypical modifications: Bg. *matemátik-a* 'mathematics'→ *matematík* 'mathematician' (vs. the conversion R. *matemátik-a* 'mathematica' → *matemátik* 'mathematician'), Bg. *ogléd-a-m* 'I inspect', 3 SG *ogléd-a* → *ógled* 'inspection' (vs. the conversion Bg. *zíd-a-m* 'I build', 3 SG *zíd-a* → *zid* 'wall'), V *iz-vír-a-m* 'I well', 3 SG *iz-vír-a* → N *íz-vor* 'well' (vs. the conversion V *raz-grom-j-á* 'I rout', 3 SG *raz-grom-í* → *raz-gróm*).

If a modification accompanies addition of morphotactic form, the change will be classified as non-prototypical addition. All non-prototypical additions can be graded for prototypicality, but here, according to the NM parameter of morphotactic transparency, the combination of addition and the least prototypical modification (type 1a above) is nearer to the prototype of addition than a combination of addition and the prototype of modification (type 2b). In other words, Bg. V *úč-a* 'I learn, study', 3 SG *úč-i* → N *úč-ene* 'learning' is an example of prototypical addition; V *uč-a* 'I learn, study', 3 SG *úč-i* → N *uč-eník* 'pupil', with a stress change, is nearer to the prototype of addition than N *učeník* 'pupil' → ADJ *učeníč-esk-i* 'pupil's', with a morphonological palatalization.

Modification can also accompany substitution of forms. In such cases, we will speak of non-prototypical substitution, e.g.: Bg. *istór-i-ja* 'history' → *istor-ík* 'historian', *ogledál-o* 'mirror' → PL *ogledal-á*, both prosodically modified, as well as Bg. *kolján-o* 'knee' → PL *kolen-á* and *kolen-é*, the latter, due to a prosodic modification (stress change) and *ja* : *e* segmental alternation, even less prototypical than the previous two.

If a modification co-occurs with a deletion of morphotactic form such as in subtraction, we postulate non-prototypical subtraction, e.g.: N *méč-k-a* 'bear' → N *meč-é* 'bear cub, teddy bear' (with a stress change) and the more non-prototypical N *găs-k-a* 'goose' → ADJ *găš-i* 'goose-' (with a palatalization of the root-final consonant).

Finally, the assumption of a scale of morphological techniques implies involvement of rules from the same morphological level, and it could happen that different techniques compete for the expression of the same morphosemantics. Consider the following instances from Bulgarian: N *krav-a* 'cow' → ADJ *krav-ø-i* 'cow-' (conversion) and ADJ *krav-ešk-i* 'cow-' (addition), N *meč-k-a* 'bear' → ADJ *meč-ø-i* 'bear-' (subtraction) and ADJ *meč-ešk-i* 'bear-' (addition). In case of competition of rules, we expect, in accordance with NM parameters, that the more natural technique will have precedence over the less natural one, the latter being restricted in some way, e.g. having smaller semantic scope, being stylistically marked, etc. If no restrictions operate on the less natural technique, the explanation could be the intervention of either typological or language-specific preferences. Instances of competition of techniques are analysed in Chapters 3 and 4.

To sum up, we have postulated a scale of morphological techniques and assumed that: (1) morphological techniques are relevant to both derivation and inflection; (2) morphological techniques are prototypical instances of morphological rules and can thus have prototypical and non-prototypical realizations; (3) prototypical occurrences of the techniques, being word-based, are the best examples of the five techniques and therefore the easiest instances to classify. Less prototypical examples of the techniques are either stem or root-based or involve modifications (except in conversion where the occurrence of a modification means that we have to do with the morphological technique of modification); and (4) since all techniques are from the same morphological level, there should be instances of competition of techniques, solved according to the naturalness conflict scenario of NM. Thus the model suggested herein has the advantages of being applicable to derivation and inflection, accounting for rules and realizations at the same time (cf. Bybee 1988), and , most importantly, being predictive.

All above assumptions and expectations will be evidenced by a detailed analysis of 'unnatural' morphology, such as conversion (Chapter 3) and subtraction (Chapter 4) with data predominantly from Bulgarian, Russian and Serbo-Croatian.

The following derivations, which involve deletion and addition of inflection only (-Ø- remains for an empty derivational slot), without being inflection (the input and the output belong to different word classes), are also relevant to the classification of morphological techniques:

(6) V *zakán-Ø-j-a (se)* 'I threaten', 3 SG *zakán-Ø-i (se)* →
N *zakán-Ø-a* 'threat'.
V *vik-Ø-a-m* 'I cry', 3 SG *vik-Ø-a* → N *vik-Ø* 'cry'

Here the verb-to-noun derivational change is signalled only by alternation of inflection, and there is a discrepancy between morphotactic expression (inflection) and morphosemantics (derivation). Such instances lead us to the next section, devoted to the differentiation of derivation and inflection.

2.5 Derivation-Inflection Continuum

In morphological theory, the idea of prototype has been applied to the classification of derivation and inflection (Dressler 1989). Similar to attributes which define the characteristic features of the category members in the framework of

2.5 Derivation-Inflection Continuum

PT, linguists elaborate sets of criteria (9 criteria in Wurzel 1984 [1989]; Dressler 1989 proposes 20 criteria; in Plank 1994 we find a set of 28 criteria; 9 criteria in Booij 2000) which, without being absolute (cf. Beard 1982; Haspelmath 1996; Rainer 1996; van Marle 1996), distinguish inflectional morphology (IM) from derivational morphology (DM). The most important of these are[9]:

(1) *Change of word class*: Since IM involves smaller meaning changes than DM, it does not change word class, DM, however, does;
(2) *Syntactic relevance*: IM serves syntax, while DM can have a syntactic function only in a very indirect way, e.g. grammatical agreement is typical for IM;
(3) *Obligatoriness*: IM is obligatory, DM is optional;
(4) *Uniformity*: The tendency towards biuniqueness plays a greater role in IM than in DM. Therefore, variation and competition of rules are typical for DM, but rare in IM;
(5) *Categories*: Inflectional categories typically form a small universal set, the language specific categories of DM being much more numerous and varying a lot cross-linguistically;
(6) *Meaning*: The meanings of IM are more abstract (relational) than those of DM;
(7) *Transparency*: IM is usually morphosemantically more transparent than DM;
(8) *Productivity*: Inflectional rules tend to be general and are therefore more productive than those of DM;
(9) *Recursivity*: IM applies only once to a word in order to fill a certain cell of the paradigm of the word. As for derivation, since each derivational step may add some additional meaning, DM is easier to reapply recursively than IM;
(10) *Paradigms*: IM is usually organized in paradigms (and in inflectional classes, when an inflectional property is expressed in more than one way), whereas the paradigmatic organization of DM is much weaker;
(11) *Substitutability*: Due to smaller meaning change and tighter paradigmatic organization, inflectional affixes are easily substitutable within the same slot (i.e. IM is usually expressed by the morphological technique of substitution, whereas DM prototypically requires affixation by addition).
(12) *Psycholinguistic status*: Derived words are likely to be stored as wholes in the mental lexicon, whereas inflected word forms are not;
(13) *Order of morphemes*: Inflectional affixes have a more peripheral position in the word form than derivational affixes.
(14) *Further suffixation* (Manova 2010): Derivation and inflection treat homophonous derivational suffixes differently. For derivational morphology homophonous derivational suffixes are different suffixes and thus allow the attachment of different sets of further derivational suffixes, whereas for inflectional morphology homophonous derivational suffixes are the same suffix and thus receive the same inflection.

---

[9]The set of criteria used in this book is based primarily on Dressler (1989) and Booij (2000).

As can be expected, there are categories that do not satisfy the criteria for being clearly either derivation or inflection, leading linguists to assume that derivation and inflection constitute a continuum, with prototypical derivation and prototypical inflection as poles[10] (except the above cited linguists see also Plank 1981, 1994; Stephany 1982; Bybee 1985; Dressler and Doleschal 1991; van Marle 1996). A list of prototypical categories is given in Dressler (1989).[11] However, the assumption of a cline from prototypical derivation to prototypical inflection is of particular importance to the classification of non-prototypical categories, since it allows for inflection-like properties of derivation and derivation-like properties of inflection (cf. Haspelmath 1996; Rainer 1996; van Marle 1996). Here, due to the formal orientation of this book, I will focus on criterion 13. According to this criterion and the generilized form of the Slavic word ((PREF)-BASE-(DSUFF)-(TM)-(ISUFF)), one expects that if a category uses the derivational slot of the word, it is derivation, and if the category exponent is in the inflectional slot of the word, the category is inflectional. However, since the generalized form of the Slavic word is based on prototypical properties, there are also derivational category changes that are expressed by inflection change only, as can be seen in example (6) above. Moreover, there are non-prototypical categories such as nominal diminutives, imperfectivization and formation of females from males, which, since having their origin in inflection, use either the inflectional (the b. examples below) or the derivational slot of the word (the a. examples below). Consider the following instances from Bulgarian:

Diminutives
(7) a. MASC *učitel* 'teacher' → DIM NEUT *učitel-č-e*
     versus
     b. MASC *kotel*, caldron' → DIM NEUT *kotl-Ø-e*;

---

[10]In current linguistic literature, the terms 'inherent inflection' and 'contextual inflection' (Booij 1996, 2000) might be seen as synonymous to Dressler's non-prototypical and prototypical inflection respectively.

> Inherent inflection is the kind of inflection that is not required by the syntactic context, although it may have syntactic relevance. Examples are the category number for nouns, comparative and superlative degree of the adjective, and tense and aspect for verbs. Other examples of inherent verbal inflection are infinitives and participles. Contextual inflection, on the other hand, is that kind of inflection that is dictated by syntax, such as person and number markers on verbs that agree with subjects and/or objects, agreement markers for adjectives, and structural case markers on nouns (Booij 1996: 2).

[11]Dressler (1989: 6) determines the following inflectional categories as prototypically inflectional: case, gender, definiteness and possessive inflection for the noun; and person, number, gender, tense, voice and mood for the verb. Non-prototypical inflection are: nominal number, gradation (comparative, superlative, excessive), verbal aspect, infinitive, participle and gerund.

2.5 Derivation-Inflection Continuum

Aspect (imperfectivization)
(8) a. PFV *pre-sto-j-a* 'I stay, remain, stop', 3 SG *pre-sto-i* →
IMPFV2 *pre-sto-jav-a-m*, 3 SG *pre-sto-jav-a*
versus
b. PFV *ob-misl-j-a* 'I think over', 3 SG *ob-misl-i* → IMPFV2 *ob-misl-Ø-ja-m*, 3 SG *ob-misl-Ø-ja*;

Gender (formation of female humans from male humans)
(9) a. MASC *pisatel* 'writer, author' → FEM *pisatel-k-a*
versus
b. MASC *săprug* 'husband' → FEM *săprug-Ø-a* 'wife'.

These examples differ from (6) above with respect to inflection. The output of derivations such as (6), like the output of derivation by overt suffixes, enters different inflection classes (i.e. Bg. *zakana* and *vik* belong to different inflection classes, cf. PL *zakan-i* but PL *vik-ove*, see Appendix A). The three pairs of examples in (7) through (9), however, belong to the same inflection class each. The point is discussed in depth in Chapter 4.

When classifying conversion and subtraction, we will further (based on criterion 1) consider that, in derivation, a morphological technique can be word-class-changing (the prototypical instance) and word-class-preserving (the non-prototypical instance).

Note that derivation-like properties of inflection and inflection-like properties of derivation do not mean that derivation and inflection are indistinguishable (cf. Wurzel 1989: 31ff.; Booij 1996). Just as categorization of non-linguistic world requires naming in all situations, whether prototypical or not, we will, herein, tend to classify categories as either derivational or inflectional. To illustrate, colours constitute a continuum, but if we have a set of colours and need red, we always have an idea whether a given colour shade is (can stand for) red or not. This understanding finds support in the NM principle of binarity and the observation by Manova (2005a) that the diachronic development of the morphological systems of Bulgarian, Russian and Serbo-Croatian has been towards either connecting in-between categories with particular inflection classes, thus inflection, or dispersing them within the whole inflection system, making them unidentifiable inflectionally, and thus derivation.

Chapter 3
Conversion

This chapter focuses on the non-iconic morphological technique of conversion. The aim is to illustrate one of the main theoretical claims of the present book, namely that a given morphological change is not a set of uniform realizations but varies and exhibits deviations that are best describable in terms of clines, the latter constitutive parts of the derivation-inflection continuum. After a discussion on terminological matters (Section 3.1), a definition of conversion is given (Section 3.2). In Section 3.3, with the help of the definition of conversion assumed, the morphological technique is set apart from lexical, (mor)phonological and morphological changes that, without being conversion, look conversion-like. Section 3.4 suggests a number of well-known and novel criteria for establishing the direction of conversion. Section 3.5 provides a classification of conversion; the various subsections treating in detail conversion in derivation, conversion in inflection and syntactic conversion, suggesting further subdivisions of these major types of conversion. In the last Section 3.6, the discussion on the classification of conversion is summarized and conclusions are drawn.

3.1 Terminology

The term conversion goes as far back as 1891 introduced by Henry Sweet:

> But in English, as in many other languages, we can often convert a word that is, to make it into another part of speech without any modification or addition, except of course, the necessary change of inflection, etc. (Sweet 1900 [1891]: 38).

At first glance this definition seems clear enough. Yet the morphological change called 'conversion' by Sweet has received a number of alternative interpretations and, as a consequence, also a number of competing labels, such as zero derivation, multifunctionality, functional change, transposition, and syntactic recategorization, the most popular of all being undoubtedly that of zero derivation. The term 'zero derivation' is connected chiefly with the studies on English word formation (Marchand 1963; 1964a, b; 1969 [1960] and his students Brekle, Kastovsky, Lipka, Hansen, Stein) from which the concept spreads to other languages, including the Slavic ones. Marchand (1969 [1960]) suggests the following definition of 'zero derivation':

> By derivation by a zero-morpheme I understand the use of a word as a determinant in a syntagma whose determinatum is not expressed in a phonic form but understood to be present in content, thanks to an association with other syntagmas where the element of content has its counterpart on the plane of phonic expression.
> ...
> We can speak of a zero morpheme only when zero sometimes alternates with an overt sign in other cases (*cash-Ø* ~ *atom-ize*). A sign always has the two facets of expression and content. Therefore zero, which is a sign, cannot just stand for content only if this content is never in any way matched by phonic form. (Marchand 1969: 359f)

In addition, Marchand makes a clear-cut distinction between 'zero derivation' and 'conversion' ('partial conversion' in Adams 1973) and reserves the latter term only for specific cases of syntactic transposition:

> What we call zero derivation is often termed 'conversion' [...]. [...]Another term that has recently come to be used is 'functional change'. I do not object to this term or to the term 'conversion' either so long as they are used to denote the syntactic transposition of the word, as that of *government* in *government job*. This is however a purely grammatical matter. The use of a sb as a preadjunct represents a regular syntactic pattern which has nothing to do with word-formation and derivation. We speak of derivation only when a word changes its word class or its lexical class (Marchand 1969: 360).

As mentioned in Chapter 1, the term 'zero derivation' entered Slavic linguistic literature after Marchand (1960), Lopatin (1966: 77f) being the first to use the zero-derivation concept for Russian data; afterwards 'zero derivation' appears in the Russian Academy Grammar (1970), Zemskaja (1973: 38) as well as Švedova et al. (1980: 219ff, 303f, cf.), i.e. the Russian Academy Grammar (1980). For 'zero derivation' in Serbo-Croatian see Babić (1991[1986]: 300ff), who mentions Zemskaja and Uluhanov; and for Bulgarian Bojadžiev (1999: 266). Unfortunately, in Bulgarian, Russian and Serbo-Croatian, the interpretations of 'zero suffix' differ. As already mentioned in Chapter 1, whereas the Russian Academy Grammar allows for the addition of inflectional material in zero suffixation, e.g. *xval-i-t'* 'to praise' → *xval-a* 'praise', *sel-i-t'sja* 'to settle' → *sel-o* 'village' (Švedova et al. 1980: 222, 224), Babić (1991) and Bojadžiev (1999) postulate zero suffixation only if after the deletion of inflectional material nothing else is added, i.e. SC. *pogled-a-ti* 'to look (at)' → *pòglēdØ* 'look, glance' (Babić 1991: 310); Bg. *zaliv-a-m* '(I) overflow', 3 SG *zaliv-a* → *zalivØ* 'bay, gulf' (Bojadžiev 1999: 266).

As for the general morphological theory, most linguists see the terms 'zero derivation' and 'conversion' either as synonymous or distributed in the way Marchand (see above) defines them. Nevertheless, there are scholars such as Lyons (1977: 523), Crocco-Galèas (1990: 27), Vogel (1996: 237ff; 258ff), Bojadžiev (1999: 266f), etc. who seek to distinguish between the labels differently from Marchand (1969: 360, see the quotation above), the main difference between the former linguists and Marchand being that the former reserve 'zero derivation' for instances where inflection intervenes (G. *besuchen* 'to visit' → *der Besuch* 'a visit' is zero derivation, but the E. *telephone* → *to telephone* is conversion (Vogel 1996: 224–70; Crocco-Galèas 1990: 27)). On the other hand, it should be stressed that many recent studies on derivational morphology reject zero suffixation analysis, cf. Aronoff (1976), Pennanen (1988), Sanders (1988), Lieber (1981a, b, 1992), Don (1993), Štekauer (1996), among others. This dominance of 'conversion' over 'zero derivation' in the present-day linguistic terminology is due to significant disadvantages in zero derivation analysis:

(1) One of the main characteristics of the zero suffix, as suggested by Marchand (1969), is the alternation with an existing overt analogue (Sanders 1988), e.g. in the above cited example from Marchand (1969) *cash-Ø* ~ *atom-ize*, the suffix *-ize* is the overt analogue of the zero suffix in *cash*. However, as noted by Sanders (1988), there exist instances of conversion without overt analogues (conversion of some proper names, for example) or with more than one analogue (for discussion and examples see Sanders 1988).

(2) Zero suffix does not behave as a real suffix

    (2a) As Lieber (1981a)[1] pointed out, all lexemes derived with the same suffix belong to the same inflectional class, but all lexemes derived with a zero suffix do not. Consider, for example, R. *lovit'* 'to hunt' → *lov-Ø* 'hunting', *rabotat'* 'to work' → *rabot-Ø-a* 'work' and *selit'sja* 'to settle' → *sel-Ø-o*. The three nouns decline in three different ways (cf. Appendix D), and it seems that we have to deal with three different zero suffixes.

    (2b) Since the output of zero derivation can belong to different word-classes (e.g. R. V *beg-a-t'* 'to run'→ N *beg-Ø* 'run' and N *sovet* 'advice, council' → V *sovet-Ø-ovat'* 'to advise'), one should postulate different nominalizing, verbalizing, etc. zeroes which lead to multiplication of non-existing forms.

    (2c) Zero derivatives of the same type (e.g. nominalization of verbal bases) cannot be described by a uniform semantic rule, as is typical of derivations from the same type of bases with the same overt affix (cf. Manova and Dressler 2005). In Bulgarian, for example, all verbal nouns derived with the suffix *-ne* are, by rule, action nouns (and seldom have other lexicalized meanings) whereas nominalisations from verbal bases are

---

[1] Lieber (1981a) also argues that there are phenomena in natural languages 'which might be counted as genuine cases of zero affixation'. She points out two such cases – Latin supin forms (abstract deverbal nouns) that seem to be zero-derived from participles and English verbal and adjectival participles, the latter derived from the former (1981a: 145ff). In both instances, the input and the output are homophonous and exhibit the same alomorphy, which Lieber sees as due to the zero affix. However, the two cases can also be explained as due to syncretism of inflectional forms since the derivational status of the supin can be doubted as well as the word-class change of the English verbal and adjectival participles. Lieber does not discuss syncretism as a possible solution.

usually event, result or concrete nouns: *stroja* 'I build, construct, erect', 3 SG *stroi* → *stroj* 'system, regime' (cf. *stroene* 'action of building), *vikam* 'I cry (out), shout (out)', 3 SG *vika* → *vik* 'cry, shout' (cf. *vikane* 'action of crying'), *zidam* 'I build (of brick/stone)', 3 SG *zida* → *zid* 'wall' (cf. *zidane* 'action of building'). Some conversions, though very few, can also have an action noun meaning with specialized semantics, e.g. *xodja* 'I go, walk', 3 SG *xodi* → *xod* 'gate, pace, tread, walk' vs. *xodene* 'going, walking'.

Therefore, from now on, we will use the term 'zero' only in relation to the following two phenomena, both concerning inflection (cf. Bybee 1985 and Mel'čuk 2002):

(1) *Zero expression* is a morphosemantically and morphotactically unmarked inflectional form. In the literature, zero expression is also called 'basic form of a paradigm' (Bybee 1985: 50), as it tends to occur in unmarked members of categories, such as NOM SG (Jakobson 1971: 220ff; 1984: 222ff; Mayerthaler 1987: 48)
(2) *Zero sign* means that a morphosemantically marked inflectional form (e.g. GEN PL of feminine nouns terminating in -*a* in Russian, see the paradigm in (1) below) is left morphotactically unmarkered (cf. Bauer 1988; Mel'čuk 2002).

Based on Mel'čuk (2002: 242), we will define zero sign as exhibiting the following three obligatory characteristics, all satisfied simultaneously:

(1) Expressiveness – a zero sign must carry some meaning or some syntactic function;
(2) Exclusiveness – there should be no other physically observable candidate to be carrier of the meaning under consideration;
(3) Contrastiveness – zero should always be contrasted with an overt item.

According to the theory of NM (Mayerthaler 1981: 43), zero sign instances are 'phonologische Störungen des konstruktionellen Ikonismus' ('phonological violations of the constructional iconicity').

When situated on the scale of morphological techniques, zero sign is a sub-case of addition, as the absence of an overt marker serves as a marker, as can be seen from the following Russian paradigm:

(1) SG   PL
     N. *cen-a* 'price' *cen-y*
     G. *cen-y*   *cen-ø*
     D. *cen-e*   *cen-am*
     A. *cen-u*   *cen-y*
     I. *cen-oj*   *cen-ami*
     L. *cen-e*   *cen-ax*

The GEN PL[2] *cen* is different from all the other forms of the paradigm and is thus seen as realization of distinctivity that is more natural than syncretism (when certain cells of a paradigm are occupied by the same word-form; for discussion on syncretism cf. Luraghi 2000 and Baerman et al. 2005). Note that the inflectional paradigm of an inflecting-fusional language, though possessing a set of various inflectional affixes, is, by rule, rich in syncretism. Consider the Russian noun paradigm where *stol* 'table' NOM SG = ACC SG; *stol-y* 'table' NOM PL = ACC PL; *cen-e* 'price' DAT SG = LOC SG; and *ceny* GEN SG = ACC PL.

As for the other terms replacing conversion in the literature, Vogel (1996: 224–70) seems to make a systematic distinction among them, speaking of: (a) multifunctionality ('Multifunktionalität') in languages such as Chinese without morphologically-defined word classes; (b) instances such as G. *treffen* → *der Treff* are called zero derivation ('(Null-) Derivation'); (c) G. *das Singen* or *der Schöne* are syntactic recategorizations ('Syntaktische Umkategorisierung'); and (d) conversion as in the English pair *taxi* → *to taxi* (for a similar classification of conversion-like changes, see Crocco-Galèas 1990: 27).

This book uses Vogel's (1996) definition of multifunctionality but classifies her syntactic recategorisation as syntactic conversion and treats both her zero derivation and conversion as conversion.

3.2 Definition

In linguistic literature, the definitions of conversion vary from very simple ones, requiring only the same form and different word classes (Bauer 1983, 1988; Ljung 1994: 758–9), to others referring to a paradigmatic change only (Smirnickij 1953, 1954; see also Dokulil 1968a), to those based on a cluster of features (called 'morphological syntactics' in Mel'čuk 1996, 2000a; cf. also Mel'čuk 1976 [1973], 1982: 102), or including a complex of semantic, paradigmatic and syntagmatic changes as in Stekauer (1996: 45–53; 1998: 11, 2000: 13f). Unfortunately, despite the great number of attempts, there is no widely accepted definition of conversion.

In this book, based on the assumption of the scale of morphological techniques, conversion is understood as being parallel to the most natural type of morphological change, i.e. that of addition, the latter representing also the most salient type (prototype) of a morphological change. Reflecting the understanding of Dressler and Manova (2002), we postulate a strict parallelism in morphosemantics of the morphological techniques of addition and conversion, due

---

[2]Nouns such as *okn-o* 'window' whose roots terminate in consonant clusters undergo a phonologic insertion of a vowel in GEN PL, thus *okon*. Other nouns, e.g. *sestr-a* 'sister', have GEN PL forms that are exceptions (Zaliznjak 1977), *sestër*. Since the vowel insertion is phonological, it does not violate the conditions for zero sign formulated by Mel'čuk (2002); exceptions are outside the scope of any morphological rule and thus also outside the scope of the zero-sign concept.

to the addition of intensional meaning. In conversion, however, since the derivational slot of the word is empty, the addition of morphosemantics is without a corresponding change in morphotactics.

Postulating morphosemantic parallelism between conversion and additon, Dressler and Manova (2002) (and Manova and Dressler 2005) abandon Marchand's purely structural treatment of conversion (zero derivation in Marchand's terminology). Recall that for Marchand, the morphotactic parallel to an existing derivation is the most important condition for establishing conversion (zero derivation):

> It is because of the parallelism with overtly marked derivatives that we speak of zero-marked derivatives or zero-derivatives, not just because of the added element of content which characterizes the transposition of the adj *clean* to the vb *clean*, etc. (Marchand 1969: 360).

In contrast, according to Dressler and Manova (2002) and Manova and Dressler (2005), conversion, as is typical for a derivational process, displays a considerable and regular change of meaning. It should be underlined here that due to the semiotic nature of linguistic signs, a parallelism in morphosemantics suggests a parallelism in morphotactics, but less so vice versa (as discussed in the chapter on subtraction, in particular in connection with root extensions). Moreover, as mentioned in the previous section, the overt analogue criterion, as Sanders (1988) calls the morphotactic parallelism between an existing affixation and a zero derivation, often does not hold and this in both directions, i.e. there are conversions without existing morphotactic parallels as well as others with more than one parallel (cf. Sanders 1988; Don et al. 2000: 946f). Therefore in this book, conversion is defined with the help of a generalized form of a Slavic word, i.e. in Slavic, the output of a derivation consists of the following slot (PREF)-BASE-DSUFF-(TM)-(ISUFF), whereas the output of conversion is (PREF)-BASE-Ø-(TM)-(ISUFF), with an empty derivational slot, which defines (Slavic) prototypical conversion as (cf. Manova 2005c):

(i) a word-class change of a base to/from which addition/substitution and deletion of inflectional affixes are allowed;
(ii) the input and the output of conversion being semantically related in a regular way (i.e. describable by a rule);
(iii) belonging to different inflectional systems of paradigms; which implies
(iv) a syntactic change.

Note, however, that this definition is formulated to capture the salient characteristics of conversion in Slavic, but the prototype of the conversion in general, similar to other morphological techniques (cf. Chapter 2), is word-based, word-class changing and does not involve any intervention of inflection. Put differently, E. *telephone* → *to telephone*, without change in inflection (of the basic forms, since there are also *telephones* and *telephoned*), is a better example of conversion and represents the prototype of the conversion rule in general.

3.2 Definition

The definition (of prototypical conversion in Slavic), that we assumed, allows for addition/substitution and deletion of inflectional affixes and classifies as conversion derivations such as R. *ucitel'* 'teacher' → *učitel-it'* 'to work as a teacher (colloq.)', which, since word-based and word-class-changing, resembles very much the above English example *telephone* → *to telephone*, but the addition in the inflectional slot of the Russian derivative *učitel-it'* makes this conversion less prototypical than the English one (cf. Fr. *gard-er* / garde/ 'to gard' → MASC *garde* /gard/ 'guard', G. *schein-en* 'to shine' → *der Schein* 'light', It. *favor-e* 'favor' → *favor-ire* 'to favor', which all also deviate from the prototype). R. N *matematik-a* 'mathematics' → N *matematik* 'mathematician', which connects semantically related input and output with different paradigms but without word-class change and with an alternation in the inflectional slot of the word, is even less prototypical than R. *ucitel'* → *učitel-it'*. If in a derivational conversion no word-class change takes place, by analogy to non-prototypical derivation, we may speak of non-prototypical conversion. For non-prototypical inflection without special suffixes (e.g. the imperfectivizatzion Bg. PFV *xvărl-ja* 'I throw', 3 SG *xvărl-i* → IMPFV *xvărl-ja-m* 'I throw', 3 SG *xvărl-ja*), where only categorical change happens and the semantic change is not as significant as in derivation, but the input and the output have different paradigms, and there is a formal analogue to conversion (the default expression of imperfectivization requires the imperfective suffix *-v-* in the derivational slot of the verb, as in PFV *izmăč-a* ' I torture', *izmăč-i* → IMPFV *izmăč-v-a-m*, *izmăč-v-a*), we postulate formal conversion. If a lexeme is used in the syntactic position of another word class (cf. (iv) above), i.e. it seems as if word-class change has happened, resulting in some restriction in semantics but without paradigmatic change, we may speak of syntactic conversion, e.g. R. *bol'noj* 'sick' is an adjective but might be used in the syntactic position of a noun meaning 'patient'.

The types of conversion described so far cover prototypical derivation (word-class-changing conversion), non-prototypical derivation (word-class-preserving conversion), non-prototypical inflection (formal conversion) and syntax (syntactic conversion). However, on the derivational-inflectional continuum, between non-prototypical inflection and syntax, stands prototypical (in the sense of Dressler 1989) inflection (such as the category of case, for example) where morphological forms can also coincide (e.g. NOM = ACC for MASC inanimates in Russian). As already mentioned, this phenomenon is known as syncretism. Syncretic forms, though morphologically equal, can be identified on the basis of their syntactic function and agreement, i.e. as in syntactic conversion, where coinciding forms are distinguishable syntactically. However, forms connected by syncretism, being from the same paradigm, have the same word-class (in contrast to syntactic conversion where the change consists of taking the syntactic position of another word class). Moreover, syncretic forms do not satisfy the requirement for different paradigms and do not involve semantic change. Put differently, syncretism satisfies neither of the conditions for conversion.

In sum, on the derivational-inflectional continuum, we can predict the following instances of conversion and conversion-like coincidences of forms:

(A) Derivation

   (1) Word-class-changing conversion
   (2) Word-class-preserving conversion

(B) Inflection

   (1) Formal conversion (in non-prototypical inflection)
   (2) Syncretism (in prototypical inflection)

(C) Syntax

   (1) Syntactic conversion

On the parameter of preference for a base of a morphological technique, conversion will be additionally graded for naturalness in terms of word-based, stem-based and root-based realizations. Word-based conversion is the most natural and the nearest to the prototype of the conversion rule, whereas all other types of conversion, as less natural, deviate from the prototype.

Section 3.5 provides a detailed account of all types of conversion found in Bulgarian, Russian and Serbo-Croatian.

3.3 Delimiting Conversion

3.3.1 Homophony, Polysemy, Metaphor, Metonymy

There are a few semantic changes, which, without being conversion, exhibit most of its characteristics. Like conversion, homophony, polysemy, metaphor and metonymy connect the same input and output forms. For example, the Modern Bulgarian word *sin* can function as an adjective meaning 'blue' as well as a noun meaning 'son'. Both lexemes *blue* and *son* belong to different word classes, share the same morphotactic form and have different paradigms. However, the noun *son* and the adjective *blue* are not semantically related, which is not the case in derivation (conversion), where the output of the rule always depends on the input semantically. Therefore, a semantically unrelated pair such as ADJ *sin* 'blue' – N *sin* 'blue' cannot be derived by morphological conversion.

The non-derivational character of the *sin* as 'blue' – *sin* as 'son' pair in Bulgarian can also be motivated diachronically. In a diachronic perspective, both *sin* 'blue' and *sin* 'son' have no semantic connection, because they developed from distinct lexemes, namely from the Old Bulgarian *sinь* 'blue' and *synъ* 'son'. Although dictionaries often use such etymological information for establishing homonymy, due to the synchronic character of this study, the etymological criterion is of no relevance to our argument.

3.3 Delimiting Conversion

Unrelatedness vs. relatedness of meaning is also traditionally invoked in drawing a distinction between homonymy and polysemy (Lyons 1990 [1977]: 551). For example, Bg. *glava* 'head (of a human body)' in *glava na semejstvo* 'head of a family' and *glava na stranica* 'top of a page' is one and the same word. It is the basic meaning of *head* 'uppermost part of a human body containing the brain' that has given rise, by a metaphorical extension, to the use of that word for a leading position in a family or for the uppermost part of a page respectively (cf. similar polysemies in other languages, e.g. based on E. *head*, G. *Kopf*, Fr. *tête*, It. *capo*). What is crucial for our argument now is the fact that the word *glava* does not change its paradigm in any of the above three usages. In contrast, in case of conversion with the same input *glava*, as in Bg. N *glav-á* 'head' → V PFV *glav-j-á*, 3 SG *glav-í*/IMPFV *glav-jáv-a-m* 'I hire, engage, take on', *glav-jáv-a*, the noun and the verb, two different lexemes with related semantics, have different paradigms. Thus, while homonymy always links semantically unrelated words, polysemy and metaphor (the latter being the most frequent reason for polysemy) connect only semantically related words. Note that semantic relatedness in polysemy and metaphor is motivated by definition: polysemy represents more definitions of the same form, and metaphor is based on the relationship of similarity between two concepts. However, forms connected by polysemy/metaphor belong to the same word class and share the same inflectional paradigm and basic semantic components, i.e. they constitute one and the same word and therefore cannot represent conversion.

Metonymy is a replacement by a related (causally, spatially or temporally) term. Therefore the two homophonous units involved in a metonymy are always semantically connected, though a methomymical semantic link is a bit vaguer than that in polysemy and metaphor. For example, the expression Bg. *glava ot naselenieto* – head-FEM-SG from population-NEUT-SG-DEF – 'capita of the population', meaning 'any citizen', is based on the very fact that every citizen possesses only one head, i.e. a particular part of a human body stands for a human being. This particular type of metonymy, when an entity is named after the name of some of its parts, is called synecdoche.

Often cited metonymy-like cases in regard to conversion include fruit and tree names in Romance languages (cf. Mel'čuk 1998: 455). In Slavic languages as well, one and the same form expresses both 'tree' and 'fruit'.

(2)   Bg. *kruša* 'pear' & 'pear tree',
      Bg. *sliva* 'plum' & 'plum tree';

(3)   R. *gruša* 'pear' & 'pear tree',
      R. *sliva* 'plum' & 'plum tree';

(4)   SC. *kruška* 'pear' & 'pear tree',
      SC. *šljiva* 'plum' & 'plum tree'

In these examples, fruits, which are parts of the respective fruit trees, are used for denoting the trees themselves. Thus, we speak of metonymy (synecdoche) instead of conversion. Moreover, the two forms, as in lexical changes such as polysemy and metaphor, belong to one and the same word class and share the same inflectional paradigm.

A bit different is the situation with the expression of the meaning 'fruit' – 'tree' in Romance languages. In these languages, fruits and trees usually have different gender, e.g. Sp. FEM *manzana* 'apple' vs. MASC *manzano* 'apple tree', *pera* 'pear' vs. *pero* 'pear-tree', *naranja* 'orange' vs. *naranjo* 'orange-tree', etc. (all conversions according to Mel'čuk 1998: 455). Due to their different forms, these Spanish examples do not fit the definition of metonymy and would be classified as formal conversion (see Section 3.5.2 below).

However, Sp. *el trombón* 'trombone' vs. *el trombón* 'trombone player', *el clarinete* 'clarinet' vs. *el clarinete* 'clarinettist' (cf. Rainer 1993: 78f) are clear cases of metonymy. Similarly, metonymy is indicated where a gender change is not formally marked in the noun as in *la trompeta* 'trumpet' vs. *el trompeta* 'trumpeter', *la viola* 'viola' vs. *el viola* 'viola player', etc. (the examples are from Rainer 1993: 78). The semantic relation in question seems to be cross-linguistically metonymical, and it is often the case that *first fiddle* in an orchestra, or *soprano*, *tenor*, etc. in the opera are used for persons playing the respective instruments or having the respecive voices. Other examples of metonymy related to a person's occupation are *a pen* 'a writer, an author' and *a gun* 'a military man' (Molhova 1976: 89).

To sum up, according to the definition of conversion, polysemy, metaphor and metonymy violate the definitional criteria of different word classes and different paradigms and therefore they cannot be conversions. In cases where a formally unmarked gender change co-occurs, the semantic pattern is taken into consideration, i.e. whether cross-linguistically the pattern is expressed by metonymy. Note, that the existence of a metonymy such as E. *a fiddle* meaning 'a fiddle player' does not contradict the existence of the suffixation *a fiddler*. These are simply two different sources of lexicon enrichment.

3.3.2 Conversion and Related Techniques

As can be expected from the assumption of the scale of morphological techniques, conversion has often been confused with its neighbour techniques, i.e. those of modification and subtraction. Therefore, in the next two sections we will try to differentiate conversion from modification and subtraction. The discussion on modification follows the scale of modifications assumed in Chapter 2 (cf. also Dressler 1987b; Manova and Dressler 2005).

3.3.2.1 Conversion vs. Modification

In the literature, prosodic and segmental modifications often have been classified as marginal (Bauer 1983: 228), minor or secondary cases of conversion, further specified as partial conversion (Bauer 1983: 229) or conversion with formal modifications (Quirk et al. 2000 [1985]; Mel'čuk 1996, 2000; Štekauer 1996). However, prosodic and segmental alternations, though non-concatenative morphology, are morphological markers, and therefore must be distinguished from conversion.

3.3.2.1.1 Prosodic Modifications

The stress change in English derivations of the type *to impórt* → *the ímport* is seen traditionally as compatible with conversion. As may be supposed, in Slavic languages, there are also instances satisfying the definition of conversion, but with a stress change. However, Slavic conversion-like examples with a stress change show some variations, since the inflectional slot of the word also comes into play. Compare the following derivations from Bulgarian whose input forms all exhibit word-final stress:

(5a) *osnov-á* 'I found', 3 SG *osnov-é* → *osnóv-a* 'base';
(5b) *otčet-á* 'I give an account', 3 SG *otčet-é* → masc. *otčét* 'an account'
(5c) *ustrem-j-á (se)* 'I rush', 3 SG *ustrem-í (se)* → *ústrem* 'a rush'

(5a), an exact parallel to E. *to impórt* → *the ímport*, clearly involves a stress change. The stress change occurring in (5b) can be seen as superficial, as the output must be stressed, but the prosodic pattern of word-final stress is preserved. In (5c), the word-final stress of the input alternates with the word-initial stress of the output, which makes (5c) the clearest case of modification. Moreover, *ústrem* (with a word-initial stress) accounts for the correctness of the assumption of no stress change in (5b), the instance of *otčét*.

Derivations with root-stressed inputs, such as Bg. *ogléd-a-m* 'I examine, look over', 3 SG *ogléd-a*, looks over' → *ógled*, represent a still more evident case of modification. Consider the verbal noun *ogléžd-a-ne* 'inspection', as well as the basic verb IMPFV1 *gléd-a-m* 'I look', 3 SG *gléd-a*, and the nouns *gléd-ka* 'view' and *gléd-a-ne* 'looking', all root-stressed.

In order to account properly for all above examples, we postulate conversion for (5b), whereas all other instances will be classified as modifications (including the derivation E. *to impórt* → *the ímport*). Thus, this distinction between different types of stress changes is a necessary step to be taken both in autosegmental theories of phonology (cf. Goldsmith 1990) and in Natural Phonology (cf. Hurch 1996).

Turning to Serbo-Croatian, the phonological system is rather complex and allows vowels to vary according to length and pitch and to be long and short. We see as crucial the fact that different sources often assign different accents to one and the same word. Therefore, for Serbo-Croatian, it is not the accentuation type but the accent placement that should be considered for classification of morphological change. In other words, for us, SC. *škōl-a* 'school' → IMPFV *škòl-ov-a-ti* 'to educate', *zlât-o* 'gold' → NEUT *zlát-i-ti* 'to gild' are conversions, but *zaštít-i-ti* 'to defend' → *zâštit-a* 'defence' is a modification.

To sum up, conversion-like instances with stress or accent placement changes that are not superficial are prosodic modifications.

3.3.2.1.2 Segmental Modifications

Although it seems that segmental changes of morphonological or allomorphic nature should be more salient cases of modification than the above discussed prosodic alternations, there are linguists (Dokulil 1968a; Lieber 1981, 1992; Bauer 1983; Štekauer 1996; Quirk et al. 1985; Mel'čuk 1996: 131, 2000a:149f) who postulate conversion even in cases of segmental modifications. The list of modifications below aims to cover as many alternations as possible, and for that reason, it contains data from non-Slavic languages as well. From now on, we will distinguish between conversion and the following segmental changes (cf. Valera 2000: 150):

(1) Voicing, as in E. *belief* → *to believe*
(2) Palatalization and depalatalization, as in R. *drug* 'friend'→ *druž-it'* 'to be a friend', SC. *skoč-i-ti* 'to jump, leap'→ *skok* 'jump, leap', R. *byt'* 'to be' → *byt* 'mode of life'
(3) Ablaut, e.g.: E. *blood* → *to bleed*, Bg. *podnasjam* 'I present, offer', *podnasja* → *podnos* 'tray'
(4) Umlaut, e.g.: G. *Kamm* 'comb' → *kämm-en* 'to comb'
(5) Consonant insertion, as in Fr. *béton* 'concrete' → V *bétonn-er* 'to concrete', *engrais* 'manure; fattening pasture or food' → V *engraisser* 'to fatten, manure' (conversions according to Mel'čuk 1996: 131; 2000a: 149f).

The correctness of the assumption of modification instead of conversion for the above instances is evidenced by competing forms derived by the two techniques, conversion and modification, from one and the same base, e.g.: R. *lov-í-t'* 'to hunt, catch' → MASC *lov* (conversion) *vs.* FEM *lóvl-ja* (modification via morphonological palatalization), both meaning 'hunting, catching' (cf. Jakobson 1971: 126 [1948]).

3.3.2.2 Conversion vs. Subtraction

It seems difficult at first to confuse conversion and subtraction. Indeed, such confusions are due more to the theoretical approach employed than to a misunderstanding of conversion. As noted in Dressler (1987a: §4.4.3–4), there might be two different solutions for the case R. *lógik-a* 'logic' → *lógik* 'logician': (1) within the stem-based morphology of Mel'čuk (1982), the derivation is a clear case of conversion, whereas (2) within the word-based morphology of Aronoff (1976), it should be understood as subtraction because the basis of any WF rule must be an occurring word-form, in our case *lógika*. For us, R. *lógik-a* 'logic' → *lógik* 'logician' is derived by conversion, as the material deleted, namely the suffix *-a* is in the inflectional slot of the input. Since the input and the output of the conversion are both nouns, the precise classification of the derivation is non-prototypical conversion.

Moreover, our theoretical framework, with the differentiation of derivational and inflectional slots in the word structure, makes possible the precise classification of derivations that, at first, appear to delete equally long segments. For example in both of the following derivations, Bg. *kot-k-a* 'cat' → *kot-e* 'kitten' and R. *dél-a-t'* 'to do, make' → *dél-o* 'affair, business, deed', a suffix is deleted, and in the inflectional slot a substitution takes place. Bg. *kot-k-a* → *kot-e* is, however, a case of subtraction, since the shortened *-k-* is in the derivational slot, whereas R. *dél-a-t'* → *dél-o* is derived by conversion, since the TM *-a-* that is deleted is not in the derivational slot of the verb *delat'*.

3.4 Direction of Conversion

Of two derivationally related items, one is recognized as the base of the derivation and the other as the derivative. Prototypically the derivative is morphotactically (as a consequence of the principle of constructional iconicity and the fact that addition is the prototype of all morphological changes) and morphosemantically motivated by its base and is characterized by a longer form and more specific semantics. Thus, the longer form is the overt signal for the derived status of a mate in a derivational pair. However, when the non-iconic technique of conversion and the anti-iconic technique of subtraction operate, no overt markers occur. This fact raises the question about the direction of a morphological change, which we will try to answer in this section.

In the literature, a number of criteria have been proposed for the determining the direction of overtly unmarked derivations (cf. Jacobini 2000), most of the criteria being formulated by Marchand (1963, 1964a, 1969, 1974). (Note that of all Marchand's criteria, that of precedence of appearance (cf. Marchand 1963), due to the synchronic character of this study, is seen as irrelevant and thus excluded from the very beginning.)

3.4.1 Marchand's Criteria

Marchand distributes the criteria for establishing direction of a derivation into two groups: (i) criteria of content and (ii) criteria of external form (Marchand 1974: 242 [1964a]).

The most important content-related criteria are those of semantic dependence and semantic range and to some extent the criterion of restriction of usage, from which we will accept only two of its five subcriteria (cf. the discussion in Bergenholtz and Mugdan 1979: 351 and in Vogel 1996: 243).

As for the form-related criteria, those of phonetic shape, morphological type, and stress, not all are applicable to our data, i.e. the criteria of phonetic shape and morphological type appear more language-specific for English than universal, and the criterion of stress has already been discussed in the section on prosodic modifications, where we concluded that stress changes are modifications.

If semantic and formal criteria make different predictions, the semantic motivation should be considered stronger.

3.4.1.1 Semantic Dependence

Marchand defined this criterion in the following way:

> The word that for its analysis is dependent on the content of the other pair member is necessarily the derivative (Marchand 1964a: 12).

According to this criterion, the verb E. *knife* is derived from the noun E. *knife* because the meaning of the verb 'wound with a knife' depends on the meaning of the noun, whereas the N *knife* does not depend on any content features of the V *knife*. Furthermore, many speakers, who commonly use the noun, never use the verb. The pair V *whistle* – N *whistle* represents the reversed case. The verb is the base because the meaning of the noun 'instrument used for whistling' entirely depends on the verb.

Although the criterion of semantic dependence works perfectly for *knife* and *whistle*, there are cases where a noun might be defined as: (1) having its own characteristics which do not depend on the respective verb, as well as (2) based on the verb, i.e. as 'an instrument used for/act of/instance of, etc. V-ing'. Indeed, the pair *saw – to saw* exemplifies this definitional problem (cf. Ljung 1977: 165; Sanders 1988: 174; Štekauer 2000: 34). (The Bulgarian equivalent of the English pair is V *kos-j-á* 'I saw', 3 SG *kos-í* vs. N *kos-á* 'saw' and also involves conversion.) Marchand (1964a) defines the N *saw* as 'a cutting instrument with a blade, having a continuous series of teeth on the edge' and V *saw* as 'use a saw, cut with a saw', i.e. he assumes that the verb is derived from the noun. Consider, however, the following observation from Sanders (1988):

> It is not literary true that "one cannot 'saw' without a 'saw,'" since it is perfectly possible to saw off a branch with a pocket knife, to saw the air with one's hand, to saw through a rope with a piece of broken glass, and so on. But it is true, nevertheless, that the normal and prototypical instrument that is used for sawing is indeed a saw[...] (Sanders 1988: 174).

For instruments like *saw* Sanders suggests the assumption of a mutual dependence of the input and the output, since it is true that *to saw* is to cut with *a saw*, but it is equally true that *a saw* is that kind of instrument prototypically used for

3.4 Direction of Conversion

sawing. A similar strategy is applied to the definition of Serbo-Croatian pairs of non-prefixed verbs and nouns in Babić (1991: 301ff). Babić notices that SC. N *brôd* 'ship, boat' could be defined as 'ono (naprava, vozilo) čime se brodi' ['sth used for sailing'], on the other hand, the V *bròditi* could be explained 'as ploviti brodom' ['to sail with a ship/boat'] (Babić 1991: 301).

An additional difficulty with the criterion of semantic dependence arises if one compares definitions by different dictionaries. For example, Cetnarowska (1993: 25) quotes the definitions of N *grin* and V *grin* as given in *Oxford English Dictionary* and *Longman Dictionary of Contemporary English* (1978). For *Oxford English Dictionary* the verb *to grin* means 'to smile showing the teeth' and the noun *a grin* 'an act of grinning, the expression produced on the face during grinning', i.e. according to the criterion of semantic dependence, the noun should be the derivative. *Longman Dictionary of Contemporary English* (1978), however, has the following definitions of the same noun and verb: *a grin* is 'a smile which shows the teeth' and the verb *to grin* is paraphrased as 'to make a grin', the verb being derived from the noun.

A later edition of *Longman Dictionary of Contemporary English* (1995) illustrates another problem with the semantic dependence criterion, i.e. it is possible to define two semantically related homophonous words as depending on a third concept. For example, according to the 1995-edition of the dictionary, *to grin* means 'to smile widely', whereas *a grin* is 'a wide smile'.

In conclusion, despite the problematic character of the criterion, we will understand it as a general principle and agree with Sanders (1988: 174) that 'in this as in all other things linguistic, unclear cases are to be expected and do not in themselves cast doubt on the appropriateness of general principles'. Where the semantic criterion appears insufficient, other criteria will be applied, which leads us to the next criterion, that of semantic range.

3.4.1.2 Semantic Range

> Of two homophonous words exhibiting similar sets of semantic features the one with the smaller field of reference is the derivative. In general terms this means that the more specific word is the derivative (Marchand 1964a: 14).

For example, a *convert* is a person that has converted to a religious or other belief, however, the verb *to convert* does not only mean 'to make a convert', but has more content features. Therefore the noun is considered a derivative from the verb.

Babić (1991: 67) motivates in a similar way the direction of the pair SC. V *braniti* 'to defend, to protect' – N *brana* 'dam, barrier', where the noun has the smaller semantic range since the verb fails the meaning 'to set a barrier'. In Slavic languages, by rule, nouns for concrete objects, if outputs of conversions, exhibit smaller semantic range (cf. Sections 3.5.1.1.1.1, 3.5.1.1.2.1, and 3.5.1.1.3.1 below).

3.4.1.3 Restriction of Usage

> If one word has smaller range of usage than its pair member, it must be considered a derivative (Marchand 1964a: 13).

The range of usage can be defined in terms of frequency and incomplete inflectional paradigm.

3.4.1.3.1 Frequency

The pair member which is more frequent is the base of the derivation, e.g. since the nouns *father* and *knife* are more frequent than their respective verbs, *to father* and *to knife* are the derivatives. A similar example from Bulgarian is the derivation N *pras-é* 'pig' → V *pras-j-á (se)* 'I farrow, litter', *pras-í*, where the noun is much more frequent than the verb.

3.4.1.3.2 Completeness vs. Incompleteness of the Inflectional Paradigm

Restriction of a pair-member to certain inflectional forms signals that it is a derivative. For example, the V *neighbour* occurs almost exclusively in *-ing* forms; and the N *thanks* is used only in the plural; therefore both are derivatives.

According to this criterion, in Bulgarian, Russian and Serbo-Croatian, pluralia tantum nouns, if related to a verb by a suffixless derivational rule, are considered to be derivatives. For example: Bg. V PFV *okov-á*, 3 SG *okov-é* 'I chain/put into chains' → PL *okóvi* 'chains'; R. V PFV *okovát'* 'to chain/put into chains' → N PL *okóvy* 'chains'; SC. V PFV *okòv-a-ti* 'to chain/put into chains'→ N PL *òkovi* 'chains'; R. V IMPFV *peregovárivat'* 'to negotiate' → N PL *peregovóry* 'negotiations' (all modifications). For further examples from Russian, see Švedova et al. (1980: 224).

3.4.2 Criteria by Other Authors

3.4.2.1 Distributional Criterion

This criterion is formulated by Aronoff (1976):

> [...] if we hypothesize that a class of words X is derived from another class of words Y, then for every x_i in X there should be listed a corresponding y_i in Y, but not vice versa [...] (Aronoff 1976: 115).

According to this criterion, Arronoff assumes noun-to-verb direction for all English *Xment* forms, such as *an/to ornament*, *an/to implement*, etc., as the nouns *element*, *figment*, *sediment*, *monument*, *garment* have no verbal mate.

Consider the following list of Bulgarian verbs and nouns, selected at random from numerous sets of simple and prefixed verbs. From most of the verbs

3.4 Direction of Conversion

below no noun can be derived, but there exists an asymmetry, insofar it is easier to derive nouns from prefixed verbs than from their non-prefixed base verbs:

(6) V → N   PREF V → PREF N
     bărša 'I wipe' → Ø   *zabărša* 'I wipe'→ Ø
     tărča 'I run' → Ø   *dotărča* 'I run up'→ Ø
     varja 'I boil' → Ø   *prevarja* 'I overboil'→ Ø
     gotvja 'I cook' → Ø   *prigotvja* ' I prepare'→ Ø
     tărsja ' I look for'→ Ø   *pretărsja* 'look through'→ Ø
     tărkam 'I rub'→ Ø   *iztărkam* 'I rub off'→ Ø
     doja 'I milk' → Ø   *nadoja* 'I milk' → *nadoj* 'yield of milk'
     stoja 'I stand, stay' → Ø stop'   *prestoja* 'stay, stop' → *prestoj* 'stay, stop'

Based on the distributional criterion, the sets of forms in (6) are evidence that in Bulgarian, the most probable direction of conversions involving verbs and nouns is that of verb-to-noun. We will postulate this direction for conversions, the direction of which could be doubted.

3.4.2.2 +/– Regular Inflectional Paradigm

Myers (1984: 58) motivates the non-derived status of a word involved in a conversion with its irregular inflectional paradigm: the nouns *man, fish, foot* and *goose* are the basic members of conversions to verbs because they all have irregular plural forms *men, fish, feet, geese*. Likewise, verbs such as *drink, hit, shake, sleep*, with irregular past tense and passive participles, are all bases of nominalizing conversions.

The observation in respect to morphological productivity – that recent borrowings and new formations always enter regular (and productive) inflectional patterns (Dressler 1997) – indirectly validates the criterion of inflectional paradigms and could explain why noun-to-verb conversions of compound items with strong verbs as second components receive regular inflection, e.g. N *joyride* 'a ride for pleasure in a vehicle, especially a stolen car' → V *joyride*, PAST = PAST PART *joyrided*, despite the irregular inflection of V *ride*, PAST *rode*, PAST PART *ridden* (the example is from Cetnarowska 1993:36).

Based on this criterion, we assume that the SC. N *potpis* 'signature' is derived from the V *potpis-a-ti* 'to sign', since the present and the infinitive stem of the verb are connected by a morphonological alternation, realized as *piš-* and *pis-* respectively, whereas the inflection of the noun follows a regular (productive) pattern.

3.4.3 Conversion with a Clear Direction

Bulgarian, Russian and Serbo-Croatian conversions (and modifications) with prefixed verbs as inputs and result nouns as outputs are representative of directed, though formally unmarked, rules, e.g. Bg. V *raz-grom-j-a* 'I rout', 3 SG *raz-grom-i* → N *raz-grom* 'rout'. In Modern Bulgarian there is an imperfective verb *grom-j-a* 'defeat, rout' which is the base of the perfective *raz-grom-j-a*. *Grom-j-a*, however, cannot be nominalized by conversion, and there is no noun **grom*, i.e. the derivation N **grom* → N *raz-grom* is impossible, which accounts for the correctness of the derivation *raz-grom-j-a* → *raz-grom* (cf. the examples in Section 3.4.2.1 above). Likewise, SC. *zapísati* 'to note' → *zápis* 'note' (there exists no **pis*), cf. Babić (1991: 304).

There are, however, a few more complicated cases with free roots as bases. Consider: Bg. V *xód-j-a*, 3 SG *xód-i*→ N *xod* vs. V *pro-xód-j-a*, 3 SG *pro-xód-i* → N *pró-xod*. It should be emphasized that such instances are rare and are, by rule, modifications (the stress pattern of *próxod* differs from that of the other member of the derivational pair). In addition, evaluation according to the semantic criterion speaks for verb-to-noun direction, as *proxod* 'passage, thoroughfare' is not a special kind of *xod* 'walk, gate, pace'. Consider also the Serbo-Croatian nouns *gòvōr* 'speech, talk, conversation' and *dògovōr* 'agreement'. Again, they can be seen formally as derived from each, but semantically *dògovōr* is not a combination of the prefix *do-* and the noun *govor*. Thus, *dògovōr* is derived from the verb *dogovòriti se* 'to agree' (Babić 1991: 304).

3.4.4 Reversible Conversion vs. Cross-Linguistic Semantic Pattern

A bidirectional approach (Lieber 1981; Ford and Sigh 1984; Müller 1993) has been suggested (Bergenholtz and Mugdan 1979: 353; Vogel 1996: 244f) for problematic cases of derivation, i.e. 'wenn ein Lexem [...], unter synchronisch-semantischem Aspekt zugleich als Produkt und Basis eines Derivationsprozesses kategorisiert werden kann, da die semantische Motivationsbeziehung die Umkehrbarkeit der Ableitungsrichtung nicht ausschließt' (Müller 1993: 53).[3] Müller calls such derivations 'reversible' ('reziproke Derivate' in Habermann 1994: 64 after von Polenz 1968: 134).

Vogel (1996) points out the possible cases involving bi-directionality:

(1) None of the pair members is motivated by its counterpart, e.g. G. *schlafen – Schlaf*.

---

[3]'when a lexeme [...] can be seen as a product and base of a derivation synchronically semantically, since semantics cannot exclude the reverse direction of the derivation' (Müller 1993: 53). (Translation by SM)

3.4 Direction of Conversion

(2) The two directions seem equally well-motivated, as in the following list of examples (from Vogel 1996: 244):

(7)
Ruf 'call'	*das Rufen (1x)* 'calling'
rufen 'to call'	*Rufe ausstoßen* 'to let out calls'
Schlag 'hit'	*das Schlagen* 'hitting'
schlagen 'to hit'	*Schläge austeilen* 'to let out hits'
Schmerz 'ache'	*wenn etwas schmerzt* 'when sth aches'
schmerzen 'to ache'	*Schmerzen verursachen* 'to cause aches'
etc.	

Indeed, the example in (1), that of G. *schlafen* 'to sleep' – *Schlaf* 'sleep', is problematic for a directional analysis in German (as well as in English and various other languages), but, for example, in Bulgarian, the noun *săn* 'dream' clearly is the base of the derivation. The latter looks in the following way: *săn* 'dream' → *săn-úv-a-m* 'I dream', *săn-úv-a* (note that *-uvam* is inflection). The argumentation of exactly this direction is simple: first, *săn* enters an unproductive inflection class (including only 5 nouns, cf. Manova and Dressler 2001), whereas *sănuvam* belongs to the most productive conjugation (that with the TM *-a-*). Thus according to the criterion of +/− regular inflection, it is more probable that the mate with the productive inflection is the derivative than vice versa. Second, in Bulgarian, modifications derived by attachment of *-uva(m)*, such as *den* 'day' → *den-úv-a-m* 'I spend the day', *den-úv-a*; *nošt* 'night' → *nošt-uv-a-m* 'I spend the night', *nošt-uv-a*; *prorók* 'prophet' → *prorok-úv-a-m* 'I prophesy', *prorok-úv-a*, all, according to the criterion of semantic dependence, have nouns as bases.

As for the examples in (7), they are not (at least not all) bidirectional. For example, the noun *Ruf* has meanings that the verb *rufen* 'to call, cry, shout' cannot motivate, such as the meaning of *Ruhm* 'fame' and that of *Berufung* 'appointment'. This could be evidence for the basic character of the noun *Ruf* in regard to the verb *rufen*.

The pair E. N *love* – V *love*/G. *Liebe* – *lieben*, which is similar to the example in (1), is a classic example of the problem with reversible derivations (cf. for English Cetnarowska 1993: 37f; for German Bergenholtz and Mugdan 1979: 353). For that conversion, Cetnarowska finds, that when applied together, the different criteria for establishing direction of a derivation clash. Nevertheless, admitting to a 'certain degree of arbitrariness', she assigns the status of base to the verb *love* (Cetnarowska 1993: 38).

In contrast to Cetnarowska, Bergenholtz and Mugdan (1979) see the members of the *love* conversion pair as semantically related, but without any direction:

[...] so können wir zwar lieb gegenüber lieblich und lieblich gegenüber Lieblichkeit als primär ansehen; lieb, lieb(en) und Liebe stehen dagegen gleichberechtig nebeneinander (wenn wir bei Liebe kein Ableitungssuffix annehmen) (Bergenholtz and Mugdan 1979: 353).[4]

In Slavic languages, the diachronic development of their morphological systems has solved the problem of direction of the conversion of *love*: for native speakers of Bulgarian, Russian and Serbo-Croatian, the noun Bg. *ljub-ov*/R. *ljub-ov'*/SC *ljub-av* 'love' is derived by suffixation from the verb Bg. *ljub-j-a, ljub-i*/R. *ljub-i-t'*/SC *ljub-i-ti* 'to love'. However, the diachronic origin of the suffix *-ov/-ov'/-av* lies in inflection: *-ov/-ov'/-av* is descendant of the old TM *-ū-* (recall that the declension systems of modern Bulgarian, Russian and Serbo-Croatian have lost TMs, which favours such reanalysis). Thus, the diachronic development of Slavic morphology confirms Cetnarowska's (Slavic!) intuition for the direction of the conversion *to love* → *love* in English. This derivation suggests the idea of the existence of cross-linguistic semantic patterns (cognitively, i.e. universally, motivated bases of word formation processes). Manova and Dressler (2005: 76) use such an approach to account for the semantic pattern 'science – scientist' expressed by three different morphological techniques in Bulgarian, Russian and Serbo-Croatian: R *matemátik-a* 'mathematics' → *matemátik* 'mathematician' (conversion); Bg. *matemátik-a* → *matematík* (due to the stress change a modification) and SC *matematik-a* → *matematič-ar* (addition), cf. also G. *Mathematik* → *Mathematiker* and E. *mathematics* → *mathematician*. We establish the directions of the Russian conversion and Bulgarian modification by analogy to the direction of the Serbo-Croatian (German and English) rule of addition, i.e. if the 'science' mate is primary for the Serbo-Croatians; the Germans and the English, it should be the base of the Russian and Bulgarian derivations as well. Although morphological theory does not recognize the criterion of a cross-linguistic semantic pattern, in doubtful instances, one can establish direction of problematic derivations with the help of universal cognitive knowledge.

Finally, the principles and assumptions of our theoretical framework imply unidirectional morphology. Therefore all derivational analyses in this study are directed.

3.5 Classification of Conversion

3.5.1 Conversion in Derivation

The classification suggested below is based on the generalized form of the Slavic word, which has slots for the following morphemes:

---

[4][...] thus we may see lieb 'dear' as a base of lieblich 'lovely' and lieblich 'lovely' as a base of Lieblichkeit 'loveliness'; lieb 'dear', leib(en) 'to love' and Liebe 'love' are, however, all at the same level (if we assume that Liebe 'love' does not possess a derivational suffix) (Bergenholtz and Mugdan 1979: 353). (Translation by SM)

3.5 Classification of Conversion

(8)   PREF – BASE – DSUFF – (TM) – ISUFF.

Recall that TMs do not occur in all word classes but only in verb morphology (see Chapter 1).

The data are organized according to the following three criteria: (1) +/− word-class change; (2) word-class of the output; and (3) type of the base (whether word, stem or root). It should be noted that since the theoretical framework of this book differs from the treatment of derivation and inflection in existing sources on Slavic morphology, the data, in order to be consistent, are taken primarily from the respective Academy grammars (for Russian Švedova et al. 1980; for Bulgarian Andrejčin et al. 1983; and Babić 1991 for Serbo-Croatian) and rearranged to fit our claims, i.e. the lists of conversions below are representative more than exhaustive. Therefore, if a conversion type is illustrated with a few examples only, this does not mean that these are the only examples that can be derived according to that pattern. Likewise, where there is no example from a given language of a particular pattern, it should be understood as meaning 'no example has been found' rather than 'no example exists'. When a considerable number of examples are given, the goal is usually to demonstrate that the pattern appears to be semantically unrestricted.

3.5.1.1 Word-Class-Changing Conversion

We call word-class-changing conversion prototypical, since it satisfies the definition of conversion (see Section 3.2 above) to a greater extent (i.e. is nearer to the prototype of conversion) than all other conversion types, i.e. word-class-changing conversion connects items belonging to different word classes, with inputs and outputs of word-class-changing conversions being semantically related in a regular way and characterized by two different systems of inflectional paradigms. The word-class-change yielded by this type of conversion implies that the latter operates in derivation, which, according to the theoretical framework of this book, means that addition, substitution and deletion of inflection are allowed. However, as already clarified in Section 3.2, word-class-changing conversions, where inflection intervenes, are less prototypical than word-based conversion without intervention of inflection. With regard to bases, of all word-class-changing conversions, word-based ones are the most prototypical, whereas the root-based subtype is least prototypical.

3.5.1.1.1 Word-Based Word-Class-Changing Conversion

Whereas languages approaching the isolating type (e.g. English) are rich in prototypical conversions (e.g. E. V *to walk* → N *a walk*), in Slavic languages which represent the inflecting-fusional type, word-based word-class-changing conversion is rare and involves addition of inflection. Put differently, if conversion in English is always word-based and of the type X→ X, i.e. can exemplify the prototype of the conversion rule, then word-based conversion in Slavic is usually X → X + ISUFF.

The intervention of inflection in Slavic causes deviation from the prototype of the conversion rule and in some instances even results in dubious cases. For example, although at first sight, the derivation Bg. *von-j-á* 'I stink', 3 SG *von-i* → *von-já* 'stink' seems to be similar to the above-cited English example V *to walk* → N *a walk*, this coincidence of verbal and nominal forms is not regular but random. Moreover, the noun *von-ja* [vonʲa] and the verb *von-j-a* [vonʲə] are, as can be seen from the respective transcriptions, only homographs. The verb and the noun have different pronunciations and cannot threfore represent word-based conversion. In fact, this is an instance of root-based conversion (Section 3.5.1.1.3 below), since the input and the output share the same root but differ in inflection. As already mentioned, in an inflecting language where even basic forms of paradigms are inflected and nouns and verbs use different sets of inflectional affixes such complete coincidence of verbal and nominal forms is unlikely.

In Slavic languages, the clearest case of word-based conversion is represented by adjective-to-noun conversions, such as SC. ADJ MASC SG *nèčist* 'dirty' → N FEM *nèčist* 'dirt'. Such conversions are, however, very few and since found only in Serbo-Croatian, are language specific. Another peculiarity of the inflecting-fusional type consists of the existence of word-based adjective-to-noun conversions of non-basic forms, e.g. Bg. ADJ MASC *blag* 'gentle, kind, sweet, mild', NEUT *blág-o*, PL *blág-i* → N SG *blág-o* 'good, welfare, wealth', PL *blag-á*. The specific features of this type of conversion are discussed in Section 3.5.1.1.1.1 below.

From a 'technical' point of view, the easiest case of word-class-changing word-based conversion is where inflectional suffixes are added to a word (base) terminating in a consonant, as in R. MASC *špion* 'spy' → IMPFV *špion-i-t'* (colloq.) 'to spy' and SC. *slȁb* 'weak, feeble' → IMPFV *slȁb-e-ti* 'to lose weight', IMPFV *slȁb-i-ti* 'to weaken' (for both types, see Section 3.5.1.1.1.2a). It may also happen that a nominal inflection suffix coincides with a verbal thematic marker. In such cases, infinitival inflection is attached to the noun that serves as a base of the conversion (Section 3.5.1.1.1.2b). The last case of word-based conversion we will deal with in this section is represented by noun-to-adjective conversions (cf. Section 3.5.1.1.1.3).

3.5.1.1.1.1 Nominalization ADJ → N

According to the inflectional properties of their output forms, adjectives-to-noun conversions can be assigned to three groups: (1) with a complete noun paradigm; (2) with an incomplete noun paradigm; and (3) with a mixed paradigm combining inflection of adjectives and nouns.

3.5 Classification of Conversion 77

(1) In Slavic, all rules the output of which are nominalizations with complete noun paradigms are unproductive.

In Serbo-Croatian, very few adjectives can serve as bases for the derivation of abstract nouns with complete inflectional paradigms. The rule exhibits the following template:

(9)   MASC SG ADJ X → FEM SG N X

This template is illustrated in (10) with examples from Babić (1990: 319). It should be emphasized, however, that other linguistic sources (dictionaries and grammars) as well as native speakers do not confirm the existence of all examples in Babić (1990).

(10)   MASC SG *nèčist* 'dirty' → FEM SG *nèčīst* 'dirt'
       MASC SG *rùmen* 'rosy' → FEM SG *rùmēn* (expressive) 'rosiness'
       MASC SG *zèlen* 'green' → FEM SG *zèlēn* (expressive) 'greens, vegetables'
       MASC SG *cŕven* 'red' → FEM SG *cŕvēn* 'the red'

As already discussed in Section 3.4.2.2, the output of conversion always takes productive inflection (Dressler 1997: 7f), and this observation provides a criterion for distinguishing between the base and the derivative of a conversion rule. The nominalizations in (10), however, enter an unproductive inflection class, that of feminines in consonants and thus challenge the criterion of regularity of the inflectional paradigm. A possible explanation of the unproductive pattern violating the criterion for regular inflection of conversion might be the fact that all nouns derived after the rule in (9) exhibit vowel lengthening (see the examples in (10)), which could be interpreted as an added modification feature. In other words, the rule may be seen as causing a regular modification of the base and thus representing modification. Note that there are no such instances in Bulgarian and Russian. (The language-specific properties of this type of conversion are further discussed in Section 5.2.1.4 where the above examples from Serbo-Croatian are compared with modifications from Russian).

Another unproductive rule of word-based nominalization takes, as input, non-basic forms of adjectives. For example: Bg. ADJ NEUT SG *sladko* 'sweet', PL *sladk-i* → N NEUT *sladko* 'jam, dessert', PL *sladk-a* and the already-mentioned ADJ MASC *blag* 'gentle, kind, sweet, mild', NEUT *blág-o*, PL *blág-i* → N SG *blág-o* 'good, welfare, wealth', PL *blag-á*. Note that in Bulgarian, this pattern, though describable in terms of a rule, is rather exceptional, as in Serbo-Croatian, where we find the same nominalizations, i.e. MASC *slàdak* 'sweet', NEUT *slàtk-o* 'sweet', INSTR SG *slàtk-īm* → NEUT *slätk-o* 'preserves, dessert', INSTR SG *slätk-om*; MASC *blâg*, NEUT *blâg-o* 'gentle, meek, mild', INSTR SG *blág-īm* → NEUT *blâg-o* 'wealth, property', INSTR SG *blâg-om*.

(2) Nominalizations of non-basic adjective forms often have incomplete inflectional paradigms, e.g.: R. ADJ NEUT *blago* → N NEUT NOM SG *blago*, GEN SG *blaga*, etc. have only the following forms in the plural: NOM *blaga*, GEN *blag*, DAT *blagam*. Likewise R. ADJ NEUT *zl-o* 'bad' → N NEUT *zl-o* 'the bad' GEN SG *zl-a*, with a single form in the plural, that of GEN PL *zol* (cf. Zaliznjak 1977: 519). Note that the outputs of these conversions are all abstract nouns. Usually, in conversions to abstract nouns, the plural part of the paradigm fails completely, as in Bg. MASC *dobăr* 'good', NEUT *dobr-o* → NEUT *dobro(-to)* 'the good', no plural form and MASC *zăl* 'evil', NEUT *zl-o* → NEUT *zlo(-to)* 'the evil', no plural inflection form. In Bulgarian, abstract nouns, derived from adjectives by conversion, are used predominantly in their definite forms (the only inflectional forms possible) *dobroto* and *zloto*. Although Bulgarian adjectives and nouns in -*o* take the same singular definite article -*to*, which makes unclear whether the abstract noun is inflected as an adjective or as a noun, the incompleteness of the paradigm will be seen as evidence for conversion, i.e. since adjectives always have plural forms, indefinite as well as definite, an incomplete paradigm signals that an abstract noun is involved.

Russian conversions to abstract nouns are typical for the literary style. Consider: MASC *tix* 'quiet', NEUT *tíxo* → NEUT *tíxo* 'the quiet', MASC *vysók* 'high, tall', NEUT *vysokó* → NEUT *vysokó* 'height (abstract)' (The examples are from Švedova et al. 1980: 226. Note, however, that informants often evaluate such conversions as unacceptable.) It should be emphasized that in Russian, conversions to abstract nouns can be derived only from short-form adjectives. Recall that Russian short-form adjectives have only a few inflectional forms: three gender forms in the singular and a single form in the plural, all following the noun inflection. In addition, short-form adjectives are homophonous with the respective neuter nominalizations, the latter, as in Bulgarian, have no plural forms. Thus, whereas Russian short-form adjectives undergo morphological conversion to abstract nouns with incomplete inflectional paradigms, long adjectives can be converted into nouns only syntactically (Section 3.5.3.1 below), i.e. they are used in syntactic positions of nouns but retain their adjectival inflection. In Russian, theoretically, two nominalizations can be derived from one and the same adjective: one by morphological conversion (e.g. *vysoko* 'height (abstract)') and one by syntactic conversion (e.g. *vysokoe* 'sth. that is high').

In Serbo-Croatian, similar examples are often dubious. It is because short (indefinite) forms of Serbo-Croatian neuter adjectives have full inflectional

3.5 Classification of Conversion

paradigms, but the latter differ from noun paradigms only in INSTR SG and GEN PL. For example:

(11) NOM SG *zlȍ*
nominal INSTR SG *zlom* vs. adjectival INSTR SG *zlīm*
nominal GEN PL *zàl-ā* vs. adjectival GEN PL *zl-ih*
all other forms being identical

As one can imagine, abstract nouns are seldom used in INSTR SG and GEN PL, i.e. though the difference in inflection, in most cases it is difficult to establish whether the inflection is nominal or adjectival. Therefore, we see Serbo-Croatian conversions of neuter adjectives to abstract nouns as in-between instances, i.e. between morphological and syntactic conversion (Section 3.5.3 below).

(3) A nominalized adjective could also have a mixed paradigm. For example, in Serbo-Croatian, one could derive by conversion the noun SC. *mlâda* 'bride' (from the adjective MASC *mlâd* 'young', FEM *mlád-a*), with the following inflectional forms: DAT, LOC SG *mlad-oj* (as is typical for an adjective, see (12)), but DAT, INSTR, LOC PL *mlad-ama* (as is typical for a noun, see (13)), cf. Anić (1991) and Halilović (1996). This paradigm mismatch is interesting since both nouns *mlada* 'bride-FEM' and *žena* 'wife-FEM', due to the same gender and termination, are expected to take the same inflection.

(12) ADJ *mlada* 'young-FEM'
SG   PL
NOM *mlad-a*   NOM *mlad-e*
GEN *mlad-e*   GEN *mlad-ix*
DAT *mlad-oj*   DAT *mlad-im(a)*
ACC *mlad-a*   ACC *mlad-e*
VOC *mlad-u*   VOC *mlad-e*
LOC *mlad-oj*   LOC *mlad-im(a)*
INSTR *mlad-om*   INSTR *mlad-im(a)*

(13) N *žena* 'woman, wife'
SG   PL
NOM *žen-a*   NOM *žen-e*
GEN *žen-e*   GEN *žen-a*
DAT *žen-i*   DAT *žen-ama*
ACC *žen-u*   ACC *žen-e*
VOC *žen-o*   VOC *žen-e*
LOC *žen-i*   LOC *žen-ama*
INSTR *žen-om*   INSTR *žen-ama*

Note that more recent sources, such as Barić et al. (1997: 180) and Anić et al. (2002), consider *mlada* 'bride' as having the usual noun inflection, i.e. that of (13) *žena*. It seems that the mixed paradigm recently has regularized, which has thus made *mlada* a clear case of morphological conversion.

Conversions of the *mlada* type are important evidence for how morphological conversion arises: a frequently used syntactic conversion can become a morphological conversion, i.e. due to the gradual organization of grammar, phenomena that are originally syntactic (such as syntactic conversion) could morphologize. The process of morphologization, since also gradual, allows for mixed inflectional paradigms containing inflection of two different word classes. Furthermore, the case of *mlada* has implications for the definition of the morphological rule of conversion, as it demonstrates the importance of the paradigm in a conversion rule.

For the sake of completeness, it should be mentioned that the semantically related conversion *stara* 'mother' (← MASC *star* 'old', FEM *stara*) has a normal nominal paradigm, such as that of *žena* in (13), but there is no diachronic evidence, to the best of my knowledge at least, for the development of the paradigm of *stara*.

In sum, according to their paradigms, adjective-to-noun morphological conversions are of three types: (1) inflected as nouns; (2) with incomplete noun paradigms and (3) with mixed paradigms combining inflection of adjectives and nouns. Conversions with mixed paradigms change towards a homogeneous (noun) inflection and are evidence for the gradual organization of morphology as well as for the importance of inflectional paradigm to the definition of conversion. Note that adjective-to-noun conversions with adjectival inlfection of the output are cases of syntactic conversion and therefore not discussed here. On syntactic conversion see Section 3.5.3.

Many linguists intuitively relate Slavic surnames to the above discussed adjective-to-noun conversions. Surnames, however, due to their highly specific semantics, exhibit many idiosyncrasies with respect to inflection and are thus less clear instances of morphological conversion than the examples cited above. For example, the plural of a surname does not have the usual meaning of a plural noun, e.g. Bg./R. *Turgenevi*, the plural form of the surname *Turgenev*, means 'the Turgenevs' and not 'many Turgenevs'. Additionally, a female person's surname, e.g. Bg./R. *Puškina*, though derived from a male person's surname, from *Puškin* in this case, does not always mean 'Puškin's wife'. *Puškina* can be Puškin's mother, daughter, niece, etc. This is, however, not the case when nouns denoting female humans are derived from nouns denoting male humans. Furthermore, the inflection of the Russian surnames depends on their termination and origin. Some surnames have mixed declension, i.e. inflect partly like nouns and partly like adjectives, e.g. surnames in -*ov*/-*ev*, such as *Turgenev*, as well as surnames in -*yn*/-*in*, such as *Puškin*. Other surnames, e.g. those in -*skij*, such as *Dostoevskij*, decline like adjectives. Foreign surnames in -*in*, e.g. *Čaplin*, have instrumental singular different from that of native surnames: *Čaplin-om* (noun inflection) but *Puškin-ym* (adjectival inflection). It should be noted that

3.5 Classification of Conversion 81

Russian surnames terminating in a consonant, i.e. surnames in *-ov/-ev* and *-yn/-in*, can be also used as place names. However, when used as place names, Russian surnames with mixed inflection, receive noun inflection, thus *Saratov* (a name of a city) has a noun inflectional paradigm and is thus a clear case of morphological conversion. Place names in *-ovo/-evo* (*-ov*-NEUT/*-ev*-NEUT) and *-yno/-ino* (*-yn*-NEUT/*-in*-NEUT), however, tend *not* to decline.

Bulgarian surnames and place names in *-ov/-ev*, *-in* and *-ski* do not suffix with the definite article, as a rule. Due to the lack of case forms in Bulgarian, surnames and place names can be seen as indeclinable in this language.

Serbo-Croatian surnames usually terminate in *-ić* and are nouns by origin. Less typical of surnames is the adjectival termination *-ski*. In Serbo-Croatian, surnames in *-ski* and adjectival-by-origin proper names and place names decline like adjectives and are thus cases of syntactic conversion. This language specific feature is discussed at the beginning of the chapter on syntactic conversion, see Section 3.5.3.

3.5.1.1.1.2 Verbalization

3.5.1.1.1.2a Zero-Inflected Input

Word-based conversions to verbs could be derived from nouns and adjectives and always require addition of verbal inflection, as can be seen from the following template:

(14)   X → V (= X + TM + ISUFF$_v$)

N → V

The following examples are noun-to-verb conversions from Bulgarian:

(15)   MASC *pečát* 'seal, stamp, press' → IMPFV *pečát-a-m* 'I print', *pečát-a*
FEM *žál* 'pity, grief, sorrow' → IMPFV *žál-j-a* 'I pity, sorry for, sorrow', *žál-i*

In Bulgarian, this type of conversion is unproductive, the rule being replaced by modifications such as *păt* 'road' → *păt-úv-a-m* 'I travel'; *săn* 'dream' → *săn-uv-a-m* 'I dream', *sănúv-a*; *den* 'day' → *den-úv-a-m* 'I spend the day', *denúv-a*; *prorók* 'prophet' → *prorok-úv-a-m* 'I prophesize', *prorok-úv-a*, etc. Recall that of the three Bulgarian conjugations, only that with the TM *-a-* is fully productive in the sense of Dressler (1997) (i.e. all borrowed verbs have the TM *-a-*), and noun-to-verb derivations (with *-uv-a*) without overt derivational suffixes belong to this conjugation.

The word-based noun-to-verb conversion rule is particularly productive in Russian, especially in the colloquial style, as can be seen from the following list of examples:

(16) MASC *par* 'steam' → IMPFV *pár-i-t'* 'to steam, stew'
MASC *špión* 'spy' → IMPFV *špión-i-t'* (colloq.) 'to spy'
MASC *sáxar* 'sugar' → IMPFV *sáxar-i-t'* (colloq.) 'to add sugar'
MASC *magnít* 'magnet' → IMPFV *magnít-i-t'* 'to magnetize'
MASC *garpún* 'harpoon' → IMPFV *garpún-i-t'* 'to harpoon'
MASC *párus* 'sail' → IMPFV *párus-i-t'* (colloq.) & *parusít'* 'to sail'
MASC *kalambúr* 'pun' → IMPFV *kalambúr-i-t'* 'to pun'
MASC *sekretár'* 'secretary' → IMPFV *sekretár-i-t'* 'to work as a secretary'
MASC *partizán* 'partisan' → IMPFV *partizán-i-t'* (colloq.) 'to be a partisan'
MASC *brigadír* 'brigade-leader' → IMPFV *brigadír-i-t'* 'to be a brigade-leader'
MASC *xuligán* 'hooligan' → IMPFV *xuligán-i-t'* 'to behave like a hooligan'
MASC *grubiján* 'rude fellow' → IMPFV *grubiján-i-t'* (colloq.) 'to be rude'
MASC *závtrak* 'breakfast' → IMPFV *závtrak-a-t'* 'to have breakfast'

In Russian, word-based noun-to-verb conversions take, by rule, the TM *-i-* and seldom the TM *-a-*, as in the last derivation of the above set of examples (cf. Švedova et al. 1980: 333–5). In informal discourse, the TM *-i-*[5] is particularly productive with nouns denoting persons 'X' from which verbs meaning 'to be a X/to work as a X/ to behave like a X' are derived.

Similar examples of word-based noun-to-verb conversions from Serbo-Croatian are:

(17) MASC *pâs* 'belt, waist' → IMPFV *pàs-a-ti* 'to put on around the waist'
MASC *krîž* 'cross' → IMPFV *kríž-a-ti* 'to cross out, intersect'
MASC *dȉm* 'to smoke' → IMPFV *dȉm-i-ti* 'smoke'
FEM *kâp* 'drop' → IMPFV *kȁp-a-ti* 'drip, drop'

---

[5]For a detailed analysis of semantics and formation of Russian *-it'* verbs see Baxturina (1966a, b).

3.5 Classification of Conversion

A sub-case of the type discussed occurs when imperfective aspectual suffixes, that seem to be in the derivational slot of the word but function as inflection class indicators, are added to nouns (on the status of imperfective suffixes in Bulgarian, Russian and Serbo-Croatian see Manova 2002 as well as Section 3.5.2.1.1 below). Such conversions are less prototypical than those involving no aspectual suffixes but change the inflection in the inflectional slot of the word and/or TMs. This means that word-based conversions can be graded in respect to their prototypicality: prototypical conversion means word-class change without any morphotactic change at all; less prototypical conversion involves addition and deletion of suffixes in the inflectional slot of the word and/or TMs; and conversion is much less prototypical if inflectional material from the derivational slot of the word such as aspectual suffixes is involved, as in the next examples of noun-to-verb conversions from Bulgarian:

(18) MASC *săvét* 'advice, council' → IMPFV *săvét-v-a-m* 'I advise', *săvetv-a*
MASC *doklád* 'report, talk, paper' → IMPFV *doklád-v-a-m* 'I report', *dokládv-a*

In accordance with the gradual organization of morphology, in the next examples from Russian and Serbo-Croatian, the old aspectual suffixes *-ov-a-* and *-ev-a-* (originally *-ov-/-ev-* + TM *-a-*) have turned into TMs (recall the discussion in Section 1.5), i.e. in modern Russian and Serbo-Croatian *-ova-* and *-eva-* cannot change the aspect of the verb any more but, as is typical of TMs, define a conjugation class (Manova 2005a), *-eva-* being an allomorph of *-ova-*:

(19) Russian
MASC *sovét* 'advice, council' → IMPFV *sovét-ova-t'* 'to advise'
MASC *špric* 'syringe' → IMPFV *špríc-eva-t'* 'to syringe'

(20) Serbo-Croatian
MASC *sáv(j)et* 'advice, council' → PFV & IMPFV *sáv(j)et-ova-ti* 'to advise'
MASC *báger* 'dredge' → IMPFV *báger-ova-ti* 'to dredge'
MASC *kämēn* 'stone' → PFV & IMPFV *kämen-ova-ti* 'to stone'

ADJ →V

Word-based adjective-to-verb conversions have the morphotactic pattern of word-based noun-to-verb conversions:

(21) Bulgarian
tópăl 'warm' → IMPFV *tópl-j-a* 'I warm', *tópl-i*
čestít 'happy' → IMPFV *čestít-j-a* 'I congratulate', *čestít-i*, and the doublet with a prosodic modification *čestit-j-á*, *čestit-í*
mắdăr 'wise' → IMPFV *mắdr-j-a* 'I think', *mắdr-i*
čist 'clean' → IMPFV *číst-j-a* 'I clean', *číst-i*
kuc 'lame, limping' → IMPFV *kúc-a-m* 'I limp', *kúc-a*

(22) Serbo-Croatian
slȁb 'weak, feeble' → IMPFV *slȁb-e-ti* 'to lose weight', IMPFV *slȁb-i-ti* 'to weaken'
bijêl 'white' → IMPFV *bijél-i-ti*, IMPFV *bijél-je-ti* 'to whiten, bleach'
kȉseo(l) 'sour' → IMPFV *kȉsel-i-ti* 'to make sour' (recall that *o* : *l* is a language-specific phonological alternation, see Section 1.2.1)
vȅdar 'clear, bright, cheerful' → IMPFV *vèdr-i-ti* 'to run the show, be the boss'
sȉtan 'small, tiny', *sȉtnī* (DEF), → IMPFV *sìtn-i-ti* 'to chop up'
stȁr 'old' → IMPFV *stȁr-je-ti* 'grow old'
žût 'yellow' → IMPFV *žút-je-ti*, IMPFV *žút-i-ti* 'to become/grow yellow'

Compare with parallel examples from Russian where the unmarked long adjectives are bases of all derivations from adjectives (except in instances such as those in 2), Section 3.5.1.1.1.1 above), e.g.: *slab-yj* 'weak, feeble' → IMPFV *slab-i-t'* 'to purge', *číst-yj* 'clean' → IMPFV *číst-i-t'* 'to clean', *star-yj* 'old' → IMPFV *stár-i-t'* 'to make old, to age', all root-based conversions (see Section 3.5.1.1.3.2b). Recall that in Russian long-form adjectives are recognized as basic because all adjectives have long forms. Moreover, the syntactic distribution of short form adjectives is restricted: long form adjectives can be used attributively and predicatively, but short form adjectives only predicatively. When used predicatively, long forms denote inherent permanent characteristics (e.g. *On bol'noj* 'He is (chronically) sick'), whereas short forms relate to temporary states (*On bolen* 'He is (temporarily) ill'). Thus, short forms appear semantically more specific, which speaks for a non-basic character.

3.5.1.1.1.2b Input with Overt Inflection
N → V
If a noun terminates in a vowel and this vowel is phonologically equal with a verb TM, the conversion rule adds only infinitival inflection, and the change is thus word-based,[6] as can be seen from the following template:

---

[6] Of course, we can assume that the final vowels of the nouns are first deleted and then attached again as part of the verb inflection. This is, however, less economical than the analysis assumed above, i.e. like Aronoff (1976, 1994) we assume that morphological rules may use already derived forms, such as words and stems. See also Section 3.5.1.1.2.2.

3.5 Classification of Conversion 85

(23) N → V (= N + ISUFF_V)

(24) Bulgarian
FEM *čétk-a* 'brush' → IMPFV *čétk-a-m* 'I brush', *čétk-a*
FEM *kótk-a* 'cat' → IMPFV *kótk-a-m* 'I butter up, pet, nurse', *kótk-a*

(25) Serbo-Croatian
FEM *vág-a* 'balance, scales' → IMPFV *vág-a-ti* 'weigh, balance'
FEM *v r̀st-a* 'kind, type, category' → IMPFV *v r̀st-a-ti* 'to (ar)range, classify'

In the next examples from Russian, the nominal inflection *-o* is reanalysed as a part of the productive inflection *-ov-a-t'*:

(26) NEUT *učítel'stv-o* 'teachers (collect.)' → IMPFV *učítelstv-ov-a-t'* 'to be a teacher'
NEUT *dovól'stv-o* 'contentment, prosperity' → IMPFV *dovól'stv-ov-a-t'* 'to supply contentment, prosperity'
NEUT *vladyčestv-o* 'dominion' → IMPFV *vladyčestv-ov-a-t'* 'to exercise dominion'

Compare with the parallel noun-to-verb conversions in Bulgarian: NEUT *učitelstv-o* 'teachers (collect.)' → IMPFV *učitelstv-a-m* 'I work as a teacher', *učitelstv-a*; NEUT *dovolstv-o* 'contentment, prosperity' → IMPFV *dovolstv-a-m* 'I prosper', *dovolstv-a*, NEUT *vladičestv-o* → Ø, all stem-based conversions (cf. Section 3.5.1.1.2.2 below).

Verbalizations corresponding to the above examples from Russian exist in Serbo-Croatian as well. Consider: NEUT *ljèt-o* 'summer' → IMPFV *ljèt-ov-a-ti* 'to spend one's summer vacation', *strànstv-o* 'foreing countries' → *strànstv-ov-a-ti* 'to wander (about)', *toržèstv-o* 'ceremony, festivity' → *toržèstv-ov-a-ti* 'to triumph'.

3.5.1.1.1.3 *Adjectivization* N → ADJ

In Serbo-Croatian, a few nouns terminating in consonants can be converted into adjectives, with the addition of the unproductive adjectival inflection *-jī*, the rule being semantically restricted to nouns denoting animals.

(27) N → A (= N + ISUFF_ADJ)

(28) jèlen 'deer' → jèlen-jī 'deer-' and jèlen-skī 'related to a deer'
bȉvo(l) 'buffalo' → bìvol-jī 'buffalo-' and bívol-skī 'related to an ox'
pȁs 'dog' → pȁs-jī 'dog-'
kȍkoš 'hen' → kȍkoš-jī 'hen-'
mȉš 'mouse' → mȉš-jī 'mouse-'
(cf. Anić et al. 2002)

Two adjective-to-noun conversions do not fit the pattern semantically: đàvō(l) 'devil' →đávol-jī 'devil-' vs. đavòl-ski, jȅsēn 'autumn' → jèsen-jī 'autumn-' vs. jèsēn-skī. However, as can be seen from these examples, in both cases, competing, more diagrammatic forms occur.

Due to the addition of the suffix -jī, the pattern often requires a segmental modification consisting in the palatalization of the final consonant of the input noun. According to Babić (1991: 405f), such modifications always have doublets derived by addition and without modifications. For example: N làv 'lion' → ADJ lȁvljī 'lion-' and lȁvov, N mèdvjed 'bear' → ADJ mèdvjeđī 'bear-' and mèdvjedov, etc. (see Section 3.5.1.1.3.3). Since -njī and -ljī are also modifications (nj and lj being the palatalized variants of n and l), the above-cited animals jèlēn and bȉvo(l) (28) also have doublets derived through the addition of the suffix -skī (Babić 1991:405). Babić (1991) explains the existence of the doublets derived by addition as a tendency towards avoiding modification (thus the more iconic technique of addition wins over modification). With respect to the use of both type of forms (derived by addition and modification respectively), as can be expected according to the principles and parameters of NM, the more iconic forms (those formed by addition) are preferred. The same holds for the single example of noun-to-adjective word-based conversion found in Russian FEM myš' 'mouse' → ADJ myšij (old) and myšinyj 'mouse-' where conversion appears archaic in comparison to addition.

3.5.1.1.2 Stem-Based Word-Class-Changing Conversion

The usual case of a stem-based conversion is when a verbal stem (ROOT + TM) fully coincides with a word form from a different word class (Section 3.5.1.1.2.1 below). In addition, derived stems (i.e. ROOT + DSUFF) can also serve as inputs of conversion (Section 3.5.1.1.2.2 below).

3.5.1.1.2.1 Nominalization V → N

The input and output of this type of conversion have the following morphotactic structure:

(29)   (PREF–)ROOT–TM–ISUFF$_V$ → (PREF–)ROOT–TM (= ISUFF$_N$)

3.5 Classification of Conversion

The TM of the verb is reanalyzed as a noun inflection suffix (i.e. the verb stem is converted into a noun), as can be seen from the following examples from Russian and Serbo-Croatian:

(30) Russian
IMPFV *igr-á-t'* 'to play, act, perform' → FEM *igr-á* 'play, acting, game, sport',
IMPFV *rabót-a-t'* 'to work' → FEM *rabót-a* 'labour, task, work, job'.

(31) Serbo-Croatian
IMPFV *ìgr-a-ti* 'to dance, play, act, perform' → FEM *ìgr-a* 'game, play(ing), dance(ing)'.
IMPFV *vlád-a-ti* 'to govern, reign' → FEM *vlád-a* 'government, reign, rule'

Since Bulgarian has no infinitive and the present tense is a base of the respective verb-to-noun derivations, the above conversion rule deletes the TM of the verb (*-e-* in the examples below), but preserves the root extension *-a-*:

(32) IMPFV *igr-á-ja* 'I play, dance, act', *igr-á-e* → FEM *igr-á* 'game, sport'
IMPFV *mečt-á-ja* 'I dream', *mečt-á-e* → FEM *mečt-á* 'dream'
IMPFV *čert-á-ja* 'I draw', *čert-á-e* → FEM *čert-á* 'line'

In these examples from Bulgarian, the bases of conversion are shorter than the actual verbal stems, but still longer than the respective roots. Therefore, we classify such instances as stem-based conversion, as also Manova and Dressler (2005) do. Recall that in Section 1.5 we define the suffix *-a-* as a root extension.

Some stem-based verb-to-noun conversions exhibit only a reduced form of the TM of the base, as in the following examples from Bulgarian:

(33) IMPFV *stro-j-á* 'I build, construct', *stro-í* → MASC *stroj* 'order, regime'
IMPFV *bro-j-á* 'I count, consider', *bro-í* → MASC *broj* 'number, copy, issue'
IMPFV *slo-j-á* 'I lay, form strata', *slo-í* → MASC *sloj* 'layer, stratum'
PFV *presto-j-à* 'I stay, stop', *presto-í*/IMPFV *prestoj-áv-a-m*, *prestoj-áv-a* → MASC *prestój* 'stay, stop'

Likewise in R. IMPFV *stro-i-t'* 'to build, tune, draw up' → MASC *stroj* 'arrangement, order, regime, tune, formation'.

To sum up, stem-based verb-to-noun conversions can have three different morphotactic structures: (1) ROOT–TM, the TM of the verb being reanalyzed as noun inflection, (2) ROOT–AMPLIFICATION, the AMPLIFICATION coincides with noun inflection; (3) ROOT–REDUCED TM, the whole form being reanalysed as a noun with zero inflection.

3.5.1.1.2.2 Verbalization N → V

Stem-based verbalizations are formed from derived nouns, the latter usually of the type ROOT–DSUFF–ISUFF. The rule substitutes the noun inflection of the base by verb inflection (TM–ISUFF), as can be seen from the following template:

(34) ROOT – DSUFF – ISUFF$_N$ → ROOT – DSUFF + TM – ISUFF$_V$

The next examples from Bulgarian are derived according to this template:

(35) NEUT *xuligán-stv-o* 'hooliganism' → IMPFV *xuligánstv-a-m* 'I behave like a hooligan', *xuligánstv-a*
NEUT *plagiát-stv-o* 'plagiarism'→ IMPFV *plagiátstv-a-m* 'I plagiarize', *plagiátstv-a*
NEUT *marodér-stv-o* 'marauding, pillage' → IMPFV *marodérstv-a-m* 'I maraud, pillage', *marodérstv-a*
NEUT *svidétel-stv-o* 'certificate, evidence, testimony' → IMPFV *svidételstv-a-m* 'I testify', *svidételstv-a*

For parallel examples from Russian and Serbo-Croatian see Section 3.5.1.1.1.2b above.

In Bulgarian, a X*stvo* noun can be the base of two verbalizations, X*stvam* and X*stvuvam* respectively. The X*stvam* and X*stvuvam* verbs are derived by conversion (-*uv*- being an unproductive ASUFF) and have the same semantic meaning. Of both groups, X*stvuvam* verbs are, however, considered archaic: *učitelstvo* 'all teachers, working as a teacher' → *učitelstvam* 'to be/work as a teacher' = *učitelstvuvam* (old) 'to be/work as a teacher'. The dominance of X*stvam* verbs over X*stvuvam* ones in Bulgarian can be explained in terms of prototypicality. As already discussed, conversions in which ASUFFs are involed (i.e. X*stvuvam* verbalizations) deviate from the prototype of conversion to a greater extent (and are therefore less stable) than conversions in which only TMs and ISUFFs intervene (i.e. X*stvam* verbalizations).

3.5 Classification of Conversion

Bulgarian *-stvam* conversions, since formed from derived nouns, are the last step of the derivational chain:

(36)   X 'X' → *X-stvo* 'all X/working as a X' → *X-stvam* 'to be/work as a X'

In some cases, especially with nouns derived with the suffix *-stv-o* from nouns denoting persons, the derivation chain in (36) represents an illogical semantic series 'X' → 'all X/working as a X' → 'to be/work as a X'. Nevertheless, the rule is fully productive. This instance appears to be a special case of conversion, since here the conversion rule does not apply directly to X (as could be expected according to the semantic change it causes 'to be/work as a X') but takes place after a diagrammatic derivation. Moreover, such conversions should, due to the unnatural length of their outputs, be unproductive.

The peculiar character of conversions with derived nouns as bases has been discussed in the literature in regard to English, where this type of conversion is unproductive,[7] though conversion, in general, is productive in English. Consider the following observation by Bauer (1983):

> The only partial restriction [on conversion] that I am aware of is that discussed by Marchand (1969: § 5.5). Marchand points out that derived nouns rarely undergo conversion, and particularly not to verbs. This is usually because of blocking. To take one of Marchand's examples, a derived noun like *arrival* will not be converted into a verb if that verb means exactly the same as *arrive*, from which *arrival* is derived. In cases where blocking is not a relevant concern, even derived nouns can undergo conversion, as is shown by the series *a sign* > *to sign* > *a signal* > *to signal* and *to commit* > *commission* > *to commission* (Bauer 1983: 226f).

The rule of blocking, as suggest by Bauer, can successfully explain instances such as Bg. *sătrudnik* 'collaborator' → *sătrudniča* 'I collaborate', *sătrudnik* 'collaborator' → *sătrudničestvo* 'collaboration' → **sătrudničestvam* 'I collaborate'. However, if we ignore the different stylistics, blocking seems to be problematic for instances such as Bg. *kljukar* 'gossiper' → *kljukarja* (colloq.) 'I gossip' and *kljukar* 'gossiper' → *klukarstvo* 'gossip(ing)' → *kljukarstvam* 'I gossip', as well as for R. *geroj* 'hero' → *geroit'* 'to behave as a hero' (occasional) and *geroj* 'hero' → *geroj-stvo* 'heroism' → *gerojstvovat'* 'to behave as a hero' (cf. Zemskaja 1996: 135). Such examples are strange since it is much more reasonable to convert 'X' into 'to be/work/behave as a X' than to have an intermediate stage. Moreover, the *-stvo* pattern is particularly productive in Bulgarian, and foreign bases also take the suffix *-stvo*, from *-stvo* nouns then *-stvam* verbs are derived, e.g.: Bg. *xuligan* 'hooligan' → *xuliganstvo* 'hooliganism' → *xuliganstvam* 'I behave like a hooligan', cf. SC. *huligan* 'hooligan' → *huluganiti* 'to behave like a hooligan' and R. *xuligan* 'hooligan' → *xuliganit'* 'to behave like a hooligan'.

---

[7]Booij (2002: 136) and Don (2005: 5) underline the unproductive character of conversion to verbs from complex nouns in Dutch and German.

The only explanation of the productivity of the Bulgarian -*stvam* conversion pattern (36) could be the total inflectional productivity of the 3rd Bulgarian conjugation (that with the TM -*a*-) to which all -*stv-a-m* verbs belong. In stem-based conversions of the type X*stvam*, the right edge of the base has been reanalyzed as a part of the class marker -*v-a*- (consisting of the ASUFF -*v*- and the TM -*a*-), which is the only fully productive (in the sense of Dressler 1997) verbal inflection in modern Bulgarian. Cf. aspectual pairs of borrowed verbs such as IMPFV & PFV *organizir-a-m* 'to organize' → IMPFV2 *organizir-v-a-m* 'to organize (colloq.)', where both verbs have the same semantics and belong to the same 3rd conjugation. Here, as in the above X*stvam* conversions, the existence of the second verb IMPFV2 *organizir-v-a-m* 'to organize (colloq.)' seems illogical and can be explained only with the extreme productivity of the inflection marker -*v-a*-. Thus, Bulgarian conversions of the type X*stvo* → X*stvam* are an interesting example of inflection-productivity dominance in derivation.

3.5.1.1.3 Root-Based Word-Class-Changing Conversion

The already-discussed types of word- and stem-based conversion often depend on certain coincidences of forms: either on homophony of adjectival and nominal inflection suffixes, as in the word-based conversion Bg. ADJ NEUT SG *sladko* 'sweet' → N NEUT *sladko* 'marmalade, dessert', or on coincidence of a verbal thematic marker and a nominal inflectional suffix, as in the stem-based conversion R. IMPFV *rabót-a-t'* 'to work'→ FEM *rabót-a* 'labour, task, work, job'. In contrast to word- and stem-based conversion, root-based conversion adds inflectional markers of the output word-class to the root of the input word form. Therefore, in inflecting languages, root-based conversion appears to be 'technically easier' than word- and stem-based conversion. In fact, root-based conversion is the most frequent type of conversion in Bulgarian, Russian and Serbo-Croatian.

The most salient feature of root-based conversion from and to verbs is the interaction of thematic material. In instances of deletion of thematic markers, a problem with establishing the base of conversion arises. For example, Russian *zamáx* 'stroke, blow' could be derived from the perfective ingressive *zamax-á-t'* 'to start to wave/strike', from the perfective semelfactive *zamax-nú-t'sja* 'to strike once', or from the imperfective IMPFV2 *zamax-ív-a-t'sja*. Diachronically the first verb is the base, and it is also the usual assumption in synchronic analyses. However, an event noun such as *zamáx* is semantically closer to the perfective verb (in our case to the perfective semelfactive). Note that in similar instances, in the list of examples below, all three verbs are cited, but the perfective verbs are meant as bases, in accordance with the understanding that all morphological processes are morphosemanticaly and morphotacticaly motivated, as postulated by NM.

3.5.1.1.3.1 Nominalization

V → N

Such conversions fall into two groups (Sections 3.5.1.1.3.1a and 3.5.1.1.3.1b). The output of the first group is a result of deletion of verbal inflection (TM and ISUFF), whereas in the second group, after the deletion of verbal inflection, nominal inflection is added.

3.5.1.1.3.1a V → Zero-Inflected N

This type of conversion shows the following morphotactic pattern:

(37) (PREF –)ROOT – TM – ISUFF$_v$ → (PREF –)ROOT

(38) Bulgarian
 IMPFV *zov-á* 'I call', *zov-é* → MASC *zov* 'call, appeal'
 IMPFV *xód-j-a* 'I go, walk', *xód-i* → MASC *xod* 'gate, pace, tread, move'
 IMPFV *bród-j-a* 'I rove, tramp, wander', *bród-i* → MASC *brod* 'ford'
 IMPFV *lov-j-á* 'I catch, hunt', *lov-í* → MASC *lov* 'hunt(ing)'
 IMPFV *vík-a-m* 'I cry', *vík-a* → MASC *vik* 'cry'
 IMPFV *bjág-a-m* 'I run', *bjág-a* → MASC *bjag* 'running, rush'

 IMPFV *tărg-úv-a-m* 'to deal in, trade', *tărg-úv-a* → *tărg* 'trade, bargain'
 PFV *razgrom-j-á* 'I rout', *razgrom-í*/IMPFV2 *razgrom-jáv-a-m*, *razgrom-jáv-a* → MASC *razgróm* 'rout'
 PFV *razdel-j-á* 'I divide, separate', *razdel-í*/IMPFV *razdél-ja-m*, *razdél-ja* → MASC *razdél* 'section, part'
 PFV *proval-j-á* 'I upset, ruin', *proval-í*/IMPFV *provál-ja-m*, *provál-ja* → MASC *provál* 'failure, ruin'
 PFV *obmen-j-á* 'I exchange', *obmen-í*/IMPFV *obmén-ja-m*, *obmén-ja* → MASC *obmén* 'exchange'
 PFV *zamáx-a-m*, *zamáx-a*/PFV SEMELFACTIVE *zamáx-n-a*, *zamáx-n-e*/IMPFV *zamáx-v-a-m*, *zamáx-v-a* 'I flap, wave' → MASC *zamáx* 'stroke, blow'

(39) Russian
 IMPFV *xvat-á-t'*, PFV *xvat-í-t'* 'to seize, snatch' → MASC *xvat* (slang) 'dashing fellow'
 IMPFV *bég-a-t'* 'to run' → MASC *beg* 'run'
 PFV INGRESSIVE *zamax-á-t'*/PFV SEMELFACTIVE *zamax-nú-t'-sja* / IMPFV *zamáx-iv-a-t'-sja* 'to raise one's hand' → MASC *zamáx* 'stroke, blow'.

PFV *ugovor-í-t'* 'to negotiate'/ IMPFV *ugovár-iv-a-t'* → MASC *ugovór* (colloq.), PL TANTUM *ugovór-y* 'negotiations'

(40)   Serbo-Croatian
IMPFV *lòv-i-ti* 'to hunt, chase' → MASC *lôv* 'hunt, chase',
IMPFV *hód-a-ti* 'to walk, pace' → MASC *hôd* 'walk, gate, pace',
IMPFV *rád-i-ti* 'to work'→ MASC *râd* 'work, labour',
IMPFV *bjèg-a-ti* 'to run' → MASC *bjêg* 'run'
IMPFV *ròj-i-ti se* 'to swarm' → MASC *rôj* 'swarm'
IMPFV *drijem-a-ti* 'to doze, take a nap' → *drijêm* 'nap'
IMPFV *ròv-a-ti* 'to ditch, trench' → MASC *rôv* 'ditch, trench'
IMPFV *pòsjed-ov-a-ti* 'to own, possess' → MASC *pòsjed* 'ownership, possession',
PFV *ùsklik-nu-ti*/IMPFV *usklik-ív-a-ti* 'to exclaim, cry out, call out, shout'→ *ùsklik* 'exclamation, shout, cry, interjection',
PFV *zamáh-a-ti*, PFV SEMELFACTIVE *zamáh-nu-ti*, IMPFV *zamah-ív-a-ti* 'to swing, wave' → *zàmah* 'swing, movement, stroke' (recall that in Serbo-Croatian native words are not stressed on the last syllable).

The suffixes *-Vv-* and *-nu-* express imperfective and perfective aspect respectively but behave as class markers (cf. Manova 2002 and Manova 2005a), i.e. aspectual suffixes occupy the derivational slot of the word (see the discussion in Section 3.5.2), but, since their status is inflectional (they mark non-prototypical inflection), their addition and deletion do not violate the notion of derivational conversion.

3.5.1.1.3.1b V → N with Overt Inflection
The outputs of this subtype of root-based verb-to-noun conversion have overt nominal inflection, either *-a* or *-o*, as can be seen from the following template and the examples below:

(41)   (PREF –)ROOT – TM – ISUFF$_V$ → (PREF –)ROOT + ISUFF$_N$

(42)   Bulgarian
IMPFV *vin-j-á* 'I blame', *vin-í* → FEM *vin-á* 'blame'
IMPFV *pil-j-á* 'I file', *pil-í* → FEM *pil-á* 'file'
PFV *zakán-j-a se* 'I threaten', *zakán-i se*/IMPFV *zakán-v-a-m se*, *zakán-v-a se* → FEM *zakán-a* 'threat'
PFV *zabráv-j-a* 'I forget', *zabráv-i*/IMPFV *zabráv-ja-m, zabráv-ja* → FEM *zabráv-a* 'forgetfulness'

3.5 Classification of Conversion   93

(43) Russian
IMPFV *dél-a-t'* 'to do, make' → NEUT *dél-o* 'affair, business, deed'
IMPFV *zavíd-ov-a-t'* 'to envy' → COMMON GENDER *zavíd-a* 'envious person'
IMPFV *sel-í-t'sja*, to settle' NEUT → *sel-ó* 'village'

(44) Serbo-Croatian
IMPFV *hrán-i-ti* 'to feed, nourish' → FEM *hrán-a* 'food, nourishment',
IMPFV *ljúb-i-ti* 'to love, be in love' → FEM *ljúb-a* 'sweetheart, girl-friend'
PFV *ràn-i-ti* 'to wound' → FEM *ràn-a* 'wound',
PFV *pòstav-i-ti* 'to place, put, set'/IMPFV *pòstavlj-a-ti* → FEM *pòstav-a* 'lining'

IMPFV *dèl-ov-a-ti* (or rare also imperfective *dèl-a-ti*) 'to work, perform'→ neut. *dèl-o* 'deed, action, act'

3.5.1.1.3.1c *ADJ → N

Conversion-like examples of this subtype were found only in Russian. Consider: R. *belyj* → *bel'*, *zelënyj* → *zelen'*, *sinij* → *sin'* (cf. Švedova et al. 1980: 224). However, a comparison with root-based verb-to-noun conversions such as R. IMPFV *xvat-á-t'*, PFV *xvat-í-t'* 'to seize, snatch' → MASC *xvat* (slang) 'dashing fellow', etc. (see Section 3.5.1.1.3.1a above) undoubtedly shows that the adjective-to-noun derivations are formed by modification via palatilization of root-final consonants.

In Bulgarian and Serbo-Croatian, adjective-to-noun root-based conversion is technically impossible, which is due to the fact that, in both languages, the basic form adjectives (MASC SG) are, by rule, zero-expressed, i.e. have no inflection at all. In the theoretical framework of this monograph, if a zero-expressed form is the base of a morphological change, the rule is always word-based (recall instances such as SC. ADJ MASC SG *zèlen* 'green' → *zëlēn* 'greens, vegetables' (cf. Section 3.5.1.1.1.1); the parallel derivation from Bulgarian, namely *zelén* 'green' → *zelen-in-á* 'greenery', is also word-based, it is a case of word-based addition).

3.5.1.1.3.2 Verbalization

(45)   ROOT – ISUFF$_X$ → ROOT + TM + ISUFF$_V$

X can be either a noun (3.5.1.1.3.2a) or an adjective (Section 3.5.1.1.3.2b).

3.5.1.1.3.2a **N → V**

(46) Bulgarian
FEM *brazd-á* 'furrow' → IMPFV *brazd-j-á* 'I furrow', *brazd-í*
FEM *pár-a* 'steam' → IMPFV *pár-j-a* 'I scald, steam', *pár-í*
NEUT *ágn-e* 'lamb' → IMPFV *ágn-j-a (se)* '(I) lamb', *ágn-i (se)*
NEUT *petn-ó* 'stain, spot' → IMPFV *petn-j-á* 'I soil, spot, tarnish', *petn-í*

FEM *vjár-a* 'belief' → IMPFV *vjár-v-a-m* 'to believe', *vjárv-a*
FEM *beséd-a* 'talk, lecture' → IMPFV *beséd-v-a-m* 'I talk, converse', *beséd-v-a*
FEM *tăg-á* 'sadness, sorrow, grief' → IMPFV *tăg-úv-a-m* 'I grieve/am sad', *tăg-úv-a*
MASC *slug-á* 'servant' → IMPFV *slug-úv-a-m* 'I am a servant', *slug-úv-a*

(47) Russian
FEM *škól-a* 'school' → IMPFV *škól-i-t'* 'to school, discipline'
FEM *špór-a* 'spur' → IMPFV *špór-i-t'* 'to spur'
FEM *žen-á* 'wife' → PFV & IMPFV *žen-í-t'(sja)* 'to marry (off)'
FEM *lopát-a* 'spade, shovel' → IMPFV *lopát-i-t'* 'to spade'
FEM *borozd-á* 'furrow' → IMPFV *borozd-í-t'* 'to furrow'
FEM *graf-á* 'column' → IMFV *graf-í-t'* 'to make columns'
FEM *struj-á* 'jet, spurt' → IMPFV *struí-t'* 'to spurt'
FEM *trub-á* 'pipe, trumpet' → IMPFV *trub-í-t'* 'to blow'
FEM *púdr-a* 'powder' → IMPFV *púdr-i-t'* 'to powder'
NEUT *serebr-ó* 'silver' → IMPFV *serebr-í-t'* 'to silver'
NEUT *stekl-ó* 'glass' → IMPFV *stekl-í-t'* 'to glaze'
NEUT *pjatn-ó* 'spot, patch, stain' → IMPFV *pjatn-á-t'* 'to spot, stain'

Compare with word-based conversions the outputs of which are *-it'* verbs (Section 3.5.1.1.1.2).

(48) Serbo-Croatian
FEM *sèstr-a* 'sister' → IMPFV *sèstr-i-ti* 'to accept as a sister'
FEM *žèn-a* 'woman, wife' → IMPFV *žèn-i-ti* 'to marry off'
FEM *píl-a* 'file' → IMPFV *píl-i-ti* 'to file'
FEM *brázd-a* 'furrow' → IMPFV *brázd-i-ti* 'to furrow'

NEUT *vèsl-o* 'oar, scull, paddle' → IMPFV *vèsl-a-ti* 'to row, paddle, scull'
NEUT *srèbr-o* 'silver' → IMPFV *srèbr-i-ti* 'to silver'
NEUT *zlât-o* 'gold' → NEUT *zlát-i-ti* 'to gild'
FEM *škōl-a* 'school' → IMPFV *škȍl-ov-a-ti* 'to educate'
FEM *sìl-a* 'power' → PFV & IMPFV *sìl-ov-a-ti* 'to rape, violate'

3.5.1.1.3.2b ADJ → V

These conversions follow the morphotactic pattern of noun-to-verb conversion in Section 3.5.1.1.3.2a, (45) above.

(49)   Russian
slab-yj 'weak, feeble' → IMPFV *slab-i-t'* 'to purge'
číst-yj 'clean' → IMPFV *číst-i-t'* 'to clean'
stár-yj 'old' → IMPFV *stár-i-t'* 'to make old, to age'
lukáv-yj 'sly, cunning' → IMPFV *lukáv-i-t'* 'to be cunning'
vtóra 'second (violin)' → IMPFV *vtór-i-t'* 'to repeat, take the second part'
xrom(-ój) 'lame, limping' → IMPFV *xrom-á-t'*, IMPFV *xrom-é-t'* 'to limp'

Corresponding ADJ → V conversions from Bulgarian and Serbo-Croatian are always word-based, cf. Section 3.5.1.1.1.2.

3.5.1.1.3.3 Adjectivization

3.5.1.1.3.3a N → A

A few feminine nouns denoting animals, birds and insects can be turned into adjectives, after addition of inflectional suffixes (compare with (27) and (28) in Section 3.5.1.1.1.3 above):

(50)   ROOT – ISUFF$_N$ → ROOT + ISUFF$_{ADJ}$

(51)   Bulgarian
kráv-a 'cow' → *kráv-i* (restricted to certain idiomatic expressions) vs. *krav-ešk-i* 'cow-'
ríb-a 'fish' → *ríb-ja* (old) vs. *ríb-en* 'fish-'
žáb-a 'frog' → *žáb-ja* (old) vs. *žab-ešk-i* 'frog-'

This pattern produces very few conversions, archaic by rule. Actually, when adjectives are derived from nouns, the more diagrammatic morphological techniques dominate over conversion. Thus in modern Bulgarian, adjective-to-noun conversion is entirely replaced by affixation (cf. (51)) and modification (such as in N *koz-á* 'goat' → ADJ *kóz-i* 'goat-', with a prosodic alternation, and N *ovc-á* 'sheep' → ADJ *óvč-i* 'sheep-', with a prosodic modification and a *c : č* morphonological alternation of the root-final consonant). In Bulgarian, adjectives corresponding to nouns denoting animals and birds might also be derived by subtraction, e.g. Bg. N *kokóš-k-a* 'hen, fowl'→ ADJ *kokóš-i* 'hen's, chicken (attr.)', with deletion of the stem-final *-k-* (cf. Section 4.4.1.1.3).

In contrast to Bulgarian, in Serbo-Croatian, adjectives derived from nouns denoting animals, birds and insects by conversion are better preserved.

(52) Serbo-Croatian
 pùr-a 'turkey. FEM'→ *pùr-jī* 'turkey-'
 òs-a 'wasp' → *òs-jī* 'wasp-'
 kòz-a 'goat' → *köz-jī* 'goat-'

As in cases of word-based conversion (Section 3.5.1.1.1.3), if modification occurs, the semantic pattern permits doublets, e.g.: N *kr̀ava* 'cow' → ADJ *kr̀avljī* 'cow-' and *kr̀avin*, *kòbil-a* 'mare' → *kóbiljī* 'mare-' and *kobilećī*. Of the two output forms, the affixed ones are preferred.

3.5.1.1.3.3b V → A

This extremely rare type of conversion has been established only in Russian, where very few verbs can be converted into adjectives. The rule has the following morphotactic structure:

(53) ROOT – TM – ISUFF$_V$ → ROOT + ISUFF$_{ADJ}$

Conversions derived according to this pattern are stylistically marked as either colloquial or poetic:

(54) *ljub-ít'* 'to love, like' → *ljúb-yj* (modification), *ljub* (poetic, colloq.) 'dear, loved, beloved' (conversion), cf. Švedova (1980: 304); Efremova (2000).

Actually, the example above is the only instance I have found in Russian that satisfies all the conditions of the definition of conversion. The pattern usually involves either a prosodic modification, as in *xvor-á-t'* 'to be ill, ailing' → *xvór-yj* (colloq.) 'ailing, sick', *tošn-í-t'* 'to feel sick; to vomit' → *tóšn-yj* 'tiresome,

3.5   Classification of Conversion   97

tedious, nauseous' or segmental and prosodic modifications, as in *vxod-í-t'* 'to enter' → *vxóž-ij* 'accepted' (Russian Academy Grammar 1980: 304).

3.5.1.2   Word-Class-Preserving Conversion

When we discussed derivation and inflection in Chapter 2, we pointed out that the former can be word-class-changing and word-class-preserving, and, since word-class change is the most salient characteristic of derivation, we call word-class-preserving derivation non-prototypical. For example, the English pair N *garden* → N *garden-er* is a non-prototypical derivation because the input and output of the derivation are nouns. What is relevant to us now is the fact that what happens in addition is expected to happen, and happens, in conversion as well, i.e. it might be the case that, in a non-prototypical derivation, no derivational affixes participate and only inflectional material is added or deleted. In such cases, we speak of non-prototypical (word-class-preserving) conversion. Non-prototypical conversion can also be root-, stem- and word-based.

3.5.1.2.1   Word-Based Word-Class-Preserving Conversion

3.5.1.2.1.1   N → N

With regard to its derivation-inflection features diminutivization is considered to be a non-prototypical morphological change. To stress the peculiar status of diminutivization in a language's morphology, Scalise (1986: 131–133) suggests the term 'evaluative morphology', i.e. neither derivation nor inflection. However, based on Manova's (2005) observation that diminutives are not identifiable inflectionally, i.e. behave rather derivation-like than inflection-like, and following Dressler and Merlini Barbaresi (1993, 1994), we will call diminutivization non-prototypical derivation. If the output of a diminutivization rule has no diminutive suffix in the derivational slot and the diminutivization change is indicated only by addition of a suffix in the inflectional slot (55), we will speak of non-prototypical conversion, as in the Bulgarian examples in (56) and (57) below.

In Bulgarian, diminutivization often requires an additional gender change from masculine to neuter. What happens in such instances ((56) and (57)) is thus more significant than inflectional class change but still less radical than word class change:

(55)   MASC N → DIM NEUT N
       X → X + ISUFF

(56)   Bulgarian
       MASC *kotél* 'caldron' → NEUT DIM *kotl-é*
       MASC *petél* 'rooster, cock' → NEUT DIM *petl-é*
       MASC *kozél* 'he-goat' → NEUT DIM *kozl-é*
       MASC *ovén* 'ram' → NEUT DIM *ovn-é*

Note that the elision of -*e* here is phonological.

(57) Dialectal forms from Bulgarian:
MASC *zăb* 'tooth' → DIM *zăb-e*
MASC *nos* 'nose' → DIM *nos-e*, etc.
(cf. Stojanov 1993: 187)

We will call these diminutives 'inflectional' in order to distinguish them from the usual diminutivization in Bulgarian that adds special diminutive (derivational) suffixes, as in:

(58) MASC *učitel* 'teacher'→ DIM NEUT *učitel-č-e*
MASC *stol* 'chair' → DIM NEUT *stol-č-e* → DIM NEUT *stol-če-nc-e*.

Due to the addition of the suffix -*e*, the inflectional diminutivization pattern is often accompanied by segmental modifications such as palatalizations (thus modification instead of conversion), e.g.: Bg. MASC *učenik* 'pupil' → DIM NEUT *učenič-e*, MASC *vojnik* 'soldier' → DIM NEUT *vojnič-e*, MASC *vălk* 'wolf' → DIM NEUT *vălč-e*. Likewise in the following derivations of the young of animals from Serbo-Croatian: FEM *lisic-a* 'fox' → NEUT *lisič-e*, FEM *ptic-a* 'bird' → NEUT *ptič-e*, MASC *zec* 'rabbit' → NEUT *zeč-e*; Bg. FEM *lisic-a* 'fox' → NEUT *lisič-e*, FEM *ptic-a* 'bird' → DIM NEUT *ptič-e*, etc. Note that the young of animals can stand for diminutives of the respective animals.

In Bulgarian linguistics, one can find two explanations of the diachronic origin of the above-cited Bulgarian inflectional diminutives. The first explanation sees them as continuants of old vocative forms (cf. Mladenov 1929:224; Mirčev 1963:150), i.e. the modern Bulgarian DIM *otče* (← *otec* 'father'), DIM *starče* (← *starec* 'old man') should be derived from the OBg. VOC *otьče*, VOC *starьče*. The second explanation, advocated by Vladimir Georgiev, connects inflectional diminutives with the Old Church Slavic *ęt*-stems (cf. Georgiev 1985:164) and seems the more probable. Georgiev motivates his claim with the plural forms of inflectional diminutives (*otče* 'father' → PL *otčeta* and *starče* 'old man' → PL *starčeta*) which, in modern Bulgarian, take the plural suffix -*ta*, as is usual for nouns originating from the OBg. *ęt*-stems (compare with the OBg. *ęt*-declension noun *tele* 'calf', NOM PL *teleta*). A second argument in favour of *ęt*-stems origin of inflectional diminutives is the fact that the OBg. *ęt*-declension was semantically related with the meaning of smallness, since *ęt*-stems originally included only the young of animals: mod. Bg. *agne*/OBg. *agne* 'lamb', mod. Bg. *kozle*/OBg. *kozьle* 'kid', etc. According to Georgiev (1985), diminutives in -*l-e* (e.g. DIM *kotl-e* ← *kotel* 'caldron') and -*č-e* (e.g. DIM *vojnič-e* ← *vojnik* 'soldier') where -*l*- and -*č*- are parts of the respective stems, served as bases for

3.5 Classification of Conversion   99

the development of the diminutive suffixes -*če* (e.g. DIM *zăb-če* ← *zăb* 'tooth') and *-le* (e.g. DIM *nos-le* ← *nos* 'nose').

Although both Russian and Serbo-Croatian are also descendants of OCS, the diminutive suffix *-e* exists only in Serbo-Croatian, where it is bound to the semantic pattern 'the young of animals', recall examples such as *lisic-a* 'fox' → *lisič-e*, *ptic-a* 'bird' → *ptič-e*, etc. As for nouns such as *vojnič-e* 'soldier-VOC' which are homophonous with the respective Bulgarian diminutives (see above), in Serbo-Croatian, these forms express vocative case, without any diminutive meaning at all. It seems that the existence of the category of vocative which often inflects with the suffix *-e* in Serbo-Croatian, has blocked the development of the diminutivization rule with the same suffix. On the other hand, modern Russian has no vocative (see, however, Section 4.2.4 in the next chapter), but even the semantics 'the young of animals' is always expressed by suffixes in the derivational slot. It is the suffix *-onok/-ënok* that usually derives young of animals in Russian, e.g. *medvež-onok* 'bear-cub', *tel-ënok* 'calf', *l'v-ënok* 'lion-cub', etc. the old *-ęt-* amplification being preserved in the plural, e.g. NOM PL *medvež-ata, tel-jata, l'v-jata*.

3.5.1.2.2 Stem-Based Word-Class-Preserving Conversion

3.5.1.2.2.1 N→N

The semantic pattern 'science' → 'scientist/specialist in', which seems to be cross-linguistically diagrammatic (e.g., E. *mathematics* → *mathematic-ian*, G: *Matematik* → *Matematik-er*, SC. *matematik-a* → *matematič-ar*), neither adds a derivational affix to the input noun nor modifies it in Russian, e.g.: N *matemátik-a* 'mathematics' → N *matemátik* 'mathematisian', *fízik-a* 'physics' → *fízik* 'physicist'. Compare with the prosodic modifications in Bulgarian *matemátik-a* 'mathematics' → *matematík* 'mathematisian' and *fízik-a* 'physics' → *fizík* 'physicist'. Russian conversions change first, the subclass of the base (from inanimate to animate), and second, its gender (from feminine to masculine). The more that class features are changed the less non-prototypical is the word-class-preserving conversion, since it thus approaches prototypical conversion. Russian word-class-preserving conversions have the following morphotactic pattern:

(59)   STEM + ISUFF$_N$→ STEM (= N)

(60)   FEM X*ik-a* 'science' → MASC X*ik* 'scientist'
       kibernétik-a 'cybernetics' → *kibernétik* 'specialist in cybernetics'
       téxnik-a 'technique' → *téxnik* 'technician'
       mexánik-a 'mechanics' → *mexánik* 'mechanic'
       informátika 'informatics' → *informátik*
       genétika 'genetics' →*genétik* 'geneticist'

Note that *kiber-, texno-*, etc. may exist alone or as parts of compounds, e.g. R. *kiber-prostranstvo* 'cyber-space', *texno(-muzyka)* 'techno-music'. This defines the bases *kibernetik, texnik* as stems (i.e. longer than the roots *kiber-* and *texno-*) and determines the above conversions as stem-based. However, this observation does not hold for conversions such as *botánik-a* 'botany' → *botánik* 'botanist', for which root-based conversion is assumed (see Section 3.5.1.2.3 below).

Although the above conversion rule seems to be semantically restricted to the pattern 'science' → 'scientist' and this semantic constraint might explain why *kalanetika* 'callanetics' and *aerobika* 'aerobics' have no *-ik* mates, it is unclear why there are sciences in *-k-a* without counterparts for scientists, e.g. R. *elektronika* 'electronics' → Ø, *kosmonavtika* 'astronautics' → Ø, *bionika* 'bionics' → Ø, *meteoritika* (derived from *meteorit* 'meteorite') → Ø. These relatively new formations (cf. Zemskaja 1992: 140), however, prove, according to the distributional criterion (cf. Section 3.4.2.1), the basic status of nouns for sciences.

3.5.1.2.3 Root-Based Word-Class-Preserving Conversion

3.5.1.2.3.1 N→N

The specifics of this type of non-prototypical conversion were discussed in the previous section. All examples of root-based word-class-preserving conversion are again ony from Russian and exhibit the following morphotactic structure:

(61)   ROOT – ISUFF$_N$ → ROOT (= N)

(62)   *botánik-a* 'botany' → *botánik* 'botanist'
       místik-a 'mysticism' → *místik* 'mystic'

The Russian conversion pattern X*ik-a* 'science' → X*ik* 'scientist' has some exceptions derived by more iconic techniques: substitutions such as R. *fonétik-a* 'phonetics' → *fonet-íst* 'phonetician'; and suffixations, e.g.: *múzyk-a* 'music' → *muzyk-ánt* 'musician' (here the base terminates in *-yk-*), *práktik-a* 'practice' → *praktik-ánt* 'practitioner', the latter two at the periphery of the semantic pattern.

Nouns in *-istika* can also be input of the above semantic pattern, their counterparts, however, terminate in *-ist*, instead of *-ik*, e.g.: R. *germanístika* 'Germanic studies' → *germaníst* 'Germanic scholar', *publicístika* 'publicism' → *publicist* 'publicist', thus subtraction (cf. Section 4.4.1.2).

3.5 Classification of Conversion

3.5.1.3 Intermediate Conclusion

In Bulgarian, Russian and Serbo-Croatian, conversion in derivation, as expected, shows various types. It can be word-class-changing (prototypical) and word-class-preserving (non-prototypical), and according to the type of its base, root-, stem- and word-based (word-based conversion being the rarest type, with root-based conversion the most frequent). In other words, in the three languages, conversion represents a strict parallel to other derivational processes such as affixation, substitution and modification. Moreover, these more iconic techniques often compete with conversion. In some instances, the competition of techniques has given rise to doublet forms. Where doublets occur, conversion is always more archaic in comparison to modification and suffixation. In other instances modification has won entirely over conversion.

In regard to the word class of the output, the most frequent, and also productive, type of conversion is conversion to verb. Conversions to verbs are easily formed by the addition of verbal inflection (TM and ISUFF) and, sometimes, of aspectual suffixes, to all possible bases, i.e. $V = X + TM + ISUFF_V$, where X is a word (noun/adjective) or a stem/root of a noun/an adjective (cf. Table 3.1 below). Conversions in which nominal inflection is reanalyzed as verbal TMs are a subtype of the previous case. Clearly, in such instances only infinitival inflection (ISUFF) is added to the base. Verbs derived by conversion take the inflectional suffixes *-i-t'*, *-a-t'*, *-ov-a-t'*/*-i-ti*, *-a-ti*, *-ov-a-ti* in Russian and Serbo-Croatian respectively, and often the TM *-a-* in Bulgarian, i.e. as expected for conversion, verbalizing conversion enters only productive inflection classes (cf. for Russian Švedova et al. 1980; Dressler and Gagarina 1999; for Serbo-Croatian Babić 1991; Dressler et al. 1996).

Conversions to nouns are produced after deletion of verbal inflection, either TM and ISUFF or ASUFF, TM and ISUFF. In rare cases, only the infinitival inflection (i.e. ISUFF) is deleted. The output of conversions to nouns either coincides with an existing noun or serves as a base to which nominal inflection is added, i.e. $N = X$ or $N = X + ISUFF_N$, where X is a root or a stem of a verb (see Table 3.1). Verb-to-noun conversions usually go into productive inflection classes such as masculines in consonant, feminines in *-a* or neuters in *-o* (cf. Švedova et al. 1980; Babić 1991; Manova and Dressler 2001). Adjective-to-noun conversions are very rare. They are word-based, and exist only in Serbo-Croatian. The output of this type of conversion belongs to an unproductive inflectional class, namely that of feminines in consonants; as a consequence, this conversion type is unproductive.

Adjectivizing conversion is the least frequent type of conversion in Bulgarian and Serbo-Croatian, and extremely rare in Russian. Noun-to-adjective conversions are word- and root-based (i.e. of the type $ADJ = X + ISUFF_{ADJ}$, where X is either a noun or a root of a noun), and since derived from nouns denoting animals, birds and insects, this conversion type is semantically restricted (cf. subtractions with the same semantic pattern, Section 4.4.1.1.3). Stem-based

Table 3.1 Types of prototypical conversion in regard to intervention of inflection

Type & subtype	→N	Deletion	Addition	→V	Deletion	Addition	→ADJ	Deletion	Addition
Word-based	<u>1.</u> ADJ > N	∅	∅	<u>2a.</u> N > V <u>2b.</u> N > V <u>3.</u> ADJ > V	∅ ∅ ∅	ISUFF TM, ISUFF TM, ISUFF	<u>4.</u> N > ADJ	∅	ISUFF
Stem-based	<u>5.</u> V > N	ISUFF	∅	<u>6.</u> N > V	TM, ISUFF	ISUFF			
Root-based	<u>7a.</u> V > N <u>7b.</u> V > N	TM, ISUFF TM, ISUFF	∅ ISUFF	<u>8.</u> N > V 9. ADJ > V	ISUFF ISUFF	TM, ISUFF TM, ISUFF	<u>10.</u> N > ADJ <u>11.</u> V > ADJ	ISUFF TM, ISUFF	ISUFF ∅

3.5 Classification of Conversion 103

conversions to adjectives have not been found. A single occurrence of root-based verb-to-adjective conversion has been attested in Russian (see Table 3.1).

To sum up: except for the few cases of coincidence of word forms, the few verb-to-noun stem-based conversions and the root-based conversion to nouns terminating in consonants, word-class-changing conversion always requires addition of inflectional suffixes (N = X + ISUFF$_N$, X ≠ N; V = X + TM + ISUFF$_V$, X ≠ V; ADJ = X + ISUFF$_{ADJ}$, X ≠ ADJ), since the output of conversion should be integrated to the morphological system of the respective (inflecting-fusional) language. Perphaps for that reason, Slavic grammars assume suffixation instead of conversion for such instances. For us, whether inflection participates or not, if the derivational slot of the word is empty, what happens is conversion. The established types of prototypical conversion with respect to the inflection involved, are summarized in Table 3.1. (Note that although addition and deletion of ASUFFs are not extra noted, they can take place in cases of deletion and addition of TMs.)

As for productivity of prototypical conversion, only N → V and V → N conversions are productive, verbalizing conversion being the more productive type of both. ADJ → V conversion is less productive than both previous types. N → ADJ and V → ADJ conversions are unproductive. The greatest productivity of conversion to verbs in comparison to the other conversion types in Slavic can be explained as a strategy for compensating the poverty of derivational suffixes in verbal morphology (Manova 2003b).

Non-prototypical conversion is, by rule, unproductive, which supports the idea of prototype organization of conversion (bad examples diminish and tend to belong to neighbouring (more prototypical) categories). Moreover, this type of conversion involves only noun-to-noun changes and is semantically restricted to two patterns only: diminutivization of nouns and the pattern of 'science' → 'scientist' (note that both patterns operate in subtraction as well, Section 4.4.1.2).

All types of conversion in derivation can be captured best in terms of a cline beginning with word-class-changing word-based conversion, extending through word-class-changing stem-based and root-based conversion to word-class-preserving word-based conversion and word-class-preserving stem-based conversion and ending with word-class-preserving root-based conversion.

3.5.2 Conversion in Inflection

3.5.2.1 Conversion and Non-prototypical Inflection: Formal Conversion

In accordance with the assumption of a derivation-inflection continuum in Chapter 2 (Section 2.5), after prototypical derivation (with word class change) and non-prototypical derivation (without word-class change), non-prototypical inflection follows. In the previous section, prototypical and non-prototypical derivation were illustrated by prototypical and non-prototypical conversion respectively. In this section, we will concentrate on categories of non-prototypical inflection such as verbal aspect and nominal gender in order to establish whether conversion ends with non-prototypical derivation or can be extended to non-prototypical inflection. It is expected that non-prototypical inflection, as neighbouring non-prototypical derivation, resembles the latter in some respects, and some occurrences of non-prototypical inflection would look like non-prototypical conversion. Let us compare instances of non-prototypical derivation, suffixation and conversion ((63a) and (63b) respectively), with examples of non-prototypical inflection ((64a), (64b), (65a) and (65b)), all from Bulgarian:

Non-prototypical derivation:
N → N
(63a)   MASC *učitel* 'teacher' → DIM NEUT *učitel-č-e*

vs. non-prototypical conversion:

(63b)   MASC *kotel* 'caldron' → DIM NEUT *kotl-Ø-e*,
        MASC *petel* 'rooster, cock' → DIM NEUT *petl-Ø-e*,

Non-prototypical inflection:
Aspect (imperfectivization):

V → V
(64a)   PFV *pre-sto-j-a* 'I stay, remain, stop', 3 SG *pre-sto-i* →
        → IMPFV2 *pre-sto-jav-a-m*, 3 SG *pre-sto-jav-a*

vs.

(64b)   PFV *ob-misl-j-a* 'I think over', 3 SG *ob-misl-i* →
        → IMPFV2 *ob-misl-Ø-ja-m*, 3 SG *ob-misl-Ø-ja*.
        PFV *xvărl-j-a* 'I throw', 3 SG *xvărl-i* →
        → IMPFV *xvărl-Ø-ja-m*, 3 SG *xvărl-Ø-ja*.

Gender (formation of females from males):

N → N
(65a)   MASC *pisatel* 'writer, autor' → FEM *pisatel-k-a*

vs.

(65b)   MASC *săprug* 'husband' → FEM *săprug-Ø-a* 'wife'

MASC *dripl-jo* 'shabby fellow' → FEM *dripl-Ø-a*.

If we evaluate the above realizations of non-prototypical derivation and non-prototypical inflection ((63) through (65)) according to the generalized morphotactic structure of the Slavic word, namely (PREF) – BASE – (DSUFF) – (TM) – (ISUFF) (TM only in verbal morphology), it becomes clear that both non-prototypical derivation and non-prototypical inflection use the derivational slot (DSUFF) of the word, as in the (a) examples above, and then only the inflectional slot (ISUFF) (ISUFF slot plus the TM slot for verbs) of a word, as in the (b) examples above. Moreover, like non-prototypical derivation, non-prototypical inflection change, such as imperfectivization and formation of females from males, is characterized by different paradigms of input and output. However, unlike non-prototypical derivation, where the semantic change of the base (due to the addition of a diminutive meaning and a gender change) signals a derivational process, non-prototypical inflection forms differ semantically only in respect to the category they express, i.e. they have only different aspectual or gender meanings. Thus, suffixless realizations of non-prototypical inflection (the (b) examples of aspect and gender), despite their different paradigms, disobey the condition of different word classes, as well as that of a significant (derivational) semantic change, as required by the definition of conversion, and should be set apart from prototypical and non-prototypical conversion. Due to the different paradigms (i.e. a formal change) of the input and output of non-prototypical inflection change, we will call suffixless expressions of non-prototypical inflection formal conversion. (On morphotactic expression of aspect and gender in Bulgarian, Russian and Serbo-Croatian, see Manova 2002; on gender in Russian, cf. Corbett 1991: 34–43).

3.5.2.1.1 Aspect

Slavic verbs might be organized in aspectual triplets, the latter consisting of a primary imperfective (IMPFV1) verb → a perfective (PFV) verb → a secondary imperfective (IMPFV2) verb, IMPFV1 as an unmarked form being the base of that triple relation (cf. Jakobson 1971[1932]: 6; Comrie 1976: 112; Bybee 1985: 147).[8] However, there are basic verbs (i.e. without prefixes or aspectual suffixes) that are perfective, for example, in Bulgarian some 80 verbs (cf. Stojanov 1993: 335). Clearly, such verbs have only the last two forms according to the aspectul triple, e.g.: Bg. PFV *xvărl-j-a* 'I throw', *xvărl-i* → IMPFV *xvărl-ja-m, xvărl-ja*; R. PFV *bros-i-t'* 'to throw'→ IMPFV *bros-a-t'*; SC. PFV *bác-i-ti* 'to throw' → IMPFV *bàc-a-ti*.

---

[8] Bybee (1985: 147) considers aspect subject to 'local markedness', since 'the more a morphological distinction affects the inherent meaning of the verb, the less clear the general markedness values will be'.

Whether the different aspect forms are forms of the same verb or different lexemes is an old problem in linguistic literature.[9] In regard to the semantic change, perfectivization is usually classified as derivation, since the choice of a prefix is lexically determined and modifies the meaning of the verb in accordance with the meaning of the prefix elsewhere in derivation. In contrast, secondary imperfectives, which are formed by suffixation from prefixed perfectives, are traditionally viewed as inflection, due to the fact that imperfectivization does not modify the semantic meaning of the perfective verb (cf. Maslov 1962b: 22, 1982: 202; Andrejčin et al. 1983: 267; Babić et al. 1991: 670; Stojanov 1993: 336, 338). As for the formal expression of verbal aspect, Slavic grammars consider perfectivizing prefixes derivation. Surprisingly, however, despite their inflectional meaning, all imperfectivizing suffixes are also listed under WF of verbs (from the aforementioned linguists see Stojanov 1993: 318; Babić 1991: 475ff).

As discussed in Section 2.5, we argue that, in a given language, a given grammatical category is either inflectional or derivational. This claim does not exclude non-prototypicality, which may have an impact on the semantics of the category as well as on its formal expression. Such understanding is based on one of the universal parameters of NM, namely that of binarity, which is seen as a main cognitive principle. For us, the debate on the status of aspect merely confirms the non-prototypical inflectional character of that category.

Note that each member of the above-postulated triplet IMPFV1 → PFV → IMPFV2 has its own morphotactic structure, but since we are interested in imperfectivization, i.e. PFV → IMPFV(2), only this step of the aspectual opposition is tackled here.

3.5.2.1.1.1 Default Expression of Imperfectivization

Secondary imperfective verbs are formed by suffixation with the aspectual suffix *-(V)v-* by default:

(66) **PFV**: PREF – ROOT – TM – ISUFF →
Bg. *pod-piš-e-š* 'you sign'; *pre-sto-i-š* 'you stay, remain, stop'
R. *pod-pis-a-t'* 'to sign'
SC. *pot-pis-a-ti* 'to sign'
→**IMPFV2**: PREF – ROOT – ASUFF – TM – ISUFF

---

[9]According to Vinogradov (1972: 395), aspect is an inflectional category. Maslov (1962: 22) recognizes only imperfectivisation as inflection. In contrast, Russian Academy grammar (Švedova et al. 1980: 584f) and Lehmann (1999: 215) interpret aspect pairs as consisting of different lexemes (i.e. as derivation). For the debate on the status of the category of aspect in Bulgarian, see Maslov (1959, 1981) and Kucarov (1983, 1999). As mentioned, Dressler (1989) has assigned verbal aspect to non-prototypical inflection. See also Comrie (1976), Bybee (1985) and Bybee et al. (1994).

3.5 Classification of Conversion

Bg. *pod-pis-v-a-š* 'you sign', *pre-sto-jav-a-š* 'you stay, remain, stop'
R. *pod-pis-yv-a-t'* 'to sign'
SC. *pot-pis-iv-a-ti* 'to sign'

Note that here 2 SG PRES of Bulgarian verbs is taken for illustration, because in this form all possible suffixes are overtly exhibited (1 SG PFV *pod-piš-Ø-a* has no thematic marker, 3 SG PFV *pod-piš-e-Ø* has no inflectional suffix), which makes that inflection form an exact parallel to the respective Russian and Serbo-Croatian infinitival forms.

3.5.2.1.1.2 Imperfectivization Without Imperfectivizing Suffix

These IMPFV(2) verbs are not marked by the suffix -*v*-, and, in accordance with the generalized morphotactic structure of the verbal form, share the following pattern (compare with the pattern in (66)):

(67) **IMPFV(2)**: (PREF –) ROOT – TM – ISUFF
Bg. PFV *za-xvárl-i-š* 'you throw away, abandon' → IMPFV *za-xvárl-ja-š*,
R. PFV *smen-í-t'* 'to change' → IMPFV *smen-já-t'*
SC. PFV *bác-i-ti* 'to throw' → IMPFV *bàc-a-ti*.

Recall that we presume to label such cases 'formal conversion' since it is a paradigmatic change only (the input and the output verbs are from different inflection classes) and the output of conversion always belongs either to the same inflection class or to two phonologically complementary classes.[10]

When aspect is expressed without a special suffix, concomitant prosodic and segmental modifications usually arise. The most typical of those are ablaut, zero/vowel alternation and palatalization. For example:

(68) Bg. PFV *pro-čet-e-š* 'you read' → IMPFV2 *pro-čit-a-š*
Bg. PFV *umr-e-š* 'you die' → IMPFV *umir-a-š*
Bg. PFV *raz-gled-a-š* 'you look at, examine' → IMPFV2 *raz-gležd-a-š*
R. PFV *za-stav-i-t'* 'to forse' → IMPFV2 *za-stavl-ja-t'*
R. PFV *vstret-i-t'* 'to meet' → IMPFV *vstreč-a-t'*
SC. PFV *is-pùst-i-ti* 'to release, miss, emit' → IMPFV2 *is-púšt-a-ti*
SC. PFV *sjèt-i-ti* 'to remember, recall' → IMPFV *sèć-a-ti*

---

[10]Thus this type of change is similar to what Lieber (1981a, b) defined as a zero affix.

Such modifications function as formal indicators of the imperfectivization change, i.e. in accordance with the iconicity scale, the more iconic morphological technique of modification blocks the less iconic formal conversion. In fact, modifications are often the case in Russian and Serbo-Croatian.

Like conversion in derivation, formal conversion also has affixation as a competitor, as can be seen from the following examples from Bulgarian:

(69) PFV *potul-i-š* 'you conceal' → IMPFV2 *potul-ja-š*
 vs. IMPFV2 *potul-v-a-š*
  PFV *podlep-i-š* 'paste (under)' → IMPFV2 *podlep-ja-š*
 vs. IMPFV2 *podlep-v-a-š*
  PFV *zakrep-i-š* 'you fix' → IMPFV2 *zakrep-ja-š*
 vs. IMPFV2 *zakrep-v-a-š*

These instances are evidence that, in a language system, a non-iconic morphological technique, whether in derivation or in inflection, is always dispreferred. In this way, the examples in (69) also support the correctness of the assumption of conversion as one of a set of morphological techniques operating in derivation and in inflection.

3.5.2.1.2 Gender

In this subsection, we will exemplify morphotactic realizations of gender that, at least in general, appear to be a formal parallel to those of aspect, though aspect and gender are semantically of an entirely different nature.

Bulgarian, Russian and Serbo-Croatian distinguish masculine, feminine and neuter gender in the singular. In the plural, in Bulgarian and Russian gender distinctions are neutralized, whereas Serbo-Croatian has preserved all three genders. The opposition we are interested in is that of formation of females from males, i.e. MASC vs. FEM of animates.

3.5.2.1.2.1 Default Pattern for Derivation of Females from Males
The rule uses the following morphotactic template where GSUFF stands for a gender suffix:

(70) MASC → FEM
   N → N – GSUFF – ISUFF

As can be seen from the next examples, Bulgarian, Russian and Serbo-Croatian possess a set of GSUFF for the derivation of females from males:

(71) Bg. *bog* 'God' → *bog-in-ja*

3.5 Classification of Conversion 109

        R. *bog* 'God' → *bog-in-ja*
        SC. *bȏg* 'God' → *bȍg-in-ja*

        Bg. *car* 'king, tsar' → *car-ic-a* 'queen'
        R. *car'* 'king, tsar' → *car-ic-a*
        SC. *cȁr* 'king, tsar' → *cȁr-ic-a*

        Bg. *uči-tel* 'teacher' → *uči-tel-k-a*
        R. *uči-tel'* 'teacher' → *uči-tel'-nic-a*
        SC. *ùči-telj* 'teacher' → *ùči-tēlj-k-a*/*uči-tèlj-ic-a*
        etc. (for a list of the Bg./R./SC. GSUFFs, see Manova 2005a)

Since GSUFFs are in the derivational slot of the word, it is possible for a GSUFF to replace a suffix that is derivational but expresses, among other possible meanings, a male pendant, e.g.: Bg. MASC *bor-ec* 'fighter' → FEM *bor-kin-ja*, R. MASC *šotland-ec* 'Scotsman' → FEM *šotland-k-a*, SC. MASC *stȁr-ac* 'old man' → FEM *stȁr-ic-a* (Bg. *bor-ec*, R. *šotland-ec*, and SC. *stȁr-ac* have zero inflection). These examples further imply that a particular morphological change is always localized in a particular word slot, be it derivational or inflectional. Therefore what takes place here is a realization of the morphological technique of substitution and not subtraction.

3.5.2.1.2.2 Derivation of Females from Males Without Gender Suffixes
This type of gender change (72) represents formal conversion and can be illustrated with the following examples:

    (72)   N → N – ISUFF (*a*)
    (73)   Bg. *săprug* 'husband' → *săprug-a* 'wife'
              R. *suprug* 'husband' → *suprug-a* 'wife'
              SC. *sùprug* 'husband' → *sùprug-a* 'wife' and
              SC. *sùpružnīk* → *sùpružnic-a*.

Most such examples of formal conversion come from Serbo-Croatian (cf. Babić 1991: 66). Consider: *brȁtučed* 'cousin' → *brȁtučed-a*, *kȗm* 'godfather' → *kúm-a* 'godmother', *râb* 'slave' → *ràb-a*, *súsjed* 'neighbour' → *súsjed-a*, *ùnuk* 'grandson' → *ùnuk-a* 'grand-daughter'.

With regard to animals, females (feminine gender) are often semantically unmarked and the direction of the gender change is from FEM to MASC, as in the following examples of formal conversion from Serbo-Croatian: *màčkā* 'cat' → *máčak* 'Tom-cat', *pȁtka* 'duck' → *pátak* 'drake' with a phonological insertion of *-a-* in the masculine forms.

As is usual for other conversion types, formal conversion might also be paralleled by affixation, e.g.: SC. *nȅćak-a* vs. *nećȁk-inj-a* 'niece' ← *nȅćak* 'nephew', *drúg-a* vs. *drug-àric-a* ← *drûg* 'frend'; consider also Bg. *vnuk-a* (old) and *vnuč-k-a* 'grand-daughter' from *vnuk* 'grandson'. As is usual in cases of competition of techniques, the more iconic affixation is preferred in Bulgarian and Serbo-Croatian (cf. Babič 1991: 66; Anić 1991). Formal conversion could be blocked by prosodic modifications (i.e. by the more iconic technique of modification), e.g.: R. *rab* 'slave' → FEM *rab-á*, Bg. *kum* 'first witness' → FEM *kum-á*. Likewise for animals, especially in Bulgarian: FEM *méčka* 'bear' → MASC *mečók* 'he-bear', FEM *kótka* 'cat' → MASC *koták* 'Tom-cat', FEM *pátka* 'duck' → MASC *patók* 'drake', etc. Such examples reveal the unproductive character (in the sense of Dressler 1997) of formal conversion, the latter a less prototypical type of conversion than non-prototypical conversion. In other words, due to deviation from the prototype, bad examples of a category (technique) diminish.

Since gender is prototypical inflection for adjectives (Dressler 1989), adjectives and participles that have undergone substantivization express gender only inflectionally: Bg. MASC *bolen* 'sick man' → FEM *boln-a*, MASC *sljap* 'blind man' → FEM *sljap-a*, MASC *zaveždašt* 'manager' → FEM *zaveždašt-a*, etc. Consider also the parallel forms from Russian: MASC *bol'n-oj* 'sick man' → FEM *bol'n-aja*, MASC *slep-oj* 'blind man' → FEM *slep-aja*, MASC *zavedujušč-ij* 'manager' → FEM *zavedujušč-aja*, etc. (cf. Manova 2002; and Spencer 2002 for Russian). In cases of false substantivization (i.e. when the adjective cannot be used as such any more, cf. Section 3.5.3.1.2.3), it is possible for a GSUFF to combine with an adjectival base, as in R. MASC *portn-oj* 'tailor' → FEM *portn-ix-a*. Such examples are, however, extremely rare.

3.5.2.2 Intermediate Conclusion

Gender and aspect represent non-prototypical inflection and as such allow for two different morphotactic realizations, either by a GSUFF/an ASUFF or by an ISUFF/a TM, respectively. Of both types of expression, the inflectional realizations are completely unproductive. Inflectional realizations of aspect and gender, since derived by conversion, are often challenged by more iconic techniques. In cases of competition of forms, like in derivational converion, the more iconic realizations are preferred. We have classified suffixless aspect and gender forms as formal conversion, since they express the respective aspect and gender alternations by a paradigmatic change, which is a formal change within the same category. Moreover, paradigmatic change distinguishes formal conversion (non-prototypical inflection) from syncretism that is coincidence of forms in prototypical inflection.

On the derivational-inflectional continuum, conversion starts with conversion in derivation, which can be prototypical (word-clas-changing) and non-prototypical (word-class-preserving). Next is inflection, where the morphological technique of conversion is realized as formal conversion. With prototypical inflection, morphological coincidence of forms (syncretism) goes into syntax where syntactic conversion arises. Syntactic conversion is very much like

3.5.3 Syntactic Conversion

In this section, we will deal with syntactic conversions such as substantivization and adjectivization. For the sake of precision, it should be noted that within the Slavic linguistic tradition, unlike modern linguistics, the terms 'substantivization' and 'adjectivization' are, by rule, used for marking syntactic changes only, i.e. they label syntactic conversions the output of which are nouns and adjectives respectively (cf. Galkina-Fëdoruk et al. 1957; Dokulil 1968a: 229ff; Zemskaja 1973: 172, 179; Rozental' and Telenkova 1976; Švedova et al. 1980; Babić 1991: 48; Barić et al. 1997: 300ff; Bojadžiev 1999: 273f). In order to avoid confusions, the term substantivization is used herein also only in regard to syntactic conversion.

Language-specific features play a significant role in syntactic conversion. For example, whereas in Serbo-Croatian both definite (long) and indefinite (short) adjectives can be used attributively and therefore substantivized by ellipsis (cf. Laškova 2001: 127), in Russian only the long forms of adjectives can be used attributively and thus substantivized after deletion of the noun, which is the head of the phrase (for long and short forms of adjectives see Section 1.2.2.2). However, the inflection of Serbo-Croatian short adjectives coincides to a great extent with nominal inflection (cf. Section 1.2.2.2 and Appendix H) and thus does not always allow for establishing conversion, since both the input and output have the same paradigm from the beginning. Moreover, if the accentuation pattern is not taken into consideration, inflection of short and long feminine adjectives in the singular and in the plural, and of masculine and neuter adjectives in the plural, also fully coincide. Perhaps for that reason, Serbo-Croatian grammars usually illustrate substantivization only with clear cases of syntactically converted long adjectives. Examples include: family names such as *Zrînskī* – GEN SG *Zrînskōga*; names of countries, e.g. *hr̀vātskā zèmlja* 'Croatian land' → *Hr̀vātskā* 'Croatia' – DAT & LOC SG *Hr̀vātskōj* (both *Zrînskī* and *Hr̀vātskā* have only long forms as adjectives); and male proper nouns, e.g. *Dòbrī* – GEN SG *Dòbrōga* (the short form of the adjective is *dòbar* 'good'). On substantivization of adjectives in Serbo-Croatian, cf. Stevanović (1964: 268–272), Babić (1991: 47–9), Barić et al.(1997: 180f).

The type of conversion (whether morphological or syntactic) could also be language-specific. For example, as mentioned in the previous paragraph, Bg. *sladko* 'marmalade, dessert, third course' (from the ADJ *sladko* 'sweet') is a case of morphological conversion, since both the noun and the adjective have different sets of inflectional endings (cf. the noun plural *sladk-a* and the adjectival *sladk-i*). However, if we convert the same adjective into a noun in Russian, it will be a syntactic conversion (substantivization) because the R. ADJ MASC *sladk-ij*,

NEUT *sladk-oe* 'sweet' and the N NEUT *sladk-oe* 'dessert, third course' take the same inflection, e.g. both the adjective and the noun have GEN SG *sladk-ogo*.

In the discussion below, as in morphological conversion, we will demonstrate that syntactic conversion is not homogeneous but encompasses different instances that constitute a cline including the following stages in substantivization:

(1) metalinguistic substantivization & substantivization of infinitives
(2) substantivization of adjectives

    (i) anaphoric substantivization
    (ii) true substantivization (lexicalization)
    (iii) false substantivization

This classification cline begins with pure syntactic changes, such as syntactic recategorizations of unchangeable forms, continues via syntactic recategorization of anaphoricaly used inflectional forms, and afterwards, true substantivization of adjectives, and concludes with false substantivization, which indicates a diachronic change of an adjective to a noun, where the converted item exhibits adjectival inflection but does not exist as an adjective synchronically, hence the label 'false substantivization'.

3.5.3.1 Substantivization

3.5.3.1.1 Metalinguistic Substantivization and Substantivization of Infinitives

The term 'metalinguistic substantivization' is used here after Dokulil (1968a: 229) and Rainer (1993:675), the latter describing this type of substantivization as follows:

> Jede sprachliche Einheit, vom Phonem bis zur Äußerung und zum Text, kann durch die bloße Voranstellung eines Artikels verobjektsprachlicht werden: *un sí, un no con entonación ascendente,* usw. (Rainer 1993: 675).[11]

In a language such as Bulgarian with a postposed (definite) article, metalinguistic substantivization is exactly as productive as in Spanish, e.g. Bg. *no-to* 'but-DEF ART', *no-ta-ta* 'but-PL-DEF ART', etc. Since Russian and Serbo-Croatian have neither definite nor indefinite articles, they use pronouns (demonstrative and possessive) for the same purpose, e.g.: R: *Vaše no / ox* 'Your "no"/"oh" '; *Èto no/ox* 'This "no"/"oh" ' (cf. Zemskaja 1973: 172). As can be seen from the examples, metalinguistic substantivization itself also constitutes a cline. In Bulgarian and Spanish, the process exhibits some degree of morphologization, which is greater in Bulgarian than in Spanish, since in Spanish the prepositional article (indefinite and definite) is a clitic, whereas in Bulgarian the postpositional definite article is an inflectional suffix. In contrast, in Russian and

---

[11] Every linguistic unit, from phoneme to sentence and text, if preceded by an article, can be used as a noun: *un sí, un no con entonación ascendente,* etc. (Rainer 1993: 675). (Translation SM)

3.5 Classification of Conversion

Serbo-Croatian the change is purely syntactic, since it is only the syntactic position of an unchangeable item that has been altered.

Another case of pure syntactic conversion is the substantivization of infinitives in Russian and Serbo-Croatian. Consider: R. *Kurit'* – *zapreščaetsja* (smoke-INF forbid-3 SG-REFL) 'No smoking'; and SC. *Čekati je teško* (wait-INF is difficult) 'It is difficult to wait'. Compare with the substantivization of infinitives in German, e.g. *les-en* 'read' → *das Lesen*. German substantivized infinitives have no plural, but can take case inflection, e.g. GEN SG *des Lesens* (cf. Dokulil 1968a: 231). Thus in German, if an infinitive is a base of a syntactic and a morphological conversion, the output of the substantivization (i.e. of syntactic conversion) cannot be pluralized whereas that of morphological conversion can, e.g.: G. *tun* 'do' → *das Tun* 'doing', PL Ø; *treff-en* 'to meet' → *das Treffen* 'meeting', PL *die Treffen* (here only die article declines) vs. the root-based morphological conversion *der Treff* 'rendezvous', PL *die Treffs*. (Thus action nouns such as *das Tun* have no plural but result nouns such as *das Treffen* can be used as plural). Cf. Italian where converted infinitives, if lexicalized, can be pluralized, e.g. *parlare* 'to speak' → *il parlar-e* 'idiom', PL *i parlar-i, sapere* 'to know' → *il saper-e* 'knowledge', PL *i saper-i*. The final step of the substantivization of infinitives that is fully morphologization is represented by English conversions such as *to walk* → a *walk, to whistle* → *a whistle*, etc. where the output nouns have all inflectional forms of a noun (cf. the syntactic conversion of gerunds, for example, *walking* as in *go walking* where the output of conversion cannot be pluralized. *The reading-s* is a case of reanalysis of syntactic conversion into a derivational suffixation, when a true nomen actionis becomes a result noun).

Among more conservative, strongly inflecting Indo-European languages such as Ancient Greek and Latin (Manova and Dressler 2005): Ancient Greek puts the definite article before the infinitive, and inflects the article but not the infinitive, e.g. *lég-ein* 'to say' → *tò légein* 'the fact of saying', GEN *toũ légein*. Pluralization is excluded. In the non-article language Latin, substantivization of infinitives is syntactic conversion, but inflection is suppletive, taking the oblique cases from the gerunds, i.e. *legere* 'to read', GEN *legend-i*. Again there is no plural. On conversion of infinitives, see also Bauer (2005).

In conclusion, substantivization of infinitives is typologically specific and represents a continuum from languages tending to the isolating type (e.g. English), i.e. from morphological conversion, via weakly inflecting languages (such as Italian and German) to strongly inflecting languages (Russian, Serbo-Croatian, Latin and Ancient Greek), i.e. to syntactic conversion.

3.5.3.1.2 Substantivization of Adjectives and Participles

Zemskaja (1973:179f) noticed for substantivization[12] of adjectives a specific transformation of the paradigm of the input, i.e. the paradigm of such an

---

[12]Similar to Marchand (1969), Zemskaja (1973) distinguishes between zero suffixation and conversion, the latter denoting substantivization.

adjective undergoes (1) quantitative change, since the noun preserves only a part of the adjectival paradigm (either the forms for one of the three genders or for the plural); and (2) qualitative change, since the dependent agreement inflection of an adjective turns into independent noun affixation (cf. Vinogradov 1947: 189). For Mel'čuk (2001: 361f), Russian substantivized adjectives are examples of 'paradigmatic, categorical and rectional conversion$_2$', i.e. in substantivization of adjectives paradigmatic, categorical and rectional changes take place. Since the main device of substantivization of adjectives is the transformation of the inflectional paradigm of the input, this type of substantivization appears to be an intermediate step between morphological conversion and a pure syntactic process, when no morphological change happens, as in cases of substantivization of infinitives in Russian and Serbo-Croatian.

In the literature, one can find different classifications of syntactic conversion, especially of substantivization of adjectives (for Russian see Galkina-Fëdoruk et al. 1957: 280–282; Švedova et al. 1980: 239: 242; Mulisch 1988: Section 1.5.3). In this book, we, in line with Galkina-Fëdoruk et al. (1957), see substantivization of adjectives as a result of ellipsis of nouns, and the classification suggested herein is based on this assumption. We speak of ellipsis when a construction of modifier + head (in either order) undergoes deletion of the head and the modifier takes on the meaning of the whole construction (Kreidler 2000: 962). Since substantivizations preserve the gender and the number of the ellipted noun, one can find substantivized adjectives in all three genders and in the plural (see Section 3.5.3.1.2.2 below).

Note that some linguists (Vogel 1996: 251) call elliptic expressions 'Pseudo-substantivierungen' 'pseudo subsantivizations' (see Section 3.5.3.1.2.1 'Anaphoric substantivization') and distinguish them from 'nicht-ellipstischen, "echten" Substantivierungen' 'non-eliptic, "true" substantivizations' (Section 3.5.3.1.2.2 'True substantivization' below), cf. also Švedova et al. (1980: 241).

3.5.3.1.2.1 Anaphoric Substantivization
We will illustrate this first step of substantivization of adjectives with a German example from Vogel (1996):

> Das Adjektiv fungiert als Anapher auf das vorerwähnte Substantiv, von dem es auch immmer sein Genus bezieht: *nachdem ich den neuen Stuhl gekauft hatte, habe ich den alten weggeworfen* (Vogel 1996: 251).[13]

Clearly, such substantivizations are possible in any of the three languages Bulgarian, Russian and Serbo-Croatian. For example in Bulgarian, the translation of the above-cited German sentence will be: *sled kato kupix novija stol, izxvărlix starija* 'after I bought the new chair, I threw out the old one'. Like in German, the second adjective *starija*-MASC.SG.DEF 'old-the' inherits the

---

[13]The adjective functions as an anaphora that refers to a previously mentioned noun and agrees in gender with the latter: *having bought the new chair*-MASC, *I threw out the old*-MASC *one* (Vogel 1996: 251). (Translation SM)

3.5 Classification of Conversion

agreement pattern of the attributively used adjective *novija*-MASC.SG.DEF 'new-the'.

3.5.3.1.2.2 True substantivization

In contrast to anaphoric substantivizations, truly substantivized adjectives, due to lexicalization, have a context-independent usage and are always thought in connection with a single noun only, as can be seen from the following expressions from Bulgarian:

(74) *Uča anglijski (ezik)* 'I am learning English (language)'.
BUT not **Pija anglijski (čaj)* 'I am drinking some English (tea)'.
(75) *Imam detska (staja)* 'I have got a children's (room)'.
BUT not **Imam detska (kniga)* 'I have got a children's (book)'.

Both substantivizations are possible in Russian (*anglijskij (jazyk)* 'English (language)', *detskaja (komnata)* 'child(ren's) (room)'), but in Serbo-Croatian only adjectives denoting languages can be substantivized in this way.

What follows is a survey of the most frequent semantic patterns of lexicalized substantivizations in Bulgarian and Russian (with some examples from Serbo-Croatian where this change is far less frequent than in Bulgarian and Russian). The classification is based on Švedova et al. (1980: 239–41), with some modifications and expansions. Substantivized adjectives are grouped according to two criteria: (i) gender and (ii) semantics.

3.5.3.1.2.2a → Masculine Nouns

(a) substantivizations denoting persons, i.e. with ellipsis of R. *čelovek*/Bg. *čovek* 'man'

(76) R. *bol'noj* 'sick (man), patient', *vzroslyj* 'adult', *rotnyj* 'company (commander)', *znakomyj* 'acquaintance', *trudjaščijsja* 'worker', *sumašedšij* 'madman';
Bg. *bolen* 'sick (man), patient', *văzrasten* 'adult', *roten* 'company (commander)', *poznat* 'acquaintance';

Cf. SC. suffixed nouns *boles-nīk* 'sick man' and *pózna-nīk* 'acquaintance'.

(b) substantivizations denoting animals

(77) R. *kosoj* 'rabbit', i.e. with ellipsis of *zajac* 'rabbit', *kosolapyj* 'bear', with ellipsis of *medved'* 'bear'

Bulgarian has no such instances.

3.5.3.1.2.2b → *Feminine Nouns*

(a) substantivizations for rooms, i.e. with ellipsis of R. *komnata*/Bg. *staja* 'room'

(78)   R. *priëmnaja* 'reception (room)', *operacionnaja* 'operating (room)', *detskaja* 'children's (room)', *ucitel'skaja*, 'teachers' (room)'.
Bg. *priemna* 'reception (room)', *operacionna* 'operating (room)', *detska* 'children's (room)', *učitelska* 'teachers' (room)'.

(b) substantivizations for documents, i.e. with ellipsis of R. *zapiska* /Bg. *zapiska* 'note'

(79)   R. *zakladnaja* 'mortgage, hypothec', *podorožnaja* (old) 'order for fresh post horses', *dokladnaja* 'report'.
Bg. *dokladna* 'report'.

(c) substantivizations denoting a part of a whole, i.e. with ellipsis of R. *čast'*/ Bg. *čast* 'part'

(80)   R. *pjataja* 'a fifth', *sed'maja* 'a seventh', *milionnaja* 'a millionth'.
Bg. *peta* 'a fifth', *sedma* 'a seventh', *milionna* 'a millionth'.

3.5.3.1.2.2c →*Neuter Nouns*

(a) substantivizations expressing general notions of characteristic features, i.e. with ellipsis of R. *čto-to (nečto)*/Bg. *nešto* 'something'

(81)   R. *prekrasnoe* '(the) beautiful', *tragičeskoe* '(the) tragic', *neizvestnoe* '(something) unknown'.
Bg. *prekrasno(to)* '(the) beautiful', *tragičesko(to)* '(the) tragic', *neizvestno(to)* '(something) unknown'.

(b) substantivizations denoting groups of persons, i.e. with ellipsis of Bg. *săštestvo* 'creature'

(82)   Bg. *staro i mlado* 'young and old', *malko i goljamo* 'young and old'.

(c) substantivizations denoting meals, courses, medicines, i.e. with ellipsis of R. *kušan'e* 'dish, food', *bljudo* 'course', *lekarstvo* 'medicine'/Bg. *jastie* 'dish', *jadene* 'eating, meal, food', *lekarstvo* 'medicine'

3.5 Classification of Conversion   117

> (83)   R. *sladkoe* 'dessert', *moroženoe* 'ice-(cream)', *pervoe* 'first
>   (course)', *vtoroe* 'second (course)', *tret'e* 'third (course)',
>   *snotvornoe* 'soporific', *slabitel'noe* 'purgative';
>   Bg. *părvo* 'first (course)', *vtoro* 'second (course)', *treto* 'third
>   (course)', *sănotvorno* 'soporific', *slabitelno* 'purgative'.

(d) substantivizations denoting plants and animals, i.e. with ellipsis of
    R. *rastenie* 'plant', *životnoe* 'animal'/Bg. *rastenie* 'plant', *životno* 'animal'.
    The substantivized adjective means the singular of 'plant' or 'animal', but
    its plural form remains for 'class of plants/animals'

> (84)   R. *bobovoe* 'bean (plant)', PL *bobovye*; *xobotnoe* 'proboscis
>   (animal)', PL *xobotnye*; *rakoobraznoe* 'crustaceous (animal)', PL
>   *rakoobraznye*;
>   Bg. *bobovo* 'bean (plant)', PL *bobovi*, *xobotno* 'proboscis (animal)', PL
>   *xobotni*, *rakoobrazno* 'crustaceous (animal)', PL *rakoobrazni*, *malko*
>   'young (of an animal)'

Cf. SC. *mlado* 'young (of an animal)')

(e) substantivizations denoting institutions, i.e with ellipsis of Bg. *upravlenie*
    'office, administration'

> (85)   Bg. *danăčno* 'tax (office)', *graždansko* 'registry (office)'.

3.5.3.1.2.2d → Pluralia Tantum

Such substantivizations are used for different types of payments, i.e. with
ellipsis of R. *den'gi* 'money'/Bg. *pari* 'money' and *nadbavki* 'allowance'

> (86)   R. *sutočnye* 'daily allowance', *naličnye* (slang) 'cash', *otpusknye*
>   'holiday (pay)', *komandirovočnye* 'travelling allowance',
>   *premial'nye* 'bonus'
>   Bg. *komandirovăčni* 'travelling allowance', *premialni* 'bonus',
>   *detski* 'child (benefit)'

The Russian Academy Grammar (Švedova et al. 1980: 241) classifies substantivizations which are outside the above-mentioned semantic patterns as 'elliptic substantivizations' (cf. Vogel 1995: 251). Examples include unique events such as R. *graždanskaja* 'a civil (war)', *Otečestvenaja* 'The patriotic (War)'; Bg. *Otečestvenata* 'The Patriotic (War)', *Vtorata svetovna* 'The Second World (War)', *Osvoboditelnata* '(The War) of Liberation'; or substantivizations with diverse semantics: R. *skoryj (poezd)* 'fast/through (train)', *uglovoj (udar)* 'corner-(kick)', *kontrol'naja (rabota)* 'control (work), test', *beloe (vino)* 'white (wine)' etc. (in Bunlgarian, *ăglov (udar)*, *kontrolna (rabota)*). It seems that the difference between these examples and the above true substantivizations is in the degree of lexicalization, i.e. these examples are less lexicalized. Cases of substantivization which are not fully lexicalized either tend toward anaphoric usage (thus anaphoric substantivization) or require a relevant context (an intermediate level between anaphoric usage and true substantivization) and thus evidence the continuum of substantivizations.

3.5.3.1.2.3 False Substanivization

The term 'false substantivization' is borrowed from Rojzenzon (1962: 123) via Vogel (1996: 36). In this book, false substantivization ('full substantivization' in Galkina-Fëdoruk et al. 1957: 281) is understood as a diachronic process involving a non-reversible change of an adjective into a noun. False substantivization shows two stages: (1) an intermediate stage between true and false substantivization; and (2) false substantivization proper. Both stages are illustrated with examples from Bulgarian and Russian below:

(1) The substantivized adjective has a unique usage and combines with a single noun only, ie. no other combinations with nouns exist:

    (87)   ADJ + N → *ADJ → N
    (88)   R. *(imja) suščestvitel'noe* 'noun', *(imja) prilagatel'noe* 'adjective', *(imja) čislitel'noe*[14] 'numeral'.
              Bg. *săštestvitelno (ime)* 'noun', *prilagatelno (ime)* 'adjective', *čislitelno (ime)* 'numeral'.

(2) The adjective existed as such only in an older period of the diachronic development of the language, ie. there is no such adjective synchronically

    (89)   *[ADJ + N] → *ADJ → N
    (90)   R. *portnoj* 'tailor'
              Bg. *vodoraslo*[15] 'see-weed', *životno* 'animal'.

Sometimes false substantivizations may have some of the typical properties of nouns. For example, false substantivizations can have feminine counterparts: R. MASC *portnoj*, GEN SG *portnogo* (adjectival inflection) → FEM *portnixa*

---

[14]For Galkina-Fëdoruk et al. (1957: 281) nouns such as *čislitel'noe* 'numeral' are translated from Latin by analogy with substantivized adjectives.

[15]*raslo* 'grown-NEUT' is a participle (*vod-* is from *vod-a* 'water', and *-o-* is a linking vowel).

(cf. MASC *vrač* 'physician' → FEM *vračixa*), GEN SG *portnixi* (with nominal inflection); or false substantivizations can function as bases for derivation of adjectives, e.g.: R. *portnoj* 'tailor' → ADJ *portnovskij*.

It should be stressed that although substantivization in Bulgartian and substantivization in Russian have much in common, it is possible that the same substantivized adjective exemplifies true substantivization in Russian but false substantivization in Bulgarian, e.g.: Bg. *životno* 'animal' (can be used neither with a nominal head nor as an adjective), PL *životni* (with adjectival inflection) → ADJ *životin-ski* 'animal-' (with the derivational suffix *-ski*) versus R. *životnoe* 'animal', GEN SG *životnogo* (a true substantivization with adjectival inflection *-ogo*) which still exists as an adjective in modern Russian. Thus, R. *životnyj myr* ' animal world' but Bg. *životinski svjat* 'animal world'.

3.5.3.2 Adjectivization

Adjectivization is another type of syntactic conversion. Since a syntactic conversion as that of *government* in E. *government job* (Marchand 1969: 360) is impossible in Slavic, Slavic sources interpret adjectivization as usage of participles as adjectives (Barić et al. 1997: 301; Bojadžiev 1999: 274, cf. also Dokulil 1968a: 231; Švedova et al. 1980: 666 speak of adjective meaning of participles instead of adjectivization of participles). Examples include: Bg. *pišešt*-MASC-SG *čovek*-MASC 'writing-PRES ACT PART man', R. *postroennyj*-MASC-SG-NOM *dom*-MASC-NOM 'built-PAST PASS PART house', SC. *osvežavajuća*-NEUT-PL-NOM *pića*-NEUT-PL-NOM 'refreshing-PRES ACT PART drinks' (the types of participles in Bulgarian, Russian and Serbo-Croatian are listed in Chapter 1, Table 1.4). As can be seen from these examples, participles, like adjectives, inflect for gender, number and case, taking adjectival inflection. Thus, when participles are used as adjectives, no paradigmatic change takes place. Therefore, we speak of syntactic conversion.

Note that the use of participles is language-specific. For example, the Bulgarian and the Russian translations of the above example from Serbo-Croatian *osvežavajuća pića* both use adjectives: Bg. *osvežitelni napitki* 'refreshing-ADJ drinks'; R. *proxladitel'nyj napitok* 'refreshing-ADJ drink'.

As in substantivization, there exist cases of false adjectivization. For example, in modern Bulgarian, all Old Bulgarian present passive participles such as *ljubim* '(be)loved', *mislim* 'sth that can be thought', etc. are adjectives. The second group of old participles completely turned into adjectives includes the Old Bulgarian present active participles. Consider the adjectives *gorešt* 'hot', *vonešt* 'stinking' (former participles) vs. the present-day participles *gorjašt* 'burning', *vonjašt* 'stinking'. Participles borrowed from Russian such as *vedušt* 'leading', *cvetušt* 'flourishing' (R. *veduščij, cvetuščij* both participles) are also adjectives in modern Bulgarian, cf. the participles *vodešt* 'leading' and *căvtjašt* 'flourishing'.

Russian, on the other hand, has developed an interesting strategy for distinguishing between participles and adjectives (cf. Dilevski 1985: 226f; Harrison and le Fleming 2000: 130f; Wade 2000: 384f). Russian past passive participles, like adjectives, distinguish between long and short forms and in both instances differ from the respective adjectives morphotactically. Consider:

(1) Long forms

> (91) Participle   Adjective
> -nn-   -n-
> ranennyj 'injured'   ranenyj
> za-žarennyj 'fried'   žarenyj
> za-morožennyj 'frosted' moroženyj

(2) Short forms
   Now the spelling is reversed, i.e. participles have one -n-, whereas adjectives retain the double -nn- in the FEM, NEUT and PL, as in the following examples:

> MASC, FEM, NEUT, PL
> (92) Participle: *obrazovan, obrazovana, obrazovano, obrazovany* 'formed'
> Adjective: *obrazovan, obrazovanna, obrazovanno, obrazovanny* 'educated'
>
> Participle: *ozaboěen, ozaboěena, ozaboěeno, ozaboěeny* 'worried'
> Adjective: *ozaboěen, ozabiěenna, ozaboěenno, ozaboěenny* 'anxious'
>
> Participle: *rassejan, rassejana, rassejano, raassejany* 'dispersed'
> Adjective: *rassejan, rassejanna, rassejanno, rassejanny* 'absent-minded'

In Russian, the difference between some present active participles and their respective adjectives is also morphotactically expressed (cf. Dilevski 1985):

> (93) Participle   Adjective
> -šč-   -č-
> koljuščij 'pricking'   koljučij 'prickly, thorny'
> letjaščij 'flying'   letučij 'flying'
> sidjaščij 'sitting'   sidjačij 'sitting'
> stojaščij 'standing'   stojačij 'standing'

Consider: R. *gorjačij vozdux* 'hot-ADJ air' and R. *gorjaščij gaz* 'burning-PRES ACT PART gas' (likewise in Bg. *gorešt văzdux* 'hot air' and *gorjašt gaz* 'burning gas').

Note that the two above-discussed rules are not absolute and hold only for a restricted number of past passive and present active participles and their respective adjectives.

Babić (1991: 47) gives two examples from Serbo-Croatian that appear similar to the above-discussed Russian participle-adjective pairs: PART *svijétlēći* 'shining' vs. ADJ *svjètlēćī*, PART *slijédēći* 'following' vs. ADJ *sljèdēćī*.

Participles which differ morphotactically from adjectives do not represent syntactic conversion, since the base and the output of the rule have different forms. In fact, such examples show a tendency towards avoiding the non-iconic conversion.

3.6 Conclusion

On the derivational-inflectional continuum, morphological conversion starts with prototypical derivation (i.e. word-class-changing conversion), continues with non-prototypical derivation (i.e. word-class-preserving conversion) and non-prototypical inflection (i.e. formal conversion), and finally is reduced to syntax, where syntactic conversion (substantivization, adjectivization) takes place.

While prototypical and non-prototypical conversion involve different paradigms and a semantic change corresponding to a derivational process, formal conversion means a paradigmatic change only. Both conversion in derivation and conversion in inflection often compete with the more diagrammatic techniques of addition, substitution and modification, which supports the correctness of the assumption of formal conversion in inflection. The more diagrammatic affixations (including addition and substitution) and modification, as expected, win over conversion, the latter being usually stylistically marked as either dialectal or archaic.

On the derivation-inflection continuum, after non-prototypical inflection prototypical inflection comes, homophonous forms of the latter representing however, syncretism. Syntactic conversion is to some extent similar to syncretism of prototypical inflection, since it also consists in coincidence of forms which can be differentiated only on the basis of their syntactic roles, but the input and output of syntactic conversion, though sharing the same inflectional paradigm, stand for different word-classes. Syntactic conversion is best described in terms of a scale beginning with false substantivization (i.e. nouns with adjectival inflection and without corresponding adjectives) which is between morphology and syntax; after false substantivization comes real substantivization, and then anaphoric substantivization. At the end of the syntactic conversion cline are metalinguistic substantivizations and substantivizations of infinitives which are pure syntactic changes.

Table 3.2 is a survey of all type of conversion found in Bulgarian, Russian and Serbo-Croatian.

Table 3.2 Types of conversion and their distribution in Bg., R. & SC

Conversion	Word-class-changing		Word-class-preserving		Formal conversion		Syntactic conversion	
Word-based								
1a. ADJ > N		SC.	12. N > N (diminutives)	Bg.	15. Gender	Bg. R. SC	17. metalinguistic usage > N	Bg. R. SC
1b. non-basic forms ADJ > N		Bg. R. SC						
2. N > V		Bg. R. SC					18. INF > N	R. SC.
3. ADJ > V		Bg. SC					19. ADJ > N	Bg. R.
4. N > ADJ		SC.					20. PART > ADJ	Bg. R. SC.
Stem-based								
5. V > N		Bg. R. SC	13. N > N science > scientist	R.				
6. N > V		Bg.						
Root-based								
7. V > N		Bg. R. SC	14. N > N science > scientist	R.	16. Aspect	Bg. R. SC.		
8. N > V		Bg. R. SC						
9. ADJ > V		R.						
10. N > ADJ		Bg. SC.						
11. V > ADJ		R.						

3.6 Conclusion

The most frequent and also productive types of morphological conversion in Bulgarian, Russian and Serbo-Croatian involve verb-to-noun and noun-to-verb changes, being predominantly root-based. In other words, the two polar and most important word classes easily convert into each other. This can be understood as a tendency for conversion to prefer morphologically different to morphologically similar input and output forms, which explains the rareness of word-class preserving and formal conversion.

Prototypical conversion means (1) word-class change that implies: (2) a semantic change; (3) a paradigmatic change and (4) a syntactic change. These features constitute a scale, and the first condition is the strongest one, the second less strong than the first but still stronger than the third and the fourth, etc. (1) defines prototypical conversion; (2) defines non-prototypical conversion; (3) is the definition of formal conversion; and if only (4) holds, we speak of syntactic conversion.

Chapter 4
Subtraction

This chapter is organized as follows: the first Section 4.1 is devoted to terminological matters and the definition of subtraction. Section 4.2 tackles subtraction-like shortenings that cannot be described in terms of morphological rules and therefore do not represent subtraction. The latter is set apart from phonological shortening, backformation, haplology, hypocoristics, clippings, blends, acronyms, subtraction of semantics, zero sign and truncation. Section 4.3 analyzes subtraction in relation to rule inversion. Section 4.4 deals with the classification of subtraction. It is shown that subtraction operates in derivation and in inflection and that subtraction in derivation can be word-class-changing and word-class preserving. Derivational and inflectional subtraction may exhibit additional phonological and morphonological modifications. The last Section 4.5 gives a brief summary of the chapter and draws conclusions.

4.1 Terminology and Definition

American structuralists are among the first who point out a linguistic element the deletion of which expresses some difference in meaning: Bloomfield (1933: 217) speaks of 'minus feature'; 'Harris (1957: 240 [1942: 170 f.]) calls it 'minus morpheme'; Hockett (1957: 110 [1947: 340]) names the deleted material 'subtraction morph'; and in Nida (1949: 75) it is a 'subtractive morpheme'. In the literature, the rule of subtraction can also be found under 'deletion', 'truncation', 'minus formation', and 'disfixation', the latter term coined on the analogy of prefixation and suffixation (Hardy and Montler 1988: 378). The most recent terminological proposal in regard to subtraction is made by Mel'čuk (cf. Mel'čuk 1991) who, with the broader term 'subtractive sign', attempts to generalize the concept and in accordance with the binary nature of linguistic signs, defines two types of subtraction: subtraction of form and subtraction of meaning. Mel'čuk's proposal is discussed in detail in Section 4.2.8 below.

As mentioned in Chapter 1, Slavic morphology does not have a special term for the categorization of subtraction as conceived in this study. Yet in some contexts, Bg. *săkraštenie* 'shortening' (cf. Bojadžiev 1999: 254f) and R. *usečenie* 'shortening (literally cutting)' (cf. Švedova et al. 1980: 421ff) could be seen as synonymous to subtraction. For the sake of precision, however, it should be stressed that both terms are hyperonyms of truncation, substitution, conversion and subtraction.

As for the nature of subtraction, the rule consists in shortening the shape of the word and can take place in derivation as well as in inflection. Prototypical subtraction deletes the final phoneme at the right edge of the base of a morphological process and is the only overt signal of the addition of some morphosemantics (cf. Dressler 2000b: 582). An exact analysis of the examples of subtraction available in the morphological theory, however, shows that there are two types of deletion of final phonemes that have been claimed to be (prototypical) subtraction: (i) deletion of single but different phonemes and (ii) deletion of the same phoneme.

The first examples of subtraction in the literature involve deletion of different phonemes (Bloomfield 1933 and Nida 1949), as in the following adjectives from French:

(1) | FEM | → | MASC | |
| --- | --- | --- | --- |
| /blãš/ | | /blã/ | 'white' |
| /grãd/ | | /grã/ | 'great, large' |
| /lõg/ | | /lõ/ | 'long' |
| /gros/ | | /gro/ | 'thick' |
| /žãtij/ | | /žãti/ | 'good' |

Bloomfield (1933: 217) and then Nida (1949: 75), following Bloomfield, consider these examples subtractive morphology, i.e. they both write that the shorter masculine forms are (presumably) derived from the longer feminine ones by a subtractive rule. Note, however, that Nida doubts the above direction of derivation and explicitly mentions that it might be incorrect. Indeed, according to the analyses in Kaye and Morin (1978) and Mel'čuk (1991), the masculine forms are the bases whereas the irregular feminine forms are suppletive and rote-learned. Moreover, Stonham (1994: 65), in view of examples such as Fr. *un bon homme* /œbɔnɔm/, concludes that what is involved here is a morphology of combination which has been complicated by the phonological rules of the system and not by subtractive morphology. Thus it has been shown that the direction of the above derivations is from MASC → FEM (as is usual for the derivation of feminine adjectives) and not as assumed by Bloomfield[1]

---

[1] Note that Bloomfield himself offers two solutions: (i) consider the masculine form as basic and assume addition of a consonant in each feminine form; or (ii) consider the feminine form as basic and derive the masculine form by the means of a minus-feature (i.e. subtractive morphology).

4.1 Terminology and Definition

and Nida. In (1), the disregard of markedness has led to the false postulation of subtraction.

Another subtraction-like example from the literature where deletion of different final phonemes takes place is the formation of perfective aspect in Papago. (Papago is a Uto-Aztecan language, spoken in Arizona and Northern Sonora, the examples below are based on Anderson 1992 and Stonham 1994).

(2) IMPFV SG → PFV SG
him 'walk'   *hi:*
hikčk 'cut'   *hikč*
gatwid 'shoot'   *gatwi*

The same relation is claimed to hold for the derivation of the plural perfectives as well:

(3) IMPFV PL → PFV PL
hihim 'walk'   *hihi*
hihikčk 'cut'   *hihikč*
gagtwid 'shoot'   *gagtwi*

For these examples, Stonham (1994: 69ff) has shown that the subtractive analysis is wrong, since there are derivations in Papago which use bases shorter than the perfective stem. Stonham, based on Zapeda (1983) and Saxton and Saxton (1969) writes that from the above cited *hikčk* 'to cut' one can derive:

(4) *hi:k* 'to clip'
hikiwoni 'to cut jaggedly'
hikčkakud 'saw'
hikşan 'to trim'
hi: 'cut hair, cut grass'

As can be seen from these examples, in Papago it is possible to derive forms on bases shorter than that of the perfective, which is evidence that the perfective is not built by subtraction. Following Stonham (1994: 73), we will conclude that the perfective form is closer to the basic and the imperfective forms are derived by addition of one of a set of suffixes. In the terminology of this book, imperfectives are derived by either addition or modification (the case of *hi:* in (2)) from their respective perfectives. Note that if we agree with Anderson (1992) that in Papago the imperfective is the base for the formation of the perfective, we will again neglect the logic of morphosematic markedness according to which imperfective aspect forms should be derived from perfective ones (at least it seems to be the usual case cross-linguistically) and not vice versa (cf. PFV → IMPFV2 formation in Slavic; E. *cut* and *is cutting*, etc.).

In the next examples of plural formation from the German Hessian dialect, classified as subtraction by many authors (cf. Dressler 2000b), the rule again deletes different final phonemes. Consider:

(5) SG → PL
    [hon̥d̥]   [hon]   'dog'
    [ʃʊk]   [ʃʊ]   'shoe'
    [d̥ɔːg̥]   [d̥ɔː]   'day'

In these examples, the rule seems to be more subtractive-like than in the case of the French adjectives (1), as now markedness holds and plural is expected to be derived from singular. Yet the Hessian short plurals have also received an alterative non-subtractive analysis in the literature. Golston and Wiese (1996) and Holsinger and Houseman (1999) demonstrate that the deletion of final consonants in some Hessian plurals is phonologically determined and affects only stems terminating either in the consonant clusters /ld/, /nd/, /ŋg/ and /rg/ or in the combination /Vg/ (the final [k] in 'shoe' (cf. (5)) being etymologically [g] (Golston and Wiese 1995: 147)). In cases of other stem terminations, the plural is expressed by addition of a suffix (be it overt or zero). Thus since the shortening is phonologically restricted, we cannot postulate a morphological rule such as that of subtraction (cf. the subtractive rule in Section 4.4.2.1 below).

To sum up, it seems that if a formal rule deletes different final phonemes, it is most probably non-subtractive.

Let us look now at instances where subtraction deletes one and the same final phoneme, as in the following examples from French:

(6) *photographie*/fotografi/ → *photographe*/fotograf/
    cartographie/kartografi/ → *cartographe*/kartograf/
    psychologie/psikoloʒi/ → *psychologue*/psikolog/
    ethnographie/ɛtnografi/ → *ethnographe*/ɛtnograf/

In these examples, the final /-i/ from the base 'X' is subtracted and the derivatives denoting 'somebody who deals professionally with X' are semantically dependent from the base.

What is crucial now is the fact (noted by Manova 2005b) that examples with deletion of the same final phoneme (as the above ones in 6) have not received non-subtractive analyses (whereas, as we could see, all instances of subtraction of different final segments, in addition to the interpretations in favour of subtraction, can been analysed as non-subtractive). This fact supports the postulation of a set of morphological techniques in which the definition of

4.1 Terminology and Definition 129

subtraction is analogous to that of affixation. Thus a subtractive rule, similar to an affixation rule with a particular suffix, is expected to delete one and the same final phoneme. This observation on the nature of subtraction is further supported by subtraction-like shortenings affecting forms longer than a phoneme, as can be seen from the following examples from Samoan (a Polynesian language, the examples are based on Bloomfield 1933: 219):

(7) ACT   PASS
    tao   ←   *taomia* 'cover'
    sao   ←   *saofia* 'collect'
    folo   ←   *fologia* 'swallow'

As for these examples, it is first unclear whether the assumed direction of derivation is correct, since cross-linguistically the active is the base for the derivation of the passive and not vice versa. Here, as in (1), (2) and (3), the subtractive analysis neglects markedness (for evidence that the longer forms are derived from the shorter ones see Krupa 1966). Note that Nida (1949) suggests as another possible analysis of those examples the postulation of an additive suffix *-ia* marking the passive). Moreover, in Samoan no word ends in a consonant, thus even if one assumes that the passive is basic, the shortening should, nevertheless, be phonological (cf. Nida 1949: 76; Hale 1973: 413–20).

To sum up, if a rule deletes different formal segments and neglects the markedness of the categories involved in the derivation, that rule is not subtractive. The same holds for instances where markedness is considered but the rule shortens different segments that cannot be seen as allomorphs.

What also should be taken into consideration for the definition of subtraction is the interaction of inflection when derivational morphotactic form is deleted. The assumption made in Chapter 1 that all derivational processes allow addition and deletion of inflectional material, since the later is irrelevant for the classification of a derivational change, holds for subtraction as well. Thus derivational subtraction is a shortening of the derivational base of the word and can be accompanied by inflectional alternations. For example: Bg. N *kót-k-a* 'cat' → N *kót-e* 'kitten' is an example of stem-based subtraction in derivation, as the subtraction of the stem-final *-k-* takes plays in the derivational slot of the noun *kotka*, whereas in the inflectional slot, the inflection *-e* substitutes the inflection suffix *-a* (i.e. N *kót-k-a* → N *kót-o-e*). Subtraction in derivation can be word-class-changing and word-class-preserving, of both word-class-changing subtraction being more prototypical (recall that the prototype of a morphological technique in derivation is word-class-changing, word-based, and without modifications).

Like the more iconic morphological techniques of addition and substitution, the subtraction of morphotactic form can give rise to phonological and morphonological modifications (see Section 2.2), and the presence of modification is another criterion for the establishing of non-prototypicality. That is, modified occurrences of subtraction are less prototypical than unmodified ones. Put differently, the above-cited Bg. N *kót-k-a* 'cat' → N *kót-e* 'kitten' is a non-prototypical subtraction, because the input and the output belong to the same word class. However, Bg. N *méč-k-a* 'bear'→ N *meč-é* 'teddy-bear' where also no word-class change takes place, is even less prototypical than *kót-k-a* 'cat' → *kót-e* 'kitten', because in the output form *mečé* a concomitant prosodic modification (a stress change) occurs. On the other hand, due to the more iconic character of the morphological technique of modification in comparison to subtraction, the relation between prototypicality and iconicity is reversed in subtraction, i.e. less prototypical subtractions, since modified, are less anti-iconic than subtractions without modifications where the morphosemantic change is signalled by shortening only. Thus, Bg. N *pát-k-a* 'duck' → ADJ *páč-i* 'duck (attr.)', since involving the additional feature of modification, is less anti-iconic and more transparent than Bg. N *méč-k-a* 'bear' → ADJ *méč-i* 'bear (attr.)'.

In the discussion below, the following criteria are taken into consideration for the classification of subtraction: (1) word-class change (for subtraction in derivation); (2) type of the base (whether word, stem or root; word-based morphology being the most natural); and (3) $+/-$ modification. In other words, we expect prototypical subtraction, which is word-based, unmodified and in WF word-class-changing, around which all other less prototypical instances to be clustered. However, since prototypical subtraction is the most unnatural type of a morphological change, it should, according to the principles of NM, be extremely rare.

Since the output of a subtraction is shorter than its input, the question about the direction of subtraction rules arises. In doubtful cases, the criteria assumed for establishing the direction of conversion (Section 3.4) will be applied to subtraction as well. In the discussion below, if a subtractive rule appears to have a problematic direction, the latter will always be explicitly motivated.

4.2 Delimiting Subtraction

As we saw in the previous section, not every shortening of form is subtraction. Furthermore, there are shortenings yielded by non-morphological causes such as articulatory restrictions or change of discourse. The non-morphological character of such shortenings makes it impossible to define them in terms of morphological rules. Therefore the ambition of the present section is to establish all non-morphological shortenings and to motivate their setting apart from the morphological technique of subtraction. Generally, we will distinguish the following types of non-subtractive shortening changes: phonological shortening, backformation, haplology, hypocoristic formation, clipping, blends, acronyms, zero sign and truncation (all discussed in detail below).

4.2 Delimiting Subtraction

4.2.1 Phonological Shortening

As we could see in the previous section, phonological shortenings have often been confused with subtraction. For that reason, now we will concentrate on the specifics of phonological shortenings. What distinguishes subtraction from phonological shortening is the fact that phonological rules are governed by phonological restrictions such as difficulty or impossibility to pronounce some combination of sounds and thus phonological rules have no exceptions. Moreover, subtraction-like phonological rules usually shorten different morphotactic segments, which, as already discussed, is not typical for morphological changes. For example in the instances below, the deletion of the root-final *d* ant *t* in the aorist past active participle in Bulgarian, the past active participle in Serbo-Croatian, and in the past tense in Russian resembles subtraction very much, but the rule is phonological.

In Bulgarian, the shortening affects I conjugation verbs with *-ox* aorist (named after the 1 SG AOR inflection) and roots terminating in *-t/-d*:

(8) PRESENT   AORIST   PAST ACT PATR
    doved-a 'I fetch', *doved-e*   *doved-o-x*   *dovel, dovela, dovelo*
    (pro)čet-a 'I read out', *(pro)čet-e*   *(pro)čet-o-x*   *(pro)čel, čela, čelo*

This deletion entirely depends on the position of the *tl/dl* consonant cluster in the word form and works only in word-final position. Since *tl/dl* is difficult to pronounce word-finally, the above shortening is exceptionless. Compare with instances where *t* and *d* are part of the root, without being word-final: Bg. FEM SG *bod-l-a* 'thorn', PL *bodli* (← V *boda* 'I prick', *bodox, bol*) and FEM SG *met-l-a* 'broom', PL *metli* (← V *meta* 'I sweep', *metox, mel*), etc.

Note that although *tla/tlo/tli* and *dla/dlo/dli* are quite normal, the forms of the past active participle that are expected to include these segments require *t/d* shortening, i.e. *čel*-MASC, *čela*-FEM/*čelo*-NEUT/*čeli*-PL instead of **četla*-FEM/**četlo*-NEUT/**četli*-PL. Thus this shortening is evidence for the organization of the inflectional paradigm (cf. Stump 2001), in our case it speaks for a block of rules deriving the forms for MASC, FEM, NEUT and PL of the past active participle, i.e. the forms *čela/o/i* can be derived only by a sequence of rules such as those in (9):

(9)   *čet-* → **četl* → *čel* → *čela/o/i*

And not by rules such as those in (10):

(10)   *čet-* →**četl* → *čel*
       čet- → **četla*
       čet- →**četlo*
       čet- →**četli*

Put differently, within the paradigm of the verb *četa*, there is a special block of rules for the derivation of the forms of the past active participle. These rules use a base of their own – the MASC SG *čel*, which means that in the paradigm of the verb *četa* there exists no single base in terms of a syntactically unspecified lexeme or stem (something like *čet-*) or an underlying form from which to derive all possible forms of the verb *četa*.

As already mentioned, in Bulgarian the rule does not delete the root-final *t/d* in the past active participles of verbs that do not belong to conjugation I (TM -*e*-); *tl* and *dl* are not word-final in such forms (11). Note that if the rule were morphological (i.e. a case of subtraction and not a phonological shortening), the non-deletion of *t/d* in conjugation II verbs (TM -*i*-) would be quite strange. Consider the following examples of past active participles of second conjugation verbs with roots in *t/d*:

(11) PRESENT   AORIST   PAST ACT PATR
      grad-j-a 'I build', *grad-i*   *grad-i-x*   *gradi-l, -a, -o*
      rabot-j-a 'I work', *rabot-i*   *rabot-i-x*   *raboti-l, -a, -o*
      let-j-a 'I fly', *let-i*   *let-ja-x*   *letja-l, -a, -o*

These examples undoubtedly show that the past active participle is formed through the addition of the suffix -*l* and not through the deletion of the root-final consonant of the verb.

For the sake of completeness, some parallel examples with shortening of the root-final *t* and *d* from Russian and Serbo-Croatian:

(12a) INF   PRES ROOT   PAST TENSE/PAST ACT PART
      R. *ves-ti* 'to conduct'   *ved-*   *vël, vëla, vëlo*
      R. *ples-ti* 'to braid'   *plet-*   *plël, plëla, plëlo*
      SC. *kras-ti* 'to rob'   *krad-*   *krao, krala, kralo*
      SC. *ples-ti* 'to knit'   *plet-*   *pleo, plela, plelo*

Thus, a precise analysis of the above rule of shortening defines it as addition: the rule produces inflection forms (past active participles) by the addition of the participle suffix -*l* in the inflectional slot of the verb, and the shortening of the root-final *t* and *d* that occurs in a few verbs is due to difficulties with the articulation of *tl/dl* clusters in word-final position. These facts determine the deletion of *t* and *d* as phonological and distinguish it from morphological subtraction.

Note that the above shortening cannot be defined as affecting athematic verbs (such as those in (12a)) only. First, there is no infinitiv in modern Bulgarian and all verbs are seen as thematic, and second, the Russian athematic verbs (those with infinitives in -*ti*) whose roots do not terminate in *t/d*, i.e. the

4.2 Delimiting Subtraction   133

majority of the Russian athematic verbs, are characterized by another peculiarity, namely they do not exhibit the past marker -*l* in their masculine past tense forms. Consider:

(12b)	*gresti*	*vezti*	*nesti*	*rasti*
	'to row'	'to convey'	'to carry'	'to grow'
MASC	*grèb*	*vèz*	*nès*	*ros*
FEM	*grebla*	*vezla*	*nesla*	*rosla*
NEUT	*greblo*	*vezlo*	*neslo*	*roslo*
PL	*grebli*	*vezli*	*nesli*	*rosli*

In these examples, in contrast to (12a), no shortening of the verb roots takes place but the past tense is zero marked in *grèb, vèz, nès* and *ros*, i.e. this is a case of a zero sign. On zero sign see Section 4.2.9.

4.2.2 Backformation

Although both backformation and subtraction can take place in derivation as well as in inflection, backformation is a diachronic rule (Marchand 1969: 391; Aronoff 1976: 27; Quirk et al. 1985: 1522; Dressler 2000b: 583), whereas for the establishing of the rule of subtraction no diachronic evidence is needed. Consider the classical example of backformation in derivation E. N *editor* → V *edit*, coined by analogy with pairs such as V *exhibit* → N *exhibitor*. If we did not know that the verb *edit* appeared in written texts much later than the noun *editor*, there would be no chance to determine the right direction of this derivation. Moreover, the semantic criterion speaks in favour of a verb-to-noun derivation, as *to edit* does not only mean 'to work as an editor', but also 'to prepare a book, piece of film, etc. for printing or broadcasting by deciding what to include and making sure there are no mistakes' (*Longman Dictionary of Contemporary English* 1995).

Backformation in inflection can be exemplified with the derivation E. *cherry* ← *cherries*. Here again only diachronic information can establish the correct direction and thus the rule of backformation: the French word for 'cherry' is *cerise*, whose medieval Normand variant was originally borrowed into English with the final /z/; this was, however, perceived as a plural marker in English, and *cherry* was created by backformation (Bauer 1988: 238).

Some linguists such as Bauer (1988) understand backformation as a synchronic rule as well, since the element deleted by backformation is or seems like a morph that exists elsewhere in the language (Bauer 1988: 33). According to Bauer, backformation can be used to produce new lexemes, and if the back-formed word is unfamiliar, then the process is noticeable. Bauer exemplifies synchronic backformation with the derivation E. *a spider* → *to spide*, as in

'*Little spider, spiding sadly...*'. However, we cannot agree that that shortening is a salient case of backformation. The derivation N *spider* → V *spide, spiding* is an occasional formation and for us it is not enough evidence for the postulation of a synchronic rule of backformation. We will consider backformation a diachronic change, since the establishing of its direction always requires some diachronic information (this even in cases of more recent formations), i.e. backformation is difficult to predict morphosemantically as synchronically the rule looks like addition (cf. the above cited *to edit* and *cherry*). Moreover, the rule of backformation seems to be word-class-sensitive, and the great majority of backformation in English are verbs (87 per cent), a fact stressed by Pennanen (1975: 217) and Bauer (1983: 230). It is unnecessary to say that such specialization is not typical for a morphological technique.

Since a diachronic rule is always unproductive, 'a frequently occurring type of back-formation may eventually develop into a subtractive rule' (Dressler 2000b: 583). For example in Polish, diminutives with the suffix -*k*-, such as *wódka* 'vodka' (lit. 'little water') from *woda* 'water' gave rise to backformations of the type *wóda* 'much/bad vodka'. In Slavic languages, nouns with stems terminating in -*k*- are usually diminutives derived by the addition of the suffix -*k*, but in Polish, such nouns have lost their diminutive semantics and now express unmarked (neutral) meanings, whereas their bases without -*k*- are felt as augmentatives. Thus synchronically, -*k*- can be deleted from any nominal stem terminating in this consonant, the result being an augmentative noun meaning either 'increasing quantity' or 'bad quantity', i.e. the more marked form semantically appears formed via deletion of morphological material, which is subtraction. The productive character of the subtraction of the stem-final -*k*- distinguishes it from backformation, which, since a diachronic change, cannot be productive.

4.2.3 *Haplology*

Haplology is the deletion of one of two identical phonological sequences. For example:

(13a) E. *sorcer-er* → *sorcer-ess*, instead of *sorcer-er-ess

Its German equivalent being:

(13b) G. *Zauber-er* → *Zauber-in*, instead of *Zauber-er-in
(13c) Cf. G. *Lehrer* teacher' → *Lehrerin*

As can be seen from these examples, haplology is a kind of a phonological process that accompanies the addition of morphotactic material. Therefore, one has to set haplology apart from the morphological rule of subtraction.

4.2 Delimiting Subtraction

As can be expected on the basis of the assumption of a prototype organization of morphological changes, the rule of haplology exhibits some variations. While in (13a) and (13b) the material causing the haplological shortening is not morphologically identical with the termination of the input, Dutch and Russian suggests instances of haplology resulting from the addition of form identical with the termination of the input item.

Dutch (Booij 2002: 185):

(14)   *kers* 'cherry' → *kers-elaar* 'cherry tree'
       pruim 'plum' → *pruim-elaar* 'plum tree'

However:

(15)   *appel* 'apple' → *appel-aar* 'apple tree'
       mispel 'medlar' → *mispel-aar* 'medlar tree'

Similar examples from Russian are:

(16a) *Tomsk* → *tomsk-ij* 'of Tomsk', not **tomskskij*

vs.

(16b) *Peterburg* → *Peterburg-skij* 'of Petersburg'

(17a) *rozov-yj* 'pink' → *rozov-atyj* 'pinkish'

vs.

(17b) *krasn-yj* 'red' → *krasn-ovatyj* 'reddish'.

Since the output of these derivations is a result of addition, in the Russian linguistics the term 'interference of morphemes' (Zemskaja 1973: 149–56) is used instead of haplology.

In Bulgarian, PFV verbs with stems terminating in *-uv-a-* represent an interesting case of blocking due to haplology. Although in Bulgarian (in contrast to all other Slavic languages) imperfectivization is generalized and nearly every PFV verb has an IMPFV2 mate, PFV verbs with *-uv-a-* fail to form secondary imperfectives. This peculiarity of the verb inflection can be explained only with the fact that the formation of IMPFV2 verbs requires the addition of the imperfectivizing suffix *-Vv-a-* (*V* stands for a vowel, *-a-* is the TM), as in (18), that is already presented in the base, as in (19a) and (19b).

(18)   IMPFV *kup-j-a* 'I buy', 3 SG *kup-i* →
       PFV *izkup-j-a* 'I buy back', 3 SG *izkup-i* →
       IMPFV2 *izkup-uv-a-m*, *izkup-uv-a*

(19a) IMPFV *păt-uv-a-m* 'I travel', 3 SG *păt-uv-a*→
PFV *propăt-uv-a-m* 'I travel all over', 3 SG *propăt-uv-a*→
IMPF2 Ø
(19b) IMPFV *săštestv-uv-a-m* 'I exist', 3 SG *săštestv-uv-a* →
PFV *prosăštestv-uv-a-m* 'survive', *prosăštestv-uv-a* →
IMPFV2 Ø

Verbs without IMPFV2 forms are formed from nouns with the addition of the unproductive imperfective (inflectional) suffix *-uv-a-* either by modification as in Bg. N *păt* 'road' → V *pătúvam* 'I travel' (with a stress change) or by conversion as in N *săštestvó* 'creature' → V *săštestvúvam* 'I exist'.

Parallel examples without IMPFV2 forms from Russian and Serbo-Croatian are R. IMPFV *suščestvovat'* → PFV *prosuščestvovat'* → IMPFV2 Ø; SC. IMPFV *putovati* → PFV *proputovati* → IMPFV2 Ø.

4.2.4 Hypocoristics

Hypocoristics are extragrammatical abbreviatory devices, distinct from true morphological rules, since their formation neither causes any morphosemantic change (cf. Dressler 2000b: 583) nor is the reduction accompanying their derivation morphologically predictable. In fact, in most cases, from a single base more than one hypocoristic output exists, e.g. Bg. *Elisaveta* → *Eli* and *Liza*. Curiously from Bg. *Elizabet* (the foreign variant of *Elisaveta*), even three hypocoristic forms are possible: *Eli, Liza,* and *Beti.*

Since deletion of form is not the only feature of hypocoristic nouns, the latter might, according to the formal rule applied to the input, be assigned to one of the following three types:

(i) displaying shortening only, e.g.: E. *Ed-ward* → *Ed, Pete-r* → *Pete*, Bg. *Drago-mir* → *Drago.*
(ii) exhibiting substitution of segments, e.g.: Hungarian *Erzs-ébet* 'Elisabeth' → *Erzs-i*, Bg. *Bo-jan* → *Bo-bi*. In the literature, this type is usually called truncation (see Section 4.2.10).
(iii) shortening plus addition or/and substitution of segments, e.g. Bg. *I-van* 'John' → *Van-jo, Di-mit-ăr* → *Mit-jo, (E)-kat-erina* → *Kat-ja.*

Hypocoristic nouns are originally used in calling and can thus stand for vocatives. However, this does not mean that hypocoristics are identical with the category of vocative and thus inflection. On the contrary, both hypocoristics and vocatives exhibit morphotactic forms of their own. For example, in modern Bulgarian, where some vestiges of vocative still exist, the vocative forms of the names cited in (iii) are *Ivan-e, Dimitr-e, (E)katerin-o/Ekaterina*, derived by addition and substitution respectively. Further evidence for the non-inflectional nature of hypocoristics comes from their syntactic behaviour, as hypocoristics behave syntactically like diminutives and not as vocatives. The syntactic criterion for distinguishing between diminutives and vocatives in Bulgarian is suggested by Georgiev (1985[1970]). This criterion takes into consideration that diminutives can, since expressing smallness, be used with the adjective *malăk* 'little', whereas vocatives, which have nothing to do with smallness, cannot. Georgiev (1985: 165) illustrates his observation with the following example:

(20a)   *Ank-e* (VOC) and *Anč-e* (DIM), both from *Anka* 'Anne'
        malk-a-ta Anč-e 'little-FEM-DEF Anče-DIM'
        **malk-a-ta Ank-e* 'little-FEM-DEF Anke-VOC'

With the aforementioned *Ekaterina* we have:

(20b)   **malk-a-ta Ekaterin-o* 'little-FEM-DEF Ekaterina-VOC'
        malk-o-to Ekaterin-če 'little-NEUT-DEF Ekaterina-DIM.NEUT'
        malk-a-ta Kat-ja 'little-FEM-DEF Katja-HYP'.

Now it seems that hypocoristics can be identified with diminutives (i.e. with morphological derivation). Moreover both hypocoristics and diminutives are semantically related as expressing familiarity. Bulgarian, however, suggests nice evidence that hypocoristics and diminutives are of two different kinds. Whereas diminutive suffixes can be attached to both full proper nouns (e.g. *Ivan-ko*, *Ivan-čo*) and shortened (hypocoristic) bases (e.g. *Van-ko*, *Van-čo*), hypocoristic endings (if existing) combine only with shortened bases, e.g. *Van-jo*, but not **Ivan-jo*. Likewise with *Ekaterin-a*: *Ekaterin-če*, *Kat-če* with the diminutive suffix *-če*, but only *Kat-ja*, *(E)katerin-ja*.

In conclusion, hypocoristics are neither inflection (vocatives) nor derivation (diminutives) but an extragrammatical abbreviatory device, and they thus differ from morphological subtraction, which operates in derivation and inflection.

A phenomenon related to hypocoristics and vocatives and nicely illustrating the gradual organization of grammar, since being between hypocoristics and vocatives, is represented by the so-called 'new vocative' in Modern Russian (Yadroff 1996; Daniel and Spencer 2009). Unlike Bulgarian and Serbo-Croatian, Modern Russian has entirely lost the Proto-Slavic vocative but has developed forms such as *Van'* (← *Vanja*), *Gal'* (← *Galja*), *Len* (← *Lena*), etc. instead. Intriguingly, these new forms are shortenings of hypochoristics.[2] *Vanja* is a

---

[2]In Russian, the usual way to address a person is either to use his/her full name and patronymic (formal discourse) or the hypocoristic form of his/her full name (informal discourse), e.g. *Elena Petrovna* and *Lena*. A very few names, e.g. *Marina*, are used in their full forms in informal discourse and consequently the full name is shortened when the new vocative form is derived, i.e. the new vocative of *Marina* is *Marin*; though the sequence *Marina* → *Marisha* → *Marish*, through the hypocoristic form, is also possible.

hypocoristic form from *Ivan*, *Galja* from *Galina* and *Lena* from *Elena*. Thus, this peculiarity of the Modern Russian vocative makes it incompatible with the Serbo-Croatian and Bulgarian vocative forms. Additionally, the Russian new vocatives are built only from proper names and kinship terms, which is a very strange restriction on case forms. These two peculiarities of the Modern Russian vocative render the latter a dubious category. Note that similar shortenings also exist in Bulgarian (e.g. *Donka* → *Doca* → *Doc*), and are possible in Serbo-Croatian (e.g. *Zoran* → *Zoki* → *Zok*), though forms with shortening of the final vowel are less frequent in these two languages than in Russian. Shortenings of hypocoristics are least typical of Serbo-Croatian. Whether due to the low frequency of the shortened forms or because in Bulgarian and Serbo-Croatian there are vocative forms that are derived by addition of vocative inflection, forms, such as Bg. *Doc* and SC. *Zok*, are not seen as vocative but as hypocoristic in the two languages. In Russian, both a hypocoristic form and its shortened variant, i.e. *Lena* and *Len*, are used as address forms, *Len* being felt more familiar. However, the hypocoristic form *Lena*, like hypocoristics in Bulgarian (recall the above-suggested criterion for distinguishing between hypocoristics and vocatives in Bulgarian), can be used with the adjective *malen'kij* 'little', while the so-called new vocatives cannot, i.e. *malen'kaja Lena* but not **malen'kaja Len*. Thus, syntactically the new vocatives behave like vocative forms.

As for the morphological analysis of the Russian new vocatives, in the theoretical framework of this book, they are not a case of subtractive morphology (contra Yadroff 1996) but of a zero sign (contra Daniel and Spencer 2009). On zero sign, see Section 4.2.9 where the concept is exemplified with zero expressed GEN PL forms of Russian nouns terminating in vowels in NOM SG. Note that the new Russian vocatives, as a rule, coincide with GEN PL formally except in two cases: (1) if 'yer vocalization' takes place in GEN PL, vocatives remain unchanged, e.g *Serjožek*-GEN PL but *Serjožk*-VOC, both forms of *Serjožka* (← *Sergej*); and (2) voiced obstruents (used to) remain voiced in VOC forms but not in GEN PL forms (Daniel and Spencer 2009: 628). Thus the new vocatives, since without any modification, are even a clearer case of a zero sign than GEN PL, the latter allows for phonological modifications and in a few instances also has forms that are not built according to any rule but are exceptions (cf. Zaliznjak 1977 and Section 4.2.9).

As for the next three types of shortening, clippings, blends and acronyms, they are even much more questionable as WF rules than the already discussed shortenings. Like hypocoristics, clippings, blends and acronyms serve to enrich the lexicon but involve no semantic change, and their output forms are members of the respective categories from which they are derived. Moreover, the next three shortenings have no recognizable morpheme structure, and thus their semantics cannot be predicted from their forms. Taking into consideration the strange character of such shortenings, Aronoff (1976: 20) suggests for them the term 'oddities'.

For the sake of precision and completeness, it should be noted that in Bulgarian, Russian and Serbo-Croatian grammars, clippings, blends and acronyms are classified under abbreviations without any further distinction of types: Bg. *săkrateni složni dumi* 'abbreviated complex words' (Andrejčin et al. 1983: 29–31); R. *abbreviatury* 'abbreviations' (Švedova et al. 1980: 255f); and SC. *skraćene riječi ili skraćenice* 'shortened words or shortenings' (Babić 1991: 46f) and *složene skraćenice (abrevijature)* 'complex shortenings (abbreviations)' in Barić et al. (1997: 299f). General morphology, on the other hand, knows many detailed descriptions of clipping, blending and acronyms, such as those in Bauer (1988); Quirk et al. (1980, 1995); Thornton (1993); Kreidler (2000); Cannon (2000), among others.

4.2.5 Clipping

A clipping is a shortening from a simple lexeme and consists of one, two, or occasionally, three syllables of that word (Kreidler 2000: 956). The shortening may occur at the beginning of the word (*phone* ← *telephone*), at the end of the word (*photo* ← *photograph*), or at both ends of the word (*influenza* ← *flu*), cf. Quirk et al. (1980: 1030). The most salient feature of clipping is the fact that the clipped form is stylistically felt as less formal (Quirk et al. 1980: 1030; Švedova et al. 1980: 256; Bauer 1988: 33; Barić et al. 1997: 300, 613; Iacobini 2000: 872), i.e. clips are augmented with the semantic-pragmatic element of familiarity (Kreidler 2000: 961f).

Typical examples of clipping from Slavic are: Bg. *psixo* ← *psixobolnica* 'psychiatry hospital', *spec* ← *specialist* 'specialist', *zam* ← *zamestnik* (vice-), *bež* ← *bežov* 'beige', *foto* ← *fotografija* 'photograph' (Bojadžiev 1999: 275); R. *psix* 'psychopath' ← *psixopat*, *spec* ← *specialist* 'specialist' (Švedova et al. 1980: 256); SC. *auto* ← *automobile* 'automobile', *kino* 'cinema' ← *kinematograf* 'cinematograph, cinema' (Barić et al. 1997: 300). It should be noted, however, that clipping is a language specific process. For example, although both Bulgarian and Serbo-Croatian have the word *avtomobil* 'car', clipping has taken place only in Serbo-Croatian (*auto* ← *automobil*), whereas in Bulgarian *avto-* is used only as the first part of complex words.

Evidence for the non-wordformational nature of clipping:

(1) In regard to inflection, clipped forms have peculiar morphological behaviour. For example: shortenings such as Bg. *kino* can be declined (as the full form *kinematograf* can). However, Bg. *foto* (← *fotografija*) can be pluralized in its full form, but when used as a clipping, its plural is problematic. The same holds for the adjective Bg. *bežov* (from Fr. *beige*, cf. Milev et al. 1978),

which has a full inflectional paradigm, whereas the clipping *bež* is indeclinable (recall that Bulgarian declines loanwords). Probably, Bg. *kino* was borrowed in its full and short forms from the very beginning and therefore the clipped form is now entirely integrated inflectionally, while *foto* and *bež* have been clipped later and are still felt as foreign and thus left either partially (the definite form *foto-to* 'photo-NEUT-DEF' is well-formed) or fully indeclinable (the case of *bež*).

In morphological theory, clipping is, by rule, illustrated by instances of clipped nouns. However, in addition to the above-cited clipped adjective Bg. *bež* (from *bežov*), Barić et al. (1997: 613) point out a few examples of clipped verbs, that are, in fact, clipped single inflection forms: SC. *gle* ← *gledaj* 'see!', *homo* ← *ho-di-mo* 'we go'. Such examples are further evidence for the particular behaviour of clipping in regard to inflection, which is not typical for the output of a morphological technique.

(2) Although formally a clipping is always derived from a single word, semantically it can correspond to a phrase. For example, E. *capital* is equivalent to *capital city*, *capital letter*, and *capital investment*; E. *pub* ← *public house*, *typo* ← *typographical error*; and Fr. *docu* ← *film documentaire* (the examples are from Kreidler 2000: 962). This phenomenon is another shortening process called ellipsis. Ellipsis consists in deletion of the head of a construction of a modifier and a head (in either order). After the deletion of the head, the modifier takes on the meaning of the whole construction.

(3) A clipping can have different interpretations in different contexts, e.g.: G. *Krimi* ← *Kriminalfilm* 'detective film', *Kriminalstück* 'detective play', and *Kriminalroman* 'detective novel'; and E. *sub* ← N *submarine*, and V *substitute* (Kreidler 2000).

Because the process of clipping appears to be very productive in modern Russian, special attention to Russian clippings is warranted. Švedova et al. (1980: 225f) and Zemskaja et al. (1981: 125f) provide the data. It should be mentioned, however, that although the two sources classify the process differently, neither uses the term 'clipping'. Švedova et al. (1980: 219, 224–6) use zero suffixation, whereas Zemskaja et al. (1981: 122–8) speak of *usečenie* 'shortening'.

Švedova et al. (1980) put forward three semantic groups of shortening:

(1) abstract state, notion, indication

>
> (21)   *serëz*   ← *serëznoe sostojanie* 'state of seriousness'
>   *intim*   ← (1) *intimnoe sostojanie* 'state of intimacy'; but also
>   (2) *intimnye vešči* 'intimate belongings';
>   (3) *intimnaja obstanovka* 'intimate environment'
>   *nervoz* ← *nervoznoe sostojanie* 'state of nervousness', etc.

4.2 Delimiting Subtraction 141

(2) person obtaining some characteristic

> (22) *intellektual* ← *intellektual'nyj čelovek* 'intellectual person'
> *nejtral* ← *nejtral'nyj čelovek* 'neutral person'
> *gumanitar* ← *gumanitarnyj specialist* 'specialist in humanities'
> *korabel* ← *korabel'nyj stroitel'* 'constructor of ships'
> *xronik* (with depalatatization) ← *xroničeskij bol'noj* 'chronically ill'
> *kosmik* (with depalatalisation) ← *specialist po kosmičeskim lučam* 'specialist in cosmic rays', etc.
> *original* ← *original'nyj čelovek* 'original person'

(3) object, substance, material, activity

> (23) *memorial* ← (1) *memorial'noe (sportivnoe) sorevnovanie v pamjat' izvestnogo sportsmena* 'memorial contest devoted to a famous sportsman',
> (2) *arxitekturno-skul'ptornyj ansambl' v pamjat' o kem-čem-n.* 'architectural-sculptural memorial'
> *sinxron* ← *sinxronnyj perevod* 'simultaneous translation'
> *central* ← *central'naja tjurma* 'central prison'
> *èlastik* (with depalatalization) ← *èlastičeskij material* 'elastic material'
> *èkzot* ← *èkzotičeskoe rastenie* 'exotic plant'
> *kiber* ← *kibernetičeskaja mašina, ustrojstvo* 'cyber machine, device'
> *fakul'tativ* ← *fakul'tativnoe zanjatie* 'facultative lesson'
> *termojad* ← *termojadernaja reakcija* 'thermonuclear reaction'
> *ul'trafiolet* ← *ul'trafioletovye luči* 'ultraviolet rays', etc.[3]

With regard to the Russian shortennings, although such formations seem subtraction-like, they show characteristics that are not typical for a morphological technique:

(1) The formal make-up of such shortenings is unpredictable. Compare output forms of shortenings derived from bases terminating in the same final segment: *kosmik* ← *kosmič(eskij)*, *ekzot* ← *ekzot(ičeskij)*, *kiber* ← *kiber (netičeskij)*. If such shortenings were derived by the morphological

---

[3]In Modern Bulgarian, the process is less productive than in modern Russian. Bulgarian examples are Bg. *liberal* 'a liberal', *fakultativ* 'facultative lesson', *nacional* 'national sportsman', etc. However, there is no serious investigation of such formations in Bulgarian. As for Serbo-Croatian, there seems to be no information relevant to the discussion, but of course, in Serbo-Croatian, there are forms such as *libèrāl* as well.

technique of subtraction, there should be some regularity in application, since for a subtractive rule it is expected to delete one and the same segment (see the discussion in Section 4.1)

(2) The semantic meaning of the above shortenings is unpredictable. For example, *central* could have meant *central'naja ploščad'* 'central square', *central'naja figura* 'central character', etc. but it means *central'naja tjurma* 'central prison'. Likewise, *sinxron* does not mean any synchronous activity, but rather 'simultaneous translation'. *Kiber* is not a specialist in cybernetics (denotes 'cyber device'), nor is *kosmik* a cosmonaut (it means 'specialist in cosmic rays'), and, surprisingly, an *original* is a person. As shown by these examples, it is even impossible to devise a superordinate abstract word-formation meaning from which the specific semantic meanings of the different shortenings to be derived, as should be the case if they were derived by a morphological technique such as subtraction.

(3) The shortenings are stylistically restricted and are typical for the colloquial style and the respective professional languages. It appears that no morphological technique shows such specialization, though clippings do (cf. the definition of clipping above). It can happen that in addition, substitution, and subtraction a given affix appears stylistically marked, so that its addition, substitution or deletion yields some stylistic change, but there is no morphological technique restricted to only two, moreover unrelated, communicative contexts.

(4) Some of the above shortenings have more than one meaning, and as is typical for elliptic clippings (Kreidler 2000), the different meanings of a shortening are semantically related (see R. *intim*). Of course an affix (recall that in Švedova et al. 1980 the above Russian shortenings are classified as zero suffixation) might also have more than a single meaning (affix polysemy), but the different meanings of an affix can be realized only in connection to different formal bases, which means different output forms and thus, by rule, does not suppose any semantic relations.

To sum up, the above Russian shortenings have many more characteristics in common with the extra-grammatical device of clipping than with any type of a word-formation rule.

Like clipping, the next two types of shortening do not involve morphemes, and because they presuppose the existence of a writing system, are therefore even more marginal than clipping.

4.2.6 Blends

Blending is the telescoping of usually two separate items into a new form, the meaning of which is restricted to the meaning of the source items, e.g. E. *Eurovision* ← *European* tele**vision**, *smog* ← *smoke* + *fog*. In contrast to this type of blending, which prototypically shortens the end of the first item and the

4.2 Delimiting Subtraction

beginning of the second one (i.e. AB + CD → AD), Slavic blends are usually of the type E. *Interpol* ← ***inter****national **pol**ice*, *telex* ← ***tele****printer **ex**change* (i.e. AB + CD → AC), which for Quirk et al. (1995) is outside the general pattern of blending in English since, 'in some respects, they more resemble acronyms' (Quirk et al. 1995: 1584), see also Bauer (1988: 40) and Plag (2003: 121–26).[4] Thus, we can say that Slavic blends are non-prototypical and thus between blending and acronyms. For example:

(24) Bg. *rabfak* ← ***rab****otničeski **fak**ultet* 'faculty for workers'
      R. *kolxoz* ← ***kol****ektivnoe **xoz**jajstvo* 'collective farm'
      SC. *Nama* ← ***na****rodni **ma**gazin* 'people warehouse'

In some cases two words are blended where they overlap (the shortening appears similar to haplology, see above), resulting in no loss of information while avoiding repetition: *slang* + *language* → *slanguage* (Bauer 1988: 39).

In Slavic, it is also possible that some of the items that participate in the input fail completely in the blended output form, e.g.: SC. *Vinteks* ← ***Vin****kovačka **teks**tilna industrija* (Barić et al. 1997: 300). Forms mixing strategies specific to the formation of acronyms (see below) and blends also exist, e.g. R. *Giprovuz* ← ***G****osudarstvennyj sojuznyj **i**nstitut **p****o **pro**ektirovaniju **v****ysšix **u****čebnyx **z**avednij* 'State union institute for projecting of high school education' (Krumova and Čoroleeva 1983).

4.2.7 Acronyms

An acronym is formed from the initial letters of words or a compound lexeme. According to Quirk et al. (1980: 1031) there are two main types of acronyms:

(1) Acronyms pronounced as sequences of letters, i.e. 'alphabetisms'.
(a) The letters correspond to full words: *FBI* – *Federal Bureau of Investigation*, *MIT* – *Massachusetts Institute of Technology*.
   Consider also:

(25) Bg. *BTA* ← *Bălgarska telegrafna agencija* 'Bulgarian telegraph agency'
      R. *MGU* ← *Moskovskij gosudarstvennyj universitet* 'Moscow State University'
      SC. *HDZ* ← *Hrvatski dijalektološki zbornik* 'A collection of Croatian dialectology'

---

[4]Plag (2003) suggests an alternative description of blends in terms of prosodic categories. However, his observations hold only for English blends of the type AB + CD → AD.

(b) The letters correspond to elements in a compound or just parts of a word: *TV – television, GHQ – General Headquarters.*
(2) Acronyms pronounced as a word, e.g.:

(26) E. *NATO – the North Atlantic Treaty Organisation*
Bg. *BAN* ← *Balgarska akademija na naukite* 'Bulgarian academy of sciences'
R. *RAN* ← *Rossijskaja akademija nauk* 'Russian academy of sciences'
SC. *HAZU* ← *Hrvatska akademija znanosti i umetnosti* 'Croatian academy of sciences and arts'

In Russian, some recent acronyms show an interesting tendency towards imitating words: *GraD* ← *Partija* '*Graždanskoe Dostojnstvo*' 'Citizen's Dignity' = *grad* 'city', *ŠARM* ← *Šou armjanskix mužčin* 'Armenian men's show' = *šarm* 'charm' (cf. Zemskaja 1996: 120).

4.2.8 Subtraction of Meaning

On the analogy of subtraction of form (i.e. when a shorter output form corresponds to more meaning), Mel'čuk (1967: 359–62 [1976: 78–93]; 1991: 287f) argues for subtraction of semantics (i.e. that a longer output form can correspond to less complex semantics). The assumption is based on the twofold character of linguistic signs, i.e. since a sign relates a signified and a signifier, subtraction might operate on both of them. Mel'čuk gives the following examples of subtraction of meaning from Russian (translations are those by Mel'čuk 1991):

(27) INF causative ~ INF*sja* reflexive
serdit' 'to make angry' [= 'to cause to be angry'] ~ *serdit'sja* 'to be angry'
udivljat' 'to astonish' [= 'to cause to be astonished'] ~ *idivljat'sja* 'to be astonished'
katat' 'to give a ride' [= to cause to ride'] ~ *katat'sja* 'to ride'
umenšit' 'to diminish' [$_{trans}$] [= 'to cause to become less'] ~
umenšit'sja 'to diminish' [$_{intrans}$] = 'to become less'

Mel'čuk (1991: 287) assumes that 'in Russian (as in many other Indo-European languages), the reflexive suffix -*sja*, when added to a causative verb, deletes the semantic component "cause" in its signified'. Thus subtraction of meaning requires addition of form. The primary function of the morphotactic form in establishing subtraction of semantics is clarified by consideration of some further examples from Russian:

4.2 Delimiting Subtraction   145

(28)   *gordit' 'to cause to be proud' ~ gordit'sja 'to be proud'
       *trudit' 'to cause to work' ~ trudit'sja 'to work'
       *smejat' 'to cause to smile' ~ smejat'sja 'to smile'
       *starat' 'to cause somebody to try, to endeavour' ~ starat'sja 'to
       try, endeavour'

In these examples, although the corresponding semantics 'to cause to...' exists (expressed by a phrase) and might be subtracted (conceivably at least), subtraction does not take place because there is no form to express it.

The Bulgarian equivalents of the examples in (27) above further contradict Mel'čuk's analysis. Consider:

(29)   sărdja ~ sărdja se
       udivljavam ~ udivljavam se
       părzaljam ~ părzaljam se
       namaljavam ~ namaljavam se

As can be seen from these examples, the Bulgarian reflexive *se* is a clitic, and it is therefore written separately from the verbs. Moreover, *se* can precede and follow the verb (e.g. *az se sărdja na nego* 'I am angry with him' and *Sărdja se na nego* 'I am angry with him') and one can place other clitics between the verb and *se* (e.g. *sărdja mu*-DAT CLITIC *se* 'I'm angry with him'), i.e. the Bulgarian *se* does not behave like an affix. Thus, in the examples given in (29), the subtraction of meaning takes place, but since there is no addition of morphological form, there is no subtraction, which once again demonstrates the primary function of the form over the meaning in the so-called 'subtraction of meaning'.

In conclusion, the above-discussed form-meaning mismatches, in respect to subtraction of semantics, invalidate Mel'čuk's argument on the subtractive character of the Russian decausatives in particular and on the existence of a morphological rule such as subtraction of semantics in general. Further evidence for the correctness of our conclusion provides research by Koontz-Garboden who has recently presented cross-linguistic arguments against the idea of any kind of semantic subtraction in argument structure alternations (Koontz-Garboden 2005, 2007a, b; Koontz-Garboden and Levin 2005).

4.2.9 Zero Sign

The term 'zero sign' was analysed in Section 3.1, but this type of expression is so often confused with subtraction that it is useful to return to it. As already discussed, the Russian GEN PL forms of the type *knig* (from FEM SG NOM *knig-a* 'book') and *okon* (NEUT SG NOM *okn-o* 'window') are examples of 'zero sign' in morphology. Yet many linguists (cf. Spencer 1991: 224f), among them even representatives of NM (Mayerthaler 1981; Wurzel 1989), have claimed that what happens in the Russian GEN PL is caused by subtraction. Recall, however, that the inflectional paradigms of *knig-a* and *okn-o* are root-based, i.e. the NOM endings *-a* and *-o* are inflectional suffixes and as such do not belong to the respective roots. Moreover, GEN PL forms, though morphotactically unmarked, differ from all other forms of the noun paradigm, i.e. the paradigm seems to use the root for the expression of a particular case value. This strategy has its parallel in NOM SG of non-derived nouns terminating in consonants, e.g. NOM SG *syn* 'son', GEN SG *syn-a*, DAT SG *syn-u*, etc., all cases except NOM SG being overtly signalled. Thus, for the GEN PL we assume expression by a zero sign, i.e. the value GEN PL is signalled by the addition of an affix that is not overtly expressed but the attachment of which derives distinctive forms within one and the same inflectional paradigm. (On zero sign see also Mel'čuk 2002).

4.2.10 Truncation

As mentioned in Section 2.4, the term truncation is introduced into linguistics by Aronoff (1976). Aronoff defines truncation as an adjustment rule consisting of deletion of an affix due to the addition of another affix (recall that within the framework of this book (Chapter 2) the process is called substitution).

While in English, there is no need to control the nature of the deleted (truncated) and the added material, since the inflectional slot of English words is empty by default, in the Slavic languages, deletion and addition can happen in the derivational as well as in the inflectional slot of the word, which means one of the following three possibilities: (i) to delete derivational form and to add inflection only; (ii) to delete inflectional material and to add derivational (plus inflectional) material; and (iii) to substitute morphotactic form in one and the same word slot (either in the derivational slot or in the inflectional slot). Of these three possibilities, only (iii) seems to correspond to what Aronoff calls truncation, and (i) and (ii) are not taken into consideration for the definition of truncation in Aronoff (1976), which leads to false analysis of data from Russian used for the illustration of truncation (Aronoff 1976: 94ff). Based on Isačenko (1972), Aronoff explains derivations such as R. *bez vred-a* 'without harm' – *bezvredn-yj* 'harmless' – *obezvred-i-t'* 'to make harmless' in terms of a sequence of forms built on each other, i.e. *bez vreda* → *bezvredn-yj* → *obezvred-i-t'*, and thus involving truncation[5] at the last step, that of the formation of the verb *obezvred-i-t'*. If we agree with Aronoff on the correctness of the direction of the

---

[5]Note that the term Isačenko used for the rule in question is *usečenie*. Recall, however, that in Russian linguistic literature (as mentioned in Section 4.1 of this chapter) *usečenie* stands for any type of shortening and can thus denote truncation, conversion, and subtraction.

4.3 Subtraction and Rule Inversion: Ethnicity Terms   147

Russian derivation chain, we should confess that after the deletion of the derivational suffix -*n*- (due to truncation according to Aronoff) in ADJ *bezv-redn-yj* → V *obezvred-i-t'*, that forms adjectives from nouns (e.g. N *vred* 'harm' → ADJ *vred-n-yj* 'harmful'), only inflection is added (the TM -*i*- and the infinitive suffix -*t'*, neither of which is derivational). Thus, it is more likely that *obezvred-i-t'* is derived by subtraction (cf. the definition of subtraction in Section 4.1 of this chapter) than by truncation.

Surprising as it may seem, the example is neither truncation (substitution in the framework of this book) nor subtraction. In fact, Aronoff's analysis of the above sequence of derivations is false, since it is not the prefix *o*- but *obez*- that has been added to form *obezvred-i-t'*. Both prefixes *o*- and *obez*- combine with verbal bases only, but there exists no *bez*- verbs in Russian, which means that there is but a single possible way to derive *obezvred-i-t'*, that in (30):

(30)   N *vred* → IMPFV *vred-it'* → PFV *obez-vred-it'*
       (cf. IMPFV2 *obez-vrež-iv-a-t'*, verbal N *obez-vreživa-nie*).

For nouns from which no verb can be derived, an empty second step can be assumed, on the analogy of the derivational chain in (30):

(31)   N *vod-a* 'water' → **vod-it'* → PFV *obez-vod-it'* 'to drain'
       (IMPFV2 *obez-vož-iv-a-t'*, verbal N *obez-vož-iv-a-nie*).

For this example, circumfixation in terms of parasynthesis is also possible: *vod-a* → *obez-vod-it'*.

Put differently, what is called truncation in Aronoff (1976) is a noun-to-verb affixation. Additionally, the phonological and morphonological alternations pointed out by Aronoff (1976: 96f) as evidence for the correctness of the direction of the derivation in question are also easily explainable within the theoretical framework of this book (Chapter 2). One simply needs to recall that affixation in its non-prototypical realizations allows for phonological and morphonological modifications.

4.3 Subtraction and Rule Inversion: Ethnicity Terms

A change in the non-linguistic world relates start conditions and end conditions and is thus always perceived as directed. This precept is the cognitive explanation of the fact that, in grammar, directed rules are preferred as they are more natural than non-directed rules. Furthermore, basic terms such as input (base) and output (derivative) presuppose directionality. In morphology, the direction of a rule can be established either on the basis of its formal side (the output of the rule shows addition of form) or as depending on the semantic change involved (the output shows addition of semantics). When features are added, form and semantics usually speak for one and the same direction. In cases where no change of form takes place (e.g. conversion) or some form is deleted (e.g. subtraction), semantics is the decisive criterion for the establishment of the direction of the derivation. It is possible, however, that the semantic direction of a pattern is well motivated in both directions. Moreover, the logic determining both directions is based on general pragmatic knowledge and does not rely on special linguistic competence. In such instances, we will speak of rule inversion. The discussion below illustrates a rule inversion pattern and aims at setting apart the phenomenon of rule inversion from morphological subtraction.

Nouns denoting inhabitants and ethnicity terms in Italian are maybe the most frequently cited examples of subtraction in WF in the literature (Dressler 1984, 1994: 4402, 2000b: 585; Rainer 1993: 694f; Naumann and Vogel 2000: 936):

(32) *Umbr-ia* → *Umbr-o/a* '(male/female) inhabitant of Umbria'
Lombard-ia → *Lombard-o/a* '(male/female) inhabitant of Lombardia'

Compare the above nouns with the following suffixations that also denote inhabitants and ethnicity terms:

(33) *Lazi-o* → *Lazi-ale*
Sicili-a → *Sicili-ano/a*
Romagn-a → *Romagn-olo/a*.

Examples of ethnicity terms in other languages also exhibit the peculiarities of the above Italian derivations. Consider:

German (Becker 1990):

(34) COUNTRY/ REGION – ETHNICITY TERM-MASC/FEM
Böhmen 'Bohemia' – *Böhm-e/in*
Dänemark 'Denmark' – *Dän-e/in*
Türkei 'Turkey' – *Türk-e/in*
Polen 'Poland' – *Pol-e/in*
Korsika 'Corsica' – *Kors-e/in*
Irland 'Irland' – *Ir-e/in*
Bulgarien 'Bulgaria' – *Bulgar-e/in*
Finnland 'Finland' – *Finn-e/in*
Serbien 'Serbia' – *Serb-e/in*
Slowenien 'Slovenia' – *Slowen-e/in*

4.3 Subtraction and Rule Inversion: Ethnicity Terms

vs.

(35) *Österreich* 'Austria' → *Österreich-er/+ -in*
      Chile 'Chile' → *Chile-n-e/in*
      Israel 'Israel' → *Israel-i*, etc.

Since English has no gender suffixes, ethnicity terms in English are even more salient examples of shortening than the above-cited ones from German:

(36) *Germany – a German*
      Turkey – a Turk
      Scotland – a Scot/Scotsman
      Czechia – a Czech
      Sweden – a Swede
      Thailand – a Thai

vs. formations such as:

(37) *Austria* → *an Austrian*
      Japan → *a Japanese*
      Iraq → *an Iraqi*
      China → *a Chinese*, etc.

When discussing subtraction, Rainer (1993: 694f) points out similar examples from Spanish:

(38) *Albania* 'Albania' – *albano*
      Arabia 'Arabia' – *árabe*
      Asturias 'Asturias' – *astur*
      Cantabria 'Cantabria' – *cántabro*
      Eslovaquia 'Slovakia' – *eslovaco*
      Etiopia 'Ethiopia' – *etíope*
      Sajonia 'Saxony' – *sajon*, etc.

vs. affixations such as:

(39) *España* 'Spain' → *español*
      Salzburgo 'Salzburg' → *salzburgués*

Slavic languages also suggest examples of ethnicity terms derived by deletion of form and affixation respectively, as can be seen from the following examples from Russian and Serbo-Croatian:

Russian

(40) *Čexija* 'Czechia' → *čex* 'a Czech'
Švecija 'Sweden' → *šved* 'a Swede'
Vengrija 'Hungary' → *vengr* 'a Hungarian'
Finnlandija 'Finland' → *finn* 'a Fine'
Uzbekistan 'Uzbekistan' → *uzbek* 'an Uzbek'
Tadžikistan 'Tajikistan' → *tadžik* 'a Tajik'

vs. affixations such as

(41) *Amerika* 'America' → *amerikanec* 'an American'
Anglija 'England' → *angličanin* 'Englishman'
Bel'gija 'Belgium' → *bel'giec* 'a Belgian', etc.

Serbo-Croatian

(42) *Engleska* 'England' → *Englez* 'Englishman'
Francuska 'France' → *Francuz* 'a French'
Hrvatska 'Croatia' → *Hrvat* 'Croatian'
Mađarska 'Hungary' → *Mađar* 'a Hungarian'

vs.

(43) *Austrija* 'Austria' → *Austrijanac* 'an Austrian'
Evropa 'Europe' → *Evropljanin* 'an European'
Bosna 'Bosnia' → *Bošnjak* 'a Bosnian', etc.

It seems that the semantic pattern 'country/region' → 'inhabitant/ethnicity term' is cross-linguistically subtractive. In order to prove the correctness of this observation, we will continue with the following relations from Bulgarian:

(44) | Country/Region | inhabitant | inhabitants/tribe |
|---|---|---|
| *Čexia* 'Czechia' | *čex* 'a Czech' | *čexi* |
| *Švecija* 'Sweden' | *šved* 'a Swede' | *švedi* |
| *Trakija* | ?*trak*/*trakiec* | *traki*/*trakijci* |

4.3 Subtraction and Rule Inversion: Ethnicity Terms   151

        Mizija   ?**miz/miziec*   *mizi/mizijci*
        Ilirija   ?*ilir   *iliri*
        Persija 'Persia'   ?**pers/persiec*   *persi/persijci*
        Ø   ?*got   *goti*
        Ø   ?*frank   *franki*
  (BUT *Francija* 'France')   *francuzin*   *francuzi*)
        Ø   ?*xun*   *xuni*
        Ø   ?*odris*   *odrisi*

As can be expected, affixation also derives nouns for inhabitants in Bulgarian:

(45)   *Avstrija* 'Austria' → *avstriec* 'an Austrian' → PL *avstrijci*
         Anglija 'England' → *angličanin* 'Englishman' → PL *angličani*
         Zair 'Zaire'→ *zairec* 'a Zairian' → PL *zairci*
         etc.

Let us now concentrate on the Bulgarian data in (44) above. As can be seen, there are instances where a noun for 'inhabitants' has no counterpart[6] in the column 'country', and in some cases even in the column 'inhabitant'. Clearly, such examples appear problematic for a uniform morphological analysis of the derivation of inhabitants in Bulgarian, though according to Aronoff's distributional criterion (Aronoff 1976; and Section 3.4.2.1 above), the direction of the above derivation pattern should be from the set with a greater number of members to the set with fewer members, as only this direction can account for all existing forms. This determines for the examples in (44) 'inhabitants' as bases and the nouns for 'country' as derivatives, which is reversed to the direction assumed for the formation of ethnicity terms/inhabitants in other languages (cf. the examples in (32)–(43)). Indeed, for the analysis of the Bulgarian data, we have the following three possibilities:

(1) We can postulate a directed rule, based on the assumption that 'ethnicity terms/inhabitants' are always derived from the respective 'countries/regions'. For the derivation of all 'ethnicity terms/inhabitants' that are morphotactically shorter than their corresponding 'countries/regions',

---

[6]Note that plural nouns without singular counterparts are typical for historical texts. For example, *traki* 'the Thracians' denotes the old Thracian tribe which inhabited the Balkan Peninsula. In historical discourse there is usually no need of the singular form of nouns such as *traki*, therefore the singular *trak* is a potential form only. However, a resident of the *Trakia* district in Bulgaria is actual, therefore expressed by the actual noun *trakiec*, PL *trakijci*. Likewise, *persi* 'the persians' has no singular in Modern Bulgarian, but an Iranian is *persiec*, and the Iranians are *persijci*, i.e. one thinks as individuals only of present-day peoples (maybe therefore *čex* 'a czech' and *šved* 'a swede' are quite normal).

that solution requires the application of subtraction. In fact, it is what Dressler (1984, 1994, 2000b), Rainer (1993), etc. do. 'Ethnicity terms/inhabitants' without corresponding 'counties/regions' should be seen as non-derived nouns that are simply listed in the lexicon.
(2) An alternative solution assumes morphotactically connected forms without any direction, 'Ableitungen ohne Basis' ('derivations without a base'), as Becker (1990: 43ff) calls them. It is how Becker derives nouns for ethnicity terms in German. For us however, that solution is unattractive, because our theoretical framework operates with bases (such as roots, stems and words), which requires directed rules, at least in the case of words as bases.
(3) The third possibility is rule inversion (cf. Dressler 2000b: 585). It means that a diachronic additive rule X → Y (= X + SUFF) turns back and becomes a synchronic additive rule of the type Y → X (= Y + SUFF). On rule inversion see also (Vennemann 1972).

Of course we can determine the direction of the pattern of ethnicity terms with the help of the semantic criterion, which, as already noted in the previous chapter, is the most important criterion for the establishing the direction of morphotactically unmarked derivations and thus seems also applicable to instances derived by deletion of form. In other words, the question now is whether Bulgaria is the Bulgarians' country or the Bulgarians are the citizens of Bulgaria? In regard to Bulgaria (*Bǎlgaria*) and the Bulgarians (*bǎlgari*), it is well-known that the country was named after the Bulgars (*bǎlgari*) when they together with the Slavs founded it. However, in Bulgarian there also exist instances such as *suapovec, trinidatec, gvineec*, etc. the direction of which is clearly from the country to the inhabitants, i.e. *Suapo* → *suapovec* (PL *suapovci*), *Trinidad* → *trinidatec* (PL *trinidatci*), *Gvineja* → *gvineec* (*gvinejci*), etc. because these inhabitants became popular after the foundation of their relatively young countries. Undoubtedly, according to the semantic criterion, in Bulgarian we have (i) nouns for countries derived from nouns for ethnicity terms/inhabitants, but also (ii) nouns for ethnicity terms/inhabitants derived from the countries where they live. In addition, the formal realization of the pattern for ethnicity terms also supports the rule-inversion solution, since (i) and (ii) have formal expressions of their own. The older pattern of (i) is either of the type ROOT*in* (e.g. *bǎlgarin* 'a Bulgarian') or a ROOT only (e.g. *čex* 'a Czech'), whereas the newer pattern, that of (ii) derives inhabitants with the suffix *-ec*. Moreover, (i) is entirely unproductive, but (ii) is fully productive.

Of course it would be helpful to know whether Bulgarian native speakers are aware of the existence of the two directions of the semantic pattern and how they process nouns such as those in (44) and (45). Or perphaps, the Bulgarians derive nationality terms unidirectionally with countries as bases and stored nouns of tribes without countries? Unfortunately, such tests have not yet been done, and psycholinguistics cannot thus help us with the answer to the question of pattern direction.

4.3 Subtraction and Rule Inversion: Ethnicity Terms   153

To sum up, ethnicity terms in Bulgarian appear to be an example of rule inversion and therefore a controversial example of subtraction. It should be noted that although the derivation of ethnicity terms in other languages has not been analysed in the way we did for Bulgarian, it does not exclude that the assumption of rule inversion would successfully work for Italian, German, English, Spanish, etc., cf. the data in (32) through (43).

The rule inversion in the derivation of ethnicity terms in Bulgarian has given rise to subtraction in the inflectional morphology of some of those nouns. As already mentioned, in Bulgarian, the actual bases of the oldest type of derivations to countries/states, were plural nouns from which singular forms were built with the help of the singulative[7] suffix *-in* (Georgiev 1969: 111–5; on Singulative in general, see Corbett 2000: 17f). Such plural-singular pairs have singular forms longer than their plural mates, e.g. PL *bălgari* – SG *bălgarin* 'a Bulgarian'. On the other hand, modern Bulgarian has lost the singulative suffix, and the singular is now the base for the derivation of the plural of all nouns. (Note also that according to the theory of universal markedness, the singular, since morphosemantically less marked than the plural, is supposed to be the base for the derivation of the plural, cf. Mayerthaler (1980: 30; 1981: 28). Though in some instances, especially when groups of persons are meant, markedness reversal (or local markedness, cf. Tiersma 1982) is also possible, i.e. the plural is unmarked, whereas the singular appears marked, e.g. G. PL *Eltern* 'parents' – SG *Elternteil* 'parent' cf. Mayerthaler 1981: 48ff). As can be seen in Table 4.1, noun plurals in modern Bulgarian are formed from the respective singular nouns either by suffixation or by substitution. Yet in the system, the short plural forms stand alongside long plurals and thus appear

---

[7]Mayerthaler (1981: 51) defined singulatives as nominal forms in which the meaning of singular is encoded through addition of a segment and gave the following examples from different languages:

(1) Nahuatl (Aztec)
   tolteca 'People from Tollan, Toltekians' – *toltecatl* 'a Toltekian'
   mexica 'Mexicans' – *mexicatl* 'a Mexican'
   ciua 'women' – *cuiatl* 'woman'

(2) Cymrian (Welsh)
   pysgod 'Fish' (PL) – *pysgodyn* 'Fish' (SG)
   moch 'swines' – *mochyn* 'swine'
   llygod 'mice' – *llygoden* 'mouse'

(3) Mongolian
   balaġad 'cities' – *balaġsun* 'city'
   -(a)d = PL exponent, *-sun* = SG exponent

(4) Arabic
   'arab 'Arabians' – *arabi* 'an Arab'
   almân 'Germans' – *almâni* 'a German'
   inkelîz 'Englishmen' – *inkelîzi* 'Englishman'.

(synchronically at least) as derived by subtraction. In inflection, due to the tighter paradigmatic organization in comparison to derivation, the diachronic primacy of the short plural forms is not felt, and for Bulgarian native speakers the old short plurals constitute a regular exception of the rule 'if the singular terminates in a consonant, the plural form is derived by suffixation' (cf. Table 4.1, macroclass 1).

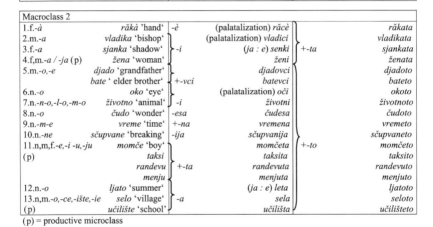

Table 4.1 Bulgarian noun inflection (based on Manova and Dressler 2001)

Macroclass 1						
singular indefinite form		plural		singular definite form		
1.m.-C	krak 'leg'	+-à	krakà			krakàt
2.m.-C	măž 'man'	+-è	măžè			măžàt
3.m.-C	săn 'dream'	+-išta	săništa			sănjat
4.m.-an	zabravan 'chuckle-head'	+-ovci	zabravanovci			zabravanăt
5.m.-j	boj 'fight'	-eve	boeve	+-ăt(-a)/-jat(-ja)		bojat
6. m.-C	vrăx 'peak'		(metathesis) vărxove			(metathesis) vărxăt
7.m.-C	grjax 'sin'	+-ove	(ja : e) grexovè			(ja : e) grexăt
8.m.-C (p)	grad 'city'		gradove			gradăt
9.f.-C	vrăv 'string'		(metathesis) vărvi			vrăvtà
10.f.-C	kost 'bone'		kosti	+-tà		kosttà
11. m.-g,k,x	učenik 'pupil'	+-i	(palatalization) učenici			učenikăt
12. m.-eC	kradec 'burglar'		(elision) kradci	+-ăt(-a)/-jat(-ja)		kradecăt
13. m.-C (p)	učitel 'teacher'		učiteli			učiteljat
14. m.-in	bălgarin 'Bulgarian'		(subtraction) bălgari			bălgarinăt

Macroclass 2						
1.f.-à	răkà 'hand'	-è	(palatalization) răcè			răkata
2.m.-a	vladika 'bishop'		(palatalization) vladici			vladikata
3.f.-a	sjanka 'shadow'	-i	(ja : e) senki	+-ta		sjankata
4.f,m.-a / -ja (p)	žena 'woman'		ženi			ženata
5.m.-o,-e	djado 'grandfather'		djadovci			djadoto
	bate ' elder brother'	+-vci	batevci			bateto
6.n.-o	oko 'eye'		(palatalization) oči			okoto
7.n.-n-o,-l-o,-m-o	životno 'animal'	-i	životni			životnoto
8.n.-o	čudo 'wonder'	-esa	čudesa			čudoto
9.n.-m-e	vreme 'time'	+-na	vremena			vremeto
10.n.-ne	sčupvane 'breaking'	-ija	sčupvanija	+-to		sčupvaneto
11.m,n,m.f.-e,-i -u,-ju	momče 'boy'		momčeta			momčeto
(p)	taksi		taksita			taksito
	randevu	+-ta	randevuta			randevuto
	menju		menjuta			menjuto
12.n.-o	ljato 'summer'		(ja : e) leta			ljatoto
13.n,m.-o,-ce,-ište,-ie	selo 'village'	-a	sela			seloto
(p)	učilište 'school'		učilišta			učilišteto

(p) = productive microclass

Examples of short plurals from Bulgarian are:

(46) SG → PL
X*in* → X*i*
bălgarin 'a Bulgarian'→ *bălgari* 'Bulgarians'
sărbin 'a Serbian' → *sărbi* 'Serbians'
xărvatin 'a Croat' → *xărvati* 'Croats'
angličanin 'an Englishman' → *angličani* 'Englishmen'
francuzin 'a Frenchman' → *francuzi* 'Frenchmen'
arabin 'an Arab' → *arabi* 'Arabs'

4.3 Subtraction and Rule Inversion: Ethnicity Terms 155

tatarin 'a Tatar' → *tatari* 'Tatars'
graždanin 'citizen' → *graždani* 'citizens'
pirdopčanin 'a resident of Pirdop'→ *pirdopčani* 'residents of Pirdop'
moskovčanin 'a resident of Moscow' → *moskovčani* 'residents of Moscow', etc.

For these nouns, in order to recognize the special status of the inflectional class *bălgarin* in the noun inflection of Bulgarian (i.e. despite singular forms in a consonant, no additive plural), Manova and Dressler (2001) postulate subtraction in the derivation of the plural. Moreover, since the short plurals terminate in -*i* (cf. the Old Bulgarian NOM PL *slověne* 'Slavs'), the change appears formally as a subtraction of the final -*n* from the singular form.

Let us now look at the singular-plural pattern of ethnicity terms in Russian and Serbo-Croatian. As mentioned in Chapter 1, Bulgarian has no category of case, but Russian and Serbo-Croatian still possess a full set of case forms. The paradigms in (47) and (48), illustrate the inflection of -*in* ethnicity terms in both languages.

(47)   R. *armjanin* 'Armenian'
       SG   PL
       NOM *armjan-ín*   *armján-e,*
       GEN *armjan-ín-a*   *armján*
       DAT *armjan-ín-u*   *armján-am*
       ACC = GEN   = GEN
       INSTR *armjan-ín-om* *armján-ami*
       LOC *ob armjan-ín-e* *ob armján-ax*

Note that in Russian, in some instances, NOM PL can also have -*y* and -*a* as exponents, as in *bolgarin* 'a Bulgarian' → *bolgár-y*, *gospodin* 'Mister' → *gospod-á*, all other forms receive the same case inflection.

(48)   SC. *Bugarin* 'a Bulgarian'
       SG   PL
       NOM *Bugar-in*   NOM/VOC *Bugar-i*
       GEN/ACC *Bugar-in-a*   GEN *Bugar-a*
       DAT/LOC *Bugar-in-u*   DAT/LOC/INSTR *Burar-ima*
       VOC *Bugar-in-e*   ACC *Bugar-e*
       INSTR *Bugar-in-om*

As in Bulgarian, Russian and Serbo-Croatian singular forms retain the suffix -*in*, whereas in all plural forms -*in* is deleted. However, in contrast to Bulgarian,

Russian and Serbo-Croatian *-in* behaves as a prototypical inflection substitutable within the same slot. For example, in Russian GEN PL has no overt marker for nouns terminating in *-a* and *-o* as well as for those terminating in *-in* (cf. NOM SG *ženščin-a* 'woman' → GEN PL *ženščin*, NOM SG *okn-o* 'window' → GEN PL *okon* and the GEN PL of *armjanin* 'Armenian' above). In Serbo-Croatian, *-in* can also be seen as a parallel to NOM noun inflection realized by vowels. In this language, it is inappropriate to claim that a subtraction of the final *-n* takes place, since only a single form (NOM/VOC) terminates in *-i* in the plural. Therefore, we will assume that in Russian and Serbo-Croatian, ethnicity terms with the suffix *-in* in the singular build their plural case forms by substitution of *-in* with plural suffixes.

4.4 Classification of Subtraction

The classification of subtraction suggested below operates with the following criteria (listed according to order of application):

(1) scope of subtraction (whether in derivation or in inflection); for subtraction in derivation the word-class of the input and the output is also considered;
(2) type of base (whether word, stem or root); and
(3) +/− modification

4.4.1 Subtraction in Derivation

4.4.1.1 Word-Class-Changing Subtraction

Examples of subtraction in derivation available in the literature are word-class-preserving subtractions.[8] However, as expected from the assumption of the scale of morphological techniques, in parallel to affixational rules, Slavic languages suggest instances of word-class-changing subtraction. The latter type usually deletes the phoneme X that follows the ROOT of the word (i.e. ROOT-X-ISUFF → ROOT-ISUFF), which means that word-class-changing subtraction is predominantly stem-based. The subtracted phoneme X does not belong to the root and might often be identified with an existing suffix placed in the derivational slot of the word, though the input is non-derived, as in examples (49)–(52) below. Word-class-changing subtraction allows for phonological and morphonological modifications.

Word-class-changing subtraction can be verbalizing:

---

[8] Assuming that action nouns in Icelandic (Anderson 1988; 1992) and Romanian (Hristea 1984) claimed to be derived by subtraction have an intermediate status within the derivation-inflection continuum.

4.4 Classification of Subtraction

4.4.1.1.1 Adjective-to-Verb Subtraction

A limited number of adjectives exhibiting the suffix *-k-* serve as input if this type of subtraction. Such adjectives, when participating as bases of morphological changes (whether derivational or inflectional, for inflection see Section 4.4.2.2), often lose the suffix *-k-*.

(49) ROOT – *k* –ISUFF → ROOT – TM – ISUFF
R. *úz-k-ij* 'narrow' → *úz-i-t'* 'to narrow' (cf. the root-based COMP *už-e* 'narrower')
R. *glád-k-ij* 'smooth' → *glád-i-t'* 'to iron, smooth out' (cf. the root-based COMP *glaž-e* 'smoother')
R. *dérz-k-ij* 'audacious' → *derz-í-t'* 'to dare' (with a stress change)

As can be expected, Bulgarian and Serbo-Croatian have similar subtractions. However, in contrast to the above-cited stem-based examples from Russian, the Bulgarian and Serbo-Croatian instances, though lesser in number than in Russian, are closer to the prototype of the morphological technique of subtraction, i.e. they are word-based (of the type ROOT-DSUFF → ROOT-TM-ISUFF). Consider:

(50) Bg. *glád-ăk* 'smooth' → *glád-j-a* 'I iron, stroke, smooth out', 3SG *glád-i*
SC. *glàd-ak* 'smooth' → *glàd-i-ti* 'to stroke, smooth out'

These examples, since exhibiting only shortening and without any modifications, are very close to the prototype of subtraction. However, the morphonological metathesis in the derivation Bg. *dắrz-ăk* 'audacious' → *drắz-v-a-m* 'I dare' yields a deviation from the prototype.

4.4.1.1.2 Noun-to-Verb Subtraction

(51) ROOT – *k* – ISUFF → ROOT – TM – ISUFF
Bg. N *kót-k-a* 'cat' → V *kót-j-a se* '(I) have kittens, kitten, litter, breed, have puppies', 3 SG *kót-i se*

It should be noted that the verb *kotja (se)* is an isolated example, which can be explained by the fact that the meaning 'to give birth to an animal' can, in Bulgarian, be expressed by the more general verb IMPFV *ražd-a-m* '(I) bear', 3 SG *ražd-a*. Consider:

(52a) *Kotkata   se   koti.*
      cat-SG-DEF   se-REFL   kitten-3 SG.PRES
      'The cat is breeding'
(52b) *Kotkata   razda.*
      cat -SG-DEF   bear-3 SG.PRES
      'The cat is breeding'.

The same verb derived by subtraction exists in Serbo-Croatian as well, but the Serbo-Croatian verb for *kotja se* exhibits a morphonological alternation:

(53)   SC. *mȁč-k-ā* 'cat' → *mác-i-ti se* 'to give birth (of a cat)'.

Note that the Russian verb *kot-í-t'sja* 'to give birth to a cat/a goat/a lamb', due to the existence of *kot* 'Tom-cat' (cf. Bg. *koták*, SC. *máčak*), appears a less convincing example of subtraction (from *kóš-k-a* 'cat').

A semantically unrelated example derived from the same morphotactic pattern is:

(54)   Bg. N *škúr-k-a* 'sandpaper' → V *škúr-j-a* 'I sandpaper',
       3 SG *škúr-i*
       R. *škúr-k-a* 'sandpaper' → *škúr-i-t'* 'to sandpaper (spec.)'.

The next instances of noun-to-verb subtraction are derived by a different morphotactic rule, cf. (55) and (57) below. The rule exists only in Bulgarian and Russian, and it is stem-based in both languages.

Bulgarian
(55)   X-*stv-i-e* → X-*stv-a-m*

X is the root, -*stv*- and -*i*- are derivationl suffixes and the stem X-*stv-i* is the base of the rule; all other suffixes (-*e*-, -*a*- and -*m*) are inflectional. Thus the rule can be represented as:

(56a) ROOT−DSUFF−DSUFF−ISUFF→ROOT DSUFF TM−ISUFF

The following are examples of such derivations from Bulgarian:

(56b) NEUT *béd-stv-i-e* 'calamity, disaster' → IMPFV *béd-stv-a-m* 'I live in poverty', *béd-stv-a*
       NEUT *blagodén-stv-i-e* 'prosperity' → IMPFV *blagodén-stv-a-m* 'I prosper, flourish', *blagodén-stv-a*

4.4 Classification of Subtraction

These Bulgarian examples represent an interesting case of reanalysis of the final phoneme (-*v*-) of the base. Originally the pattern derived output verbs by the addition of the unproductive aspectual suffix -*uv-a*-, i.e. the first forms were *bedstvuvam*, *blagodenstvuvam*, cf. (57). Later on, however, the -*uv-a*- was omitted, and the final -*v*- of the base conceived as a part of the productive aspectual suffix -*v-a*- (for a discussion on the -*uv-a* → -*v-a*- change in Bulgarian see Section 5.2.1.2). Although the pattern in (54) is productive in general, there are pairs such as *spokojstvie* 'calmness' → *spokojstvam, *našestvie* 'invasion' → *našestvam, with failing verbal mates (Manova 2006). Indeed, X*stvie* nouns without verbal counterparts are very few, but of particular importance for our analysis, since they, according to Aronoff's distributional criterion (cf. Chapter 3), support the correctness of the assumed direction of derivation and thus the subtractive character of the rule.

As already said, similar derivations exist in Russian as well:

(57) X-*stv-i-e* → X-*stv-ov-a-t'*

(58a) ROOT –DSUFF – DSUFF – ISUFF →
ROOT – DSUFF – ASUFF – TM – ISUFF

(58b) NEUT *napút-stv-i-e* 'advice' → IMPFV *napút-stv-ov-a-t'* 'to advise'
NEUT *privet-stv-i-e* 'greeting' → IMPFV *privet-stv-ov-a-t'* 'to greet'

The two patterns in (55) and (57) appear formally related to noun-to-verb conversions in Bulgarian (such as N*stv-o* → V*stv-a-m*) and in Russian (such as N*stvo* → V*stvovat'*), cf. Sections 3.5.1.1.1.2b and 3.5.1.1.2.2.

In Bulgarian and Serbo-Croatian, word-class-changing subtraction sometimes derives adjectives.

4.4.1.1.3 Noun-to-Adjective Subtraction

Although there are very few nouns from which adjectives can be derived by subtraction, the rule shows some generality (as in some of the examples above, consists of the deletion of the suffix -*k*- from the derivational slot of the input); the formal structure of the patter is given in (59). As is typical for a WF change, the rule is sensitive to the semantic meaning of the base and operates only on nouns denoting animals.

(59) ROOT-*k-a* → ROOT -*i*
(-*a* and -*i* are inflectional suffixes)

(60) Bg. N *kokóš-k-a* 'hen, fowl'→ ADJ *kokóš-i* 'hen's, chicken (attr.)'
Bg. N *miš-k-a* 'mouse' → *miš-i* 'mouse (attr.)'
SC. *màč-k-ā* 'cat'→ ADJ *màč-jī* 'cat (attr.), cat-like'

The adjectives formed by this subtractive pattern often have competing forms derived by more iconic techniques, e.g.: Bg. N *méč-k-a* 'bear'→ ADJ MASC *méč-i* 'bear (attr.), bearish'/*méč-ešk-i* 'bear (attr.), bear-like', Bg. N *mráv-k-a* 'ant'→ *mráv-i*/*mráv-č-i*/*mráv-ešk-i* 'formic, ant (attr.)'; SC. *gùs-k-a* 'goose' → *gùs-jī*, *gùš-č-jī* 'goose (attr.)'. As already discussed in Chapter 2, the more diagrammatic forms have a wider semantic scope than subtractions, the latter, since diachronically older, participating in idiomatic expressions.

The noun-to-adjective subtractive rule is sometimes accompanied by modifications, as in the following examples:

(61) Bg. *gǎ́s-k-a* 'goose' → ADJ *gǎ́š-i* 'goose (attr.)'
Bg. *pát-k-a* 'duck' → ADJ *páč-i*/*pat-ešk-i* 'duck (attr.)'. The second form *pat-ešk-i* is derived by substitution.
SC. *pàt-k-a* 'duck' → ADJ *pàč-jī* 'duck (attr.)'

Cf. also Bg. *kot-k-a* 'cat' → subtraction *koč-i* (old) 'cat (attr.)' vs. substitution *kot-ešk-i* 'cat (attr.)', *koči* is now considered archaic and therefore has been replaced by *koteški* in modern Bulgarian.

4.4.1.2 Word-Class-Preserving Subtraction

4.4.1.2.1 Noun-to-Noun Subtraction

The next subtractive pattern, that in (62), derives nouns from other nouns, e.g.: Fr. *photographie* 'photography' → *photographe* 'photographer', i.e. we have to do with non-prototypical subtraction in derivation. The rule is, perhaps, the classical case of word-formational subtraction in the literature. Examples of that type can be found in Dressler (2000b: 584) from French; in Rainer (1993: 80 f., 695–7) from Spanish; in Hristea (1984: 75f) from Romanian; and in Iacobini (2000), among others.

(62) Bg., R., SC. N X-*i-ja* → N X
(-*ja* is an inflectional suffix)

The semantics of this pattern can be described in general as 'science, illness, process of' → 'specialist in/representative of/carrying out X*ija*', X being usually trisyllabic. Rainer (1993: 696) motivates the direction of the pattern with derivations such as G. *Mikrobiologie* 'microbiology' → *Mikrobiologe* 'microbiologist' where microbiologist does not mean a very small biologist but a specialist in microbiology. Thus the non-compositional semantics of *Mikrobiologe* is evidence for its derived (subtractive) character, i.e. *Mikrobiologe* is derived from *Mikrobiologie* by subtraction. We will agree with Rainer on the direction of the rule in general, though in cases such as Bg. *filosof* 'philosopher'

4.4 Classification of Subtraction

– *filosofija* 'philosophy' a rule inversion is also possible (cf. Section 4.3 above). Cf. E. *philosophy – philosopher* and G. *Philosophie – Philosoph*.

The examples below are from Bulgarian, Russian and Serbo-Croatian. By rule, such subtractions show no modification in Bulgarian but are prosodically modified (by a stress change) in Russian[9] and Serbo-Croatian. Note that since stress changes are irrelevant for the establishing of subtraction, in (63), they are ignored. In the discussion below, only nouns with morphotactically different forms in one of the three languages are extra indicated.

(63)　*oligarx-i-ja* → *oligarx*, SC. *oligarh-i-ja* → *oligarh*
　　　psixiatr-i-ja → *psixiatăr* R. *psixiatr*, SC. *psihijatr-i -a* → *psihijatar*
　　　geograf-i-ja → *geograf*
　　　psixolog-i-ja → *psixolog*, SC. *psiholog-i-ja* → *psiholog*
　　　astronom-i-ja → *astronom*
　　　oligofren-i-ja → *oligofren*
　　　filosof-i-ja → *filosof*, SC. *filozof-i-ja* → *filozof*
　　　strateg-i-ja 'strategy' → *strateg* 'strategist' (with diachronic rule inversion from the Ancient Greek *stratēgós* → *stratēgía*)
　　　logoped-i-ja → *logoped*
　　　psixopat-i-ja → *psixopat*, SC. *psihopat-i-ja* → *psihopat*

Unlike Rainer (1993) who distributes the above nouns into different groups such as nouns in *-iatria, -ocracija, -ografija, -ologija*, etc., we, in order to generalize the pattern, assume that all above subtractions are of the type 'X-*i-ja* → X'. The only instance we will separate from the group of nouns in (63) is that of nouns in *-cija* which, with the subtraction of *-ija*, change the final consonant of the base *c* into *t*, as in *demokrac-i-ja* → *democrat*.

In the literature, subtraction is usually defined as a shortening of the base of a morphological change without any connection to the length of the base of the rule, though on the parameter of optimal length of a word, as postulated by NM (cf. Dressler 2000a), one could expect that subtraction should prefer longer bases. In fact, it is the case with X-*i-ja* nouns. For such nouns a formal constraint concerning the number of the syllables of the base of the subtractive rule X-*i-ja* → X can be formulated, namely subtraction prefers as bases words (X-*i-ja*) which consist of more than four syllables (cf. the examples in (63) where only *strategija* 'strategy' is four-syllabic). In case of shorter bases, the semantic pattern uses either addition or substitution, as can be seen from the following examples:

(64)　Bg., R. X-*i-ja* → X*ik*
　　　SC. X-*i-ja* → X*ičar*

---

[9] For the stress pattern of the Russian nouns in *-graf* and *-olog* see Comrie et al. (1996: 94–96).

(65)   *istor-i-ja* 'history' → *istorik* 'historian', SC. *histor-i-ja* → *historičar*
xim-i-ja 'chemistry' → *ximik* 'chemist', SC *hem-i-ja/kem-i-ja* → *hemičar/kemičar*
man-i-ja 'mania' → *maniak* /SC. *manijak* 'maniac'

A form longer than *-ik/-ičar* is affixed in Bg./R: *teor-i-ja* 'theory' → *teor-etik* 'theorist' and SC. *teor-etičar*.

In accordance to the above-formulated constraint, derivations with bases terminating in *manija* use subtraction, e.g. *meloman-i-ja* 'melomania' → *meloman*, *narkoman-i-ja* → *narkoman*, *piroman-i-ja* → *piroman*, etc., though *man-i-ja* 'mania' → *maniak*, SC. *manijak* 'maniac'. However, derivations in which *ximik/* SC. *hemičar/kemičar* participates always have the suffix *-ik* irrespective of the number of the syllables of the base, e.g. *bioximija*, SC. *biohemija/biokemija* 'biochemistry' → *bioximik/*SC. *biohemičar/biokemičar* 'biochemist'.

The number of the syllables of the base seems irrelevant if illnesses serve as input. Regardless of the number of syllables of the illness, the corresponding ill person is derived either by suffixation (66) or by subtraction (67):

(66)   *šizofren-i-ja* → *šizofrenik* (SC. also *šizofreničar*)
xipoxondr-i-ja → *xipoxondrik*, SC. *hipohondr-i-ja* → *hipohondar* (subtraction) and *hipohondrik* (suffixation)
melanxol-i-ja → *melanxolik*, SC. *melankol-i-ja* → *melankolik*
epileps-i-ja → *epileptik* (SC. also *epileptičar*)
etc.

vs. subtractions such as

(67)   *oligofren-i-ja* → *oligofren*
psixopat-i-ja → *psixopat*, SC. *psihopat-i-ja* → *psihopat*
etc.

In addition to the formal constraint in regard to the number of syllables of the base, a semantic constraint can also be formulated: if the meaning of a word terminating in *-logija* is different from 'science, illness, process of', that word cannot be paired according to the pattern X*ija* → X.

(68)   *antologija* 'anthology' → Ø
trilogija 'trilogy' → Ø
haplologija 'haplology' → Ø

4.4 Classification of Subtraction

The same holds for nouns in *-log* with a semantic meaning different from 'specialists in/representatives of/caring out X', they also do not have *-logija* mates:

(69)   *catalog* 'catalogue', *dialog* (SC. *dijalog*) 'dialogue', *monolog* 'monologue', *prolog* 'prologue',
(cf. also *metronom* 'metronome', *paragraf* 'paragraph', etc.)

This semantic restriction is a nice illustration of the semantic core of derivational rules (be they additional or subtractive) and thus a proof against theories such as Beard (1995), who postulates a morphological spelling component which implements formal processes parallel to our morphological techniques but having only grammatically determined referents, without semantics.

The complex suffix *-olog-i-ja*, by rule, combines with nominal bases of foreign origin but in neologisms, *-ologija* could be found attached to native non-nominal bases. For example, in Russian, some verbs of native origin can function as bases of *-ologija* neologisms from which, by subtraction, *-olog* nouns might be derived, as in V *boltat'* 'to chat, gossip' → *boltologija* → *boltolog*; V *trepat'sja* 'to talk nonsense' → *trepologija* → *trepolog* (cf. Zemskaja 1992: 120, 142).

In the next example, *-ologija* attaches to a pronominal base. Consider: Bg. PRO *vsičko* 'everything' → *vsičkologija* 'science of everything' and the potential form ?*vsičkolog*, and R. PRO *vse* 'all' → *vseologija* and *vseolog* (for Russian, see Zemskaja 1992: 120, 142).

The next case of subtraction also expresses the semantics 'science' → 'scientist' but with a different morphotactic structure:

(70)   Bg./R./SC. X-*ist-ika* → X-*ist*
germanistika 'German studies' → *germanist*
lingvistika 'linguistics' → *lingvist*
slavistika 'Slavic studies' → *slavist*

In Bulgarian, Russian and Serbo-Croatian, the complex suffix *-ist-ik-a* is particularly productive with bases denoting countries and peoples, e.g. *ispanistika* 'Spanish studies'/SC. *španistika*, *portugalistika* 'Portugal studies', *katalonistika* 'Catalan studies', etc., and all such nouns have counterparts in *-ist*.

As in the case of *-olog-ija* → *-olog* (cf. (68) and (69)), if new formations in both *-ist-ik-a* and *-ist* contradict semantically the pattern 'science' → 'scientist', they have no counterparts. For example:

(71) Russian
èmotivistika (from emotion) → Ø
erundistika (from *erunda* 'nonsense') → Ø
zubristika (from *zubrit'* 'to cram') → Ø,
but there is *zubrila* 'crammer'
(for this type of neologisms in Russian see Zemskaja 1992: 142).

For the opposite direction:

(72) Bg./R. *pianist* (SC. *pijanist*) 'pianist' → Ø
telefonist 'telefone operator'→ Ø
etc.

The Slavic equivalent of *-ologija* is *-vedenie*. The Russian *-vedenie* originated from the old verb R. *vedat'* 'to know' (Zemskaja 1992: 142f), which is connected semantically with the verb *znat'* 'to know'. In modern Russian, the rule X*ved-enie* → X*ved* derives by subtraction examples such as *jazykovedenie* 'linguistics' → *jazykoved* 'linguist', *naukovedenie* 'science + knowledge, i.e. science' → *naukoved*, *čelovekovedenie* 'man + knowledge, i.e. psychology' → *čelovekoved*, etc. As Zemskaja (1992) noted, there is a complimentary distribution of the two suffixes *-ologija* and *-vedenie*. The suffix *-vedenie* combines with native bases only, whereas *-ologija* prefers foreign bases. An example is *grafologija* 'graphology' vs. the native Russian *počerkovedenie*.

In Bulgarian, only X*ved* nouns denoting scientists such as *literaturoved* 'expert in literature/literary critic', *ezikoved* 'linguist', *izkustvoved* 'art expert/ critic', etc. exist. These nouns are undoubtedly under Russian influence, and their respective sciences have as a second part the Bulgarian noun *znanie* 'knowledge', instead of the expected Russian *-vedenie*. Examples include: *literaturoznanie* 'theory of literature' but *literaturoved* 'expert in literature/literary critic', *ezikoznanie* 'linguistics' but *ezikoved* 'linguist' as well as *lingvistika* → *lingvist*, *izkustvoznanie* 'science of art/ art criticism' but *izkustvoved* 'art expert/ critic', etc. In these examples, since the input and the output exhibit morphotactically unrelated forms, the rule is not subtractive. In fact, we have an interesting example of suppletion in word-formation.

Note that in Serbo-Croatian, there exist neither X*vedenie* nor X*ved* nouns.

The next examples of subtraction belong to the periphery of the above-discussed semantic pattern 'science' → 'scientist'. The template of the rule is given in (73):

(73) Bg. X*vădstvo*/R. X*vodstvo* 'X-breeding/growing' → X*văd* / X*vod* 'specialist in X; X-breeder/grower'

4.4 Classification of Subtraction   165

(74a)   Bulgarian
        rastenievădstvo 'plant-growing' → *rastenievăd* 'plant-grower'
        ovcevădstvo 'sheep-breeding' → *ovcevăd* 'sheep-breeder'
        konevădstvo 'horse-breeding' → *konevăd* 'horse-breeder', etc.

(74b)   Russian
        rastenievodstvo 'plant-growing' → *rastenievod* 'plant-grower'
        ovcevodstvo 'sheep-breeding' → *ovcevod* 'sheep-breeder'

Such pairs are relatively new formations. In fact, the pattern became productive under socialism, and its precise semantics is 'X-growing/breeding in a socialist manner' → 'X-grower/X-breeder/specialist in X'. The specific semantics of the pattern explains the existing parallel forms such as Bg. *ovčar*/R. *ovčar'* 'shepherd' and Bg. *ovcevăd*/R. *ovcevod* 'sheep-breeder', Bg. *konjar* 'groom' and *konevăd* 'horse-breeder'. While *ovčar* and *konjar* denote non-organized breeders of X, *ovcevăd* and *konevăd* remain designations for persons working in socialist collective farms. Note that the nouns in *-văd* are more respectful. We will see the connection of the pattern with the development of socialist collective farms as evidence for its subtractive character, i.e. since both the input and the output appear at the same time, the derivatives can be reliably established according to the semantic criterion of dependence of meaning. In our case, due to the meaning, 'specialist in breeding/growing', breeders/growers, though shorter in form, are undoubtedly the derivatives.

As for the productivity of the rule, although Zemskaja (1992: 120) evaluates the pattern as productive (due to examples such as R. *vodoraslevodstvo* 'seaweed-growing' → *vodoraslevod* 'seaweed-grower'; R. *norkovodstvo* 'minkbreeding' → *norkovod* 'mink-breeder'), with the end of socialism the rule seems to become unproductive.

The next group of examples is derived by shortening of the stem-final *-k-* from the input noun, i.e. ROOT-*k*-ISUFF → ROOT-ISUFF. The output nouns are either diminutives or augmentatives.

4.4.1.2.2 Diminutives

(75)   Bg. *pát-k-a* 'duck' → DIM *pát-e* 'duckling'
        Bg. *kót-k-a* 'cat' → DIM *kót-e* 'kitten'
        SC. *màč-k-ā* 'cat' → DIM *màč-e* 'kitten' (Barić et al. 1997: 315)

The pattern allows for prosodic and segmental modifications:

(76)   Bg. *méč-k-a* 'bear' → DIM *meč-é* and *méč-e* 'Teddy bear'
        SC. *pàt-k-a* 'duck' → DIM *pàč-e* 'duckling' (Barić et al. 1997: 315)

4.4.1.2.3 Augmentatives

All the examples of augmentatives derived by subtraction come from the West Slavic language Polish, where the subtraction of the stem-final -*k*- expresses the meaning 'much/big bad quantity' (Mel'čuk 1991: 299; Dressler 1994, 2000b; Dressler and Merlini Barbaresi 1994: 485–7), as in the next two examples:

(77)   *wód-k-a* 'vodka' → AUG *wód-a* 'much bad vodka'
         łapów-k-a 'bribe' → AUG *łapów-a* 'big bad bribe'

As can be expected, like the diminutives in (76), some of the augmentatives derived by subtraction of the stem-final -*k*- exhibit modifications (cf. Dressler 2000b: 584):

(78)   *pias-ek* → AUG *piach* 'sand' (this example is word-based)
         flasz-k-a → AUG *flax-a* 'bottle'

Uluhanov (2000: 291) mentions two examples of occasional formations from Russian, which appear parallel to the above Polish augmentatives: R. *čaš-k-a* 'cup' → *čaša* 'big cup', *lož-k-a* 'spoon' → *log-a* 'big spoon'. However, the reductive character of these examples is less clear than that of the Polish rule of augmentative formation. First, no other source considers those Russian examples subtractive and second, the direction of derivation suggested by Uluhanov for *čaša* seems incorrect, as from the diachronic point of view it is more probable that *čaška* was derived from *čaša* with the diminutive suffix -*k*- than vice versa (cf. Ožegov and Švedova 1995: 866).

For the sake of completeness, one should add that Bulgarian and Serbo-Croatian do not have augmentatives derived by subtraction.

4.4.2 Subtraction in Inflection

4.4.2.1 Subtraction in Inflection Without Modifications

The first type of subtraction in inflection is word-based, derives plural forms and has the following morphotactic structure:

4.4.2.1.1 Plural

(79)   ROOT*in* 'ethnic noun' → ROOT*i*
         Bg. *bǎgarin* '(a) Bulgarian' → *bǎlgari* 'Bulgarians'.
         (see the examples in (46))

4.4 Classification of Subtraction   167

Indeed, the singular suffix -*in* already has been dealt with in detail in Section 4.3. For that reason only brief discussion is included here.

For the definition of the -*in* subtractive rule, it is of particular importance that in Bulgarian, nouns in -*in* which are not ethnicity terms (for semantic elements in Bulgarian nominal inflection, cf. Manova 2003a) have lost the singulative suffix -*in*, and now the short plurals seem to be derived by addition of the plural suffix -*i* attached to the new singular forms without -*in*. Examples include SG *advokatin* (old) vs. *advokat* 'lawyer' → PL *advokati*, SG *oficerin* (old) vs. *oficer* 'military officer' → PL *oficeri*, *tiranin* (old) vs. *tiran* 'tyrant' → *tirani*, and likewise with all borrowings from Turkish which had the suffix -*in*: *bakalin* vs. *bakal* 'grocer' (T. *bakkal*) → PL *bakali*, *dušmanin* vs. *dušman* 'enemy' (T. *düsman*) → PL *dušmani*, *kasapin* vs. *kasap* 'butcher' (T. *kasap*) → PL *kasapi*, *kalpazanin* vs. *kalpazan* 'good-for-nothing, rascal' (T. *kalpazan*) → PL *kalpazani*, etc. Undoubtedly, when all these nouns were borrowed from Turkish, the singulative suffix -*in* was productive (in the sense of Dressler 1997). Afterwards, however, the suffix -*in* lost its productivity, and due also to the isolated character of such singular-plural pairs in the declension system of Bulgarian (cf. the discussion in Section 4.3, and Table 4.1), the singular forms lost their final -*in*. This change makes from the previous subtracted plurals diagrammatic forms suffixed with the most productive inflection for polysyllabic nouns in consonants, the suffix -*i*. This diachronic change towards iconicity is thus evidence for the marked (subtractive) character of the short plurals of ethnicity terms in the noun inflection system of Bulgarian and indirectly supports the correctness of the postulation of subtraction of -*n* in the case of ethnicity terms. Moreover, the fact that only nouns with semantics different from ethnicity terms have lost -*in*, defines the pattern in (79) semantically.

It should also be noted that Bulgarian subtractive plurals clearly differ from the above-discussed Hessian plurals (cf. (5)), where the rule, since phonologically governed, is not subtractive. In Bulgarian (in contrast to Hessian German), the -*in* termination of a noun does not automatically mean subtraction (Manova 2003a: 112), e.g. *ispolin* 'colossus' → PL *ispolin-i*, since *ispolin* contradicts the pattern of ethnicity terms semantically.

4.4.2.2 Subtraction in Inflection with Modifications

4.4.2.2.1 Plural

In Bulgarian, there is an isolated example fitting formally and semantically the pattern in Section 4.4.2.1 but with a morphonological alternation (isolated paradigm according to Manova and Dressler 2001): *turčin* → *turci*.

4.4.2.2.2 Comparatives

Comparatives in Russian and Serbo-Croatian are formed by default with the help of the morphological techniques of substitution and addition respectively (cf. Section 1.2.2.2), e.g.: R. *trudn-yj* 'difficult' → *trudn-ee* 'more difficult', *dorog-oj* 'dear' → *dorož-e* 'dearer', *star-yj* 'old' → *star-še* 'older'; SC. *tužan* 'sad' → *tužn-iji* 'sadder', *suh* 'dry' → *suš-i* 'drier', *mek* 'soft' → *mek-ši* 'softer'. However, some Russian and Serbo-Croatian adjectives terminating in the (non-inflectional) suffix -*k*- or in an epenthetic vowel plus -*k*- (-*Vk*) delete this suffix in the comparative degree. Consider the following templates:

(80)   SC. ROOT – (V)*k* → ROOT-*j*-ISUFF
R. ROOT – *k* – ISUFF → ROOT-*j*-ISUFF
-*j*- indicates palatalization of the root-final consonant

The rule affects only adjectives continuants of the old Indo-European short comparatives and is entirely unproductive.

In Serbo-Croatian, adjectives with comparative forms derived by subtraction terminate in -*(a)k*, -*(e)k*, -*(o)k*,[10] as can be seen from the following examples:

(81)   POSITIVE → COMPARATIVE
ROOT – V*k* → ROOTj + ISUFF
(i.e. word-based subtraction)
blizak 'near' → *bliži* 'nearer'
dalek 'far' → *dalji* 'farther, further'
dubok 'deep' → *dublji* 'deeper'
gladak 'smooth' → *glađi* 'smoother'
kratak 'short' → *kraći* 'shorter'
nizak 'low' → *niži* 'lower'
plitak 'shallow' → *plići* 'shallower'
rijedak 'rare' → *rjeđi* 'rarer'
širok 'wide' → *širi* 'wider'
sladak 'sweet' → *slađi* 'sweeter'
tanak 'slim' → *tanji* 'slimmer'
težak 'heavy' → *teži* 'heavier'
uzak 'narrow' → *uži* 'narrower'
visok 'high' → *viši* 'higher'
žestok 'cruel' → *žešći* 'crueller'
(cf. Težak and Babič 1992: 104f; Barić et al. 1997: 182).

As is usual for an unproductive rule, and since subtraction is an anti-diagrammatic technique, exceptions and competing forms, both following productive rules, accompany this subtractive pattern. There are adjectives which despite the suffix -*ak*, build additive comparative forms, e.g.: *gor-ak*

---

[10]The vowels are phonologically inserted, since 'consonant + k' is difficult to pronounce word-finally.

4.4 Classification of Subtraction

'bitter' → *gorč-i, krep-ak* 'strong' → *krepć-i*, also *krepk-iji, ljub-ak* 'cute' → *ljupk-iji, drzak* 'impudent' → *drsk-iji*. Other adjectives have doublet forms built either by subtraction or by addition, e.g.: *žid-ak* 'viscous' → *žid-i* and *žitk-iji*, *mrz-ak* 'hateful' → *mrž-i* and *mrsk-iji, krot-ak* 'tame' → *kroč-i* and *krotk-iji* (cf. Barić et al. 1997: 182f.).

Russian adjectives with subtracted comparative forms are parallel to the above-cited examples from Serbo-Croatian. There is a distinction between Russian and Serbo-Croatian, however, regarding superlatives. In Russian some superlative forms of adjectives with subtracted comparatives are also derived by subtraction. All such forms are noted in the list of examples from Russian below. (For the derivation of comparative and superlative forms of Russian adjectives see Section 1.2.2.2).

(82) POSITIVE → COMPARATIVE
      ROOT –*k*– ISUFF → ROOTj + ISUFF
      (i.e. stem-based subtraction)
      bliz-k-ij 'near' → *bliž-e* 'nearer', *bliž-ajšij* 'nearest'
      dalë-k-ij 'far, remote' → *dal'-še* 'farther, remoter', *dal-ee*
                                          (no -*ajšij* superlative)
      gad-k-ij 'bad, wicked' → *gaž-e* 'worse' (no -*ajšij* superlative)
      glad-k-ij 'plane, smooth' → *glaž-e* 'planer, smoother'
                         (no -*ajšij* superlative)
      korot-k-ij 'short' → *koroč-e* 'shorter', BUT *kratč-ajšij* 'shortest'
      niz-k-ij 'low' → *niž-e* 'lower', *niž-ajšij* 'lowest'
      red-k-ij 'rare' → *rež-e* 'rarer', BUT *redč-ajšij* 'rarest'
      slad-k-ij 'sweet' → *slašč-e* 'sweeter',
                   BUT *sladč-ajšij* 'sweetest (metaph.)'
      ton-k-ij 'fine, thin' → *ton-še* 'finer, thinner',
                   BUT *tonč-ajšij* 'finest (metaph.)'
      uz-k-ij 'narrow' → *už-e* 'narrower' (no -*ajšij* superlative)
      žid-k-ij 'liquid' → *žiž-e* 'more liquid' (no -*ajšij* supperlative)
      (cf. Švedova et al. 1980: 565)

The whole suffix -*ok* is subtracted only in *vys-ok-ij* 'high' → *vyš-e* 'higher' and *šir-ok-ij* 'wide' → *šir-e* 'wider'.

As in Serbo-Croatian, some Russian adjectives with the suffix -*k*- have either two comparative forms derived by subtraction and modification, e.g.: *merz-k-ij* 'loathsome' → *merz-ee* and *merz-č-e, gor'-k-ij* 'bitter' → *gor-še* and *gor'-č-e*; or they have only forms built by modification, e.g.: *krep-k-ij* 'solid, strong' → *krep-č-e, grom-k-ij* 'loud' → *grom-č-e*.

Unpredictable subtractive shortenings occur in *dolg-ij* 'long' → *dol'-še* 'longer' and *dol-ee* 'longer' (both root-based subtractions); *kras-iv-yj* 'beautiful'

→ *kraš-e* and *kras-iv-ee,* both forms meaning 'more beautiful', and in *pozdn-ij* 'late' → *pozž-e, pozdn-ee,* both meaning 'later'.

Note, however, that in modern Russian, *-ee* and *-še* comparatives often differ either lexically or stylistically. For example, *dol'še* is the comparative form of *dolgij,* whereas *dolee* expresses adverbial meaning. *kraše* is poetic, whereas *krasivee* is stylistically neutral, etc. (cf. Russian Academy Grammar 1980: 565).

A case when a subtraction of an inflectional affix changes word class is theoretically impossible because, as assumed (cf. Chapters 2 and 3), if a deletion of an inflectional suffix gives rise to a word-class change and no modification co-occurs, we speak of conversion, e.g.: Bg. V *razgrom-j-á* 'I rout', 3 SG *razgrom-í* → N *razgróm* 'rout' is a case of conversion. Recall that a similar word-class-changing rule with a concomitant modification will be classified as modification (according to the assumptions in Chapter 2), e.g., Bg. V *izved-á* 'I bring out, work out', 3 SG *izved-é* → N *ízvod* 'conclusion' with a stress change is a case of modification. No instance has been attested wherein the reduction of a part of an inflection suffix yields a word class change.

4.5 Conclusion

Subtraction is defined herein as a morphological technique consisting of deletion of the final segment of the base of a morphological rule. On the analogy of the rule of affixation, it has been assumed and demonstrated that a subtractive rule deletes the same final segments, be they a particular phoneme or longer than a single phoneme. A further comparison with affixation has shown that the morphological technique of subtraction also has realizations in derivation and in inflection (see Table 4.2), with word-class-changing and word-class-preserving realizations in derivation; and that subtraction operates on roots, stems and words (see Table 4.3).

In regard to the languages under consideration, in Bulgarian, Russian and Serbo-Croatian, subtraction in derivation is predominantly stem-based (cf. Table 4.3), i.e. the rule exhibits the morphotactic structure ROOT – X – ISUFF → ROOT – ISUFF, where the deleted element X, though a single

Table 4.2 Types of subtraction according to their scope

Subtraction					
	In derivation			In inflection	
No	Word-class-changing		Word-class-preserving	Category	Language
1.	N > V	Bg., R., SC.	N > DIM N Bg., SC.	PL ethnicity terms	Bg.
2.	N > ADJ	Bg., SC.	N 'science' > N 'scientist' Bg., R., SC.	COMP	R., SC.
3.	ADJ > V	Bg., R., SC.	N > N ethnicity terms (rule inversion) Bg., R., SC.	SUP	R.

4.5 Conclusion

Table 4.3 Types of subtraction according to their bases

Base	Subtraction			
	Subtraction in derivation		Subtraction in inflection	
Root			COMP	R.
Stem	N > V	Bg., R., SC.	COMP & SUP	R.
	N > ADJ	Bg., SC.		
	ADJ > V	R.		
	N > DIM N	Bg., SC.		
Word	N 'science'> N 'scientist'	Bg., R., SC.		
	ADJ > V	Bg., SC.	PL ethnicity terms	Bg.
	N > N ethnicity terms (rule inversion)	Bg., R., SC.	COMP	SC.

phoneme, usually coincides with a morpheme and can therefore be identified as having some semantics. As expected according to the principles of NM, word-class-changing word-based subtraction without modifications is rare. Even rarer, however, is root-based subtraction (recall that roots are the most unnatural type of bases). Indeed, root-based subtraction is the rarest type of subtraction in the three languages (see Table 4.3), and no such examples have been found in derivation. It seems that there exists a transparency constraint that preserves the root against the anti-iconic subtraction but not against the weakly iconic modification (recall examples such as Bg. N *pat-k-a* → ADJ *pač-i*, N *găs-k-a* → ADJ *găš-i*, both word-class-changing stem-based subtractions with modified roots. Likewise in inflection, R. *bliz-k-ij* 'near' → COMP *bliž-e*, SUP *bliž-ajšij*, SC. *bliz-ak* 'near' → COMP *bliž-i*, etc.). Subtraction in inflection affects only non-prototypical inflection (the categories of plural and comparatives) and is either word-based (the plural of ethnicity terms in Bulgarian and the comparative forms of some Serbo-Croatian adjectives) or stem-based (comparatives and superlatives in Russian), cf. Tables 4.2 and 4.3. A single instance of root-based subtraction has been found in Russian where from the adjective *dolg-ij* 'long' one derives by subtraction of the root-final consonant the comparative form *dol'-še* 'longer' and the adverb *dol-ee* 'longer' (an old comparative).

Furthermore, similar to affixation by addition, subtraction is sensitive to the semantics of the bases on which operates; this has been observed in derivation as well as in inflection.

The examples analysed evidence that subtraction has its sources in: (1) language-specific system-adequate diachronic change; (2) preservation of old unproductive forms; and (3) rule inversion.

(1) In Old Church Slavic, due to the shift to gender-oriented declension, the suffix *-k-* was added to some feminine nouns denoting animals such as *myšb'* 'mouse', *gosb'* 'goose' which after the amplification with *-k-a* (cf. modern Bulgarian *miška, găska*) received the morphotactic make-up of feminine nouns in *-a* (Ivanova-Mirčeva and Xaralampiev 1999: 100). On the other

hand, the old verbs and adjectives related to the nouns extended by -*k*- have remained unchanged, and they are now in derivational connection with bases that are longer (due to the -*k*- extension), which, from the synchronic point of view, can be explained only in terms of subtraction.

(2) Preserved old forms (such as the short Russian and Serbo-Croatian comparatives) derived by an already entirely unproductive rule are the second source of subtraction. Nowadays the short comparatives and superlatives which are remnants of the root-based Indo-European/Old Church Slavic comparatives stay in the morphological systems of Russian and Serbo-Croatian alongside all new comparatives, the latter formed either by addition or by substitution, and therefore the short forms are felt as subtraction.

(3) In the diachronic development of a language some rules changed their direction. The result is a reanalysis of forms that, at the synchronic level, might be considered subtraction, i.e. a diachronic additive rule X → Y (= X + SUFF) turns over for pragmatic reasons and becomes a synchronic rule Y → X (= Y + SUFF). Both the diachronic and the synchronic rule are additive, but synchronically the output of the diachronic rule appears subtractive. Due to the additive nature of the synchronic and the diachronic rule, the subtractive character of the process can be doubted.

In Bulgarian, Russian and Serbo-Croatian, subtraction is unproductive, whereas extragrammatical shortenings such as clippings and acronyms are productive, especially in Russian.

Since subtraction is unproductive and anti-iconic, diagrammatic techniques often compete with subtraction for the expression of one and the same meaning. In some such instances diagrammatic forms have fully replaced subtractive formations, and the latter are now felt as archaic. These competition and replacement of rules support the idea that subtractive rules belong to the level of the other morphological techniques and thus explain the assumption of a cline of morphological techniques.

Chapter 5
Typological and Language-Specific Adequacy of Conversion and Subtraction

This chapter focuses on the typological and language-specific characteristics of conversion and subtraction. After a brief discussion of the typological adequacy of subtraction, conversion is tackled (Section 5.1). The typological perspective in regard to conversion is primarily in relation to its bases in the two polar morphological types – the isolating and the inflecting-fusional, though examples from agglutinating languages are also considered. In Section 5.2, cases of conversion and subtraction are explained with language-specific features such as system-adequate stress-patterns, language-specific inflectional productivity, etc. Bulgarian, Russian and Serbo-Croatian belong to the Slavic family and possess nearly the same sets of morphemes, presupposing the same or at least similar morphological solutions. At times, however, the same semantic meaning may be expressed by different morphological techniques in the three languages. Such instances are also in the scope of the chapter.

5.1 Typological Adequacy of Conversion and Subtraction

As already mentioned many times in this book, there is not much research on subtractive rules in the literature. As might be expected, no typologically oriented investigation of subtraction exists. However one, somewhat intuitively, relates an anti-diagrammatic morphological rule, such as subtraction, to the inflecting-fusional morphological type, since the associated with this language type cumulative exponence of morphological features is expected to give rise to subtractive morphology. Indeed in Chapter 4, we could demonstrate that subtraction appears typical of the inflecting-fusional language type, though the fusion of morphemes does not seem to have any role in subtraction. Additionally, the fact that subtraction operates in the inflecting-fusional type does not mean that one cannot find examples of subtraction from other language types in the literature (see, for example, Melčuk 1991). Subtractions from agglutinating and incorporating languages are, however, highly questionable, which is not because of the morphological organization of these two language types but is due to the fact that examples of subtractive morphology usually come from underdescribed languages. In most of the cases, only single examples are pointed out and there is no reliable grammar (there often exists only a single grammar, if any, where subtraction is, by rule, not mentioned), which allows for alternative interpretations of the same data by different scholars and makes it impossible to judge whose analysis is correct and whose is just speculative. Thus, since there are not enough data, the question about the typological adequacy of subtraction is not easy to answer convincingly and we prefer to leave it open.

As regards conversion, it is analysed either mainly in relation to languages tending to the isolating type (e.g. English) or in weakly inflecting languages such as Dutch, German and French, and only rarely in strongly inflecting languages, such as the Slavic ones. In the ideal isolating type, multifunctionality is assumed instead of conversion, since there are no morphologically defined word-classes (cf. Vogel 1996: 228ff) and no competing affixations or modifications (Manova and Dressler 2005). It should be emphasized, however, that the morphological technique of conversion, though not clearly connected with a given language type, seems to exhibit specific preferences with respect to the base of the rule in the different types. A brief discussion of this point follows.

Conversion in languages such as English, is word-based only, while inflecting languages, as we saw in Chapter 3, also use bases shorter than words. The more a language approaches the inflecting-fusional type, the more root-based and stem-based conversion appears, whereas word-based conversion decreases and even vanishes (Manova and Dresser 2005).

Kastovsky (1989, 1994, 2005, as well as in other publications) attributes English word-based conversion to typological changes in Old and Middle English morphology that led from root-based through stem-based to word-based morphological rules. Kastovsky understands stem-formatives as 'doing double duty' (in his terms) derivational and inflectional elements, but classifies them as derivation, which allows him to assume zero derivation, i.e. 'replacing something by nothing' (2005: 46). According to Kastovsky, the stem-formative *-oj-/-o-* (of the Pre-OE Class 2 weak verbs) converts the noun *wund* into a verb (therefore a derivational role), and at the same time makes it a member of a particular inflectional class (thus an inflectional role). However, such understanding of stem-formatives (TMs in the terminology of this book), cannot be applied to Slavic languages which, like Old and Middle English, represent the inflecting-fusional type. If we assume that the TM is what turns a noun to a verb and that it then is followed by the obligatory inflection, it is unclear why there are instances in which verbalizing conversion seems to happen without the attachment of stem-formatives, e.g. Bg. *četk-a* 'brush' → *četk-a-m* 'I brush', SC. *vag-a* 'balance' → *vag-a-ti* 'to balance', etc. (Kastovsky does not attest such instances in the diachronic development of English). An additional problem arises with the analysis of verb-to-noun and noun-to-adjective morphological conversion in Slavic where there are no stem formatives in declension. In other words, if Kastovsky's analysis is correct and it is the stem-forming element that changes the word-class of the base, verb-to-noun and noun-to-

5.1 Typological Adequacy of Conversion and Subtraction

adjective conversions should be impossible. However, such conversions exist. Therefore, in this book, in order to have a unified account of conversion, we have assumed that TMs in verbalizations are inflection, i.e. TMs, like pure inflectional affixes, are obligatory for the syntactic well-formedness of the verb. In fact, irrespective of whether Kastovsky's analysis of stem forming elements holds or not, it does not reflect on the correctness of the final observation, namely that conversion in modern English is word-based (while Old English morphology is root-based and stem-based).

The second reason for word-based conversion in English, according to Kastovsky, is the loss of ablaut derivatives in contradistinction to German. Thus morphophonological alternations became exceptional, characterizing 'irregular patterns' (cf. Kastovsky 1989: 289 and passim) and derivational relations regularized. Such a tendency has not been observed in Slavic languages.

In morphological theory, conversion in agglutinating and incorporating languages has been underrated. If it is understandable for the incorporating languages wherein, due to the long complex forms often incorporating stems of different word classes, defining conversion is extremely difficult, it is not quite clear why conversion has been seen as incompatible with agglutinating languages. Thus, though belated, recent analyses of data from the agglutinating type (Kiefer 2005) have shown that this language type also allows for conversion.

Kiefer (2005) establishes the following types of conversion in Hungarian:

(1) Noun-to-adjective conversion (with the following subtypes according to the semantics of the base: nouns referring to persons, e.g. *vitéz* 'champion' → *vitéz* 'courageous'; nouns referring to animals *kutya* 'dog' → *kutya* 'bad, miserable' (cf. the Bulgarian root-based conversion *kuč-e* 'dog' → *kuč-i* 'dog-; bad, miserable'); and ethnic names *Magyar* '(a) Hungarian' → *Magyar* 'Hungarian')
(2) Adjective-to-noun conversion, e.g. *gazdag* 'rich', *a lusták* 'the lazy-PL'
(3) Participle-to-adjective conversion, e.g. *felkavaró* 'disturbing', *kiábrándito* 'disappointing'

Of these three types, only noun-to-adjective conversion is morphological, the last two types being cases of syntactic conversion.

Syntactic conversion is, in Hungarian (and cross-linguistically), word-based, except in one instance defined by Kiefer as conversion of active root to passive root, e.g. *megolható* 'solvable', *kikapcsolható* 'releasable'. The participles with the suffix *-ható* have a passive meaning (*a megalható feladat* 'the solvable task'), though the complex suffix *-ható* consists of the possibility suffixes *-hat* and the suffix of the present participle *-ó*. Kiefer points out two possible analyses of such passive participles:

(i) active root → passivization → + *-hat* → + *-ó* (the analysis Kiefer assumes)
(ii) active root → + *-hat* → passivization → + *-ó*

According to the type of the base on which passivization operates, these two rules are root-based (i) and stem-based (ii) respectively. However, there is also a third, word-based, possibility, namely:

(iii) active root → + -*hat* → + -*ó* → passivization
(or active root → + -*ható* → passivization).

This third solution seems to be much more in line with the word-based nature of syntactic conversion in Hungarian (and cross-linguistically). In other words, for us, an agglutinating language, such as Hungarian, possesses only word-based conversion, be it morphological or syntactic.

In Finnish, another agglutinating language (though less agglutinating than Hungarian), noun-to-adjective morphological conversion is rare but also word-based, e.g. *pöllö* 'owl' and 'stupid'. All other conversion types typical of Hungarian are well presented. Consider adjective-to-noun syntactic conversion, such as (*Englanti* 'England' →) *englantilainen* 'English' → N *englantilainen* 'Englishman', as well as the following adjectives that can remain for persons: F. *vieras* 'foreign' (H. *idegen*); F. *sokea* 'blind' (H. *vak*); F. *mykkä* 'mute' (H. *néma*); F. *rikas* 'rich' (H. *gazdag*); F. *köyhä* 'poor' (H. *szegény*); F. *vaalea* 'blond' (cf. H. *a szókék* 'the blond-PL'), etc.

In Finnish, like in Hungarian, one can use participles as adjectives, e.g. *kuolla* 'to die' → *kuollut* 'died' can be used as adjective meaning 'dead'. Participles can also be substantivized, e.g. *kuollut* can also mean 'death'. Consider also *syntyä* 'to be born' → *syntynyt* 'born', *syntyneitä*-PL 'newly-born children'.

However, the less agglutinating Finnish (with some properties of the inflecting-fusional type) in comparison to Hungarian, has derivations such as F. *emä* 'mother' → DIM *emo*; *jän-is* 'rabit' → DIM *jän-ö*, *kats-o-a* 'to look' → *kats-e* 'a look', *huut-a-a* 'to shout' → *huut-o* 'a shout', *mail-i* 'e-mail' → *mail-a-ta* 'to e-mail', *faks-i* 'fax' → *faks-a-ta* 'to fax'. Although these derivations resemble conversion in Slavic, their analysis is problematic, since the Finnish stem-forming elements are terminal (word-final) in NOM, which is not typical of TMs, and often preserved in the whole paradigm of the output item, which makes it difficult to establish whether they are derivational or inflectional.[1] The last two verbalizations, however, appear to be clear cases of conversion. It is traditionally assumed that the suffix -*i* forms nouns from verbs via derivation, e.g. *kasv-a-a* 'to grow' → *kasv-i* 'plant', *paist-a-a* 'to roast' → *paist-i* 'roast meat', etc., but *mail-i* 'e-mail' and *faks-i* 'fax' are non-derived borrowings from which the respective verbs *mail-a-ta* 'to e-mail' and *faks-a-ta* 'to fax' are derived. Therefore we assume that -*i* in *mail-i* and *faks-i* differs from the derivational suffix -*i* in *kasv-i* and *paist-i*.

As for morphological conversion in the inflecting-fusion type (represented by Bulgarian, Russian and Serbo-Croatian), we saw in Chapter 3 that it can be word-based, stem-based and root-based, the latter type being the most frequent

---

[1] Although these Finnish instances differ from the English examples for which Kastovsky suggests 'double duty' stem forming elements (TMs are not terminal in English), Kastovsky's analysis might make sense here.

and most productive. As in English, Hungarian and Finnish, syntactic conversion is very productive in Slavic (and in the inflecting-fusional type in general) and always word-based.

In sum, whereas subtraction is primarily related to the inflecting-fusional type, morphological conversion operates in isolating and agglutinating languages as well. In languages tending to the last two types, conversion is word-based, whereas languages showing characteristics of the inflecting-fusional type allow for root-based, stem-based and word-based conversion rules. All three language types have productive syntactic conversion rules that are word-based.

5.2 Language-Specific Adequacy of Conversion and Subtraction

Although Bulgarian, Russian and Serbo-Croatian are genealogically and typologically related, their morphological systems show many specific characteristics. For example, Bulgarian has almost completely lost the category of case, and there is no infinitive in its verbal morphology. In contrast, Russian and Serbo-Croatian have preserved both the case and the infinitive but have lost the old dual the continuant of which the count plural still exists in Bulgarian, etc. (for the specific morphological characteristics of the three languages see Section 1.2). As noted in Chapter 2, language-specific characteristics are investigated by the third subtheory of NM, that of language-specific system-adequacy which, as elaborated by Wurzel, focuses on the inflectional organization of a language. However, in this chapter we will demonstrate that not only inflectional categories may exemplify language-specific features but that each language behaves in its own way with regard to morphological techniques. In other words, it often happens that a morphosemantic pattern expressed by conversion or subtraction in one language, uses (an)other technique(s) in the other two languages.

For a morphological pattern to be system-adequate, it should exhibit some peculiar characteristics, be they prosodic or segmental, which are typical for and normal in a particular language. Thus in this chapter, we will discuss different morphosemantic patterns and compare the solutions of the three languages. Indeed, during the discussion so far we have noted language-specific phenomena, but now these will be put together, the aim being to give a uniform account of the language-specific features of the three languages.

Language-specific restrictions due to loss of categories will not be dealt with, since it is clear that if Bulgarian has lost the infinitive, there is no substantivization of infinitives in that language. Due to the fact that existing features are communicatively much more important than non-existing ones, we will concentrate on occurring categories and specific characteristics rather than on non-occurring ones, unless there is evidence that the lack of a category or structural property has significant impact on system-adequacy. However, even in such instances, we have to keep in mind the soundness of the old philological scepticism against argumenta ex silentio.

5.2.1 Conversion as a Language-Specific Morphological Technique

5.2.1.1 The (Un)Stressed Suffix -*ik*

In this section, we will concentrate on Russian and Bulgarian agent nouns in -*ik* (SC. -*ičar*) denoting scientists, such as R. *matemátika* 'mathematics' → *matemátik* 'mathematician', Bg. *matemátika* → *matematík*. The analysis will elaborate on Dressler (1987a: 71–3). In the course of the discussion data from Serbo-Croatian, where the semantic pattern in question is affixational, will also be considered.

The Bulgarian and Russian -*ik* nouns for scientists have their origin in Ancient Greek and Latin. Examples such as Bg. *akadémija* → *akademík*, R. *akadémija* → *akadémik* show that the Latin type *academia* 'academy' – *academicus* 'academician' were borrowed into Bulgarian and Russian (as well as into other Slavic languages whereby the exact historical path of loaning is of no interest here) as a derivation by the suffix -*ik*, which means that the Latin inflectional suffix -*us* (Latin *o*-stems, NOM in -*us*) was rendered by zero, and the -*ik* scientists were assigned to the only productive inflectional classes for masculine nouns in Bulgarian and Russian. In Serbo-Croatian, such borrowings also enter the inflectional class of masculine in consonants. However, in this language they are derived by addition of the suffix -*(ič)ar*, thus *akademija* → *akademičar*. During the Renaissance, each of the three languages borrowed Latin nouns in -*icus* according to its own language-specific pattern, i.e. Lat. *academicus* → Bg. *akademík*/R. *akadémik*/SC. *akademičar*, which resulted in the awkward synchronic derivation: Bg. *fízika* 'physics' → *fizík* 'physicist', R. *fízika* → *fízik* vs. SC. *fizika* → *fizičar*. As can be seen from these examples, Russian and Bulgarian agent nouns in -*ik* differ in their stress-pattern, showing language-specific conspiracies in their prosodic make-up. The conversion pattern *lógika* 'logic' → *lógik* 'logician' is, in Russian, in consonance with the unstressed -*ik* (which is the default stress-pattern for -*ik* nouns in Russian) and its allomorphs, e.g.: *(s)pút-nik* '(fellow-)traveller', *kolxóz-nik* 'collective-farmer', *razvéd-čik* 'scout, secret service man', and *nabór-ščik* 'compositor'. Consider also neologisms such as *jadér-ščik* 'specialist in nuclear physics' (*jadro* 'nucleus'), *infárkt-nik* 'infarction ill' (*infarkt* 'heart attack'), *verojátnost-nik* 'specialist in the calculus of probability' (*verojatnost'* 'probability'), *ènèló-šnik* (*NLO* [en-el-o] = UFO) 'interested in UFOs', *cèrèú-šnik* (*CRU* [ce-re-u] = FBI) 'FBI officer', etc. (cf. Zemskaja 1992: 97ff).

In Russian, clippings terminating in -*ik* (cf. Section 4.2.5) also exhibit the same stress pattern, though in such formations -*ik* is not a suffix:

(1) *xrónik* ← *xroníčeskij bol'noj* 'chronically ill'
 èlástik ← *èlastíčeskij material* 'elastic material'
 kósmik ← *specialíst po kosmíčeskim lučám* 'specialist in cosmic rays', etc. (cf. Švedova et al. 1980: 225–6).

5.2 Language-Specific Adequacy of Conversion and Subtraction   179

In contrast, in Bulgarian where the suffix -*ík* and its allomorph -*ník* are, by default, stressed in native words (cf. Stojanov 1993: 175), the stress of all -*ik* scientists is on -*ík*. Compare: *uč-en-ík* 'pupil' (cf. V *úč-a* 'I learn', 3 SG *úč-i*, ADJ *úč-en* 'scholar'), *grozn-ík* 'ugly man' (cf. ADJ *grózen* 'ugly'), *măčen-ík* 'martyr' (cf. N *măka* 'pain, torture', V *măč-a* 'I torture', 3 SG *măč-i*, ADJ *măčen* 'difficult'), *čist-ník* 'fastidious person' (from the ADJ *čist* 'clean') to *logika* 'logic' → *logík* 'logician', *matemátika* 'mathematics' → *matematík* 'mathematician', *téxnika* 'technique' → *texník* 'technician', etc. Thus, -*ik* scientists in Bulgarian, due to the stress change in comparison to the stress of the base (the respective science), are derived by (prosodic) modification.

As mentioned above, in Serbo-Croatian, the semantic pattern 'scientist, specialist in' is expressed by a suffixation with the suffix -(*ič*) *ar*, e.g. *matematika* → *matematičar*, *fizika* → *fizičar*, *tehnika* → *tehničar*, etc. Bulgarian and Russian also have the suffix Bg. -*ar*/R. -*ar'*. Consider: Bg. *ovc-a* 'sheep' → *ovč-ar* 'shepherd', *strug* 'lathe' → *strug-ar* 'turner', etc., cf. R. *ovčar'* 'shepherd', *tokar'* 'turner', etc. However, the Bulgarian and the Russian suffix -*ar*/-*ar'* has been semantically specialized for the derivation of agent nouns denoting low-educated persons, as in the above-cited examples. The very old nouns such as Bg. *lekar*/R. *lekar'* (old or irrespective in Russian) 'medical doctor', Bg. *aptekar*/R. *aptekar'* 'chemist' show that originally -*ar*/-*ar'* was not restricted semantically. Note that now both nouns, in both languages, have more respectful sounding doublets: Bg. *doktor*/R. *vrač* for Bg. *lekar*/R. *lekar'* and Bg./R. *farmacevt* for Bg. *aptekar*/R. *aptekar'*.

In sum, each of the three languages uses its own language-specific pattern for the derivation of 'scientist, specialist in' from nominal bases in -*ika* denoting 'sciences': Russian prefers the morphological technique of conversion, which fits the default stress pattern of nouns in -*ik* in this language; Bulgarian derives such nouns by prosodic modification (word-final stress, which is the default pattern for -*ik* nouns in Bulgarian); and Serbo-Croatian suffixes with -(*ič*) *ar*.

5.2.1.2 Noun-to-Verb Conversion

As already discussed in Chapter 3, the most productive strategy for derivation of verbs by conversion in Russian and Serbo-Croatian consists of the attachment of a TM and an ISUFF to nominal and adjectival bases. The added material is of the type R.-*Vt'*/ SC.-*Vti*, where -*V*- is a TM, and -*t'* and -*ti* the language-specific infinitive endings:

(2)   R. N *špión* 'spy' → IMPFV *špión-i-t'* (colloq.) 'to spy'
      ADJ *číst-yj* 'clean' → IMPFV *číst-i-t'* 'to clean', etc.
      SC. N *dȉm* 'smoke' → IMPFV *dȉm-i-ti* 'to smoke'
      ADJ *stȁr* 'old' → IMPFV *stȁr-je-ti* 'grow old', etc.

A less productive strategy for derivation of conversions in Russian and Serbo-Croatian adds to nominal bases ASUFF + TM + ISUFF, as in the following examples:

(3) N(= X*stv-(o)*) → V(= R. X*st-ov-a-t'*, SC. X*st-ov-a-ti*)
R. *učítel'stv-o* 'teachers (collect.)' → *učítelstv-ov-a-t'* 'to be a teacher'
R. *dovól'stv-o* 'contentment, prosperity' → *dovól'stv-ov-a-t'* 'to supply contentment, prosperity'
SC. *strànstvo* 'foreing countries' → *strănstv-ov-a-ti* 'to wander (about)'
SC. *toržèstvo* 'ceremony, festivity' → *toržèstv-ov-a-ti* 'to triumph'

The output of both (2) and (3) is assigned to productive inflection classes.

In Bulgarian, however, the only productive inflection class is that of *-am* verbs, in which all verbs derived with the imperfectivizing suffix *-(V)va-* belong. However, the vowel *-V-* of the suffix *-(V)va-*, if overt, is usually stressed, which means that the addition of the suffix *-Vva-* to a base automatically changes its stress-pattern, as in the following examples:

(4) *săn* 'dream' → IMPFV *sănúv-a-m* 'I dream', 3 SG *sănuv-a*
(cf. R. *son* → *sn-í-t'sja*, SC. *sàn* → IMPFV *sánj-a-ti*)
prorók 'prophet' → IMPFV *prorok-úv-a-m* 'I prophesy', 3 SG *prorok-úv-a*
(cf. R. *prorók* → *proróč-i-t'*, SC. *prórok* → IMPFV *prorîc-a-ti*)

Thus the Bulgarian IMPFV verbs, that are output of the derivations in (4), are all formed by modification, and not by conversion as in Russian and Serbo-Croatian (see (3)). In Bulgarian, the language-specific development of the verbal system has impact on the inflection class productivity, which has led to derivations of verbs by modification instead of conversion. Coincidences of the stress-patterns of the base and the output of a derivation (i.e. conversions) are extremely rare, as in Bg. NEUT *škol-ó* (old) 'school' → *škol-úv-a-m*. In Bulgarian, such derivations are much rarer than in Russian and Serbo-Croatian (cf. R. FEM *škól-a* 'school' → IMPFV *škól-i-t'* 'to school, discipline'; SC. FEM *škôl-a* 'school' → IMPFV *škŏl-ov-a-ti* 'to educate').

However, the modification character of the *-uv-a(-m)* pattern does not mean that Bulgarian lacks a productive pattern for noun-to-verb conversions. On the contrary, if the imperfectivizing suffix has no vowel, i.e. is realized as *-v-a-*, no stress-change takes place. Intriguingly, conversions to verbs prefer nouns derived by the suffix *-stv-(o)*, where they reanalyse the final *-v-* as a part of the productive imperfectivazing suffix *-v-a-*, as in:

(5) NEUT *plagiát-stv-o* 'plagiarism' → IMPFV *plagiátstv-a-m* 'I plagiarize', *plagiátstv-a*
NEUT *marodér-stv-o* 'marauding, pillage' → IMPFV *marodérstv-a-m* 'I maraud, pillage', *marodérstv-a*
NEUT *svidétel-stv-o* 'certificate, evidence, testimony' → IMPFV *svidételstv-a-m* 'I testify', *svidételstv-a*

In Bulgarian, the rule N*stvo* → V*stvam* might apply to all nouns terminating in *-stv-(o)*, with a very few exceptions. As for the suffix *-stv-(o)*, it can be attached to native as well as to foreign bases following the template X 'X' → X*stvo* 'being a X'. Conversions to verbs from *-stv(o)* nouns are extremely productive, especially if X is a person:

(6) N (= X*stv-(o)*) → V (= X*st-v-a-m*)
pisátel-stv-o 'being a writer' → *pisátelst-v-a-m* 'I am/behave as a writer', *pisátelst-v-a*
pirát-stv-o 'being a pirate' → *pirátst-v-a-m* 'I am/behave as a pirate', *pirátst-v-a*
tirán-stv-o 'being a tyrant' → *tiránst-v-a-m* 'I am/behave as a tyrant', *tiránst-v-a*
xuligán-stv-o 'being a hooligan, hooliganism' → *xuligánst-v-a-m* 'I am/behave as a hooligan', *xuligánst-v-a*, etc.

Thus in modern Bulgarian, the productive pattern for noun-to-verb conversions requires nouns with the suffix *-stv-(o)*, from which, after reanalysis of the final *-v-* of the suffix *-stv-(o)*, verbs are derived. The pattern is language-specific and system-adequate, since its productivity is due to the suffix *-v-a-*, which is the most productive verbal inflection in Bulgarian (note that in Russian and Serbo-Croatian imperfectivize suffix *-v-a-* is unproductive). In fact, the right edge of the base coincides with a highly productive verbal inflection and is therefore reanalyzed as verbal inflection. Note that the verbs in (6) have archaic forms with *-uva-*, e.g. *pisatelstvuvam, piratstvuvam, tiranstvuvam*, etc. The aspectual suffix *-uva-*, however, is no more productive in Modern Bulgarian and has been deleted from the verbs, which is further evidence for reanalysis because of coincidence of the final edge of the noun with a productive inflectional suffix. Thus this type of conversion is an interesting example of inflectional productivity that gives rise to derivational productivity.

5.2.1.3 The Suffix *-e*: Bulgarian Diminutives

Of the three Slavic languages focused on, Bulgarian possesses a language-specific rule that derives diminutives from nominal bases by conversion (cf. Chapter 4, Section 5.1.2.1). Recall the pattern MASC N X → NEUT DIM X*e* as in:

(7) MASC *kotel* 'caldron' → NEUT DIM *kotl-e*
MASC *petel* 'rooster, cock'→ NEUT DIM *petl-e*
MASC *oven* 'ram' → NEUT DIM *ovn-e*
etc.

According to Georgiev (1985 [1970]: 164–8; 1985 [1976]: 159), such forms are continuants of the Old Bulgarian *-et-* stems which included only nouns denoting the young of the man and young of animals: *děte* 'child', *otroče* 'infant', *agne* 'lamb', *žrebe* 'colt', *kozьle* 'kid', *tele* 'calf'. Georgiev assumes a diminutive suffix *-et-*, which later phonologically coincided with the vocative suffix *-e*: *otče* from the OB *otьče* (Vocative form of *otьcь* 'father'), and *otče* from the OB **otьče* (diminutive of *otьcь*, where *e* → *e* in modern Bulgarian). In contrast, Mladenov (1929: 224) and Mirčev (1963: 150) argued for reanalyzed old vocative forms.

According to Georgiev (1985), diminutives in *-l-e* (e.g. DIM *kotl-e* ← *kotel* 'caldron') and *-č-e* (e.g. DIM *vojnič-e* ← *vojnik* 'soldier') where *-l-* and *-č-* are parts of the respective stems, served as bases for the development of the diminutive suffixes *-če* (e.g. DIM *zăb-če* ← *zăb* 'tooth') and *-le* (e.g. DIM *nos-le* ← *nos* 'nose'). Thus in modern Bulgarian, the inflection *-e* has become a formal analogue to diminutive suffixes that terminate in *-e* and are gender-changing, as in the following examples:

(8a) MASC *brat* 'brother' → NEUT DIM *brat-le* and
NEUT DIM *brat-če*
MASC *vrat* 'neck' → NEUT DIM *vrat-le*
MASC *nos* 'nose' → NEUT DIM *nos-le*
FEM *knig-a* 'book' → NEUT DIM *kniž-le*

(8b) MASC *dvor* 'yard' → NEUT DIM *dvor-če*
MASC *koš* 'basket' → NEUT DIM *koš-če*
MASC *nož* 'knife' → NEUT DIM *nož-če*
MASC *slon* 'elephant' → NEUT DIM *slon-če*, etc.

In Bulgarian, a nominal base often takes more than one diminutive suffix, and if the first suffix terminates in *-e*, the next one(s) also end(s) in *-e*:

(9) MASC *stol* 'chair' → NEUT DIM *stol-če* →
→ NEUT DIM *stol-če-nce* →
→ NEUT DIM *stol-če-nce-nce*.

5.2 Language-Specific Adequacy of Conversion and Subtraction   183

The same holds for examples of second-level diminutives from the diminutives in (8a), derived with the suffix *-le*: NEUT DIM *brat-le, brat-če* → NEUT DIM *brat-le-nce, brat-če-nce*, FEM *knig-a* 'book' → NEUT DIM *kniž-le* → NEUT DIM *kniž-le-nce*.

Some diminutives, also terminating in *-e*, are formed by modification involving a *k : č* palatalization:

(10) X*k*-(ISUFF) → NEUT DIM X*č-e* (palatalization)
      MASC *učeník* 'pupil' → NEUT DIM *učeníč-e*,
      MASC *krak* 'leg' → NEUT DIM *krač-é*,
      MASC *bik* 'bull' → NEUT DIM *bič-é*,
      FEM *devojk-a* 'maiden' → NEUT DIM *devojč-e*.

Such modifications are much more frequent than the conversions in (7) due to (i) the palatalizing character of *-e*; (ii) the old origin of the pattern when the palatalizations still worked; and (iii) the great number of nouns terminating in *-k*(-ISUFF) in Bulgarian.

Finally, there are even parallel subtractions in *-e*: FEM *méčk-a* / MASC *mečók* 'bear' → NEUT DIM *meč-é*, FEM *pátk-a* / MASC *patók* 'duck' → NEUT DIM *pát-e*, all also terminating in *-e*.

All this evidence is indicative of the high system-adequacy of *-e* in regard to diminutivization in Bulgarian and explains the stability of the inflectional diminutives derived by conversion (7) and subtraction (see below). A more iconic variant of the pattern (with stress change) shows some productivity in colloquial Bulgarian: FEM *čánta* 'bag' → NEUT DIM *čanté*, FEM *bába* 'grandmother' → NEUT DIM *babé*, MASC *číco* 'uncle' → NEUT DIM *čičé*, etc. and the conversion NEUT *paltó* 'coat' → NEUT DIM *palté*.

5.2.1.4 Palatalized vs. Non-palatalized Final Consonants

If an adjective is converted into a noun, irrespective of whether the change is morphological or syntactic, the noun usually inherits the morphosyntactic properties of the adjective. In syntactic substantivization, the base of the rule does not change its paradigm by definition and the output of conversion is thus automatically specified for categories such as number and gender. In adjective-to-noun morphological conversion, this input-output relation with respect to morphosemantics is best visible in conversions of non-basic forms such as Bg. ADJ NEUT SG *sladko* 'sweet' → N NEUT SG *sladko* 'marmalade, dessert', where the adjective and the noun have the same number and gender.

Surprisingly, in Russian and Serbo-Croatian, a few masculine adjectives serve as input of derivations (conversions and modifications) to abstract feminine nouns. The pattern is entirely unproductive in both languages and constitutes an exception since the output of the rule enters unproductive inflection classes, which is unusual for conversion. In Serbo-Croatian, adjective-to-noun conversions receive the language-specific inflection of feminines in consonants, such as *glâd* 'hunger', *mâst* 'revenge', *mîsao* 'thought', *mlãdōst* 'youth', etc. (most of them abstract nouns), and terminate in non-palatalized consonants, i.e. ADJ MASC SG *nèčist* 'dirty' → N FEM SG *nečīst* 'dirt', ADJ MASC SG *rùmen* 'rosy' → N FEM SG *rùmēn* (expressive) 'rosiness', ADJ MASC SG *zèlen* 'green' → N FEM SG *zêlēn* (expressive) 'greens, vegetables'. As can be seen from the examples, the adjectives that are bases of derivation and the nouns that are outputs fully coincide phonologically and have the same accent patterns, though with different contours and vowel lengthening in the nouns. In Russian, by contrast, feminine nouns in consonants have, as a language-specific feature, palatalized final consonants (cf. the inflection class of *kost'* 'bone', *noč'* 'night', *molodost'* 'youth', *krasivost'* 'beauty', etc.). Thus, ADJ MASC SG *zelënyj* 'green' → N FEM SG *zélen'* 'greens, vegetables', ADJ MASC SG *nóvyj* 'new' → N FEM SG *nov'* 'virgin soil', both with palatalized final consonants, which determines these Russian derivations as clear cases of modification.

In sum, following the language-specific segmental patterns, masculine-adjective-to-feminine-noun derivations behave differently in Serbo-Croatian and in Russian, being formed by conversion in Serbo-Croatian and by modification in Russian.

Recall that in Bulgarian, no such examples exist.

5.2.2 Subtraction as a Language-Specific Morphological Technique

It is not only with regard to conversion that Bulgarian, Russian and Serbo-Croatian show language-specific system-adequate characteristics. Subtractive patterns, whether in derivation or in inflection, also can be language-specific. In fact, since subtraction is anti-iconic (i.e. expected to be dispreferred), the most frequent reason for the preservation of subtractive patterns is their system-adequacy.

5.2.2.1 Nouns in -k-(a) Denoting Animals

According to their gender, nouns for animals with an overt suffix -*k*- are masculine and feminine. As discussed in Chapter 3, such nouns can be associated either by formal conversions (as in Serbo-Croatian) or by prosodic modification (as in Bulgarian), see Table 5.1 below. In both instances the feminine nouns are bases for the masculine ones (cf. Section 3.5.2.1.2.2). The assumption of the feminine gender as basic is motivated by the theory of markedness (cf. Battistella 1990, 1996; Ludwig 2001): while masculine nouns denote only the male spouse, feminine nouns can stand for both the female and

5.2 Language-Specific Adequacy of Conversion and Subtraction 185

the male pendant, which speaks for their unmarked status. For example in Bulgarian, if one has a picture of an animal, the answer of the question 'What is this?' will be *mečka* 'bear-FEM', *kotka* 'cat-FEM', etc.; and if one answers the question with *mečok* 'bear-MASC', *kotak* 'cat-MAC', etc., one underlines that it is a picture of a male animal. In other words, the Bulgarian feminine nouns in Table 5.1 are semantically unmarked in Jakobsonian terms. This holds in all instances, except 6 and 9 where the female and the male exemplars look differently, in 6 ('hen') the different appearance of the male and the female spouses is iconicaly expressed by suppletive forms, *petel* and *kokoška* respectively.

In Serbo-Croatian, feminine nouns with the suffix *-ka* are bases for the masculine ones in examples 3, 4 & 5 (Table 5.1).

(For convenience, all forms exhibiting *-k-* in the three languages are marked in grey in Tables 5.1, 5.2, and 5.3).

Note that the basic character of the Bulgarian feminine nouns is confirmed by the distributional criterion, a formal criterion used for determining the base of a derivation (cf. Section 3.4.2.1), i.e. since not all feminine forms have masculine counterparts, the feminine nouns are the bases for the masculine ones and not vice versa.

As seen in Table 5.1, in Russian and Serbo-Croatian the relations between the masculine and feminine forms of the nouns in question are much more complex than in Bulgarian. This is due to the fact that both languages have preserved most of the Old Church Slavic forms without the suffix *-k-*. Thus, in cases such as 'bear' (2), the masculine noun is morphosemantically and morphotactically unmarked and a base of the feminine one, i.e. R. *medved'* → *medvedica*, SC. *medvjed* → *medvjedica*. However, in the case of 'cat' R. *koška*/SC.

Table 5.1 Feminine and masculine nouns with the suffix *-k-(a)* denoting animals

Category	FEM			MASC		
Translation/Lang.	Bg.	R.	SC.	Bg.	R.	SC.
1. Ant	mráv-ka	Ø	Ø	Ø	muravej	mrâv
2. Bear	méč-ka	medvédica	mèdvjedica, mèčka	meč-ók	medved'	mèdvjed
3. Cat	kót-ka	kóš-ka	mȁč-kā	kot-ák, kot-arák	kot	máč-ak
4. Duck	pát-ka	út-ka, útica	pȁt-ka	pat-ók	Ø	pát-ak
5. Goose	gắs-ka	Ø	gùs-ka	gắs-ók	gus', gusak	gùs-ak, gùsan
6. Hen	kokóš-ka	kúrica	kȍkōš, kòkōška	Ø	kur (old)	Ø
7. Louse	vắš-ka	voš'	ûš	Ø	Ø	?ušénac
8. Mouse	miš-ka	myš'	mìšica	miš-ók	Ø	mìš
9. Turkey	púj-ka	indéj-ka, indjúš-ka (coll.)	pùra	púj-ak	indj-uk	pùrān

Table 5.2 Diminutives from nouns in -k-(a) denoting animals

Category	FEM			MASC			DIM 'young of X'		
Translation/Lang.	Bg.	R.	SC.	Bg.	R.	SC.	Bg.	R.	SC.
1. Ant	mrav-ka	∅	∅	∅	muravej	mrȃv	?mravč-e	∅	mrȁvič
2. Bear	meč-ka	medved-ica	mȅdvjed-ica, mȅčka	meč-ok	medved'	mȅdvjed	meč-e	medvež-onok	mȅče, mȅčić, mȅdvjedić
3. Cat	kot-ka	koš-ka	mȁč-kā	kot-ak, kot-arak	kot	mȃč-ak	kot-e	kot-ënok	mȁče, mȁčić
4. Duck	pat-ka	ut-ka, utica	pȁt-ka	pat-ok	∅	pȁt-ak	pat-e	ut-ënok	pȁče, pȁčić
5. Goose	gås-ka	∅	gȕs-ka	gås-ok	gus', gusak	gȕs-ak, gȕsan	gås-e	gus-ënok	gȕšče, gȕščić
6. Hen	kokoš-ka	kurica	kȍkōš, kȍkōška	∅	kur (old)	∅	∅	kur-ënok	∅
7. Louse	vǎš-ka	voš'	ȗš	∅	∅	∅	∅	∅	∅
8. Mouse	miš-ka	myš'	mȉšica	miš-ok	∅	mȉš	miš-le	myš-onok	mȉšić
9. Turkey	puj-ka	indej-ka, indjuš-ka (coll.)	pūra	puj-ak	indj-uk	pūrān	pujč-e	indjuš-onok	pūre, purānčić

5.2 Language-Specific Adequacy of Conversion and Subtraction 187

Table 5.3 Adjectives from nouns in -k-(a) denoting animals

Category	FEM			MASC			ADJ 'X-like, X (attr.)'		
Translation/Lang.	Bg.	R.	SC.	Bg.	R.	SC.	Bg.	R.	SC.
1. Ant	mrav-ka	∅	∅	∅	muravej	mrȃv	mravi, mravci	muravʹinyj	mrȁvljī
2. Bear	meč-ka	medved-ica	mèdvjed-ica, mèčka	meč-ok	medvedʹ	mèdvjed	meči, mečeški	medvežij	mèdvei
3. Cat	kot-ka	koš-ka	mȁč-kā	kot-ak, kotarak	kot	mȁč-ak	koči, koteški	košačij, košečij (old), kotinyj	mȁčjī
4. Duck	pat-ka	ut-ka, utica	pȁt-ka	pat-ok	∅	pȁt-ak	pači, pateški	utinyj, utjačij (coll.)	pȁčjī
5. Goose	găs-ka	∅	gȕs-ka	găs-ok	gusʹ, gus-ak	gȕs-ak, gȉsan	găsi	gusinyj	gȕščjī, gȕsjī
6. Hen	kokoš-ka	kurica	kȍkōš, kȍkōška	∅	kur (old)	∅	kokoši	kurjačij, kurinyj, kuricyn	kokȍšjī, kokȍšinjī
7. Louse	văš-ka	vošʹ	ȕš	∅	∅	?ušènac	∅	∅	∅
8. Mouse	miš-ka	myšʹ	mȉšica	miš-ok	∅	mȉš	miši, miškin	myšij (old), myšinyj	mȉšjī
9. Turkey	puj-ka	indej-ka, indjuš-ka (coll.)	pȕra	puj-ak	indj-uk	purȃn	pujči, pueški	indjušačij	pȕrečī, pȕrjī

mačka the feminine gender is semantically unmarked. Moreover, neither the set of masculine forms nor that of feminine ones is full, which makes the application of the distributional criterion (Section 3.4.2.1) unreliable. In other words, in Russian and Serbo-Croatian, though masculine forms seem to be dominating, it is difficult to formulate a rule with a given gender form as basic. In the two languages each case appears to be for itself.

As a result of language-specific, system-adequate diachronic development, Bulgarian has regularized the derivation of animals (Table 5.1) from which one can regularly derive diminutives (young of animals) (Table 5.2) and adjectives (Table 5.3). For the sake of completeness, the respective Russian and Serbo-Croatian diminutives and adjectives are also cited in Tables 5.2 and 5.3.

In Bulgarian, offspring derived from *-k-(a)* nouns lack *-k-* (see Table 5.2) and since *-k-* is not in the inflection slot of the noun, the only plausible synchronic explanation is that the respective offspring (all NEUT nouns) are derived by subtraction. More precisely, in Table 5.2 diminutives 1 and 9 are modifications, 8 is an instance of a substitution and the four remaining forms are subtractions. For pragmatic reasons, there is no term for louse offspring. Although it is possible to say *văščica* for a little louse, this noun is a diminutive only and does not express an offspring relation.

As can be seen in Table 5.2, all Russian offspring forms are affixations derived with the suffix *-onok/-ënok*.

In Serbo-Croatian, examples 1 and 8 are affixations. In the rest of the cases, affixation competes with modification and subtraction. The more diagrammatic forms usually express the meaning 'offspring of X' and diminutiveness, whereas the subtractions often combine hypocoristic and diminutive meaning (for details see Babić 1991: 136f).

Thus, subtraction occurs systematically only in Bulgarian. The preservation of the subtractive forms in Bulgarian is due to their system-adequacy: the subtractions terminate in *-e*, like all other gender-changing diminutive suffixes (cf. the discussion and the examples in Section 5.2.1.3 above). Moreover, as Manova and Dressler (2001) and Manova (2003a) showed, the termination of the noun plays a great role in Bulgarian nominal morphology.

The suffix *-k-* in nouns denoting animals is also subtracted when adjectives are derived (Table 5.3).

In Bulgarian, adjectives from nouns for animals might be derived either by subtraction (examples 5, 6 in Table 5.3) or by subtraction and other diagrammatic techniques such as addition (8), substitution (2, 3, 4, 9) and modification (1). Since all adjectives terminate in *-i* (an archaic adjective suffix vestige of the Old Bulgarian long adjectives), the adjectives formed by subtraction are less system-adequate than the above-discussed diminutives which all end in the system-adequate suffix *-e*. Perhaps for that reason, the adjectivizing rule is less stable than the diminutivizing one and derives only two pure subtractions.

Russian usually forms adjectives by affixation and substitution, but in some instances old and colloquial forms are built by modification and conversion.

As can be seen from Table 5.3, in Serbo-Croatian, adjectives from nouns denoting animals may be derived by all of the techniques (affixation, substitution, modification, conversion and subtraction).

To sum up, due to language-specific system-adequate regularization of nouns denoting animals with the amplification -*k-(a)*, Bulgarian has generalized rules for derivation of diminutives and adjectives from those nouns. The diminutives and the adjectives are usually derived by a stem-based subtraction rule of the type ROOT-*k-a* → ROOT + ISUFF. Since this rule does not really hold for Russian and Serbo-Croatian, we acknowledge it as language-specific for Bulgarian. However, only the derivation of diminutives is an example of a system-adequate pattern, as diminutives formed by subtraction terminate in -*e*, which is the most frequent inflection of diminutive nouns in Bulgarian. The system-inadequate pattern of adjectives is almost entirely replaced by more diagrammatic morphological techniques.

5.2.2.2 Singular Nouns in -*in* Denoting Ethnicity Terms

The second instance of a language-specific subtractive pattern is inflectional. It derives plural forms from nouns for ethnicity terms with singular forms terminating in -*in*. Although the case was discussed in detail in Sections 4.3 and 4.4.2, we return to it because it is an interesting example of a language-specific subtractive rule. As established in the previous chapter, in Bulgarian, such plural nouns are formed according to the rule ROOT*in* → ROOT*i*. We have classified the pattern as subtractive only in Bulgarian, since the paradigm structure condition of Bulgarian noun inflection associates the plural of any singular noun in a consonant with the morphological technique of addition (Manova and Dressler 2001; Manova 2003b). The only exception to that rule are singular nouns in -*in* denoting ethnicity terms. The plural forms of ethnicity terms in -*in* are shorter than the respective singular ones, which speaks for derivation by subtraction. Though formed by subtraction, such plurals are system-adequate. They terminate in -*i* which is the default plural inflection for masculine polysyllabic nouns with singular forms in consonants.

The rule of subtraction in question is semantically restricted and works only for ethnicity terms (cf. Manova 2003b), the plural forms of which appear semantically unmarked in comparison to the singular ones. This instance of markedness reversal has been discussed in Mayerthaler (1981: 48ff 'Markiertheitsumkehrung' 'markedness reversal'), Tiersma (1982) and Bybee (1985: 74–7), the latter two labeling the phenomenon 'local markedness'. The markedness reversal principle is evidenced by nouns terminating in -*in* but with contrasting semantics. Such nouns have either (1) diagrammatic plural forms, e.g. *ispolin* 'giant, colossus' → *ispolini*, *domakin* 'household, host'→ *domakini*, *magazin* 'shop' → *magazini*, *tramplin* 'spring-/plunge-board' → *tramplini*; or (2) doublet forms in the singular: old forms terminating in -*in* such as *oficerin* 'military officer', *tiranin* 'tyrant', *dušmanin* 'enemy', etc. and more recent forms without -*in*, i.e. *oficer, tiran, dušman*, etc., the latter with diagrammatic plurals:

oficeri, tirani, dušmani. Note that in modern Bulgarian, the explicit norm accepts only the forms without *-in*, whereas the old *-in* forms can be found in old literary texts only.

Taking into consideration the system-adequate termination of the pattern Bg. ROOT-*in* 'ethnicity term' → ROOT-*i* in the plural, we speak of a language-specific system-adequate subtractive pattern in inflection. (For nouns denoting ethnicity terms in Russian and Serbo-Croatian and their place in the respective declension systems, see Section 4.3).

5.3 Conclusion

Although subtraction is usual in the inflecting-fusional type, the question of its typological adequacy is difficult to answer. Conversion is registered in all language types except the incorporating one. The morphological technique of conversion shows preferences in regard to the type of bases it uses in the different language types. Morphological conversion is word-based in languages tending to the isolating type as well as in languages tending to the ideal agglutinating type. Languages that exhibit features of the inflecting-fusional type have word-based, stem-based and root-based conversion. The more a language approaches the inflecting-fusional type, the more root-based and stem-based conversion appears, whereas word-based conversion decreases.

When a given language prefers the non-iconic conversion or the anti-iconic subtraction, they should be in consonance with the specific features of its morphological system. Thereby output forms are often either prosodically or segmentally modified, thus modification instead of conversion. As for subtraction, only patterns whose output is system-adequate have a clear subtractive character. If the output of a subtractive language-specific rule is system-inadequate, other more diagrammatic morphological techniques compete with subtraction for the realization of the rule.

Chapter 6
Conclusions

We have assumed that all morphology is word-based semantically. With respect to morphological form, however, we have recognized three different types of bases: roots, stems and words. All morphological rules can be described with the help of five morphological techniques. Morphological techniques correspond to all possible cognitive operations that can be performed on an existing form, i.e. they include addition, substitution, modification, conversion and subtraction. Morphological techniques operate in derivation and in inflection and are prototypical instances of morphological rules. In other words, a morphological rule is a concrete realization of a morphological technique. All realizations of a given technique might be graded according to their prototypicality. The latter depends on the type of base (whether word, stem or root), the involvement of modification and, in derivation, it is of particular importance whether word-class change takes place. Unmodified word-based realizations either represent the prototype or approach it rather closely, at least more closely than unmodified stem-based and root-based realizations of a technique, the prototype of a derivation rule being unmodified, word-based and word-class-changing.

Subsequently, we have positioned the non-iconic conversion and anti-iconic subtraction on the inflection-derivation continuum, i.e. with hard-to-analyse non-iconic and anti-iconic data from Bulgarian, Russian, Serbo-Croatian and other languages, we have attempted to demonstrate that the above cognitively drawn assumptions hold.

The analysis of conversion and subtraction takes into consideration the fact that Slavic morphology is inflecting-fusional. One of the salient characteristics of inflecting-fusional morphology is the paradigmatic and syntagmatic distinction between derivation and inflection suffix slots. Thus for a Slavic word a template form with the following slots has been assumed: (PREF)-ROOT-(DSUFF)-(TM)-(ISUFF), further generalized as (PREF)-BASE-(DSUFF)-(TM)-(ISUFF). Of all slots, only the ROOT (BASE) is obligatorily occupied, and the TM slot is relevant only to verbs. Prototypical derivational processes take place in the derivational slot and prototypical inflectional processes in the inflectional slot. The inflecting character of Slavic morphology often requires an overt suffix in the inflectional slot. Therefore we allow suffixes to be added, substituted or deleted in both slots at the same time, which does not ignore the fact that the derivational slot governs the choice of the inflection suffix. Put differently, we have allowed for addition/substitution/deletion of inflectional material in cases of derivation. In fact, addition/ substitution/deletion of inflectional affixes is the most characteristic feature of word-formational conversion and subtraction in Bulgarian, Russian and Serbo-Croatian. Since we assume that one discovers morphological rules when comparing words, the data presentation involves templates (based on the generalized form of the Slavic word) that connect well-formed words (basic forms of words) as input and output. This approach allows 'to discover' what happens in conversion and subtraction in Slavic. Templates of rules relating basic forms work successfully for all cases analysed, except for conversions of the type Bg. ADJ NEUT SG *sladko* 'sweet' → N NEUT SG *sladko* 'jam, dessert', since the basic form of an adjective in Bulgarian is MASC SG. However, markedness reversal can suggest a plausible explanation why neuter adjectives are the input of conversion: the neuter gender prototypically expresses inanimacy. Therefore when converted to inanimate neuter nouns, neuter adjectives appear unmarked (cf. G. *das Übel* 'evil', *das Gut* 'the good, property', *das Hoch* '(meteor.) high', *das Tief* '(meteor.) depression', etc.). Moreover, both neuter adjectives and neuter nouns are homophonous. Further evidence that basic forms are of importance to morphology comes from verbalizing conversion that has as output imperfective verbs only (recall that the imperfect is the semantically unmarked member of the category of aspect).

We have defined prototypical conversion as (1) word-class change that implies (2) a semantic change, (3) a paradigmatic change and (4) a syntactic change. These features constitute a scale, the first condition being the strongest one, the second less strong, the third still less so and so forth. Of all the features, (1) defines prototypical conversion; (2) defines non-prototypical conversion and (3) formal conversion. If only (4) is satisfied, we speak of syntactic conversion, where a word is used only in the syntactic position of another word-class. In some instances, syntactic conversion causes semantic and paradigmatic restrictions of the input (e.g. in substantivization where, due to ellipsis of a noun, the substantivized adjective is fixed to one gender and to a given semantic pattern). Such restrictions, however, differ from the morphotactic and morphosemantic changes that take place in morphological conversion.

Although conversion exhibits four occurrences with different features, its various realizations are not unrelated. All conversions can be situated on the derivation-inflection continuum, and in so doing, we could establish that conversion itself constitutes a continuum (beginning with prototypical conversion, continuing via non-prototypical conversion, to formal conversion, and ending with syntactic conversion). Since some of the four points of the above-postulated scale can be satisfied only partially, each of the four conversion types may be graded further. For example, there are word-class-changing conversions the outputs of which have only a part of the inflectional paradigm of the new word class, or others with mixed paradigms comprising inflection forms of the input

Conclusions

and output of the conversion. Undoubtedly such conversions are less prototypical than word-class-changing conversions the output and the input of which exhibit full and independent paradigms.

Neither are non-prototypical conversions all of exactly the same type. Both instances of non-prototypical conversion found in Bulgarian and Russian illustrate the point: Bulgarian diminutivization by conversion alters the gender and thus the inflectional class, whereas the Russian 'science' → 'scientists' pattern affects gender (thus inflectional class change) and animacy of the base, which mirrors the greater semantic change in Russian non-prototypical conversions in comparison to Bulgarian ones. Thus diminutivization in Bulgarian is much non-prototypical than the Russian pattern, i.e. the latter approximates prototypical conversion, while the former is closer to formal conversion.

Both instances of formal conversion (derivation of females from males and imperfectivization) differ from each other as well. Whereas in derivation of females from males the input and output have different referents and are seen as different lexemes (i.e. as in derivation) by some linguists, imperfectivization produces word-forms of the same lexeme. Hence, gender change without a gender suffix approaches non-prototypical morphological conversion to a greater extent than aspect change without an aspectual suffix. The latter neighbours syntactic conversion. (There are, perhaps, linguists, such as Smirnickij 1954, Maslov 1981[2], Mel'čuk 2001, Bojadžjiev 1999, who therefore assume conversion for derivation of female humans from male humans but not for aspect, except Dokulil 1968a who postulates a conversion change in both cases).

At the end of the conversion continuum is syntactic conversion that can also be graded, i.e. false substantivization is between morphological and syntactic conversion (being neither of the two), followed by true substantivization, anaphoric usage and finally, metalinguistic use of unchangeable items. Some of the latter can have a single inflectional form of a noun (either the definite or the plural) or no inflectional forms at all, as in cases of substantivizations of infinitives in Russian and Serbo-Croatian, which are thus the best example of a pure syntactic change. Substantivizations of infinitives in English, German, Italian, Latin and Ancient Greek add further intermediate steps to the continuum of syntactic conversion and thus further support the idea of a conversion cline.

We have established that conversion in derivation and inflection operates on different types of bases, such as words, stems and roots. Since word-based conversion is the most prototypical type we expected that it would be the most productive. However, as can be seen in Table 6.1, word-based conversion is either unproductive or productive in only one or two of the three languages. In contrast, stem-based and especially root-based conversions show greater productivity. Such behaviour of conversion is typologically motivated: the more a language approaches the strongly inflecting type, the more root- and stem-based conversion appears, whereas word-based conversion vanishes.

With regard to stem-based conversion, only two conversion patterns in Bulgarian, Russian and Serbo-Croatian operate on stems. Moreover, stem-based

Table 6.1 Word-, stem- and root-based conversion in Bg., R. & SC

Conversion					
Word-class-changing		Word-class-preserving		Formal conversion	
Word-based					
ADJ > N (u)	Bg. R. SC	N > DIM N (u)	Bg.	Gender (u)	Bg. R. SC
N > V (?p)	Bg. R. SC				
ADJ > V (?u)	Bg. SC				
N > ADJ (u)	SC.				
Stem-based					
V > N (?u)	Bg. R. SC	N*ka* > N*k* (?u)	R.		
N > V (p)	Bg.				
Root-based					
V > N (p)	Bg. R. SC	N*ka* > N*k* (?p)	R.	Aspect (u)	Bg. R. SC.
N > V (p)	Bg. R. SC				
ADJ > V (?p)	R.				
N > ADJ (u)	Bg. SC.				
V > ADJ (u)	R.				

Note: (p) stands for a productive type of conversion; (?p) is to be understood as 'the type is not fully productive', i.e. it is productive only in one or two of the three languages and/or does not occur with loanwords; (u) means unproductive type; (?u) means slightly less unproductive type.

conversion to nouns in Bulgarian is less prototypical than in Russian and Serbo-Croatian, since in Bulgarian, the output of the conversion retains the root-amplification vowel, e.g. Bg. *igra-ja, igra-e* 'I play, act' → *igr-a*' 'play, game, acting', but omits the TM of the verb (in this case the TM is *-e-*). Compare R. *igr-a-t'* → *igra* / SC. *igr-a-ti* → *igr-a*. Thus, the Bulgarian conversions are between stem- and root-based morphology and show that even morphotactic rules have no sharp boundaries.

The only productive stem-based conversion pattern is illustrated by the Bulgarian noun-to-verb conversions of the type X*stv-o* 'all Xs/working as a X' → X*stv-a-m* 'I am/work/behave as a X'. Nouns derived by the suffix *-stv-o* serve as input of conversion. The pattern is language-specific and its productivity is due to the inflection *-v-a-*. The latter is the most productive verbal inflection in modern Bulgarian. Indeed, the right edge of the base coincides with a highly productive verbal inflection and is therefore reanalyzed as verbal inflection. Thus this type of conversion is an interesting example of inflectional productivity that causes derivational productivity. The same holds for Russian word-based conversions X*stvo* 'all Xs/working as a X' → X*stv-ov-a-t'* 'to be/work/behave as a X'.

Of all root-based conversion types, only conversions to nouns and to verbs are productive. Similar to the above-discussed stem-based conversions, all root-based verb-to-noun and noun-to-verb conversions enter productive inflectional classes, except for a single language-specific conversion pattern that derives feminine abstract nouns terminating in consonants from masculine adjectives in Serbo-Croatian. Conversions from and to verbs, especially word- and root-based ones, may involve addition and deletion of aspectual suffixes. The latter are in the derivational slot of a prototypical word yet behave as inflection, i.e. always combine only with the TM -*a*- (in the infinitive), thus the combination -ASUFF-*a*- seems as a complex TM. The complex TM serves to assign a verb to a particular inflection class and all verbs that exhibit the combination -ASUFF-*a*- belong to the same conjugation class in Bulgarian and Russian and to two phonologically complementary conjugation classes in Serbo-Croatian (Manova 2005a). The fact that a TM and an ASUFF merge adds further support to the idea of fuzzy boundaries of morphological rules.

With regard to the word class of the output of conversion, it has been observed that verbalizing conversion is usually productive, nominalizing conversion is less productive, and adjectivizing conversion always unproductive (cf. Table 6.1). This observation is in line with what Bauer (1983: 229) observes for English.

If in nominalizing and verbalizing conversion, it seems that the mere attachment of a productive inflectional suffix to a base gives rise to conversion, in adjectivizing conversion inflectional productivity does not play any role. For example, in Russian the basic form of an adjective is the long form MASC SG that is always inflected. This means that conversion to adjectives should be easily formed after addition of productive adjectival inflection to a base belonging to another word class. However, this is not the case. In Russian, adjectivization by conversion is extremely unproductive and has only a single occurrence. The rule derives the long-form adjectives *ljúb-yj* (prosodic modification), short form *ljub* (conversion) 'dear, loved, beloved (old, poetic & colloq.)' from the verb *ljubít'* 'to love, like'. However, as mentioned above, the basic form of a Russian adjective (i.e. the most probable output of adjectivization) is the long one, which makes the rule of conversion unconvincing (due to the modification in the long-form adjective). All conversions to adjectives in Serbo-Croatian have as output definite (long) adjectives without short forms, i.e. the output of a conversion is always inflected with the (only possible) inflectional suffix *ī*. Nevertheless, conversions to adjectives in Serbo-Croatian are unproductive and have very few occurrences.

The observed difference in productivity of verbalizing, nominalizing and adjectivizing conversion seems to be fairly general in the languages of the world and can be explained by the central role of verbs in syntax and sentence semantics on the one hand, and to the relatively marginal role of adjectives on the other.

As for the word-class of the input, productive conversions involve noun-to-verb and verb-to-noun patterns. Of all conversions where adjectives participate as input, only conversions to verbs show some productivity, especially in Russian and Serbo-Croatian (Bauer 1983: 230 also notices the relatively unproductive character of adjective-to-noun conversion in English). In Serbo-Croatian, where a clear differentiation between long- and short-form adjectives exists and both types of forms can be basic (i.e. might serve as bases of conversion), definite (long) and indefinite (short) adjectives behave differently with respect to conversion. Short-form adjectives usually undergo morphological conversion (e.g. *nèčist* 'dirt' and *blâgo* 'wealth, property'), whereas long form adjectives convert syntactically (e.g. *Hr̀vātskā* 'Croatia'). This pattern may be due to the morphotactically different basic forms and declensions of long adjectives and nouns, whereas short forms entirely coincide with the basic forms of the nouns and have nearly the same declension.

In sum, the most frequent types of conversion in Bulgarian, Russian and Serbo-Croatian resemble the prototype of a derivation rule and involves verb-to-noun and noun-to-verb changes, i.e. the two polar and most important word classes easily convert into each other. There exists a clear tendency for conversion to prefer morphologically and semantically different to morphologically and semantically similar input and output. This makes non-prototypical word-class preserving and formal conversion rare (cf. Table 6.1). Indeed, non-prototypical conversion is restricted to two semantic patterns: (1) diminutives from nominal bases in Bulgarian, and (2) the pattern 'science' → 'scientist' in Russian (the Bulgarian rule of diminutivization by conversion being entirely unproductive).

We have defined paradigmatic (inflection class) change as formal conversion. Due to its high non-prototypicality, this type of conversion is very rare, i.e. gender and aspect changes without gender and aspect suffixes are entirely unproductive in Bulgarian, Russian and Serbo-Croatian.

With regard to subtraction, we have established that, as usual for a morphological technique, it operates on different bases (words, stems, roots), and this in derivation as well as in inflection (see Table 6.2). Thus, Slavic languages contribute instances of stem- and root-based subtraction to morphological theory (all the examples of subtraction cited in the literature so far are word-based subtractions, cf. Dressler 2000b). The same holds for word-class changing subtraction.

Table 6.2 Root-, stem- and word-based subtraction in Bg., R. & SC

Base	Subtraction			
	Subtraction in Derivation		Subtraction in Inflection	
Root			COMP	R.
Stem	N>V	Bg., R., SC.	COMP, SUP	R.
	N > ADJ	Bg., SC.		
	ADJ > V	R.		
	N > DIM N	Bg., SC.		
Word	N 'science'> N 'scientist'	Bg., R., SC.	PL ethnicity terms	Bg.
	ADJ > V	Bg., SC.		
	N > N ethnicity terms (rule inversion)	Bg., R., SC.	COMP	SC.

Derivational subtractions in Bulgarian, Russian and Serbo-Croatian are word-based and stem-based (cf. Table 6.2), stem-based subtraction being the more frequent (i.e. word-based subtraction approaches the prototype of the anti-iconic subtraction rule more closely than stem-based subtraction, making word-based subtraction more anti-iconic and therefore less frequent than stem-based subtraction). Stem-based subtraction has the morphotactic structure ROOT – X – ISUFF → ROOT – ISUFF, where X is a single phoneme, but usually coincides with a morpheme and therefore might be identified as having some semantics. Since all derivational subtractions are either stem-based or word-based, it seems that, in word formation, there exists a transparency constraint that preserves the root against the anti-iconic subtraction. In contrast, the weakly iconic modification often affects the root in cases of subtraction in derivation, e.g. Bg. N *pat-k-a* 'duck' → ADJ *pač-i* 'duck-', N *găs-k-a* 'goose' → ADJ *găš-i* 'goose'. In this way modification contributes some iconicity to subtraction.

Like conversion, subtraction in derivation can be word-class-changing and wor-class-preserving (see Table 6.3 below). Moreover, non-prototypical conversion and subtraction are often associated with the same semantic change, namely diminutivization and science-to-scientist derivations.

Subtraction in inflection affects only non-prototypical inflection (plural, comparatives and supperlatives) and can be word-based (plural of ethnicity terms in Bulgarian and comparatives in Serbo-Croatian), as well as stem-based (comparatives and superlatives in Russian).

Root-based subtraction is the least natural instance of subtraction according to the NM parameters of iconicity and of a base of a morphological rule, which makes this subtraction type extremely rare. The only example of root-based subtraction found is from Russian. It is the comparative of the adjective *dol'g-ij* 'long' → COMP *dol'še* and *dol-ee* (now an adverb), the final phoneme of the root is deleted in both forms.

In Bulgarian, Russian and Serbo-Croatian, anti-iconic subtraction is, as expected, unproductive, except in two cases where it shows some partial productivity (cf. Table 6.3):

Table 6.3 Types of subtraction and their productivity

Subtraction					
In Derivation				In Inflection	
No	Word-class-changing		Word-class-preserving	Category	Language
1.	N > V (?u)	Bg., R., SC.	N > DIM N (u)	Bg., SC. PL ethnicity terms (u)	Bg.
2.	N > ADJ (u)	Bg., SC.	N 'science' > N 'scientist' (?p)	Bg., R., SC. COMP, SUP (u)	R., SC.
3.	ADJ > V (u)	Bg., R., SC.	N > N ethnicity terms (u) (rule inversion)	Bg., R., SC.	

Note: u – unproductive; ?u – slightly less unproductive; ?p – not fully productive

(1) Word-class-changing subtraction of the type X*stv-i-e* → Bg. X*stv-a-m*/R. X*stv-ov-a-t'*

This type of subtraction has to do with inflectional productivity (as the productivity of the conversion pattern Bg. X*st-v-o* → X*st-v-a-m*/R. X*stv-o* → X*stv-o-va-t'*).

(2) Word-class-preserving subtraction of the type 'science' → 'scientist'

The productivity of this pattern is mainly due to the complex suffix *-olog-i-ja* (i.e. X*ologija* → X*olog*). This suffix, by rule, combines with nominal bases of foreign origin, as well as with verbs of native origin in colloquial Russian where from *-ologija* neologisms one could derive by subtraction *-olog* nouns (V *boltat'* 'to chat, gossip' → *boltologija* and *boltolog*; V *trepat'sja* 'to talk nonsense' → *trepologija* and *trepolog*).

Unlike anti-iconic subtraction, extragrammatical shortenings (hypocoristics, clippings, blends and acronyms) are productive in Bulgarian, Russian and Serbo-Croatian. An extreme productivity of clippings has been attested in Russian.

As for the sources of subtraction in Bulgarian, Russian and Serbo-Croatian, we have established that those could be system-adequate diachronic change, preservation of old unproductive forms and rule inversion.

For some cases of subtraction, a formal restriction depending on the number of the syllables of the base has been observed. Subtraction takes place with relatively long bases, whereas suffixation occurs when the base is shorter. Thus, Bg./R./SC. *biolog-ija* 'biology' → *biolog* 'biologists', but Bg./R. *xim-ija* / SC. *hemija* 'chemistry' → Bg./R. *ximik* / SC. *hemičar* 'chemist'. In such cases, according to the NM parameter of the optimal shape of morphological words, subtraction shows some naturalness.

Prototypical subtraction in derivation (i.e. word-based word-class-changing subtraction without any (mor)phonological modification) is the most unnatural type of derivation rule, and therefore very rare. In inflection, where the semantic change is smaller than in word-formation, subtraction was found with and without concomitant modifications.

Due to their cognitively complex nature (i.e. low degree of naturalness), conversion and subtraction are often challenged by more iconic morphological techniques such as addition, substitution and modification. Where doublets occur, conversion and subtraction are stylistically marked as either poetic or archaic in comparison to the more iconic forms. In some cases, even a full replacement of conversion and subtraction, by more natural techniques, has taken place. The preservation of archaic conversion and subtraction forms is always due to language-specific system-adequacy. System-adequacy also has a significant impact on productivity of conversion and subtraction patterns.

Thus with regard to conversion and subtraction, one can conclude that they both behave as any other morphological technique:

(1) They operate in derivation as well as in inflection.
(2) In derivation, conversion and subtraction have prototypical (word-class-changing) and non-prototypical (word-class-preserving) realizations.

Conclusions 199

(3) Both techniques can be applied to different bases such as words, stems and roots.
(4) Like affixation and substitution, subtraction is often accompanied by phonological and morphonological modifications (modifications are not allowed in conversion, since their occurrences are realizations of the morphological technique of modification).
(5) Conversion and subtraction often compete with more diagrammatic techniques such as affixation, substitution and modification for the expression of same semantics. This is evidence for the correctness of the assignment of conversion and subtraction to the cognitive level of the other morphological techniques.

Appendix A
Bulgarian Noun Inflection

SG	'city'	'law'	'Bulgarian'	'woman'	'village'	'sea'
INDEF	*grad*	*zakon*	*bălgarin*	*žena*	*selo*	*more*
DEF	*grada/ gradăt*	*zakona/ zakonăt*	*bălgarina/ bălgarinăt*	*ženata*	*seloto*	*moreto*
PL						
INDEF	*gradove*	*zakoni*	*bălgari*	*ženi*	*sela*	*moreta*
DEF	*gradovete*	*zakonite*	*bălgarite*	*ženite*	*selata*	*moretata*

Appendix B
Bulgarian Adjective Inflection

	MASC	FEM	NEUT	PL	
INDEF	*krasiv*	*krasiva*	*krasivo*	*krasivi*	'beautiful'
DEF	*krasivijat*	*krasivata*	*krasivoto*	*krasivite*	
INDEF	*măžki*	*măžka*	*măzko*	*măžki*	'man-'
DEF	*măžkijat*	*măžkata*	*măžkoto*	*măžkite*	

Appendix C
Bulgarian Verb Inflection (Synthetic Forms)

PRESENT

	'read'	'shave'	'play'	'sing'	'walk'	'build'	'think'	'organize'
1SG	četa	brăsna	igraja	peja	vărvja	stroja	mislja	organiziram
2SG	četeš	brăsneš	igraeš	peeš	vărviš	stroiš	misliš	organiziraš
3SG	čete	brăsne	igrae	pee	vărvi	stroi	misli	organizira
1PL	četem	brăsnem	igraem	peem	vărvim	stroim	mislim	organizirame
2PL	četete	brăsnete	igraete	peete	vărvite	stroite	mislite	organizirate
3PL	četat	brăsnat	igrajat	pejat	vărvjat	strojat	misljat	organizirat

AORIST

1SG	četox	brăsnax	igrax	pjax	vărvjax	stroix	mislix	organizirax
2SG	čete	brăsna	igra	pja	vărvja	stroi	misli	organizira
3SG	čete	brăsna	igra	pja	vărvja	stroi	misli	organizira
1PL	četoxme	brăsnaxme	igraxme	pjaxme	vărvjaxme	stroixme	mislixme	organiziraxme
2PL	četoxte	brăsnaxte	igraxte	pjaxte	vărvjaxte	stroixte	mislixte	organiziraxte
3PL	četoxa	brăsnaxa	igraxa	pjaxa	vărvjaxa	stroixa	mislixa	organiziraxa

IMPERFECT

1SG	četjax	brăsnex	igraex	peex	vărvjax	strojax	mislex	organizirax
2SG	četeše	băsneše	igraeše	peeše	vărveše	stroeše	misleše	organiziraše
3SG	četeše	brăsneše	igraeše	peeše	vărveše	stroeše	misleše	organiziraše
1PL	četjaxme	brăsnexme	igraexme	peexme	vărvjaxme	strojaxme	mislexme	organiziraxme
2PL	četjaxte	brăsnexte	igraexte	peexte	vărvjaxte	strojaxte	mislexte	organiziraxte
3PL	četjaxa	brăsnexa	igraexa	peexa	vărvjaxa	strojaxa	mislexa	organiziraxa

IMPERATIVE

2SG	četi	brăsni	igraj	pej	vărvi	stroj	misli	organiziraj
2PL	četete	brăsnete	igrajte	pejte	vărvete	strojte	mislete	organizirajte

Appendix D
Russian Noun Inflection[1]

SG				
NOM	*zakon* 'law'	*komnata* 'room'	*mesto* 'place'	*kost'* 'bone'
GEN	*zakona*	*komnaty*	*mesta*	*kosti*
DAT	*zakonu*	*komnate*	*mestu*	*kosti*
ACC	*zakon*	*komnatu*	*mesto*	*kost'*
INST	*zakonom*	*komnatoj*	*mestom*	*kost'ju*
LOC	*zakone*	*komnate*	*meste*	*kosti*

PL				
NOM	*zakony*	*komnaty*	*mesta*	*kosti*
GEN	*zakonov*	*komnat*	*mest*	*kostej*
DAT	*zakonam*	*komnatam*	*mestam*	*kostjam*
ACC	*zakony*	*komnaty*	*mesta*	*kosti*
INST	*zakonami*	*komnatami*	*mestami*	*kostjami*
LOC	*zakonax*	*komnatax*	*mestax*	*kostjax*

---

[1] The order of cases is that of the Russian Academy Grammar (1980).

Appendix E
Russian Adjective Inflection

staryj 'old'

Long form declension

SG	MASC	NEUT	FEM	PL
NOM	*staryj*	*staroe*	*staraja*	*starye*
GEN	*starogo*		*staroj*	*staryx*
DAT	*staromu*		*staroj*	*starym*
ACC	= NOM or GEN	*staroe*	*staruju*	= NOM or GEN
INST	*starym*		*staroj*	*starymi*
LOC	*starom*		*staroj*	*staryx*

Short form declension

	star	*staro*	*stara*	*stary*

Possessive Adjective Declension

djadin 'uncle's'

SG	MASC	NEUT	FEM	PL
NOM	*djadin*	*djadino*	*djadina*	*djadiny*
GEN	*djadinogo*		*djadinoj*	*djadinyx*
DAT	*djadinomu*		*djadinoj*	*djadinym*
ACC	= NOM or GEN	*djadino*	*djadinu*	= NOM or GEN
INST	*djadinym*		*djadinoj*	*djadinymi*
LOC	*djadinom*		*djadinoj*	*djadinyx*

Appendix F
Russian Verb Inflection (Synthetic Forms)

INF	čitat'	sovetovat'	belet'	kriknut'	govorit'
	'to read'	'to advise'	'to whiten'	'to cry'	'to speak'
NON-PAST					
1SG	čitaju	sovetuju	beleju	kriknu	govorju
2SG	čutaeš'	sovetueš'	beleeš'	krikneš'	govoriš'
3SG	čitaet	sovetuet	beleet	kriknet	govorit
1PL	čitaem	sovetuem	beleem	kriknem	govorim
2Pl	čitaete	sovetuete	beleete	kriknete	govorite
3Pl	čitajut	sovetujut	belejut	kriknut	govorjat
PAST					
SG MASC	čital	sovetoval	belel	kriknul	govoril
FEM	čitala	sovetovala	belela	kriknula	govorila
NEUT	čitalo	sovetovalo	belelo	kriknulo	govorilo
PL	čitali	sovetovali	beleli	kriknuli	govorili
IMPERAT					
2SG	čitaj	sovetuj	belej	krikni	govori
2PL	čitajte	sovetujte	belejte	kriknite	govorite

Appendix G
Serbo-Croatian Noun Inflection

SG					
NOM	grâd 'city'	zákon 'law'	žèna 'woman'	sèlo 'village'	stvâr 'thing'
GEN	grâda	zákona	žènē	sèla	stvâri
DAT	grâdu	zákonu	žèni	sèlu	stvâri
ACC	grâd	zákon	žènu	sèlo	stvâr
VOC	grâde	zákone	žèno	sèlo	stvâri
LOC	grádu	zákonu	žèni	sèlu	stvári
INST	grâdom	zákonom	žènōm	sèlom	stvârju/stvâri
PL					
NOM	gràdovi	zákoni	žène	sèla	stvâri
GEN	gràdōvā	zákōnā	žènā	sêlā	stvárī
DAT	gràdovima	zákonima	žènama	sèlima	stvárima
ACC	gràdove	zákone	žène	sèla	stvâri
VOC	gràdovi	zákoni	žène	sèla	stvâri
LOC	gràdovima	zákonima	žènama	sèlima	stvárima
INST	gràdovima	zákonima	žènama	sèlima	stvárima

Appendix H
Serbo-Croatian Adjective Inflection

stȁr 'old'

Short form declension

SG	MASC	NEUT	FEM
NOM	*stȁr*	*stȁro*	*stȁra*
GEN	*stȁra*		*stȁrē*
DAT	*stȁru*		*stȁrōj*
ACC	as NOM or GEN	*stȁro*	*stȁru*
VOC	*stȁr*	*stȁro*	*stȁra*
LOC	*stȁru*		*stȁrōj*
INST	*stȁrīm*		*stȁrōm*

PL			
NOM	*stȁri*	*stȁra*	*stȁre*
GEN		*stȁrīh*	
DAT		*stȁrīm(a)*	
ACC	*stȁre*	*stȁra*	*stȁre*
VOC	*stȁri*	*stȁra*	*stȁre*
LOC		*stȁrīm(a)*	
INST		*stȁrīm(a)*	

Long form declension

SG	MASC	NEUT	FEM
NOM	*stârī*	*stârō*	*stârā*
GEN	*stârōga*		*stârē*
DAT	*stârōme*		*stârōj*
ACC	as NOM or GEN	*stârō*	*stârū*
VOC	*stârī*	*stârō*	*stârā*
LOC	*stârōme*		*stârōj*
INST	*stârīm*		*stârōm*

PL			
NOM	*stârī*	*stârā*	*stârē*
GEN		*stârīh*	
DAT		*stârīma*	
ACC	*stârē*	*stârā*	*stârē*
VOC	*stârī*	*stârā*	*stârē*
LOC		*stârīma*	
INST		*stârīma*	

Appendix I
Serbo-Croatian Verb Inflection (Synthetic Forms)

	pèvati[1] 'to sing'	sávetovati[2] 'to advise'	nòsiti 'to carry'	víknuti 'to cry'
PRESENT				
1SG	pèvām	sávetujēm	nòsīm	víknēm
2SG	pèvāš	sávetujēš	nòsīš	víknēš
3SG	pèvā	sávetujē	nòsī	víknē
1PL	pèvāmo	sávetujēmo	nòsīmo	víknēmo
2PL	pèvāte	sávetujēte	nòsīte	víknēte
3PL	pèvajū	sávetujē	nòse	víknū
AORIST				
1SG	pèvah	sávetovah	nòsih	víknuh
2SG	pèva	sávetovā	nòsī	víknū/víknu
3SG	pèva	sávetovā	nòsī	víknū/víknu
1PL	pèvasmo	sávetovasmo	nòsismo	víknusmo
2PL	pèvaste	sávetovaste	nòsiste	víknuste
3PL	pèvašē	sávetovaše	nòsiše	víknuše/víknušē
IMPERFECT				
1SG	pèvāh	sávetovāh	nòšāh	this verbs is PFV
2SG	pèvāše	sávetovāše	nòšāše	and has no IMPF forms
3SG	pèvāše	sávetovāše	nòšāše	
1PL	pèvāsmo	sávetovāsmo	nòšāsmo	
2PL	pèvāste	sávetovāste	nòšāste	
3Pl	pèvāhū	sávetovāhu	nòšāhu	
IMPER				
2SG	pèvāj	sávetūj	nòsi	víkni
1PL	pèvājmo	sávetūjmo	nòsimo	víknimo
2PL	pèvājte	sávetūjte	nòsite	víknite

---

[1] *Pjèvati* in Bosnian, Croatian and the jekavian dialect of Serbian.
[2] *Sávjetovati* in Bosnian, Croatian and the jekavian dialect of Serbian.

References

Adams, Valerie. 1973. *An Introduction to Modern English Word-Formation*. London: Longman.
Anderson, Stephen R. 1988. Morphological Theory. In *Linguistics: The Cambridge Survey, Vol. I: Linguistic Theory: Fondations*, ed. Frederick J. Newmeyer, 146–191. Cambridge, MA: Cambridge University Press.
Anderson, Stephen R. 1992. *A-morphous Morphology*. Cambridge, MA: Cambridge University Press.
Andrejčin, Ljubomir. 1962. K morfologičeskoj xarakteristike vidovoj sistemy sovremennogo bolgarskogo jazyka. In *Voprosy glagol'nogo vida*, ed. Jurij Maslov, 231–237. Moskva: Izdatel'stvo inostrannoj literatury.
Andrejčin, Ljubomir. 1978. *Osnovna bălgarska gramatika*. Sofija: Nauka i izkustvo.
Andrejčin, Ljubomir, Petja Asenova, Elena Georgieva, Kalina Ivanova, Ruselina Nicolova, Petăr Pašov, Xristo Părvev, Rusin Rusinov, Valentin Stankov, Stojan Stojanov, and Kristalina Čolakova. 1983. *Gramatika na săvremennija bălgarski knižoven ezik. Tom II. Morfologija*. Sofija: Izdatelstvo na BAN.
Andrejčin, Ljubomir, L. Georgiev, St. Ilčev, N. Kostov, Iv. Lekov, St. Stojkov, and Cv. Todorov. 1999. *Bălgarski tălkoven rečnik*, IV izdanie, dopălneno i preraboteno ot D. Popov. Sofija: Nauka i izkustvo.
Anić, Vladimir. 1991. *Rječnik hrvatskoga jezika*. Zagreb: Novi Liber.
Anić, Vladimir, Dunja Brozović Rončević, Ivo Goldstein, Slavko Goldstein, Ljiljana Jojić, Ranko Matasovič, and Ivo Pranjković. 2002. *Hrvatski enciklopedijski rječnik*. Zagreb: Novi Liber.
Aronoff, Mark. 1976. *Word Formation in Generative Grammar*. Cambridge, MA: MIT Press.
Aronoff, Mark. 1994. *Morphology by Itself: Stems and Inflectional Classes*. Cambridge, MA: MIT Press.
Aronoff, Mark and Nanna Fuhrhop 2002. Restricting suffix combinations in German and English: Closing suffixes and the monosuffix constraint. *Natural Language and Linguistic Theory* 20, 451–490.
Assenova, Petja 2002. *Balkansko ezikoznanie*. V. Tărnovo: Faber.
Babić, Stjepan. 1991 [1986]. *Tvorba riječi u hrvatskom književnom jeziku: nacrt za gramatiku*. 2 izd. Zagreb: Djela Hrvatske akademije znanosti i umjetnosti.
Babić, Stjepan, Dalibor Brozović, Milan Moguš, Slavko Pavešić, Ivo Škarić, and Stjepko Težak. 1991. *Povijesni pregled, glasovi i oblici hrvatskoga književnog jezika: nacrt za grammatiku*. Zagreb: Djela Hrvatske akademije znanosti i umjetnosti.
Baerman, Matthew, Dunstan Brown, and Greville G. Corbett. 2005. *The Syntax-Morphology Interface: A Study of Syncretism*. Cambridge, MA: Cambridge University Press.
Barić, Eugenija, Mijo Lončarić, Dragica Malić, Slavko Pavešić, Mirko Peti, Vesna Zečević, and Marija Znika. 1997 [1995]. *Hrvatska gramatika*. II. promijeneno izdanje. Zagreb: Školska knjiga.

Battistella, Edwin L. 1990. *Markedness. The Evaluative Superstructure of Language*. Albany, NY: State University of New York Press.
Battistella, Edwin L. 1996. *The Logic of Markedness*. New York, NY: Oxford University Press.
Bauer, Laurie. 1983. *English Word-formation*. Cambridge, MA: Cambridge University Press.
Bauer, Laurie. 1988. *Introducing Linguistic Morphology*. Edinburgh: Edinburgh University Press.
Bauer, Laurie. 2005. Conversion and the notion of lexical category. In *Approaches to Conversion/Zero-Derivation*, eds. Laurie Bauer and Salvador Valera, 19–30. Münster/New York: Waxmann.
Baxturina, R.V. 1966a. Značenie i obrazovanie otimennyx glagolov s suffiksom -Ø- // -i-(t'). In *Razvitie slovoobrazovanija sovremennogo russkogo jazyka*, eds. Elena A. Zemskaja and D. N. Šmeleva, 74–112. Moskva: Nauka.
Baxturina, R. V. 1966b. Morfonologičeskie uslovija obrazovanija otymennyx glagolov s suffiksom -Ø- // -i-(t'). In *Razvitie slovoobrazovanija sovremennogo russkogo jazyka*, eds. Elena A. Zemskaja and D. N. Šmeleva, 113–126. Moskva: Nauka.
Beard, Robert. 1982. The plural as a lexical derivation. *Glossa* 16(2), 133–148.
Beard, Robert. 1987. Morpheme order in a lexeme/morpheme-based morphology. *Lingua* 72, 1–44.
Beard, Robert. 1995. *Lexeme-Morpheme Base Morphology*. Albany, NY: State University of New York Press.
Becker, Thomas. 1990. *Analogie und morphologische Theorie*. München: Fink.
Becker, Thomas. 1993. Back-formation, cross-formation, and 'bracketing paradoxes' in paradigmatic morphology. In *Yearbook of Morphology 1993*, eds. Geert Booij and Jaap van Marle, 1–25. Dordrecht: Kluwer.
Bergenholtz, H. and J. Mugdan. 1979. Ist liebe primär? – Über Ableitung und Wortarten. In *Deutsche Gegenwartssprache*, ed. Peter Braun, 339–354. München: Fink.
Berlin, Brent and Paul Kay. 1969. *Basic Color Terms. Their Universality and Evolution*. Berkeley, Los Angeles, CA: University of California Press.
Blevins, J. P. 2005. Word-based declensions in Estonian. In *Yearbook of Morphology 2005*, eds. Geert Booij and Jaap van Marle, 1–25. Dordrecht: Springer.
Blevins, J. P. 2006. Word-based morphology. *Journal of Linguistics* 42, 531–573.
Bloomfield, Leonard. 1933. *Language*. New York, NY: Holt [British edition 1935]: London: Allen and Unwin.
Bojadžiev, Todor, Ivan Kucarov, and Jordan Penčev. 1999. *Săvremenen bălgarski ezik. Fonetika. Leksikologija. Slovoobrazuvane. Morfologija. Sintaksis*. Sofija: P. Beron.
Bojadžiev, T. 1999. Slovoobrazuvane. In *Săvremenen bălgarski ezik. Fonetika. Leksikologija. Slovoobrazuvane. Morfologija. Sintaksis*, eds. Bojadžiev, Todor, Ivan Kucarov, and Jordan Penčev, 227–276. Sofija: P. Beron.
Booij, G. 1996. Inherent versus contextual inflection and the split morphology hypothesis. In *Yearbook of Morphology 1995*, eds. Geert Booij and Jaap van Marle, 1–16. Dordrecht: Kluwer.
Booij, G. 2000. Inflection and derivation. In *Morphology. An International Handbook on Inflection and Word-Formation*. Vol. 1, eds. Geert Booij, Christian Lehmann, and Joachim Mugdan, 360–369. Berlin: Walter de Gruyter.
Booij, Geert. 2002. *The Morphology of Dutch*. Oxford: Oxford University Press.
Booij, Geert, Christian Lehmann, and Joachim Mugdan. (eds.). 2000. *Morphology. An International Handbook on Inflection and Word-Formation*, Vol. 1. Berlin: Walter de Gruyter.
Browne, W. 1993. Serbo-Croat. In *The Slavonic Languages*, eds. Bernard Comrie and Greville G. Corbett, 306–387. London: Routledge.
Bulgarian Academy Grammar = Andrejčin et al. (1983).
Bybee, Joan L. 1985. *Morphology. A Study of the Relation between Meaning and Form*. Amsterdam: Benjamins.
Bybee, J. L. 1988. Morphology as lexical organization. In *Theoretical Morphology*, eds. Michael Hammond and Michael Noonan, 119–141. San Diego, CA: Academic Press.

Bybee, Joan L. and Carol L. Moder. 1983. Morphological classes as natural categories. *Language* 59, 251–270.
Bybee, Joan, R. Perkins, and W. Pagliuca. 1994. *The Evolution of Grammar. Tense, Aspect, and Modality in the languages of the World.* Chicago: University of Chicago Press.
Cannon, G. 2000. Blending. In *Morphology. An International Handbook on Inflection and Word-Formation*, Vol. 1, eds. Geert Booij, Christian Lehmann, and Joachim Mugdan, 952–956. Berlin: Walter de Gruyter.
Carstairs-McCarthy, Andrew. 1992. *Current Morphology*. London: Routledge.
Carstairs-McCarthy, Andrew. 2000. Lexeme, word-form, paradigm. In *Morphology. An International Handbook on Inflection and Word-Formation*, Vol. 1, eds. Geert Booij, Christian Lehmann, and Joachim Mugdan, 595–607. Berlin: Walter de Gruyter.
Cetnarowska, Bozena. 1993. *The Syntax, Semantics and Derivation of Bare Nominalisations in English*. Katowice: Uniwersytet Śląski.
Coleman, Linda and Paul Kay. 1981. Prototype semantics: The English verb lie. *Language* 57/1, 26–45.
Comrie, Bernard. 1976. *Aspect*. Cambridge, MA: Cambridge University Press.
Comrie, Bernard. 1981. *Language Universals and Linguistic Typology*. Oxford: Blackwell.
Comrie, Bernard. 1990. Russian. In *The Major Languages of Eastern Europe*, ed. Bernard Comrie, 63–81. London: Routledge.
Comrie, Bernard. 2001. Different views of language universals. In *Language Typology and Language Universals*, Vol. 1, eds. Martin Haspelmath, Ekkehard König, Wulf Oesterreicher, and Wolfgang Raible, 25–39. Berlin: Walter de Gruyter.
Comrie, Bernard and Greville G. Corbett. (eds.). 1993. *The Slavonic Languages*. London: Routledge.
Comrie, Bernard, Gerald Stone, and Maria Polinsky. 1996. *The Russian Language in the Twentieth Century*, 2nd ed., Revised and Expanded, of *The Russian Language Since the Revolution*, eds. Bernard Comrie and Gerald Stone [1978]. Oxford: Clarendon Press.
Corbett, G. G. 1990. Serbo-Croat. In *The Major Languages of Eastern Europe*, ed. Bernard Comrie, 125–143. London: Routledge.
Corbett, Greville G. 1991. *Gender*. Cambridge, MA: Cambridge University Press.
Corbett, Greville G. 2000. *Number*. Cambridge, MA: Cambridge University Press.
Corbett, Greville G. and Norman M. Fraser. 1993. Network morphology: A DATR account of Russian nominal inflection. *Journal of Linguistics* 29, 113–142.
Crocco-Galèas, G. 1990. Conversion as morphological metaphor. In *Naturalists at Krems*, eds. J. Méndez Dosuna and C. Pensado, 23–32. Salamanca: Acta Salamanticensia (Estudios Filológicos 227).
Daniel, M. and A. Spencer. 2009. The vocative – an outlier case. In *The Oxford Handbook of Case*, eds. Andrej Malchukov and Andrew Spencer, 626–634. Oxford: Oxford University Press.
De Bray, R. G. A. 1951. *Guide to the Slavonic Languages*. London: Dent. (Third edition 1980 in three volumes: *Guide to the South Slavonic Languages; Guide to the West Slavonic Languages; Guide to the East Slavonic Languages*. Columbus, OH: Slavica).
Dilevski, Nikolaj. 1985. *Ruska gramatika*. Sofija: Nauka i izkustvo.
Di Sciullo, Anna M. and Edwin Williams 1987. *On the Definition of Word*. Cambridge, MA: MIT-Press.
Dokulil, Miloš. 1968a. Zur Frage der Konversion und verwandter Wortbildungsvorgänge und –beziehungen. *Travaux linguistiques de Prague* 3, 215–239.
Dokulil, M. 1968b. Zur Frage der sog. Nullableitung. In *Wortbildung, Syntax und Morphologie*, eds. Herbert E. Brekle and Leonard Lipka, 55–64. The Hague: Mouton.
Dokulil, Miloš. 1968c. Zur Theorie der Wortbildungslehre. Wissenschaftliche Zeitschrift der Karl-Marks-Universität Leipzig. *Gesellschafts- und sprachwissenschaftliche Reihe* 17, 203–211.
Doleschal, Ursula. 2000. *Das Phänomen der Unflektierbarkeit in den slawischen Sprachen*. Wien, Wirtschaftsuniv., Habil.-Schrift.

Don, Jan. 1993. *Morphological Conversion*. Utrecht: OTS (Research Institute for Language and Speech, University of Utrecht).
Don, Jan. 2005. On conversion, relisting and zero-derivation: A comment on Rochelle Lieber: English word-formation processes. *SKASE Journal of Theoretical Linguistics* 2(2), 2–16.
Don, J., M. Trommelen, and W. Zonneveld. 2000. Conversion and category indeterminacy. In *Morphology. An International Handbook on Inflection and Word-Formation*, Vol. 1, eds. Geert Booij, Christian Lehmann, and Joachim Mugdan, 943–952. Berlin: Walter de Gruyter.
Dressler, Wolfgang U. 1984. Subtraction in word formation and its place within a theory of natural morphology. *Quaderni di Semantica* 5, 78–85.
Dressler, Wolfgang U. 1985a. Typological aspects of natural morphology. *Wiener Linguistische Gazette* 36, 3–26 [= *Acta Linguistica Hungarica* 35, 1987, 51–70].
Dressler, Wolfgang U. 1985b. *Morphonology*. Ann Arbor, MI: Karoma Press.
Dressler, Wolfgang U. 1987a. Subtraction in a polycentristic theory of Natural Morphology. In *Rules and the lexicon*, ed. E. Gussmann, 67–78. Lublin: Redakcja Wydawnictw Katolickiege Uniwersytetu Lubelskiego.
Dressler, Wolfgang U. 1987b. Word formation (WF) as part of natural morphology. In *Leitmotifs in Natural Morphology*, eds. Wolfgang U. Dressler, Willi Mayerthaler, Oswald Panagl, and Wolfgang U. Wurzel, 99–126. Amsterdam: Benjamins.
Dressler, W. U. 1988. Preferences vs. strict universals in morphology: Word-based rules. In *Theoretical Morphology*, eds. Michael Hammond and Michael Noonan, 143–154. San Diego, CA: Academic Press.
Dressler, Wolfgang U. 1989. Prototypical differences between inflection and derivation. *Zeitschrift für Phonetik, Sprachwissenschaft and Kommunikationsforschung* 42, 3–10.
Dressler, W. U. 1990a. Sketching submorphemes within natural morphology. In *Naturalists at Krems*, eds. J. Méndez Dosuna and C. Pensado, 33–41. Salamanca: Acta Salamanticensia (Estudios Filológicos 227).
Dressler, Wolfgang U. 1990b. The cognitive perspective of "naturalist" linguistic models. *Cognitive Linguistics* 1–1, 75–98.
Dressler, Wolfgang U. 1994. Subtraction. In *The Encyclopedia of Language and Linguistics*, ed. Robert E. Asher, 4401–4402. Oxford: Pergamon Press.
Dressler, Wolfgang U. 1997. On productivity and potentiality in inflectional morphology. *CLASNET Working Papers* 7, 2–22.
Dressler, Wolfgang U. 1999. What is natural in natural morphology? *Prague Linguistic Circle Papers*, Vol. 3. Amsterdam: Benjamins, 135–144.
Dressler, Wolfgang U. 2000a. Naturalness. In *Morphology. An International Handbook on Inflection and Word-Formation*, Vol. 1, eds. Geert Booij, Christian Lehmann, and Joachim Mugdan, 288–296. Berlin: Walter de Gruyter.
Dressler, Wolfgang U. 2000b. Subtraction. In *Morphology. An International Handbook on Inflection and Word-Formation*. Vol. 1, eds. Geert Booij, Christian Lehmann, and Joachim Mugdan, 581–587. Berlin: Walter de Gruyter.
Dressler, Wolfgang U. 2005. Word-formation in natural morphology. In *Handbook of Word-Formation*, eds. Pavol Štekauer and Rochelle Lieber, 267–284. Dordrecht: Springer.
Dressler, Wolfgang U., Willi Mayerthaler, Oswald Panagl, and Wolfgang U. Wurzel. 1987. *Leitmotifs in Natural Morphology*. Amsterdam: Benjamins.
Dressler, Wolfgang U. and Ursula Doleschal. 1991. Gender agreement via derivational morphology. *Acta Linguistica Hungarica* 40(1–2), 115–137 (1990–1991).
Dressler, Wolfgang U. and L. Merlini Barbaresi. 1993. Italian diminutives as non-prototypical word formation. In *Natural Morphology. Perspectives for the Nineties*, eds. Livia Tonelli and Wolfgang U. Dressler, 21–29. Padova: Unipress.
Dressler, Wolfgang U. and Lavinia Merlini Barbaresi. 1994. *Morphopragmatics. Diminutives and Intensifiers in Italian, German, and Other Languages*. Berlin: Mouton de Gruyter.

References

Dressler, Wolfgang U., Katarzyna Dziubalska-Kołaczyk, and Antigona Katičić. 1996. A contrastive analysis of verbal inflection classes in Polish and Croatian. *Suvremena lingvistika* 22(41/42), 127–138.
Dressler, Wolfgang U. and N. V. Gagarina. 1999. Basic questions in establishing the verb classes of contemporary Russian. In *Essays in Poetics, Literary History and Linguistics. Presented to V. V. Ivanov on the Occasion of His Seventieth Birthday*, eds. L. Fleishman et al., 754–760. Moscow: OGI.
Dressler, Wolfgang U. and Maria Ladányi. 2000. Productivity in word formation (WF): A morphological approach. *Acta Linguistica Hafniensia* 47, 103–144.
Dressler, Wolfgang U. and Stela Manova. 2002. Conversion vs. modification and subtraction. *Paper Presented at the Seminar on Conversion/Zero-Derivation*. Szentendre, Hungary, May 2002.
Efremova, T. F. 2000. *Novyj slovar' russkogo jazyka. I, II. Tolkovo-slovoobrazovatel'nyj*. Moskva: Russkij jazyk.
Evgen'eva, A. P. (ed.). 1981–1984. *Slovar' russkogo jazyka v četyrex tomax*. Izdanie vtoroe, isparevlennoe i dopolnennoe. Moskva: Russkij jazyk.
Filipović, Rudolf. 1986. *Teorija jezika u kontaktu*. Zagreb: Školska knjiga.
Ford, A. and R. Singh. 1984. Remarks on the directionality of word formation processes. In *Proceedings of the Eastern State Conference on Linguistics (ESCOL)* 1, 205–213, Columbus, Ohio.
Fraser, N. M. and G. G. Corbett. 1995. Gender, animacy, and declensional class assignment: A unified account for Russian. In *Yearbook of Morphology 1994*, eds. Geert Booij and Jaap van Marle, 123–150. Dordrecht: Kluwer.
Galkina-Fëdoruk, Evdokija M., K. V. Gorškova, and N. M. Šanskij. 1957. *Sovremennyj russkij jazyk: Leksikologija, fonetika, morfologija*. Moskva: Gos. uchebno-pedagog. izd-vo.
Georgiev, Vladimir I. 1969. *Osnovni problemi na slavjanskata diaxronna morfologija*. Sofija: BAN.
Georgiev, Vladimir I. 1970. Preosmisleni padežni formi. *Bălgarski ezik* 20, kn. 2–3, 153–157. Reprinted in Georgiev, Vladimir. 1985. *Problemi na bălgarskija ezik*. Sofija: BAN, 164–168.
Georgiev, Vladimir I. 1976. Njakoi osobenosti na bălgarskite zvatelni formi. *Bălgarski ezik* 26, kn. 1–2, 56–59. Reprinted in Georgiev, Vladimir. 1985. *Problemi na bălgarskija ezik*, Sofija: BAN, 157–160.
Georgiev, Vladimir I. 1985. *Problemi na bălgarskija ezik*. Sofija: BAN.
Givón, T. 1986. Prototypes: Between Plato and Wittgenstein. In *Noun Classes and Categorization*, ed. Colette Craig, 77–102. Amsterdam: Benjamins.
Goldsmith, John A. 1990. *Autosegmental and Metrical Phonology*. Oxford: Blackwell.
Golston, C. and R. Wiese. 1996. Zero morphology and constraint interaction: subtraction and epenthesis in German dialects. In *Yearbook of Morphology 1995*, eds. Geert Booij and Jaap van Marle, 143–159. Dordrecht: Kluwer.
Greenberg, Joseph H. 1963 (ed.). *Universals of Language*. Cambridge, MA: MIT Press.
Habermann, Mechthild. 1994. *Verbale Wortbildung um 1500: eine historisch-synchrone Untersuchung anhand von Texten Albrecht Dürers, Heinrich Deichslers und Veit Dietrichs*. Berlin (Wortbildung des Nürnberger Frühneuhochdeutsch 2).
Hale, K. 1973. Deep-surface canonical disparities in relation to analysis and change: An Australian example. In *Current Trends in Linguistics 11: Diachronic, Areal, and Typological Linguistics*, ed. Thomas Sebeok A, 401–458. The Hague: Mouton.
Halilović, Senahid. 1996. *Pravopis bosanskoga jezika*. Sarajevo: Kulturno društvo Bošnjaka Preporod.
Hardy, H. K. and T. R. Montler. 1988. Alabama radical morphology: H-infix and disfixation. In *Honor of Mary Haas. From the Haas Festival Conference on Native American Linguistics*, ed. William Shipley, 377–409. Berlin: Mouton de Gruyter.
Harris, Zellig S. 1942. Morpheme alternants in linguistic analysis. *Language* 18, 169–180. [Reprinted in: Joos, Martin. (ed.). 1957. *Readings in Linguistics: The development of*

Descriptive Linguistics in America since 1925. New York, NY: American Council of Learned Societies, 109–115]
Harrison, William and Stephen le Fleming. 2000. *Intermediate Russian Grammar.* Cardiff: University of Wales Press.
Haspelmath, M. 1996. Word-class-changing inflection and morphological theory. In *Yearbook of Morphology 1995*, eds. Geert Booij and Jaap van Marle, 43–66. Dordrecht: Kluwer.
Hockett, Charles F. 1947. Problems of morphemic analysis. *Language* 23, 321–343. [Reprinted in: Joos, Martin. (ed.). 1957. *Readings in Linguistics: The development of Descriptive Linguistics in America since 1925.* New York, NY: American Council of Learned Societies, 229–242]
Holsinger, D. J. and P. D. Houseman. 1999. Lenition in Hessian: Cluster reduction and 'subtractive plurals'. In *Yearbook of Morphology 1998*, eds. Geert Booij and Jaap van Marle, 159–174. Dordrecht: Kluwer.
Horálek, Karel. 1992. *An introduction to the Study of the Slavonic Languages*, Vol. 1 and 2. Nottingham: Astra Press.
Hristea, Theodor. 1984 [1972]. *Sinteze de limba română.* Bucureşti: Albatros.
Hurch, B. 1996. Morphoprosody: Some reflections on accent and morphology. In *Trubetzkoy's Orphan. Proceedings of the Montréal Roundtable "Morphonology: Contemporary responses" (Montreal, September 30 – October 2, 1994)*, ed. Rajendra Singh, 189–221. Amsterdam: Benjamins.
Iacobini, C. 2000. Base and direction of derivation. In *Morphology. An International Handbook on Inflection and Word-Formation*, Vol. 1, eds. Geert Booij, Christian Lehmann, and Joachim Mugdan, 865–876. Berlin: Walter de Gruyter.
Isačenko, A. V. 1972. Rol' usečenija v russkom slovoobrozovanii. *International Journal of Slavic Linguistics and Poetics* 15, 95–125.
Isačenko, A. V. 1982. *Die russische Sprache der Gegenwart.* Formenlehre. 4 Auflage. München: Max Hueber Verlag.
Ivanova-Mirčeva, Dora and Ivan Xaralampiev 1999. *Istorija na bălgarskija ezik.* V. Tărnovo: Faber.
Jakobson, Roman. 1932. Zur Struktur des russischen Verbums. Reprinted in *Selected Writings II*, 1971, 3–15.
Jakobson, Roman. 1939. Signe zéro. Reprinted in *Selected Writings II*, 1971, 211–219.
Jakobson, Roman. 1948. Russian conjugation. *Word IV.* Reprinted in *Selected Writings II*, 119–129.
Jakobson, Roman. 1971. *Selected Writings II. Word and Language.* The Hague: Mouton.
Jakobson, Roman. 1984. *Russian and Slavic Grammar* (Studies 1931–1981), eds. Linda R. Waugh and Morris Halle. Berlin: Mouton.
Kastovsky, Dieter. 1968. *Old English Deverbal Substantives Derived by Means of a Zero Morpheme.* Esslingen/N.: B. Langer.
Kastovsky, Dieter. 1989. Typological changes in the history of English word-formation. In *Anglistentag 1988 Göttingen. Vorträge*, eds. Heinz-Joachim Müllenbrock and Renate Noll-Wiemann, 281–293. Tübingen: Niemeyer.
Kastovsky, Dieter. 1994. Typological differences between English and German morphology and their causes. In *Language Change and Language Structure: Old Germanic Languages in a Comparative Perspective*, eds. Toril Swan, Endre Mørck and Olaf Jansen Westvik, 135–158. Berlin: Mouton de Gruyter.
Kastovsky, Dieter. 2005. Conversion and/or zero: word-formation theory, historical linguistics, and typology. In *Approaches to Conversion/Zero-Derivation*.Bauer, eds. Laurie Bauer and Salvador Valera, 31–50. Münster/New York: Waxmann.
Kay, Paul and C. K. McDaniel. 1978. The Linguistic Significance of the Meanings of the Basic Color Terms. *Language* 54/3, 610–647.
Kaye, J. D. and Y.-C. Morin. 1978. Il n'y a pas de règles de troncation, voyons! In *Proceedings of the Twelfth International Congress of Linguistics. Vienna, August 28 – September 2, 1977*,

eds. Wolfgang U. Dressler and Wolfgang Meid, 788–792. Innsbruck: Institut für Sprachwissenschaft der Universität Innsbruck.
Kiefer, F. 2005. Types of conversion in Hungarian. In *Approaches to Conversion/Zero-Derivation* eds. Laurie Bauer and Salvador Valera, 51–66. Münster/New York: Waxmann.
Kiparsky, P. 1982. Lexical morphology and phonology. In *Linguistics in the Morning Calm: Selected Papers from SICOL-1981*, Linguistic Society of Korea. Seoul: Hanshin, 3–91.
Kleiber, Georges. 1998 [1993]. *Prototypensemantik.* [*La sémantique du prototype* (1990)] Übersetzt von Michael Schreiber. 2 überarb. Aufl. Tübingen: Narr.
Kondrašov, N. A. 1986. *Slavjanskie jazyki.* Moskva: Prosveščenie.
Koontz-Garboden, A. 2005. On the typology of state/change of state alternations. In *Yearbook of Morphology 2005*, eds. Geert Booij and Jaap van der Marle, 3–117. Dordrecht: Springer.
Koontz-Garboden, Andrew. 2007a. *States, Changes of State, and the Monotonicity Hypothesis.* Unpublished Ph.D. Dissertation, Stanford University.
Koontz-Garboden, Andrew. 2007b. Aspectual coercion and the typology of change of state predicates. *Journal of Linguistics* 43, 115–152.
Koontz-Garboden, Andrew and B. Levin. 2005. The morphological typology of change of state event encoding. In *Online Proceedings of the Fourth Mediterranean Morphology Meeting (MMM4), Catania, 21–23 September 2003*, eds. Geert Booij, Emilio Guevara, Angelliki Ralli, Salvatore Sgroi and Sergio Scalise, 185–194. Università degli Studi di Bologna. <http://morbo.lingue.unibo.it/mmm/mmm4-proceedings.php>
Kreidler, C. W. 2000. Clipping and acronymy. In *Morphology. An International Handbook on Inflection and Word-Formation*, Vol. 1, eds. Geert Booij, Christian Lehmann, and Joachim Mugdan, 956–963. Berlin: Walter de Gruyter.
Krumova, L. and M. Čoroleeva. 1983. *Rečnik na săkraštenijata v bălgarskija ezik.* Sofija: Nauka i izkustvo.
Krupa, Viktor. 1966. Rules of occurrence of the passive suffix alomorphs in Maori. *Asian and African Studies* 2, 9–13.
Kucarov, Ivan. 1983. Po văprosa za kategorialnata xarakteristika na glagolnija vid v săvremennija bălgarski ezik. *Naučni trudove na Plovdivskija universitet "Paisij Xilendarski"*, t. 21, kn. 5 – Filologija, 45–54.
Kucarov, I. 1999. Morfologija. In *Săvremenen bălgarski ezik. Fonetika. Leksikologija. Slovoobrazuvane. Morfologija. Sintaksis*, eds. Todor Bojadžiev, Ivan Kucarov, and Jordan Penčev, 277–497. Sofija: P. Beron.
Kuznetsova, Ariadna I. and Tatjana F. Efremova. 1986. *Slovar' morfem russkogo jazyka.* Moskva: Russkij jazyk.
Lakoff, George. 1973. Hedges: A study in meaning criteria and the logic of fuzzy concepts. *Journal of Philosophical Logic* 2, 458–508.
Langacker, Ronald W. 1987. *Foundations of Cognitive Grammar. Vol. I. Theoretical Prerequisites.* Stanford: Stanford University Press.
Langacker, Ronald W. 1991. *Foundations of Cognitive Grammar. Vol. II. Descriptive Application.* Stanford: Stanford University Press.
Langacker, Ronald W. 1999. *Grammar and Conceptualization.* Berlin: de Gruyter.
Langacker, Roland W. 2002 [1991]. *Concept, Image and Symbol. The Cognitive Basis of Grammar*, 2nd edition. Berlin: Mouton de Gruyter.
Lappe, Sabine. 2007. *Prosodic Morphology.* Dordrecht: Springer.
Laškova, Lili. 2001. *Sărbo-xărvatska gramatika.* Sofija: IK EMAS.
Lehmann, V. 1999. Aspekt. In *Handbuch der sprachwissenschaftlichen Russistik und ihrer Grenzdisziplinen*, ed. H. Jachnow (Hrsg.), 214–242. Wiesbaden: Harrassowitz (Slavistische Studienbücher; N.F., Bd. 8).
Libben, G. and R. G. de Almeida. 2002. Is there a morphological parser? In *Morphology 2000. Selected papers from the 9th Morphology Meeting, Vienna, 24–28 February 2000*, eds. Sabrina Bendjaballah, Wolfgang U. Dressler, Oskar E. Pfeiffer, and Maria D. Voeikova, 213–226. Amsterdam: Benjamins.

Lieber, Rochelle. 1981a. *On the Organisation of the Lexicon*. Bloomington, IN: Indiana University Linguistic Club.
Lieber, Rochelle. 1981b. Morphological conversion within a restricted theory of the lexicon. In *The Scope of Lexical Rules*, eds. Moortgat, Michael, Harry van der Hulst, and Toen Hoekstra. Dordrecht: Foris.
Lieber, Rochelle. 1992. *Deconstructing Morphology: Word Formation in Syntactic Theory*. Chicago and London: The University of Chicago Press.
Ljung, M. 1977. Problems in the derivation of instrumental verbs. In *Perspektiven der Wortbildungsforschung*, eds. H. E. Brekle and D. Kastovsky, 165–179. Bonn: Bouvier Verlag Herbert Grundmann.
Ljung, M. 1994. Conversion. In *The Encyclopedia of Language and Linguistics*, ed. Robert E. Asher, 758–759. Oxford: Pergamon Press.
Longman Dictionary of Contemporary English. 1995. 3rd edn. München: Langenscheidt-Longman.
Longman Dictionary of Contemporary English. 1978. In Procter, P. (ed.). London: Longman.
Lopatin, Vl. 1966. Nulevaja affiksacija v sisteme russkovo slovoobrazovanija. *Voprosy jazykoznanija* 1, 76–87.
Ludwig, R. 2001. Markiertheit. In *Language Typology and Language Universals*, Vol. 1, eds. Martin Haspelmath, Ekkehard König, Wulf Oesterreicher, and Wolfgang Raible, 400–419. Berlin: Walter de Gruyter.
Lukatela, Geogije, Claudia Carello, and M. T. Turvey. 1987. Lexical representation of regular and irregular inflected nouns. *Language and Cognitive Processes* 2, 1–17.
Luraghi, S. 2000. Syncretismus. In *Morphology. An International Handbook on Inflection and Word-Formation*, Vol. 1, eds. Booij, Geert, Christian Lehmann, and Joachim Mugdan, 638–647. Berlin: Walter de Gruyter.
Lyons, John. 1977. *Semantics*, Vol. 1 and 2. Cambridge, MA: Cambridge University Press.
Manova, Stela. 2002. Between inflection and derivation: on morphotactic expression of aspect and gender in Bulgarian, Russian and Serbo-Croatian. *Wiener Slavistisches Jahrbuch* 48, 203–217.
Manova, Stela. 2003a. An input-oriented approach to inflection class assignment illustrated with Bulgarian nominal inflection. *Wiener Slavistisches Jahrbuch* 49, 103–118.
Manova, Stela. 2003b. *Conversion and Subtraction in Bulgarian, Russian and Serbo-Croatian*. Ph.D. Dissertation, University of Vienna.
Manova, S. 2005a. Derivation versus inflection in three inflecting languages. In *Morphology and its Demarcations. Selected Papers from the 11th International Morphology Meeting, Vienna, February 2004*, eds. Wolfgang U. Dressler, Dieter Kastovsky, Oskar Pfeiffer, and Franz Rainer, 233–252. Amsterdam: Benjamins.
Manova, Stela. 2005b. Towards a theory of subtraction. *Paper Presented at the 38th Societas Linguistica Europaea Congress*, 7–10 September 2005, Valencia, Spain (*Abstracts/Resúmenes*, 163–164).
Manova, Stela. 2005c. Towards a theory of conversion in Slavic: Evidence from Bulgarian, Russian and Serbo-Croatian. *Glossos* 6. http://seelrc.org/glossos/issues/6/manova.pdf. Accessed 26.01.2010.
Manova, Stela. 2006. Subtrakcijata kato vid morfologična texnika. *Săpostavitelno ezikoznanie/Contrastive linguistics* 2005: 3, 41–56.
Manova, S. 2008. On some recent changes in Bulgarian conjugation. In *Bulgarian Language and Literature at the Crossroads of Cultures*, Vol. 1, ed. István, Ferincz, 22–29. Szeged: Szegedi Egyetemi Kiadó. http://homepage.univie.ac.at/stela.manova/publications/Manova_Paper_Szeged.pdf. Accessed 26.01.2010.
Manova, Stela. 2010. Suffix combinations in Bulgarian: Parsability and hierarchy-based ordering. *Morphology* 20: 1, 267–296. DOI: 10.1007/s11525-010-9148-3.
Manova, Stela and Wolfgang U. Dressler. 2001. Gender and declensional class in Bulgarian. *Wiener Linguistische Gazette* 67–69, 45–81.

Manova, S. and W. U. Dressler. 2005. The morphological technique of conversion in the inflecting-fusional type. In *Approaches to Conversion/Zero-Derivation*, eds. Laurie Bauer and Salvador Valera, 67–102. Münster/New York: Waxmann.
Marchand, Hans. 1963. On a question of contrary analysis with derivationally connected but morphologically uncharacterised words. *English Studies* 44, 176–187.
Marchand, Hans. 1964a. A set of criteria for the establishing of derivational relationship between words unmarked by derivational morphemes. *Indogermanische Forschungen* 69, 10–19.
Marchand, Hans. 1964b. Die Ableitung desubstantivischer Verben mit Nullmorphem im Englischen, Französischen und Deutschen. *Die neueren Sprachen*, N. F. 10, 105–118.
Marchand, Hans. 1969 [1960]. *The Categories and Types of Present-Day English Word-Formation*, 2nd completely revised and enlarged edition. München: Beck.
Marchand, Hans. 1974. *Studies in Syntax and Word-Formation. Selected Articles. On the Occasion of his 65th Birthday*, ed. Dieter Kastovsky. München: Fink.
Mareš, František V. 1980. Die Tetrachotomie und doppelte Dichotomie der slavischen Sprachen. *Wiener Slavistisches Jahrbuch* 26, 33–45.
Marle, J. van. 1996. The unity of morphology: On the interwovenness of the derivational and inflectional dimensions of the word. In *Yearbook of Morphology 1995*, eds. Geert Booij and Jaap van Marle, 67–82. Dordrecht: Kluwer.
Martin, Jack. 1988. Subtractive morphology as dissociation. *Proceedings of the West Coast Conference on Formal Linguistics* 7, 229–240. Stanford: CSLI Publications.
Martin, Jack. 1994. Implications of Plural Reduplication, Infixation and Subtraction for Muskogean Subgrouping. *Anthropological Linguistics* 36, 27–55.
Maslov, Jurij S. 1959. Glagol'nyj vid v sovremennom bolgarskom literaturnom jazyke (značenie i upotreblenie). In *Voprosy grammatiki bolgarskogo literaturnovo jazyka*, ed. Bernštejn, S. S., 157–312. Moskva: Nauka.
Maslov, Jurij S. (ed.). 1962a. *Voprosy glagol'nogo vida*. Moskva: Izdatel'stvo inostrannoj literatury.
Maslov, Jurij S. 1962b. Voprosy glagol'nogo vida v sovremennom zarubežnom jazykoznanii. In *Voprosy glagol'nogo vida*, ed. Jurij S. Maslov, 7–32, Moskva: Izdatel'stvo inostrannoj literatury.
Maslov, Jurij S. 1981. *Grammatika bolgarskogo jazyka*. Moskva: Vysšaja škola. [Bulgarian translation: 1982. *Gramatika na bălgarskija ezik*. Sofija: Nauka i izkustvo].
Matthews, Peter H. 1972. *Inflectional Morphology: A Theoretical Study Based on Aspects of Latin Verb Conjugation*. Cambridge, MA: Cambridge University Press.
Mayerthaler, Willi. 1980. Ikonismus in der Morphologie. *Zeitschrift für Semiotik* 2, 19–37.
Mayerthaler, Willi 1981. *Morphologische Natürlichkeit*. Wiesbaden: Athenaion [English translation: 1988. *Morphological Naturalness*. Ann Arbor, MI: Karoma].
Mayerthaler, W. 1987. System-independent morphological naturalness. In *Leitmotifs in Natural Morphology*, eds. Wolfgang U. Dressler, Willi Mayerthaler, Oswald Panagl, and Wolfgang U. Wurzel, 25–58. Amsterdam: Benjamins.
Mel'čuk, Igor A. 1967. K ponjatiju slovoobrazovanija. *Izvestija Akademii Nauk SSSR, Serija literatury i jazyka* 26, 352–362. Reprinted in Mel'čuk, Igor A. 1976. *Das Wort* [Zum Begriff der Wortbildung (Derivation)], 63–88.
Mel'čuk, Igor A. 1973. Konversija kak morfologičeskoe sredstvo. Reprinted in Mel'čuk, Ingor A. 1976. *Das Wort* [Die Konversion als morphologisches Mittel], 288–318.
Mel'čuk, Igor A. 1976. *Das Wort*. München: Fink (Internationale Bibliothek für allgemeine Linguistik 9).
Mel'čuk, Igor A. 1982. *Towards a Language of Linguistics*. Munich: Fink.
Mel'čuk, Igor A. 1991. Subtraction in Natural Language. In "*Words are physicians for an ailing mind*". *For Andrzej Boguslawski on the Occasion of His 60th Birthday*, eds. Miciej Grochowski and Daniel Weiss, 279–293. München: Sagner (Sagners Slavistische Sammlung 17).

Mel'čuk, Igor A. 1993. *Cours de morphologie générale*, Vol. 1. Montréal: Les Presses de l'Université de Montréal [Russian translation: see Mel'čuk 1997a].
Mel'čuk, Igor A. 1994. *Cours de morphologie générale*, Vol. 2. Montréal: Les Presses de l'Université de Montréal [Russian translation: see Melčuk 1998].
Mel'čuk, Igor A. 1996. *Cours de morphologie générale*, Vol. 3. Montréal: Les Presses de l'Université de Montréal [Russian translation: see Mel'čuk 2000a].
Mel'čuk, Igor A. 1997a. *Kurs obščej morfologii*. Tom I. Moskva – Vena: Wiener Slawistischer Almanach, Sonderband 38/1.
Mel'čuk, Igor A. 1997b. *Cours de morphologie générale*, Vol. 4. Montréal: Les Presses de l'Université de Montréal [Russian translation: see Melčuk 2001].
Mel'čuk, Igor A. 1998. *Kurs obščej morfologii*. Tom II. Moskva – Vena: Wiener Slawistischer Almanach, Sonderband 38/2.
Mel'čuk, Igor A. 2000a. *Kurs obščej morfologii*. Tom III. Moskva – Vena: Wiener Slawistischer Almanach, Sonderband 38/3.
Mel'čuk, Igor A. 2000b. *Cours de morphologie générale*, Vol. 5. Montréal: Les Presses de l'Université de Montréal.
Mel'čuk, Igor A. 2001. *Kurs obščej morfologii*. Tom IV. Moskva – Vena: Wiener Slawistischer Almanach, Sonderband 38/4.
Mel'čuk, Igor A. 2002. Towards a formal concept 'zero linguistic sign'. Applications in typology. In *Morphology 2000. Selected papers from the 9th Morphology Meeting, Vienna, 24–28 February 2000*, eds. Sabrina Bendjaballah, Wolfgang U. Dressler, Oskar E. Pfeiffer, and Maria D. Voeikova, 241–258. Amsterdam: Benjamins.
Milev, Al., B. Nikolov and J. Bratkov. 1978. *Rečnik na čuždite dumi v bălgarskija ezik*. IV preraboteno i dopălneno izdanie. Sofija: Nauka i izkustvo.
Mirčev, Kiril. 1963. *Istoričeska gramatika na bălgarskija knižoven ezik*. Vtoro izdanie. Sofija: Nauka i izkustvo.
Mladenov, Stefan. 1929. *Geschichte der bulgarischen Sprache*. Berlin: Walter de Gruyter & Co.
Molhova, Jana. 1976. *Outlines of English Lexicology*, 3rd revised edition. Sofija: Nauka i izkustvo.
Mrazović, Pavica and Zora Vukadinović. 1990. *Gramatika srpskohrvatskog jezika za strance*. Sremski Karlovci: Izdavačka knjižarnica Zorana Stojanovića; Novi Sad: Dobra vest.
Mulisch, Herbert. (ed.). 1988. *Morphologie*. 1. Aufl. d. Neufassung. In *Russische Sprache der Gegenwart*, Bd. 2, ed. Gabka, Kurt Leipzig: Verlag Enzyklopädie.
Müller, Peter O. 1993. *Substantiv-Derivation in den Schriften Albrecht Dürers*. Berlin: Walter de Gruyter.
Myers, S. 1984. Zero derivation and inflection. In *Papers in Morphology*, eds. M. Speas and R. Sproats, 53–69. Cambridge, MA: Department of Linguistics and Philosophy, MIT.
Naumann, B. and P. M. Vogel. 2000. Derivation. In *Morphology. An International Handbook on Inflection and Word-Formation*, Vol. 1, eds. Booij, Geert, Christian Lehmann, and Joachim Mugdan, 929–943. Berlin: Walter de Gruyter.
Nida, Eugene A. 1949 [1946]. *Morphology: The descriptive Analysis of Words*. Ann Arbor, MI: University of Michigan Press.
Oxford English Dictionary 1933. Oxford: Clarendon.
Ožegov, S. I. and N. Ju. Švedova. 1995. *Tolkovyj slovar' russkogo jazyka*. Moskva: Azъ.
Pennanen, E. V. 1975. What happens in back-formation? In *Papers from the Second Scandinavian Conference of Linguistics*, ed. E. Hovdhaugen, 216–229. Norway: University of Oslo.
Pennanen, Esko V. 1988. Word-formation revisited. Topical aspects of English word-formation. *Studia Anglica Posnaniensia* 21, 123–144.
Peirce, Charles S. 1965. *Collected Papers*. Cambridge, MA: Harvard University Press.
Plag, Ingo. 2003. *Word-Formation in English*. Cambridge, MA: Cambridge University Press.
Plank, Frans. 1981. *Morphologische (Ir-)Regularitäten. Aspekte der Wortstrukturtheorie*. Tübingen: Narr.

Plank, Frans. 1994. Inflection and derivation: In *The Encyclopedia of Language and Linguistics*, ed. Robert E. Asher, 1671–1678. Oxford: Pergamon Press.
Polenz, Peter von. 1968. Ableitungsstrukturen deutscher Verben. *Zeitschrift für deutsche Sprache* 24, 1–15 and 129–160.
Quirk, Randolph, Sidney Greenbaum, Geoffrey Leech, and Jan Svartvik. 1980. *A Grammar of Contemporary English*. London: Longman.
Quirk, Randolph, Sidney Greenbaum, Geoffrey Leech, and Jan Svartvik 1985/1995. *A Comprehensive Grammar of the English Language*. London: Longman.
Rainer, Franz. 1993. *Spanische Wortbildungslehre*. Tübingen: Niemeyer.
Rainer, Franz. 1996. Inflection inside derivation: Evidence from Spanish and Portuguese. In *Yearbook of Morphology 1995*, eds. Geert Booij and Jaap van Marle, 83–91. Dordrecht: Kluwer.
Rojzenzon, L. I. 1962. K tipologii substantivirovannyx prilagatel'nyx i pričastij v russkom jazyke. *Trudy Samarkanskogo universiteta* 118, 121–139.
Rosch, Eleanor. 1973. On the internal structure of perceptual and semantic categories. In *Cognitive Development and the Acquisition of Language*, ed. Timothy E. Moore, 111–144. New York, NY: Academic Press.
Rosch, Eleanor. 1975. Cognitive Representations of Semantic Categories. *Journal of Experimental Psychology: General* 104, 192–233.
Rosch, Eleanor. 1977. Human Categorization. In *Studies in Cross-cultural Psychology*, Vol. 1, ed. Neil Warren, 1–49. London: Academic Press.
Rosch, Eleanor. 1978. Principles of categorization. In *Cognition and Categorization*, eds. Eleanor Rosch and Barbara B. Lloyd, 27–47. Hillsdale, NJ: Erlbaum.
Rozental', D. È. and M. A. Telenkova. 1976. *Spravočnik lingvističeskix terminov*. Izdanie 2oe, ispravlennoe i dopolnennoe. Moskva: Prosveščenie.
Russian Academy Grammar 1970 = *Grammatika sovremennnogo russkogo literaturnogo jazyka*. Moskva: Nauka (Izdatel'stvo Akademii Nauk SSSR).
Russian Academy Grammar = Švedova et al. (1980).
Sanders, G. 1988. Zero derivation and the overt analogue criterion. In *Theoretical Morphology. Approaches in Modern Linguistics*, eds. Michael Hammond and Michael Noonan, 155–175. San Diego, CA: Academic.
Sassen, A. 1981. Morfologische produktiviteit in het licht van niet-additieve woodafleidung. *Forum der Letteren* 22, 126–142.
Saxton, Dean and Leslie Saxton. 1969. *Dictionary, Papago and Pima to English, English to Papago and Pima*. Tuscon: University of Arizona Press.
Scalise, Sergio. 1986. *Generative Morphology*. Dordrecht: Foris.
Schaner-Wollas, Chris. 1992. *Spracherwerb trotz Down-Syndrom. Eine vergleichende Studie über die modulare Organisation der Grammatik*. Universität Wien, Habilitationsschrtift.
Schaner-Wollas, C. and H. Haider. 1987. Spracherwerb und Kognition – Eine Studie über interpretative Relationen. In *Grammatik und Kognition*, ed. J. Bayer. Opladen: Westdeutscher Verlag.
Schenker, Alexander M. and Stankiewicz, Edward. (eds.). 1980. *The Slavic Literary Languages: Formation and Development*. New Haven, CT: Yale Concilium on International and Area Studies.
Serbo-Croatian Academy Grammar = Babić (1991).
Skalička, Vladimir. 1979. *Typologische Studien*, ed. P. Hartmann. Wiesbaden: Braunschweig.
Smirnickij, A. I. 1953. Tak nazyvaemaja konversija i čeredovanie zvukov v anglijskom jazyke. *Inostrannnye jazyki v škole* 5, 21–31.
Smirnickij, A. I. 1954. Po povodu konversii v anglijskom jazyke. *Inostrannnye jazyki v škole* 3, 12–24.
Spencer, Andrew. 1991. *Morphological Theory: An Introduction to Word Structure in Generative Grammar*. Oxford: Blackwell.
Spencer, Andrew. 1998. Morphological operations. In *The Handbook of Morphology*, eds. A. Spencer and A. Zwicky, 123–143. Oxford: Blackwell.

Spencer, Andrew. 2002. Gender as an inflectional category. *Journal of Linguistics* 38, 279–312.
Stampe, D. 1973a. On chapter nine. In *Issues in Phonological Theory*, eds. Michael Kenstowicz and Charles Kisseberth, 44–52. The Hague: Mouton.
Stampe, David. 1973b. *A Dissertation on Natural Phonology*. New York, NY: Garland.
Stankiewicz, Edward. 1986. *The Slavic Languages: Unity in Diversity*. Berlin: de Gruyter.
Stephany, Ursula. 1982. Inflectional and lexical morphology: A linguistic continuum. *Glossologia* 1, 27–55.
Stevanović, Mihailo. 1978. *Gramatika srpskohrvatskog jezika*. Osmo izdanje. Obog-Cetinje.
Stojanov, Stojan. 1993 [1964]. *Gramatika na bălgarskija knižoven ezik*. V izdanie. Sofija: Universitetsko izdatelstvo "Sv. Kl. Oxridski".
Stonham, John T. 1994. *Combinatorial Morphology*. Amsterdam: Benjamins.
Stump, Gregory T. 2001. *Inflectional Morphology. A Theory of Paradigm Structure*. Cambridge, MA: Cambridge University Press.
Sweet, Henry. 1900 [1891]. *A New English Grammar. Part I: Introduction, Phonology and Accidence*, 2nd edition. Oxford: Clarendon Press.
Štekauer, Pavol. 1996. *A Theory of Conversion in English*. Frankfurt am Main: Peter Lang.
Štekauer, Pavol. 1998. *An Onomasiological Theory of English Word-Formation*. Amsterdam: Benjamins.
Štekauer, Pavol. 2000. *English Word-Formation. A History of Research (1960–1995)*. Tübingen: Narr.
Štekauer, Pavol and Rochelle Lieber. (eds.). 2005. *Handbook of Word-Formation*. Dordrecht: Springer.
Švedova, Natalija Ju. et al. 1980. *Russkaja grammatika. Tom I. Fonetika, Fonologija, Udarenie, Intonacija, Slovoobrazovanie, Morfologija*. Moskva: Izdatel'stvo 'Nauka' (Izdatel'stvo Akademii Nauk SSSR).
Taylor, John R. 2003. *Cognitive Grammar*. New York, NY: Oxford University Press.
Težak, Stjepko and Stjepan Babić. 1992. *Gramatika hrvatskoga jezika: priručnik za osnovno jezično obrazovanje*. 8. popravljeno izdanije. Zagreb: Školska kniga.
Thornton, A. M. 1993. Italian blends. In *Natural Morphology. Perspectives for the Nineties*, eds. Livia Tonelli and Wolfgang U. Dressler, 143–155. Padova: Unipress.
Tiersma, P. M. 1982. Local and general markedness. *Language* 58, 832–849.
Timberlake, Alan. 1993. Russian. In *The Slavonic Languages*, eds. Bernard Comrie and Greville G. Corbett, 827–886. London: Routledge.
Travaux linguistiques de Prague 2 (1966). *Les problèmes du centre et de la périphérie du système de la langue*. Prague: Académie Tchécoslovaque des sciences.
Trubetzkoy, Nikolaj S. 1931. Die phonologischen systeme. *Travaux du Cercle Linguistique de Prague* 4, 96–116.
Tuggy, D. 2005. Cognitive approach to word-formation. In *Handbook of Word-Formation*, eds. Pavol Štekauer and Rochelle Lieber, 233–266. Dordrecht: Springer.
Uluhanov, I. S. 2000. Wortbildungsarten. In *Handbuch zu den modernen Theorien der Russischen Wortbildung*, eds. Jelitte Herbert and Nina Schindler, 287–311. Frankfurt am Main: Peter Lang.
Ungerer, Friedrich and Hans-Jörg Schmid. 1996. *An Introduction to Cognitive Linguistics*. London: Longman.
Valera, Salvador. 2000. Conversion and onomasiological theory. Review article of Pavol Štekauer, *A theory of conversion in English*. Frankfurt am Main: Peter Lang, 1996. *Journal of Linguistics* 36, 145–155.
Valgina, N. S, D. È. Rozental', M. I. Fomina, and V. V. Capukevič. 1964. *Sovremennyj ruskij jazyk*. 2 izdanie. Moskva: Vysšaja škola.
Vennemann, Teo. 1972. Rule Inversion. *Lingua* 29, 209–242.
Vinogradov, Viktor V. 1972 [1947]. *Russkij jazyk (grammatičeskoe učenie o slove)*. Izdanie II. Moskva: Izdatel'stvo "Vysšaja škola".

Vogel, Petra M. 1996. *Wortarten und Wortartenwechsel*. Berlin: Walter de Guyter.
Wade, Terence. 2000 [1992]. *A Comprehensive Russian Grammar*, 2nd edition, revised and expanded. Oxford: Blackwell.
Williams, Edwin. 1981. On the notions "Lexically related" and "Head of a Word". *Linguistic Inquiry* 12, 245–275.
Wittgenstein, Ludwig. 1953. *Philosophical investigations*. New York, NY: MacMillan.
Wurzel, Wolfgang U. 1984. *Flexionsmorphologie und Natürlichkeit*. Berlin: Akademie-Verlag. [English translation: 1989. *Inflectional Morphology and Naturalness*. Dordrecht: Kluwer]
Wurzel, Wolfgang U. 1987. System-dependent morphological naturalness in inflection. In *Leitmotifs in Natural Morphology*, eds. Wolfgang U. Dressler, Willi Mayerthaler, Oswald Panagl, and Wolfgang U. Wurzel, 59–98. Amsterdam: Benjamins.
Wurzel, Wolfgang U. 1993. Morphology, natural. In *The Encyclopedia of Language and Linguistics*, ed. Robert E. Asher, 2590–2598. Oxford: Pergamon Press.
Yadroff, Michael. 1996. Modern Russian vocatives: A case of subtractive morphology. *Journal of Slavic Linguistics* 4, 133–153.
Zaliznjak, Andrej A. 1977. *Grammatičeskij slovar' russkogo jazyka: slovoizmenenie*. Moskva: Izdatel'stvo 'Russkij jazyk'.
Zapeda, Ofelia. 1983. *A Papago Grammar*. Tuscon: University of Arizona Press.
Zemskaja, Elena A. 1973a. *Sovremennyj russkij jazyk: slovoobrazovanie*. Moskva: Prosveščenie.
Zemskaja, Elena A. (ed.). 1973b. *Russkaja razgovornaja reč*. Moskva: Nauka.
Zemskaja, Elena A. 1992. *Slovoobrazovanie kak dejatel'nost'*. Moskva: Nauka.
Zemskaja, Elena A. 1996. Aktivnye procesy sovremennogo slovoproizvodstva. In *Russkij jazyk konca XX stoletija (1985–1995)*, eds. V. L. Voroncova, M. Ja. Golovinskaja, E. I. Golanova, O. P. Ermakova, E. A. Zemskaja, N. E. Il'ina, M. V. Kitajgorodskaja, E. V. Kakorina, L. P. Krysin, and N. N. Rozanova, 90–141. Moskva: Jazyki russkoj kul'tury.
Zemskaja, Elena A., M. V. Kitajgorodskaja, and E. N. Širjaev. 1981. *Russkaja razgovornaja reč. Obščie voprosy. Slovoobrazovanie. Sintaksis*. Moskva: Nauka.
Zwicky, A. M. 1985. How to describe inflection. In *Proceedings of the Eleventh Annual Meeting of the Berkeley Linguistics Society*, eds. Mary Niepokuj, Mary Van Clay, Vassiliki Nikiforidou, and Deborah Feder, 372–386. Berkeley, CA: Berkeley Linguistics Society.

Author Index

A
Adams, V., 56
Anderson, S. R., 3, 5, 127, 156
Andrejčin, L., 6, 22, 38, 75, 106, 139
Anić, V., 79–80, 86, 110
Aronoff, M., 5, 16, 25, 40, 45–48, 57, 67, 70, 84, 133, 139, 146–147, 151, 159
Assenova, P., 10, 19

B
Babić, S., 6–8, 13, 15–16, 56, 69, 72, 75, 77, 86, 101, 106, 109–111, 121, 139, 168, 188
Barić, E., 6–7, 15–16, 80, 111, 119, 139–140, 143, 165, 168–169
Battistella, E. L., 184
Bauer, L., 25, 35, 37, 58–59, 65–66, 89, 113, 133–134, 139, 143, 195
Baxturina, R. V., 82
Baerman, M., 59
Beard, R., 5, 51, 163
Becker, T., 47, 148, 152
Bergenholtz, H., 68, 72–74
Berlin, B., 42
Blevins, J. P., 28–29
Bloomfield, L., 125–126, 129
Bojadžiev, T., 6–8, 56, 111, 119, 126, 139, 193
Booij, G., 25–26, 35, 51–53, 89, 135
Browne, W., 16
Bybee, J. L., 43–44, 50, 52, 58, 105–106, 189

C
Cannon, G., 139
Carstairs-McCarthy, A., 25, 35, 37
Cetnarowska, B., 5, 69, 71, 73–74
Coleman, L., 42
Comrie, B., 10, 16, 20, 22, 39, 105–106, 161

Corbett, G. G., 10, 16, 20, 28, 105, 153
Čoroleeva, M., 143
Crocco-Galèas, G., 56–57, 59

D
Daniel, M., 19, 137–138
De Almeida, R. G., 2
De Bray, R. G. A., 10
Dilevski, N., 119–120
Di Sciullo, A. M., 5
Dokulil, M., 5, 59, 66, 111–113, 119, 193
Doleschal, U., 20, 52
Don, J., 5, 57, 60, 89
Dressler, W. U., 3–5, 20, 35–37, 39–42, 44–46, 48, 50–52, 57, 59–61, 64, 66, 71, 73–74, 77, 81, 87, 90, 97, 101, 106, 110, 113, 126, 128, 133–134, 136, 148, 152, 154–155, 160–161, 166–167, 174, 178, 188–189, 196

E
Efremova, T. F., 96

F
Filipović, R., 20
Ford, A., 72
Fraser, N. M., 16
Fuhrhop, N., 48

G
Gagarina, N. V., 101
Galkina-Fëdoruk, E. M., 111, 114, 118
Georgiev, V. I., 98–99, 137, 153, 182
Givón, T., 42–43
Goldsmith, J. A., 65

Golston, C., 128
Greenberg, J. H., 13

H
Habermann, M., 72
Haider; H., 41
Hale, K., 129
Halilović, S., 79
Hardy, H. K., 125
Harrison, W., 119
Harris, Z. S., 125
Haspelmath, M., 51–52
Hockett, C. F., 125
Holsinger, D. J., 128
Horálek, K., 12, 18
Houseman, P. D., 128
Hristea, T., 156, 160
Hurch, B., 65

I
Iacobini, C., 139, 160
Isačenko, A. V., 21, 33, 146
Ivanova-Mirčeva, D., 171

J
Jakobson, R., 16, 19, 24, 35, 37, 58, 66, 105, 185

K
Kastovsky, D., 5, 174–175
Kaye, J. D., 126
Kay, P., 42, 126
Kiefer, F., 175
Kiparsky, P., 5
Kleiber, G., 42
Kondrašov, N. A., 10
Koontz-Garboden, A., 145
Kreidler, C. W., 114, 139–140, 142
Krumova, L., 143
Krupa, V., 129
Kucarov, I., 18, 38, 106

L
Ladányi. M., 40
Lakoff, G., 42
Langacker, R. W., 42–43
Lappe, S., 47
Laškova, L., 111

Le Fleming, S., 119
Lehmann, V., 106
Libben, G., 2
Lieber, R., 3, 5, 25, 35, 57, 66, 72, 107
Ljung, M., 59, 68
Lopatin, Vl, 6, 56
Ludwig, R., 184
Lukatela, G., 28
Luraghi, S., 59
Lyons, J., 56

M
Manova, S., 3, 20, 22, 32, 36, 45, 53, 57, 59–60, 73, 83, 92, 101, 103, 105, 109–110, 128, 155, 159, 167, 188–189, 195
Marchand, H., 5, 6, 55–57, 60, 67–70, 89, 113, 119, 133
Mareš, F. V., 10
Martin, J., 5
Maslov, J. S., 6–7, 22, 106, 193
Matthews, P. H., 3
Mayerthaler, W., 27, 36, 58, 146, 153, 189
McDaniel, C. K., 42
Mel'čuk, I. A., 5, 58–59, 63–67, 114, 125–126, 144–146, 166, 193
Merlini Barbaresi, L., 97, 166
Mirčev, K., 98
Mladenov, S., 98
Moder, C. L., 43, 44
Molhova, J., 64
Montler, T. R., 125
Morin, Y.-C., 126
Mrazović, P., 22, 24
Mugdan, J., 68, 72–74
Mulisch, H., 114
Müller, P. O., 72
Myers, S., 71

N
Naumann, B., 148
Nida, E. A., 125–126

O
Ožegov, S. I., 166

P
Peirce, C. S., 35, 37
Pennanen, E. V., 57, 134

Plag, I., 143
Plank, F., 51–52

Q
Quirk, R., 65–66, 133, 139, 143

R
Rainer, F., 51–52, 64, 112, 148–149, 152, 160–161
Rojzenzon, L. I., 118
Rosch, E., 42
Rozental', D. È, 111

S
Sanders, G., 57, 60, 68–69
Sassen, A., 47
Saxton, D., 127
Saxton, L., 127
Scalise, S., 97
Schaner-Wollas, C., 41
Schenker, A. M., 10
Schmid, H.-J., 41–43
Skalička, V., 3, 17, 39
Smirnickij, A. I., 6, 59, 193
Spencer, A., 47, 110, 146
Stampe, D., 35
Stankiewicz, E., 10, 19
Štekauer, P., 5, 35, 57, 59, 65–66, 68
Stephany, U., 52
Stevanović, M., 6
Stojanov, S., 6, 38, 98, 105–106, 179
Stonham, J. T., 126–127
Stump, G. T., 3–4, 28–30, 40, 131
Švedova, N. J., 6–8, 33, 56, 70, 75, 78, 82, 93, 96, 101, 106, 111, 114–115, 117, 119, 126, 139–140, 142, 166, 169, 178
Sweet, H., 55

T
Telenkova, M. A., 111
Težak, S., 168
Thornton, A. M., 139

Tiersma, P. M., 153, 189
Timberlake, A., 16
Trubetzkoy, N. S., 35
Tuggy, D., 41

U
Uluhanov, I. S., 8, 166
Ungerer, F., 41, 43

V
Valera, S., 66
Valgina, N. S., 7
van Marle, J., 51–52
Vennemann, T., 152
Vinogradov, V. V., 6, 21, 106
Vogel, P. M., 5–6, 56–57, 59, 68, 72–73, 114, 117–118, 148, 174
von Polenz, P., 72
Vukadinović, Z., 22, 24

W
Wade, T., 119
Wiese, R., 128
Williams, E., 5, 30
Wittgenstein, L., 42
Wurzel, W. U., 36, 40, 51, 53, 146

X
Xaralampiev, I., 171

Y
Yadroff, M., 19, 137–138

Z
Zaliznjak, A. A., 59, 78, 138
Zapeda, O., 127
Zemskaja, E. A., 6, 89, 100, 140, 144, 163–165, 178
Zwicky, A. M., 3

Subject Index

A

Acronyms, 9, 125, 130, 138–139, 143–144, 172, 198
Addition, 2–5, 7–8, 12, 14, 17, 21, 28, 31, 34–35, 37–38, 40, 42, 45–51, 55–56, 58–61, 67, 72, 74–76, 78, 81, 83, 85–86, 92–93, 95, 97–98, 101–103, 105, 121, 126–129, 132, 134–136, 138, 140, 142, 144–146, 148, 152–153, 159, 161–162, 167, 169, 171–172, 178, 180, 188–189, 191–192, 195, 198
Aspectual suffix, 31–34, 83, 92, 101, 105–106, 159, 181, 193, 195

B

Backformation, 9, 125, 130, 133–134
Balkan Sprachbund, 10
Blends (blending), 9, 41, 125, 130, 138–139, 142–143, 198
Bosnian, 4–5, 13, 150
Bulgarian (Bg.), 4–28, 30–32, 36–38, 45–46, 48–50, 52–53, 56–57, 62, 65, 68, 70–75, 77–78, 81, 83–85, 87–99, 101, 104–108, 110, 112, 114–115, 118–119, 121, 123, 131–132, 135–141, 143–145, 151–155, 157–161, 163–167, 170–173, 175–185, 188–198

C

Clipping, 9, 125, 130, 138–142, 172, 178, 198
Cognitive linguistics (abbreviated as CL in the text), 2, 8, 35–36, 41–42, 44–45
Conversion
    in derivation, 55, 74–103, 108, 110, 121, 193
        word-class-changing, root-based, 90–97
        word-class-changing, stem-based, 86–90
        word-class-changing, word-based, 75–81, 198
        word-class preserving, root-based, 62, 97–100, 121
        word-class preserving, stem-based, 99–100
        word-class preserving, word-based, 97–99
    in inlfection (formal conversion), 80
        aspect (imperfectivization), 9, 105, 107, 108, 110, 122, 192–194
        gender (derivation of females), 9, 64, 108–110, 122, 184, 192–193
    syncretism, 57, 59, 61–62, 110, 121
    syntactic conversion, 6, 9, 55, 59, 61–62, 78–81, 110–119, 121–123, 175–177, 192–193
        adjectivization, 111, 119–121
        substantivization, 6, 9, 110–114, 119, 121, 177, 192–193
Croatian, 4, 6–7, 13, 111, 143, 150

D

Derivation, 2–7, 9, 12–13, 29–31, 35, 39, 41, 45–48, 50–53, 55–57, 59–62, 65, 67, 70, 72–106, 108–110, 119, 121, 125–127, 129–130, 132–133, 136–137, 147–148, 151, 153–166, 169–171, 174, 176, 178–180, 184–185, 188–189, 191–193, 196–198
Derivational-inflectional continuum (or derivation-inflection continuum), 50–53, 55, 61–62, 103, 110, 121, 192
Diagrammaticity, 37, 40

238   Subject Index

Diminutives, 3, 52, 97–99, 105, 122, 134, 137,
     165–166, 181–183, 186, 188–189,
     196
Direction of conversion
     criteria for establishing, 55, 67, 73
          cross-linguistic semantic pattern,
               72–74
          distributional criterion, 70–71, 100,
               151, 159, 185, 188
          frequency, 70, 138
          (in)complete inflectional paradigm,
               70, 77
          (ir)regular inflectional paradigm, 71
          restriction of usage, 68, 70
          semantic dependence, 69
          semantic range, 68–69
     reversible conversion, 72–74

E

English (E.), 5–6, 26, 36–38, 40, 43, 48, 55, 57,
     59, 61, 65, 68–70, 73–76, 89, 97,
     113, 115, 133–134, 143, 146,
     149–151, 153–154, 174–176, 193,
     195

F

Finish (F.), 8
French (Fr.), 126, 128, 133, 150, 154, 160, 174

G

German (G.), 1, 48, 73–74, 89, 113–114, 128,
     134, 148–149, 152–153, 163, 167,
     174–175, 193
(German) Hessian, 167

H

Haplology, 9, 125, 130, 134–136, 143
Homonymy, 46, 62–63
Hungarian (H.), 136, 150, 175–177
Hypocoristics, 9, 125, 130, 136–139, 198

I

Iconicity, 2–3, 8, 13, 35–37, 47, 58, 67, 108,
     130, 167, 197
Inflection, 3–7, 9–10, 12–17, 19–20, 24–28,
     32–36, 39–41, 45–53, 55–56, 58,
     60–62, 71, 73–81, 83–85, 87–88,
     90–93, 101–114, 118–119, 121, 126,
     129, 132–133, 135–140, 146–147,
     154–157, 166–171, 174–175,
     180–184, 188–198
Italian (It.), 27, 113, 148, 153, 193

L

Latin (Lat.), 16–17, 57, 113, 118, 178, 193

M

Metaphor, 9, 37, 62–64
Metonymy, 9, 62–64
Modification
     prosodic (stress change), 49
     segmental, 48, 65–66, 86, 98, 107, 165
Morphological technique, 3–4, 8–9, 29, 35,
     40, 44–51, 53, 55, 58–60, 62, 64, 74,
     96, 108–110, 128–130, 134,
     140–142, 156–157, 163, 167, 170,
     172–174, 177–191, 196, 198–199
Morphology
     generative, 35
     natural (abbreviated as NM in the text),
          2, 8, 13, 28, 35–41, 44, 48–50, 53,
          58, 86, 90, 106, 130, 146, 171, 198
     root-based, 29–31, 48, 194
     stem-based, 29–30, 48, 67
     word-based, 29–30, 67, 130
Morphonology, 4, 8, 11–13, 27, 36, 38, 45,
     48–49, 66, 71, 96, 125, 129, 147,
     156–158, 167, 199

N

Naturalness
     language-specific, 36, 39–41, 198
     typological, 36, 39, 41
     universal, 36–39, 41

O

Old Bulgarian (Obg.), 10–11, 36, 62, 98, 119,
     155, 182, 188
Old Church Slavic (OCS), 10, 16, 19, 98–99,
     171–172, 185
Old English, 175
Old Greek, 113, 161, 178, 193

P

Palatalization, 4, 12–13, 28, 36–37, 40, 49, 66,
     86, 98, 107, 141, 168, 183

Subject Index 239

Papago, 127
Phonological shortening, 9, 125, 130–133
Phonology, 35, 39, 43, 65
    accentuation (Serbo-Croatian), 11–12, 66
Polish, 10, 134, 166
Polysemy, 9, 62–64, 142
Prototype theory (abbreviated as PT in the text)
    cline, continuum, 2, 8–9, 35, 43, 50, 103
    gestalt, 43
    prototype, 42–44
    schema, 30

R

Romanian, 10, 156, 160
Root extension, 31–34, 60, 87
Rule inversion, 9, 125, 147–156, 161, 170–171, 198
    ethnicity terms, 147–156
Russian (R.), 4–28, 32–34, 48, 50, 53, 56, 58–59, 61–62, 70, 72, 74–75, 77–78, 80–88, 90–91, 93–97, 99–101, 103, 105–108, 111–115, 118–121, 131–133, 135–142, 144–147, 150, 155–159, 161, 163–173, 176–181, 183–185, 188–198

S

Samoan, 129
Semiotics, 35
Serbian (S.), 5, 10, 13, 18, 154
Serbo-Croatian (SC.), 4–28, 32, 34, 46, 50, 53, 56, 62, 66, 69–70, 72, 74–79, 81–85, 87–88, 90, 92–96, 98–99, 101, 105, 107–109, 111–115, 119, 121, 123, 131–132, 136–139, 141, 150, 155–159, 161, 163–164, 166–173, 176–181, 183–185, 188–198
Spanish (Sp.), 64, 112, 149, 153, 160, 163

Substitution, 2–3, 8, 14, 35, 40, 45–47, 49, 51, 60–61, 67, 75, 101, 109, 121, 126, 129, 136, 142, 146–147, 153, 156, 160–161, 167, 172, 188–189, 191–192, 198–199
Subtraction
    in derivation, 46, 125, 129–130, 156–166, 170–171, 196–198
        word-class-changing, 53, 61–62, 75–76, 90, 101, 103, 129–130, 156–160, 170, 192–195, 198
        word-class-preserving, 160–166
    in inflection, 154, 166–171, 196–197
        with modifications, 167–170
        plural of ethnicity terms, 171, 197
        superlatives, 52, 171, 197
        without modifications, 166–167
Subtraction of meaning
    causatives, 144–145
    reflexives, 144–145
Suppletion, 45, 164

T

Thematic marker, 7, 14–17, 24, 27, 31–34, 40, 76, 90, 107
Truncation, 8–9, 45–47, 125–126, 130, 136, 146–147
Turkish (T.), 23, 167

V

Vocative, 19–20, 98–99, 136–138, 182
    new Russian vocative, 138

Y

Young of animals, 98–99, 182, 188

Z

Zero sign, 9, 34, 58–59, 125, 130, 133, 138, 145–146

Printed by Printforce, the Netherlands